W9-AKP-461

Eat Raw,
Eat Well

Eat Raw, Eat Well

400 Raw, Vegan & Gluten-Free Recipes

Douglas McNish

Robert
ROSE

For complete cataloguing information, see page 374.

Disclaimer

The recipes in this book have been carefully tested by our kitchen and our tasters. To the best of our knowledge, they are safe and nutritious for ordinary use and users. For those people with food or other allergies, or who have special food requirements or health issues, please read the suggested contents of each recipe carefully and determine whether or not they may create a problem for you. All recipes are used at the risk of the consumer.

We cannot be responsible for any hazards, loss or damage that may occur as a result of any recipe use.

For those with special needs, allergies, requirements or health problems, in the event of any doubt, please contact your medical adviser prior to the use of any recipe.

Design and Production: Kevin Cockburn/PageWave Graphics Inc.
Editor: Judith Finlayson
Copy Editor: Gillian Watts
Recipe Tester: Jennifer MacKenzie
Proofreader: Gillian Watts
Indexer: Gillian Watts
Nutritional Consultant: Doug Cook, RD, MHSc
Food Photography: Colin Erricson
Associate Photographer: Matt Johannsson
Food Styling: Kathryn Robertson and Jill Snider
Prop Styling: Charlene Erricson

Farmers' market photos: © iStockphoto.com/Alison Stieglitz

Cover image: Pesto-Coated Carrot and Parsnip Fettuccine (page 236)

We acknowledge the financial support of the Government of Canada through the Book Publishing Industry Development Program (BPIDP) for our publishing activities.

Published by Robert Rose Inc.
120 Eglinton Avenue East, Suite 800, Toronto, Ontario, Canada M4P 1E2
Tel: (416) 322-6552 Fax: (416) 322-6936
www.robertrose.ca

Printed and bound in Canada

2 3 4 5 6 7 8 9 FP 20 19 18 17 16 15 14 13 12

Contents

Acknowledgments

First and foremost I want to thank my mother and father for encouraging me to read at an early age. Without them I would not have been able to write this book.

To Candice for teaching me to be present and to enjoy what you have while you have it. You help to keep me grounded. Thank you, baby.

I also want to thank all of the people that have ever had a meal prepared by me, come to a restaurant I worked at, attended a cooking demonstration or taken a class with me. I do what I do for many reasons but the main one is to show people that healthy food has the ability to change your life.

To Arpi Magyar for teaching me the ropes of a professional kitchen and treating me like a son. You showed me that food truly is an art and in order to be successful you cannot be a shoemaker. You are not only a wonderful chef but also a great man.

To Bob Dees for his business savvy.

To Judith Finlayson for the hours upon hours that we spent editing the book. Thank you for your sense of humor and astonishing attention to detail.

Thanks to the group at PageWave Graphics, especially designer Kevin Cockburn. Also to photographer Colin Ericcson, asssociate photographer Matt Johannsson, prop stylist Charlene Erricson and food stylist Kathryn Robertson. And also to copy editor Gillian Watts.

I also want to thank Jimmy and Harula for the opportunity at Raw Aura and for allowing me the creative freedom to broaden my skills.

Last but not least, Lisa Borden for being there for me whenever I need it, day or night. Not only are you a mentor and business advisor to me but I am proud to call you my friend. You are a truly good human being with a heart of gold.

Introduction

When I first heard the words "raw food," like most people I conjured up images of thinly sliced sashimi and carrot and celery sticks. Soon, though, I came to understand that there was an entire world of raw food that I knew nothing about. It tasted great, was beautifully presented and exploded with flavors and textures I had never experienced before. The dishes seemed so fresh and vibrant. Essentially, they were full of life.

My raw food journey was a gradual one. Throughout my teens I was overweight and suffered from acne and migraine headaches. Interestingly, the doctors I saw prescribed drugs for my acne but none ever suggested changing my diet or working out. When I was fifteen, I began to cook, just for fun, and in the process discovered I was good at it, so after leaving high school I attended culinary school and became a chef. At one point I was a grill chef, cooking a couple of hundred steaks every night. I felt terrible and knew I needed to change my lifestyle, so I started going to the gym and working out.

I switched to a vegan diet and lost more than 100 pounds (45 kg) over the course of two years. But my efforts were seriously undermined when I got a job as a chef in a vegan café. Although I was eating vegan food, many of my food choices were very poor, and I gained back much of the weight I had lost.

During this time I became interested in raw foods. I got a job in a restaurant that served raw food and began to eat more and more raw food myself. I also started experimenting with developing raw food recipes. Amazingly, not only did my food taste better, which meant I was enjoying it more, but I also seemed to have a lot more energy. One visible result was that my skin cleared up!

When I began to consume raw food on a more regular basis, I felt a sense of well-being and improved mental clarity. I continued to work out and noticed that as my consumption of raw food increased, I was building more muscle mass and my cardiovascular level was improving. Within three months I had lost the 40 pounds (18.2 kg) I had gained back while making poor vegan food choices. I was lighter on my feet and felt amazing.

At that point I was spending a great deal of time in New York. Visiting the raw food restaurants and cafés in that city, I discovered "gourmet" raw food — restaurants where real chefs were preparing delicious multicourse raw meals in beautiful settings. I remember thinking that the people creating those recipes must be magicians. Who could make great-tasting chocolate or whipped cream without using dairy or refined sugars? How could a burger not contain meat and, even more amazingly, also be completely uncooked? I became determined to learn the tricks of this trade.

Over the course of several years I educated myself about the potential benefits of raw food and slowly learned how to create delicious raw food dishes for my friends and family as well as for myself. While transitioning to a raw food diet, I was testing some of the theory on myself. Through trial and error I discovered that the more raw food I consumed, the less sluggish I felt and the fewer digestive problems I had.

While the scientific evidence justifying a raw food diet is in its preliminary stages, there is reason to believe that, as we learn more about food enzymes and the process of digestion, we will discover many benefits to increasing our consumption of raw foods. Certainly many people have discovered, as I did, that eating a raw food diet increases their vitality and sense of well-being. Some studies show that heat — above a certain temperature — can degrade specific enzymes (such as myrosinase and alliinase) that help the body utilize phytochemicals. My own kitchen experiments provided visual confirmation of what I'd been reading. While gently cooking kale or spinach, for example, I'd notice the color change from bright green to dark brown. Seeing vegetables lose their vibrant color when cooked helped to make me a raw food convert. I perceived it as the loss of "living" qualities, and it was enough to make me believe what I had read about the effects of heat on food. I was a believer and ready to transform my diet.

In general terms, raw food has not been heated beyond 118°F (48°C). Most people who follow raw food diets are vegetarians (people who don't eat meat or fish but may consume eggs, milk and/or cheese) or vegans (who don't eat any animal products). I am a vegan because I am deeply concerned about the welfare of all living creatures. I am also very opposed to factory farming and the many ways in which it is contributing toward the destruction of our environment. In addition, I strongly believe that there are many health benefits to eating a whole-foods plant-based diet.

Many people assume that vegetarians and vegans enjoy healthy diets, but this is not necessarily the case. Many consume foods (for instance, processed foods or those containing a large amount of refined flour, sugar and salt) that are not beneficial for their bodies. I experienced this myself. As mentioned previously, while working as a chef in a vegan café, I gained 40 pounds (18.2 kg) because of poor vegan food choices.

The raw food diet I follow today is plant-based and vegan. It contains whole, unprocessed foods, fruits and vegetables, nuts and seeds and a selection of legumes and grains. My aim as a chef is to provide recipes that deliver not only flavor but an abundance of nutrients that will help to keep you feeling vibrant. Recipes that contain ingredients such as hemp seeds, avocados and flax oil are all good examples of nutrient-dense cuisine. I believe that when you eat raw unprocessed foods that have all their enzymes intact, your body can use the energy it saves for other things.

The idea underlying a raw food diet is the promotion of health. It should not become a dogmatic way to live, along the lines of a religion. You'll notice the beneficial effects if you simply add raw food to your diet every day. The important thing is that the way you eat helps you to feel good about yourself. It doesn't need to become a strict way of life.

In this book I have created recipes that are simple to follow and require minimal preparation time. Some use special equipment such as an electric food dehydrator or a spiral vegetable slicer (spiralizer), which are explained in Equipping a Raw Food Kitchen (pages 13 to 14). While I recommend purchasing these tools at some point along your raw food journey, you can certainly become familiar with raw food and make many of the recipes in this book without their assistance.

Although raw food is relatively new in contemporary society, I believe it's here to stay. I'm walking testimony to the fact that it can have a profound effect on your life, both physically and mentally. The important thing to remember is that transitioning to a raw food diet — assuming that's what you decide to do — should be taken one day at a time. I like to use the analogy of dating. If you're serious, it is important to take your time to get to know raw food, just as you would get to know a potential mate. If you rush into this new way of eating, chances are you will have a breakup and go back to a diet that treated you poorly. But if you take your time and get to know and understand raw food, you will gradually learn how your body interacts with it and become comfortable with the relationship. If you slip up, that's okay. There is always the next day and the next recipe to try.

I believe — and my own experience confirms it — that eating a whole-foods plant-based diet is one way to prevent illness and stay healthy. A vegan diet of unprocessed foods has changed me not only as a chef but also as a human being. It helped me appreciate that food is an excellent medicine and that we can heal ourselves through eating a nutritious balanced diet. It's an experience that many people have shared with me, and I welcome you to become one of them.

— *Douglas McNish*

Raw Food Know-How

What Is a Raw Food Diet?

A traditional raw food diet is vegetarian or vegan. The term "raw food" typically refers to any unprocessed whole food in its purest form. Uncooked avocados, apples, oranges and kale are all examples of raw food. Raw food cuisine is based on combining raw ingredients to create a dish. It can be as simple as a kale and tomato salad or as complex as a sprouted buckwheat pizza crust with uncooked tomato sauce, almond cheese and assorted raw vegetables.

A raw food diet contains whole, unprocessed fruits and vegetables, nuts and seeds and select legumes and grains that have not been heated past 118°F (48°C). Although there is some debate in the raw food community about what the maximum temperature should be, it is generally agreed that food should not be heated above this temperature.

Enzymes

All food in its whole, unprocessed form contains enzymes, which basically help the plant to sustain life. Our bodies produce enzymes too — substances, usually proteins, that help to digest food, absorb nutrients and promote health, among other functions. Although there is a great deal of controversy regarding the relationship between food enzymes and health, many people in the raw food community believe that when food is heated or cooked past 105°F (41°C), the natural enzymes begin to break down and the food loses a significant component of its nutritional value.

Organic Produce

Since most people are interested in raw food because of its health benefits, it is important to use organic produce whenever possible. Food that is grown organically has not been exposed to chemical fertilizers, herbicides and pesticides. At the very least, we do not know the long-term effects these chemicals have on our bodies. For the best-tasting, most nutritious food (because it is likely to be freshly picked or harvested), look for seasonal produce that is grown locally by real farmers. In the short term it may be more expensive than food produced by agribusiness, but over the long term it is the most sustainable and healthful option.

To help you make informed food choices, the following list — the "Dirty Dozen" — provided by the Environmental Working Group (www.ewg.org) and Food News (www.foodnews.org), lists the 12 foods identified as being most contaminated by pesticide residues when not grown organically. Also listed are those that are least likely to be contaminated when not grown organically.

The 12 Most Contaminated Foods

- Peaches
- Apples
- Sweet bell peppers
- Celery
- Nectarines
- Strawberries
- Cherries
- Pears
- Grapes (imported)
- Spinach
- Lettuce
- Potatoes

The 12 Least Contaminated Foods

- Onions
- Avocado
- Sweet corn (frozen)
- Pineapples
- Mango
- Asparagus
- Sweet peas (frozen)
- Kiwifruit
- Bananas
- Cabbage
- Broccoli
- Papaya

Eating Raw in Cold Weather

One of the stigmas associated with raw food is that much of it is served at room temperature, cool or cold. While this may not be an issue in warmer climates or during the summer, it can play a vital role in how we eat when it is cold outside. In chilly weather we tend to gravitate toward warmer foods because they feel comforting. When eating raw food, adding seasoning may help to compensate for the fact that it isn't warm. For instance, studies show that adding a pinch of cayenne pepper or minced fresh chile pepper makes us feel warm by boosting our metabolic rate. Capsaicin, the substance in chiles that gives them their heat, also helps to improve digestion. Ginger is another ingredient that works to help us feel warmer in cooler months, and it too is an effective digestive aid.

Another technique for warming raw food is to use a dehydrator. Place the food on a nonstick dehydrator sheet and turn the dehydrator to 105°F (41°C) for 20 to 30 minutes, until the food is warmed through. Lastly, many recipes such as sauces and soups can be placed in a high-powered blender or food processor and processed for 45 to 60 seconds, until they are slightly warm.

Tips for Transitioning to a Raw Food Diet

Transitioning to a raw food diet can be overwhelming at first. Here are some quick and easy tips to get you going on your way.

- Start slowly. Take your new diet day by day, slowly incorporating new elements and techniques as you progress.
- When going out to eat, have something before you leave. By eating beforehand you are nourishing your body with the food you want to eat. This will also limit the amount of explaining you need to do about why you are not eating very much.
- When hunger hits, snack on a handful of raw, unsalted almonds. They will provide protein, healthy fats and fiber and help to balance blood sugar levels.
- Do not be scared of healthy fats, such as those provided by avocados or seeds and nuts. They leave you feeling nourished and can actually help you lose weight when consumed in moderation.
- When craving sweets, try eating one or two dates. This will curb your cravings and help you on your way toward eliminating processed sugars.
- If you are watching your sodium intake, try using dried kelp or dulse in a recipe instead of salt.
- Snack on fresh fruit throughout the day to keep blood sugar levels balanced.
- Replace your morning coffee with fresh juice.
- Keep berries in the freezer at all times so you can easily make a quick and nutritious smoothie.
- Drink smoothies regularly. As time goes by, start making smoothies (or juices) that contain green vegetables.
- Write out a week-long meal plan before you go grocery shopping.
- As soon as you bring home your produce from the farmers' market or store, wash and store it for easy access.
- Search for an online community or meet up with other people transitioning to a raw food diet.
- Look for restaurants in your surrounding area that offer raw food classes to gain a better understanding of a raw food diet.

Techniques and Terms for a Raw Vegan Kitchen

Living Food

Living food is similar to raw food. It is also whole, unprocessed food that is in its purest form. The difference is that living food has been activated by soaking, which brings out its natural enzymes. All nuts, seeds and grains are in their dormant state when ingested naturally. Soaking brings them to life, making the proteins and carbohydrates easier for the body to break down. All nuts, seeds and grains benefit from being soaked, as this aids digestion. For more on bringing foods to life, see Tips, page 99.

Sprouting

Sprouting is activating the germ in a grain and/or legume. Research shows that sprouting can make foods more digestible and improve the quality of the protein they contain. Not only is the food soaked, it is left in the water long enough to grow and develop into a sprout. Sprouting can be done in various ways. You can buy special equipment that requires electricity. However, the simplest method is to soak the ingredient for a specified period of time, then to place it in a colander and periodically rinse it under cold running water. The objective is to make sure that the food is kept damp but not wet.

Marinating

Marinating is a common technique in raw food cuisine. It helps to break down raw fruits or vegetables, giving them the look and mouth feel of being slightly cooked or steamed. Marinating foods such as carrots, beets, kale or any green vegetable for a short time can help to make them seem more like cooked food.

Juicing

Juicing is the process of running fruits, vegetables and/or herbs through a juicer, separating the liquid, which contains most of the nutrients, from the solids. Juicing is an important part of a raw food diet because it allows your body to assimilate nutrients more quickly and efficiently than when they are consumed as whole foods.

Dehydrating

Dehydrating is the act of removing water from foods at a slow, controlled rate in order to preserve the maximum amount of enzymes and nutrients. It is a fairly common practice in raw food kitchens because it significantly increases the range of recipes you can create. It is also relatively convenient. Although dehydrated recipes need to be started one to two days ahead of time, they don't require much, if any, attention while dehydrating. They also keep well once dehydrated. Removing the water entirely from foods greatly extends their storage life. Even if dehydrated foods retain some moisture, they may be made ahead and stored in the refrigerator for varying periods of time.

Dehydrated recipes are usually built around foods such as nuts and seeds, which are higher in protein. However, dehydrating is often used to soften or change the texture of other foods such as fruits and vegetables. For most of the recipes in this book, I have kept the dehydrating temperature at 105°F (41°C) for the sake of nutrition. Raw food theory holds that once foods are exposed to internal temperatures above that level, proteins are damaged, phytonutrients are destroyed and the overall nutritional benefits diminish. To make the dehydrated recipes in this book, you will need an electric food dehydrator (see page 14).

Raw Breads

Raw breads can be a large part of a raw food diet, especially when transitioning from a cooked or vegan/vegetarian/gluten-free diet. Raw breads are not actual leavened breads (which most people are familiar with) but a mixture of various ingredients bound together until a dough forms, and then dehydrated. Raw breads have a texture similar to that of grain-based baked breads and can be very filling.

Equipping a Raw Food Kitchen

You won't need a lot of special equipment to get started on a raw food diet. In fact, your kitchen probably already has most of what is required. For instance, a good **cutting board** is an important component of a raw food kitchen. One made of solid wood is ideal, as plastic will dull knives much more quickly. For convenience, buy a large board at least 2 feet (60 cm) long. If you are chopping a substantial amount of food, you can leave it in piles at the edges as completed and continue working seamlessly.

I recommend having at least two good **sharp knives**: a chef's knife for chopping and a paring knife for most other jobs. Since you will get the best results from many recipes by producing thin, even slices, I also suggest that you purchase a **mandoline**. This handy kitchen tool doesn't have to be expensive. It is essentially a blade attached to a frame that allows you to slice vegetables or fruits evenly and very thinly. I also recommend a **sharp-toothed grater**, such as those made by Microplane. This handy tool purées gingerroot and makes easy work of zesting citrus, which is used to enhance the flavor in many recipes.

If you don't already have one, you should also invest in a **colander**, a large strainer that can be placed in a sink. Soaked and, to a lesser degree, sprouted nuts, seeds and grains are used widely in this book, and you'll need a colander for draining these foods. You'll also need a good sturdy **vegetable peeler**. In addition to its obvious uses, this tool can be used for making raw "pasta" from vegetables such as carrots and parsnips (see page 236). There are two types of vegetable peelers: the more traditional type, with blades that run lengthwise, and a Y-shaped ("slingshot") version, which has blades across the top. The latter is the vegetable peeler of choice for raw cuisine because its shape allows you to peel long strips off vegetables in a continuous downward motion. When using a traditional vegetable peeler, you constantly need to realign the blade, which can be time-consuming.

You'll certainly need a **blender** to make smoothies and many of the dips, sauces and dressings in this book. In addition to a blender, the only other slightly expensive small appliance you'll need to get started is a **food processor**. Like a blender, it is used for puréeing and blending ingredients. The difference is, a food processor can handle denser foods and doesn't require as much liquid as a blender. You'll want a machine that has a capacity of at least 10 cups (2.5 L). The shredding and slicing blades that come with most models are very useful and can take the place of a mandoline for many jobs. A mini-bowl attachment is helpful for processing small quantities such as some dressings and sauces.

If you make the transition to a raw food diet, you should think about purchasing a **high-powered blender**. These machines have very powerful motors and have been designed so you can adjust the settings to achieve maximum results for specific tasks, such as making smoothies, sauces or dips. They are so powerful they can easily make a completely smooth purée of any nut, seed, vegetable or fruit. They can make delicious creamy sauces or butters from soaked nuts. For some recipes it is simply not possible to achieve the ideal smooth and creamy consistency using a regular household blender.

Juicing plays an important role in raw food cuisine because fresh juices are very nutrient-dense. If you're transitioning to a raw food diet, I suggest you consider investing in a **juicer** once you begin to consume lighter foods on a regular basis. Many different kinds of juicers are available. Read up on their features and look for one that fits your price range and meets your needs.

A **nut milk bag**, which is used to squeeze the liquid from the pulp when making nut or seed milks, is fairly specific to raw food.

Typically they are made from nylon mesh. They are available from specialty raw food dealers and most health food stores. If you do not have a nut milk bag, line a sieve with two layers of cheesecloth and place it over a bowl or pitcher. Add the puréed nut-and-water mixture and strain. Use a wooden spoon to press out the liquid, extracting as much of it as possible. Collect the corners of the cheesecloth and twist them to form a tight ball. Using your hands, squeeze out the remaining liquid. Discard the solids or save for another use.

It is important to invest in **glass storage containers** when setting up a raw food kitchen. I also suggest you use glass or stainless steel mixing bowls. Most plastic contains a substance called bisphenol A (BPA), which is now deemed a toxic substance and should be avoided whenever possible.

A **spiral vegetable slicer** (often referred to as a spiralizer) is a device that is used in raw food cuisine to make "pasta" from vegetables. They come in different shapes and sizes and have a variety of blades. Depending on the brand you purchase, it will cut vegetables into pasta-like strands or paper-thin slices; some will even make curlicues. The best prices are available online, but you can also look for them in natural foods stores, raw food specialty stores or, if there is one, your local Chinatown.

As you transition further to a raw food diet, you will likely want to invest in an **electric food dehydrator**, a kind of low-heat mini oven that enables you to soften foods and concentrate their flavors without destroying nutrients. It also allows you to create desirable textures in certain dishes. An electric food dehydrator is an appliance specifically designed to remove the water content from food at very low temperatures.

There are many different models on the market. To make the recipes in this book that require a dehydrator, you will need one with an adjustable thermostat and a fan to circulate the air (if it doesn't have a fan, it takes longer to dry the food and the results may be uneven).

Food dehydrators come in various shapes, sizes, models and brands. You can purchase them in either food-grade plastic or stainless steel. If you are purchasing stainless steel, make sure the parts are made of high-quality, non-toxic materials. Dehydrators that are square or rectangular are recommended for raw food cuisine because the straight walls allow the user to create shapes and sizes that can be stored easily.

Dehydrators have racks with mesh liners or trays with mesh-like slats that allow the air to circulate around the food. Dehydrators with mesh-like trays also have optional fine-mesh liners that are placed on top. These are useful for preventing smaller pieces of food from falling through the mesh. There are also solid nonstick sheets (Paraflexx is one brand) that can be placed on the racks or on top of the trays when dehydrating very moist foods or mixtures. Most machines come with one or two of these nonstick sheets, and extras can be purchased as well. The nonstick sheets are often used in the first stage of dehydrating, when it is necessary to remove most of the moisture to eliminate stickiness. Once they are dry enough to be handled, foods are transferred to the mesh sheets for further drying. If you don't have these specialized sheets, you can use parchment paper cut to fit your dehydrator trays. Electric food dehydrators are available at raw food specialty suppliers or online.

Breakfast

When you think of raw food, breakfast isn't usually the first thing that comes to mind. And that's too bad, because there are so many great things you can enjoy for breakfast that don't need to be cooked. In fact, on a raw food diet, in addition to traditional smoothies and juices, delicious facsimiles of all your favorite cooked breakfast foods are possible.

I agree with nutritionists who say that breakfast is the most important meal of the day. Ideally, to get off to a good start, your body needs a balance of healthy fats, protein and carbohydrates, all of which are very easy to obtain from nutritious raw food. Using the recipes in this book, you'll be able to start off every day with a well-balanced breakfast that will keep you energized and support your busy, active life.

These days many people don't have time to prepare breakfast and as a result give it a pass. Perhaps surprisingly, some raw food recipes (for instance, those made in a dehydrator) are a great solution to this problem. Although most don't require a lot of involved prep work, dehydrator recipes take a long time to make and should be started a day or two before you want to eat them. But once they are ready, most dehydrated foods can be stored in an airtight container for up to two weeks. If you want to serve them slightly warm, just pop them into the dehydrator for 15 or 20 minutes.

Quick and delicious, a smoothie or freshly made juice is one of the easiest ways to get your day off to a nutritious start. In this chapter I've included two simple smoothie recipes and one for a "green juice," all of which have been designed with ease of preparation in mind. They are basic and forgiving, so you can substitute ingredients according to the seasons and to accommodate what you're likely to have on hand. Other smoothies that I think are especially good for breakfast can be found in Smoothies, Juices and Other Drinks (page 43). They include the Cinnamon Toast Crunch (page 48), Choco-Hemp-Aholic (page 65), Bodybuilder (page 65) and Kitchen Sink (page 67) Smoothies.

The most important thing to know about a raw food breakfast is that whether it is a simple smoothie or something more involved, such as Buckwheat Toast (page 36) spread with Sunflower Seed Miso Butter (page 20), you are starting your day with some of the healthiest food possible. Because your body and your mind are so well nourished, you will be setting yourself up to have a wonderful day.

Basic Nut Milk Smoothie

This basic smoothie, made with nut milk, mango and banana, is a good source of potassium and vitamin C. Orange fruits such as mangoes are an excellent source of beta-carotene, a powerful antioxidant. Bananas are a good source of a type of fiber that helps to maintain healthy bacteria in your gut. To boost the protein content of this smoothie, you can add your favorite nut butter and/or a scoop of protein powder, using a brand that meets raw criteria.

Makes 2 servings

Tips

In many recipes, almond milk is an alternative to cow's milk. Although lower in protein, almond milk contains the phytochemicals found in almonds, as well as trace amounts of potassium, magnesium, manganese, phosphorus and B vitamins.

To peel and chop a mango, cut a small slice from the top and bottom of the fruit to make flat ends. Using a vegetable peeler, carefully peel away the skin. Stand the mango on a cutting board and, using a chef's knife, run the blade through the flesh, taking approximately three slices from each of the four sides. When you are close to the stone, use a paring knife to remove any remaining flesh from around the middle.

I like to keep frozen organic berries on hand to help sweeten smoothies and make them cold. When your favorite fruit is in season, purchase it in bulk and freeze some to use in smoothies throughout the year.

1½ cups	Almond Milk (page 45, and see Tips, left)	375 mL
1	mango, peeled, seeded and chopped (see Tips, left)	1
1	banana	1
4	strawberries	4

1. In a blender, combine almond milk, mango, banana and strawberries. Blend at high speed until smooth.

Variations

Substitute an equal quantity of Cashew Milk (page 46), Coconut Milk (page 47) or Hemp Milk (page 47) in this smoothie.

Substitute other fleshy orange fruits for the mango. In season, use 2 peaches or nectarines or 4 apricots, with stones removed. An orange tropical fruit such as papaya will also work well.

You can substitute other berries for the strawberries. Try blueberries, raspberries, blackberries or even a "bumbleberry" combination of berries. If the fruit is not as sweet as you would like or if you prefer a sweeter drink, add a pitted soft date.

To boost the protein content, add 1 to 2 tbsp (15 to 30 mL) of your favorite nut butter and/or some protein powder (see page 373).

Basic Berry Smoothie

> This smoothie is high in potassium, which is provided mainly by the orange juice and banana. It is also an excellent source of vitamin C and healthy carbohydrates.

Makes 2 servings

Tip

Buy organic frozen berries in bulk and keep them in your freezer to use as needed. You can add frozen berries to your smoothie to chill your drink instead of ice. Frozen berries are generally cheaper when you purchase them in larger quantities.

1 cup	freshly squeezed orange juice	250 mL
12	strawberries	12
8	blackberries	8
1	banana	1
1	pitted soft date, chopped	1

1. In a blender combine orange juice, strawberries, blackberries, banana and date. Blend at high speed until smooth.

Variations

Substitute pineapple juice for the orange juice.

Try different mixes of berries. I like using blueberries, blackberries and strawberries.

Perfect Green Juice

> This juice is a perfect tonic. It is rich in healthful components that are susceptible to high temperatures and are water-soluble, which means their nutritional benefit is maximized when eaten raw. Vary the leafy greens to suit your taste. Try spinach, arugula, or even slightly bitter dandelion greens.

Makes 1½ cups (375 mL)

Tip

When juicing vegetables that contain lower amounts of water, such as kale, follow them through the juicer with vegetables or fruits, such as cucumber, that are higher in water. Sometimes the liquid from less juicy vegetables gets left in the gears of the juicer. Following with a vegetable with high water content helps to flush it out.

- **Electric juicer**

1	bunch kale, divided	1
1	English cucumber, sliced, divided	1
4	leaves romaine lettuce, divided	4
½	bunch parsley, divided	½
4	stalks celery, divided	4
¼	lemon, skin on	¼
1	piece gingerroot (½ inch/1 cm), skin on	1

1. In a juicer, process 2 leaves of kale, one-quarter of the cucumber, 1 leaf of lettuce, one-quarter of the parsley, 1 stalk of celery, lemon and ginger. Repeat three times, increasing the quantity of kale in the final step.

Superfood Almond Butter Delight

This is a smooth and creamy spread, sinfully delicious, with a velvety mouth feel. The mixture of slightly sweet coconut oil and smooth-textured almond butter is a perfect pairing. It makes an ideal topping for a morning side such as Cinnamon Raisin Flax Bagels (page 33) or Buckwheat Toast (page 36), or even crisp apple slices. It is loaded with nutrients, including healthy fats.

Makes 2½ cups (625 mL)

2 cups	almond butter (see Tips, left)	500 mL
½ cup	melted coconut oil (see Tips, left)	125 mL
¼ cup	raw agave nectar (see Tips, left)	60 mL
2 tbsp	raw shelled hemp seeds	30 mL

1. In a bowl, combine almond butter, coconut oil, agave nectar and hemp seeds. Mix well. Place in an airtight container and refrigerate for up to 2 weeks.

Variations

Substitute ½ cup (125 mL) Date Paste (page 80) for the agave nectar in this recipe.

Substitute cashew butter for the almond butter. It too will produce a nutrient-dense spread.

Tips

A 2 tbsp (30 mL) serving of almond butter contains about 190 calories. In addition to being a good source of protein, it is high in phosphorus and is a source of calcium, potassium and fiber. Although it's high in calories, you don't need a large amount to feel full.

Coconut oil is solid at room temperature. To melt it, place near a source of heat — it has a melting temperature of 76°F (24°C), so it is easy to liquefy. You can also place the required amount of coconut oil in a shallow bowl and set it in a dehydrator at 100°F (38°C) for 5 to 6 minutes, until melted. If you do not have a dehydrator, place the oil in a shallow glass bowl over a pot of simmering water.

When purchasing agave nectar, be sure to look for products labeled "raw." Most of the agave nectar on the market has been heated to a high temperature and does not qualify as raw food. If you have concerns, ask your purveyor.

Making Nut Butters

I do not recommend making your own nut butters because they inflict too much wear and tear on most machines, except those with a commercial motor. Although some people successfully make nut butters using a food processor, it is thought that this method may heat the product to the point where it is no longer considered a raw food. As a result, the use of industrial equipment is usually recommended when making nut butters for a raw food diet. The best place to purchase nut butters is bulk food stores, as they can be quite pricey when purchased in small quantities. When purchasing nut butters, make sure they are raw and organic. Find a favorite brand or source and stick with it.

Sunflower Seed Miso Butter

This delicious dairy alternative is so rich and creamy that no one will be able to tell the difference if someone asks you to pass the butter. It's perfect on Buckwheat Toast (page 36). On weekends, when I create large brunch meals and am often craving something creamy, I like to make this recipe. With the addition of chopped fresh herbs, you can also use this recipe as the base for a raw butter to use as a dip for breads and crackers or carrot and celery sticks, or with a plate of crudités.

Makes 4 cups (1 L)

Tips

To soak the sunflower seeds for this recipe, place in a bowl and add 2 cups (500 mL) water. Cover and set aside for 30 minutes. Drain, discarding water and any shells or unwanted particles.

The key to making the spread taste delectable is using high-quality extra virgin olive oil. Although extra virgin olive oil should, by definition, be cold-pressed, it is worth checking the label. Some olive oils are extracted using a centrifuge system, which spins the olives at a very high rate. This heats the olives and the resulting oil, depriving it of its raw status.

Apple cider vinegar has long been used in folk medicine. Is a great digestive aid, among its other benefits. When purchasing apple cider vinegar, make sure it is raw, made from organically grown apples and contains the "mother," which is a source of healthy bacteria and enzymes.

1 cup	raw sunflower seeds, soaked (see Tips, left)	250 mL
½ cup	filtered water	125 mL
3 tbsp	apple cider vinegar (see Tips, left)	45 mL
2 tbsp	brown rice miso paste	30 mL
2 cups	cold-pressed (extra virgin) olive oil (see Tips, left)	500 mL

1. In a food processor fitted with the metal blade, process soaked sunflower seeds, water, vinegar and miso paste for 3 to 4 minutes or until sunflower seeds have been completely broken down and mixture is smooth.
2. With the motor running, add olive oil through the feed tube in a slow, steady stream until mixture is emulsified (see box, below). Transfer to a container, cover and refrigerate for up to 4 days.

Variation

Add any fresh or dried herb to this butter for additional flavor. One of my favorite combinations is 1 tbsp (15 mL) dried dill weed and 2 tsp (10 mL) freshly squeezed lemon juice. Add these in Step 1.

Making Emulsions

An emulsion results when a liquid and a fat amalgamate to form a sauce. The ingredients are usually combined very slowly while whisking or beating vigorously. This forces the fat molecules to surround the cell walls of the liquid. The key is to start emulsification very slowly, usually drop by drop. Using a food processor makes easy work of this process.

Coconut Water Strawberry Jam

This spread is as good and as sweet as store-bought jam but contains none of the refined sugars and preservatives. Use it any way you would use traditional jam. High-quality coconut water, which is rich in electrolytes, will help to give your body the natural salts and sugars it needs to thrive.

Makes 2 cups (500 mL)

Tips

To soak the figs and dates for this recipe, place them in a container and add water to cover. Set aside for 1 hour. Drain, discarding soaking water.

Coconut water, which is the watery liquid inside a young coconut, is nature's electrolyte replacer. It is full of naturally occurring salts and sugars, which help to regulate many bodily functions. It is also a great source of potassium. The best kind is straight from a young organic coconut, but if that is not available the next best thing is pure organic coconut water in cans not lined with bisphenol A (BPA) or Tetra Paks. If you're purchasing coconut water, look for high-quality products that don't contain additives or preservatives (many prepared coconut waters have added sugar and other ingredients).

Dates provide iron, fiber and potassium. They are also a good source of antioxidants. Although dates are a healthy whole food, they are high in sugar and calories (about 25 calories each, depending on the variety).

½ cup	dried figs, soaked and drained (see Tips, left)	125 mL
¼ cup	chopped pitted dates, soaked and drained	60 mL
3 cups	chopped hulled strawberries	750 mL
¼ cup	coconut water (see Tips, left)	60 mL

1. In a food processor fitted with the metal blade, process strawberries and coconut water until smooth. Add soaked figs and dates and process until smooth. (To ensure proper smoothness, you will need to stop the motor, remove the lid and stir once, using a rubber spatula.) Serve immediately or cover and refrigerate for up to 2 days.

Variations

Substitute different berries in the same quantity. A version made only with raspberries is delicious, and I also like a blend of blueberries, blackberries and strawberries.

Cinnamon Applesauce

This applesauce couldn't be easier to make. To make it taste as delicious as your grandmother's homemade version, process in the food processor long enough to create a smooth purée. It can be used as a simple sweetener on virtually any breakfast cereal in place of table sugar. I like to use it on Buckwheat Porridge (page 24) and as a dip for Morning Energy Bars (page 35).

Makes 3 cups (750 mL)

Tip

To remove the skin and core from an apple, cut a small amount from both the top and bottom of the apple. Use a vegetable peeler to remove the skin. Cut into four equal parts and, using a paring knife held on an angle, remove the core.

4 cups	chopped peeled apples	1 L
1 tsp	freshly squeezed lemon juice	5 mL
2 tsp	ground cinnamon	10 mL

1. In a food processor fitted with the metal blade, process apples, lemon juice and cinnamon until smooth, stopping the machine once or twice to scrape down the sides of the work bowl. Transfer to a bowl. Serve immediately or cover and refrigerate for up to 4 days.

Variation

Substitute pears for the apples and add a pinch of freshly grated nutmeg.

Blueberry Date Syrup

This nutritious version of breakfast syrup goes well with Pear and Walnut Pancakes (page 38). It is also delicious drizzled over sliced fresh fruit. In fact, a perfect breakfast is sliced fruit drizzled with this syrup and a bowl of Breakfast Muesli (page 29).

Makes 3 cups (750 mL)

Tip

To soak the dates for this recipe, combine 2 cups (500 mL) pitted dates and 3 cups (750 mL) filtered water in a bowl. Cover and set aside for 30 minutes. Drain.

2 cups	chopped pitted dates, soaked (see Tip, left)	500 mL
¾ cup	blueberries	175 mL
2 tbsp	raw agave nectar	30 mL
2 tbsp	filtered water	30 mL
1 tsp	freshly squeezed lemon juice	5 mL

1. In a food processor fitted with the metal blade, combine soaked dates and blueberries. Process until slightly broken down. Add agave nectar, water and lemon juice and process until smooth and slightly runny. Transfer to an airtight container and refrigerate for up to a week.

Variations

Substitute other berries for the blueberries. I like using a mixture of ⅓ cup (75 mL) each strawberries and raspberries to create a mixed-berry date syrup.

Mixed Fruit, Chia and Flaxseed Porridge

This simple mixture is extremely nutritious. It is quick to prepare and will leave you feeling well satisfied throughout the morning.

Makes 2 to 3 portions

Tips

To soak flax seeds, submerge them in double the amount of liquid. For this recipe, soak 3 tbsp (45 mL) flax seeds in 6 tbsp (90 mL) water. Set aside for 30 minutes. Drain and rinse under cold running water.

Flax seeds must be soaked or ground so your body can absorb the nutrients. In this recipe I prefer to use soaked whole flax seeds because they add body to the porridge. Otherwise, it would be runny.

The chia seeds in this recipe do not need to be soaked because they are used to add a slightly crunchy texture to the porridge. Because they are so small, chia seeds can be consumed without soaking or grinding. When soaked, they absorb liquid and swell quickly.

To remove the membrane from an orange, use a chef's knife to remove a bit of the skin from the top and the bottom. Using the tip of the knife, remove the skin and as much of the white pith as possible without losing flesh. Cut the orange in half and then cut into ½-inch (1 cm) cubes for this recipe.

3 tbsp	whole flax seeds, soaked (see Tips, left)	45 mL
½ cup	Coconut Milk (page 47)	125 mL
¼ cup	chopped apple	60 mL
¼ cup	chopped banana	60 mL
¼ cup	chopped orange, skin and membrane removed (see Tips, left)	60 mL
¼ cup	chopped hulled strawberries	60 mL
¼ cup	blueberries	60 mL
3 tbsp	chia seeds (see Tips, left)	45 mL
½ tsp	raw vanilla extract (see Tips, page 38)	2 mL

1. In bowl, toss together coconut milk, apple, banana, orange, strawberries, blueberries, soaked flax seeds, chia seeds and vanilla. Set aside for 5 minutes so the chia seeds can swell and absorb some of the liquid.

Variation

Use ⅓ cup (75 mL) chia seeds and 1 tbsp (15 mL) flax seeds soaked in 2 tbsp (30 mL) water. The result will have a very similar texture and flavor but a higher content of omega-3 fatty acids, because the chia seeds contain more omega-3 fats than the flax seeds.

Soaking Nuts or Seeds

When soaking nuts or seeds, the least amount of time required is 30 minutes, unless you are using the seeds to add texture to a recipe and want them to be crunchy. Ideally, to fully activate the enzymes and reap the greatest digestive benefit, soak nuts or seeds for 8 hours, changing the water every 3 to 4 hours. If you are soaking nuts or seeds overnight and can't change the water, place them in the refrigerator to reduce the potential for spoilage.

Buckwheat Porridge

A creamy take on classic morning oatmeal, this is the perfect comfort food on a cool day when your body is craving something more substantial than a salad or fruit. Be sure to allow an hour for soaking the buckwheat.

Makes 3 cups (750 mL)

Tips

Be sure to use raw buckwheat groats, not kasha, which has been toasted.

To soak the buckwheat for this recipe, combine 1 cup (250 mL) buckwheat with 2 cups (500 mL) water. Set aside for 60 minutes. Drain, discarding soaking water. Rinse under cold running water until the water runs clear.

When soaking buckwheat, it is important to change the water every 30 minutes to ensure it does not begin to ferment. Because buckwheat is extremely high in protein it is very easy for it to become sour and grow bacteria. Always use cool water to soak, and if any bubbles start to form, immediately change the water.

Be aware that coconut water is the liquid from inside the coconut, not coconut milk, which is very different. Coconut water is widely available. The best brands, which contain no added sugar or other additives, are available at natural foods stores, or you can use the liquid from a young organic coconut.

1 cup	buckwheat groats, soaked (see Tips, left)	500 mL
½ cup	coconut water (see Tips, left)	125 mL
¼ cup	raw agave nectar (see Tips, page 25)	60 mL
2 tbsp	Date Paste (page 80)	30 mL
2 tsp	ground cinnamon	10 mL
1 tsp	raw shelled hemp seeds	5 mL
Pinch	fine sea salt	Pinch

1. In a food processor fitted with the metal blade, process soaked buckwheat until it begins to break down. Stop the motor, scrape down the sides using a rubber spatula and pulse 4 or 5 times.

2. Add coconut water, agave nectar, date paste, cinnamon, hemp seeds and sea salt. Process until smooth. Taste and adjust seasonings. This porridge is best served immediately. If you have leftovers, transfer to an airtight container and refrigerate for up to 2 days.

Variations

Instead of the buckwheat, substitute 1 cup (250 mL) sunflower seeds soaked in 2 cups (500 mL) water for 30 minutes.

Try flavoring the porridge with different spices, such as 1 tsp (5 mL) chopped ginger and a pinch of ground nutmeg — a nice addition when the body is craving warmer foods.

Pear and Pumpkin Porridge

This porridge is heavily spiced and very stimulating for the digestive system. I enjoy it in the morning with a tall glass of Almond Milk (page 45) and a side of Buckwheat Toast (page 36).

Makes 6 cups (1.5 L)

Tips

To soak the buckwheat for this recipe, combine buckwheat with 1 cup (250 mL) water in a large bowl (it needs room to "grow"). Cover and set aside for 1 hour, changing the water once. Drain, discarding soaking water. Rinse under cold running water until the water runs clear.

To soak the cashews and pumpkin and sunflower seeds for this recipe, combine in a large bowl and add 1 cup (250 mL) water. Cover and set aside for 30 minutes. Drain and rinse under cold running water until the water runs clear.

To shred pumpkin or squash for this recipe, remove the peel and use the large holes of a box grater or a food processor fitted with the shredding blade.

When purchasing agave nectar, be sure to look for products labeled "raw." Most of the agave nectar on the market has been heated to a high temperature and does not qualify as raw food.

½ cup	buckwheat groats, soaked (see Tips, left)	125 mL
¼ cup	raw cashews, soaked (see Tips, left)	60 mL
¼ cup	raw pumpkin seeds, soaked	60 mL
¼ cup	raw sunflower seeds, soaked	60 mL
2 cups	chopped pears	500 mL
1 cup	shredded pumpkin or squash	250 mL
½ cup	Almond Milk (page 45)	125 mL
3 tbsp	raw agave nectar (see Tips, left)	45 mL
1 tbsp	ground cinnamon	15 mL
¼ tsp	freshly grated nutmeg	1 mL
Pinch	ground cloves	Pinch
Pinch	fine sea salt	Pinch

1. In a food processor fitted with the metal blade, process soaked buckwheat, cashews, pumpkin and sunflower seeds and pears, until slightly broken down but no longer completely smooth.
2. Add shredded pumpkin and almond milk and pulse 3 to 4 times to break down the squash. Add agave nectar, cinnamon, nutmeg, cloves and salt and pulse 3 to 4 times, until combined. Serve immediately, if possible, or cover and refrigerate for up to 2 days.

Variations

Try using various nuts and/or seeds in this recipe in the same quantities called for. For instance, replace the cashews with Brazil nuts and substitute Hemp Milk (page 47) for the Almond Milk.

Chocolate, Fruit and Buckwheat Almond Granola Bowl

This is a perfect summer bowl of fresh fruit and buckwheat seasoned with chocolate. The trick for maximizing flavor is to use perfectly ripe peaches, picked at the height of the growing season.

Makes 4 servings

Tips

To soak the buckwheat for this recipe, combine with 2 cups (500 mL) water. Cover and set aside for 30 minutes. Drain, discarding soaking water. Rinse under cold running water until the water runs clear.

To soak the almonds, combine with 1 cup (250 mL) water. Cover and set aside for 30 minutes. Drain, discarding soaking water. Rinse under cold running water until the water runs clear.

To soak the dates and figs for this recipe, place in a bowl and add enough water to cover them by at least 2 inches (5 cm), as they will swell. Drain.

- **Electric food dehydrator**

Crisp

1 cup	buckwheat groats, soaked (see Tips, left)	250 mL
½ cup	raw whole almonds, soaked (see Tips, left)	125 mL
⅓ cup	raw agave nectar, divided	75 mL
1 tsp	finely grated lemon zest	5 mL
1 tsp	raw vanilla extract (see Tips, page 38)	5 mL
Pinch	fine sea salt	Pinch

Fruit

5	chopped pitted dates, soaked (see Tips, left)	5
5	dried figs, soaked	5
1	peach, sliced	1
¾ cup	blueberries	175 mL
2 tbsp	raw cacao powder (see Tips, page 35)	30 mL
2 tsp	freshly squeezed lemon juice	10 mL
1 tsp	ground cinnamon	5 mL

1. *Crisp:* In a food processor fitted with the metal blade, pulse soaked buckwheat and almonds until slightly broken down, about 10 pulses (you do not want a purée; it should be chunky). Transfer to a bowl and toss with 3 tbsp (45 mL) agave nectar, lemon zest, vanilla and salt. Spread mixture on a nonstick dehydrator sheet in a single layer and dehydrate at 105°F (41°C) for 10 to 12 hours or until crispy. (The crisp can be made ahead of time, cooled and stored in an airtight container for up to 2 weeks.)

2. *Fruit:* In a clean food processor fitted with the metal blade, process soaked dates and figs, peach, blueberries, cacao powder, lemon juice and cinnamon until almost smooth (you want to keep some texture). Transfer to a bowl.

3. Using your hands, gently break up the buckwheat crisp and toss with the peach and blueberry mixture. Serve immediately, if possible, or cover and refrigerate for up to 2 days.

Apple, Almond and Ginger Chia Seed Bowl

This tart and creamy breakfast dish is an excellent source of protein. It is also very high in calcium, omega-3 fats, fiber, phosphorus, manganese and copper. Ginger has traditionally been used as a digestive aid, and now this benefit has some scientific support.

Makes 4 servings

Tip

Apples come in many different flavors and textures. Some hold up better for making purées or if you're trying to achieve softer textures, and some are better for slicing because they hold their texture. I like using Royal Gala apples for this particular recipe because I find they work for both functions. They create a good texture when puréed but also hold up when used in recipes that call for whole pieces, providing texture and crunch.

2	apples, peeled, cored and chopped	2
1 cup	raw whole almonds	250 mL
1/4 cup	Almond Milk (page 45)	60 mL
2 tbsp	chopped gingerroot	30 mL
2 tsp	ground cinnamon	10 mL
2	apples, sliced	2
3/4 cup	chia seeds	175 mL
2 tbsp	raw shelled hemp seeds	30 mL
Pinch	fine sea salt	Pinch

1. In a food processor fitted with the metal blade, process chopped apples, almonds, almond milk, ginger and cinnamon until apples have been puréed and the almonds are still somewhat chunky. Transfer to a bowl.
2. Add sliced apples, chia seeds, hemp seeds and salt. Stir well and set aside for 10 minutes to allow the chia seeds to absorb the liquid and swell. Serve immediately or transfer to an airtight container and refrigerate for up to one day.

Variations

Substitute an equal quantity of walnuts for the almonds.

In season, add 1/4 cup (60 mL) sliced peach in Step 1 for a nice summery flavor.

Experiment with various nut milks to see which flavor you like the most.

Buckwheaty Hemp Chocolate Granola

I love to eat this for breakfast with a tall glass of Almond Milk (page 45). It also makes a great snack at any time of the day. This cereal is so delicious you will never buy ready-made granola again. It takes a minimal amount of time to prepare and will keep for up to a month in an airtight container.

Makes 3 cups (750 mL)

Tips

To soak the buckwheat for this recipe, combine with 2 cups (500 mL) water. Cover and set aside for 3 hours, changing the water every 30 minutes to make sure it doesn't begin to ferment. Drain, discarding soaking water. Rinse under cold running water until the water runs clear.

Because buckwheat is extremely high in protein it is very easy for it to become sour and grow bacteria. Always use cool water to soak, and if any bubbles start to form, immediately change the water. If you are short of time or want to soak your buckwheat overnight, do so in the refrigerator, where it can be soaked for longer without fear of fermentation.

To soak the almonds for this recipe, place in a bowl and add ½ cup (125 mL) water. Cover and set aside for 30 minutes. Drain, discarding soaking water. Rinse under cold running water until the water runs clear.

- **Electric food dehydrator**

1 cup	buckwheat groats, soaked (see Tips, left)	500 mL
¼ cup	raw whole almonds, soaked (see Tips, left)	60 mL
½ cup	Date Paste (page 80)	125 mL
¼ cup	raw cacao powder (see Tips, page 35)	60 mL
3 tbsp	raw shelled hemp seeds	45 mL
1 tbsp	sesame seeds	15 mL

1. In a food processor fitted with the metal blade, pulse date paste, cacao powder and soaked almonds until almonds are slightly broken down (do not overprocess; you want the almonds to retain chunkiness and texture).

2. Transfer to a bowl. Add soaked buckwheat and hemp and sesame seeds and mix well.

3. Transfer to a nonstick dehydrator sheet and, using your hands, spread evenly. Dehydrate at 105°F (41°C) for 4 to 5 hours or until completely dry. Allow to cool. Transfer to an airtight container and store at room temperature for up to one month.

Variations

Standard recipes for raw granola usually use buckwheat as a base. Use this quantity of buckwheat as your base and vary the recipe to suit what you have on hand. I like to use ¼ cup (60 mL) walnuts and 2 to 3 tbsp (30 to 45 mL) pumpkin seeds, sunflower seeds, chia seeds or pine nuts instead of the hemp and sesame seeds.

This recipe is not overly sweet. If you prefer, add 3 tbsp (45 mL) raw agave nectar in Step 2.

Breakfast Muesli

You will go back time and time again for this delicious muesli. Serve it with Almond Milk (page 45) and a big handful of fresh berries for a delicious and nutritious breakfast.

Makes 4 large servings

Tips

When soaking buckwheat, keep in mind that the dry amount you start with will double in size. To soak the buckwheat for this recipe, combine 1 cup (250 mL) buckwheat with 2 cups (500 mL) water. Cover and set aside for 30 minutes. Drain, discarding soaking water. Rinse under cold running water until the water runs clear.

To soak the sunflower seeds, place in a bowl and add 1 cup (250 mL) water. Cover and set aside for 30 minutes. Drain, discarding water and any shells or unwanted particles.

To soak the almonds, walnuts and pecans for this recipe, combine in a bowl and cover with 3 cups (750 mL) water. Cover and set aside for 30 minutes. Drain, discarding soaking water, and rinse under cold running water until the water runs clear.

- **Electric food dehydrator**

1 cup	buckwheat groats, soaked (see Tips, left)	250 mL
½ cup	raw sunflower seeds, soaked (see Tips, left)	125 mL
½ cup	raw whole almonds, soaked (see Tips, left)	125 mL
½ cup	walnuts, soaked	125 mL
½ cup	pecans, soaked	125 mL
¼ cup	raisins	60 mL
2 tbsp	raw shelled hemp seeds	30 mL
2 tsp	ground cinnamon	10 mL
½ tsp	fine sea salt	2 mL
¼ cup	melted coconut oil (see Tips, page 40)	60 mL
3 tbsp	raw agave nectar	45 mL

1. In a food processor fitted with the metal blade, combine soaked buckwheat, sunflower seeds, almonds, walnuts and pecans. Pulse until roughly chopped (you want to make sure they are slightly broken down but not smooth). Transfer to a bowl.

2. Add raisins, hemp seeds, cinnamon, salt, coconut oil and agave nectar and stir well. Divide mixture into two batches and spread out on two nonstick dehydrator sheets. Dehydrate at 105°F (41°C) for 2 to 3 hours, until dry and crisp. Allow to cool. Transfer to an airtight container and store at room temperature for up to 2 weeks.

Variation

You may substitute any type of nut or seed for the ones called for in this recipe. Keep in mind that because nuts contain more fat than seeds, it is important not to substitute seeds for too many nuts, or the mixture will become dry and not as filling.

Apple, Banana and Flax "Oatmeal"

> Although this recipe is very simple to prepare, it will leave you feeling very nourished because of the healthy fats, protein and fiber it contains. For added flavor and nutrition, try adding a handful of fresh blueberries as a garnish.

Makes 2 servings

Tips

To soak this quantity of flax seeds, place in a bowl and add 1½ cups (375 mL) water. Cover and set aside for 30 minutes. Drain.

For a slightly different flavor, add a pinch of freshly grated nutmeg and a dash of raw vanilla extract along with the cinnamon.

¾ cup	whole flax seeds, soaked and drained (see Tips, left)	175 mL
1 cup	fresh apple juice	250 mL
½ cup	chopped peeled apple	125 mL
½ cup	chopped banana	125 mL
2 tsp	ground cinnamon	10 mL
Pinch	fine sea salt	Pinch

1. In a blender, combine apple juice, apple and banana. Blend at high speed until smooth.
2. Add soaked flax seeds, cinnamon and salt. Blend at low speed until seeds are coarsely ground and cinnamon is thoroughly combined. Serve immediately or cover and refrigerate for up to 2 days.

Chocolate Chia Seed Pudding

> This creamy chocolate pudding is high in protein as well as omega-3 fatty acids, provided by the chia seeds. It is a good source of calcium, potassium, phosphorus and fiber. Preliminary research shows that a chemical contained in chocolate may promote a positive and calming mood.

Makes 2 main or 3 side servings

Tip

Cacao powder is powdered raw chocolate. Is it similar to cocoa powder but tastes even better. Because it has not been heated, it maintains all of its healthy antioxidants and is much more easily digested. Cacao powder is available in well-stocked supermarkets, natural foods stores and online. In a pinch, substitute an equal quantity of good-quality cocoa powder.

4 cups	Almond Milk (page 45)	1 L
1½ cups	chia seeds (see Tips, page 79)	375 mL
2 tbsp	raw agave nectar	30 mL
1 tbsp	raw cacao powder (see Tip, left)	15 mL
Dash	raw vanilla extract	Dash

1. In a large bowl, combine almond milk, chia seeds, agave nectar, cacao powder and vanilla. Mix well, using a wire whisk. Set aside for 10 minutes so the chia seeds can absorb the liquid and swell. Serve immediately, if possible, or cover and refrigerate for up to 2 days.

Variation

Substitute the Almond Milk with a combination of 3½ cups (875 mL) Cashew Milk (page 46) and 1 cup (250 mL) raspberries, puréed in a blender.

Warm Coconut Creamed Goji Berries

Loaded with goji berries, which are rich in antioxidants, this combination is a great way to start your morning on a cold winter day.

Makes 3 cups (750 mL)

Tips

Coconut butter is a blend of coconut oil and coconut meat. It is high in healthy fats and adds creaminess to smoothies and sauces. It is available in the nut butter section of natural foods stores or well-stocked supermarkets. Don't confuse it with coconut oil, because they are different.

If you store this in the refrigerator, it will firm up slightly. To soften, stir over hot water until the desired consistency has been achieved.

1¼ cups	unsweetened dried shredded coconut, divided	300 mL
1 cup	dried goji berries, divided	250 mL
2 tbsp	raw shelled hemp seeds	30 mL
1 tbsp	coconut butter (see Tips, left)	15 mL
¾ cup	hot filtered water	175 mL
Pinch	fine sea salt	Pinch

1. In a bowl, combine 1 cup (250 mL) coconut, ½ cup (125 mL) goji berries and the hemp seeds. Add 2 cups (500 mL) water. Cover and set aside for 30 minutes. Drain, discarding soaking water.

2. In a blender, combine soaked coconut, goji berries and hemp seeds with the coconut butter and hot water. Blend at high speed until smooth.

3. Transfer to a bowl. Stir in remaining coconut and goji berries and salt. Serve immediately, if possible, or cover and refrigerate for up to 2 days (see Tips, left).

Variations

Add 1 tsp (5 mL) ground cinnamon along with the salt.

Before serving, stir in a combination of nuts and/or seeds to taste.

Blueberry Scones

In addition to protein, fiber and good carbs, this healthy take on a traditional breakfast pastry provides calcium, beneficial fatty acids and antioxidants. Serve with Coconut Water Strawberry Jam (page 21) or a big spoonful of almond butter.

Makes 6 to 8 scones

Tips

You can purchase almond flour at well-stocked supermarkets. Just check to ensure it has been made from whole raw almonds. Or you can make your own. Place almonds in a food processor fitted with the metal blade and process until they become flour-like in consistency. The key is to process them long enough that no large pieces remain but not to overprocess, which causes the fats to break down, in which case you will start to get something similar to almond butter.

I prefer to use golden flax seeds in this recipe, as it keeps the color light. If you prefer, use brown flax seeds, which produce a darker product.

If you prefer perfectly circular scones, use a round biscuit cutter instead of a knife to cut the dough. Reroll the scraps for a final scone or two.

The trick to getting these scones just right is to make sure they do not dehydrate long enough to become crispy throughout. You want them to be a little soft in the center.

- **Electric food dehydrator**
- **Rolling pin**

½ cup	blueberries	125 mL
¼ cup	raw agave nectar (see Tips, page 35)	60 mL
2 tbsp	coconut butter (see Tips, page 31)	30 mL
2 tbsp	filtered water	30 mL
2 tsp	finely grated lemon zest	10 mL
1 tbsp	freshly squeezed lemon juice	15 mL
½ tsp	raw vanilla extract (see Tips, page 38)	2 mL
2 cups	almond flour (see Tips, left)	500 mL
3 tbsp	ground flax seeds (see Tips, left)	45 mL
½ tsp	ground cinnamon	2 mL
¼ tsp	fine sea salt	1 mL

1. In a food processor fitted with the metal blade, process blueberries, agave nectar, coconut butter, water, lemon zest and juice and vanilla, until smooth, stopping the motor once and scraping down the sides of the bowl.

2. In a bowl, combine almond flour, flax seeds, cinnamon and sea salt. Mix well.

3. Add blueberry mixture to almond flour mixture and mix well. Set aside for 10 to 15 minutes to allow the flax to absorb some of the liquid and swell.

4. Place the dough between two nonstick dehydrator sheets or parchment paper and, using a rolling pin, roll into a square ½ inch (1 cm) thick. Remove the top sheet and, using a knife (see Tips, left), cut the dough into 6 to 8 equal scones. If necessary, slide parchment into dehydrator. Place scones about 2 inches (5 cm) apart. Dehydrate at 105°F (41°C) for 10 to 12 hours, until scones are firm enough to handle. Transfer to the mesh sheet, space evenly and dehydrate for 4 to 5 hours or until dry on the outside and slightly soft in the middle. Serve warm or allow to cool, then transfer to an airtight container and refrigerate for up to 3 days. To serve, place on a nonstick dehydrator sheet and warm at 105°F (41°C) for 20 to 30 minutes.

Cinnamon Raisin Flax Bagels

The key to making these bagels perfect is to dehydrate them as long as possible to remove all moisture from the dough. They can be stored in an airtight container for up to a month, which makes them a perfect anytime snack. They are delicious served with almond butter or Cashew Scallion Cream Cheese (page 104).

Makes 8 bagels

Tips

When making raw breads in the dehydrator, you have options in terms of texture. For crispier, firmer bread, dehydrate until all of the moisture has been removed. This will make storing the bread easy, as it can't spoil without moisture. For softer, more chewy bread, dehydrate for less time, retaining moisture in the middle of the bread. Make sure to store breads that contain moisture in the refrigerator, because bacteria can grow when water is present.

When spreading out raw breads on a dehydrator sheet, have a small bowl containing room-temperature water handy. Use this to wet your hands intermittently to prevent the dough from sticking.

Use ground golden flax seeds rather than brown flax to achieve a lighter-colored bagel.

- **Electric food dehydrator**

4 cups	ground flax seeds (see Tips, left)	1 L
3 tbsp	ground cinnamon	45 mL
1 tsp	fine sea salt	5 mL
2 cups	water	500 mL
¼ cup	raisins	60 mL

1. In a large bowl, combine flax seeds, cinnamon and salt. Add water and raisins and mix well.
2. Using an ice cream scoop or a small ladle, drop 8 equal portions of dough onto a nonstick dehydrator sheet, distributing evenly, and shape into rounds. Using your index finger, make a hole in the center of each bagel.
3. Dehydrate at 105°F (41°C) for 4 to 5 hours, until firm enough to handle. Flip and transfer to the mesh sheet. Dehydrate for 3 to 4 hours or until dry throughout. Serve warm or allow to cool. Transfer to an airtight container and store for up to one month.

Variations

Sesame Garlic Bagels: Substitute ½ cup (125 mL) white sesame seeds, ¼ cup (60 mL) shredded yellow onion and 4 cloves garlic, minced, for the raisins and cinnamon.

Lemon Dill Poppy Seed Bagels: Substitute the ground cinnamon and raisins in this recipe with 3 tbsp (45 mL) each lemon juice and poppy seeds and 1 tbsp (15 mL) dried dill weed.

Apple and Celery Flaxseed Crackers

These crackers are a great morning snack, full of heart-healthy flax seeds. They are delicious spread with Cashew Scallion Cream Cheese (page 104) and accompanied by a Thank You Berry Much Smoothie (page 60).

Makes 16 crackers

Tips

To soak the whole flax seeds for this recipe, place in a bowl and combine with 4 cups (1 L) water. Cover and set aside for 30 minutes so the flax can absorb the liquid and swell. Drain, discarding soaking water. Rinse under cold running water until the water runs clear.

When spreading out raw breads or crackers on a dehydrator sheet, keep a small bowl of room-temperature water off to the side. Use this to wet your hands intermittently to prevent the dough from sticking to your hands.

I like to use brown flax seeds when making this recipe because they produce a darker-colored cracker.

- **Electric food dehydrator**

2 cups	whole flax seeds, soaked (see Tips, left)	500 mL
1 cup	chopped peeled, cored apple	250 mL
1/2 cup	chopped celery	125 mL
1 tsp	freshly squeezed lemon juice	5 mL
1/2 tsp	fine sea salt	2 mL
1 cup	ground flax seeds (see Tips, left)	250 mL
1 cup	(approx.) filtered water	250 mL
1/4 cup	chopped parsley	60 mL

1. In a food processor fitted with the metal blade, process apple, celery, lemon juice and salt until smooth.
2. In a large bowl, combine soaked whole flax seeds, ground flax seeds, water and parsley. Add apple mixture and mix well. The dough should be thick enough to spread but not so thick that it is difficult to stir. If needed, add up to 1/4 cup (60 mL) additional water.
3. Transfer mixture to a nonstick dehydrator sheet and, using your hands, spread evenly in a thin layer, approximately 1/2 inch (1 cm) thick, across the entire area of the sheet. Using a small knife, cut into 16 equal portions. Dehydrate at 105°F (41°C) for 10 to 12 hours or until crispy. Allow to cool, then transfer to an airtight container. Store at room temperature for up to 2 weeks.

Morning Energy Bars

These bars are the perfect way to start your day, as they contain proteins, healthy fats and carbohydrates and an abundance of micronutrients such as calcium, magnesium and potassium.

Makes 9 bars

Tips

There are numerous varieties of dates, but Medjool are my favorite. Although they are generally more expensive, they are larger, softer and ideal for using in raw food recipes.

Cacao powder is powdered raw chocolate. Is it similar to cocoa powder but tastes even better, with a deeper, richer flavor. Cacao powder is available in well-stocked supermarkets, natural foods stores and online. If you are transitioning to a raw foods diet or can't find it, substitute an equal quantity of good-quality cocoa powder.

When purchasing agave nectar, be sure to look for products labeled "raw." Most of the agave nectar on the market has been heated to a high temperature and does not qualify as raw food. If you have concerns, ask your purveyor.

2 cups	chopped pitted dates	500 mL
2 tbsp	raw cacao powder (see Tips, left)	30 mL
3 tbsp	raw agave nectar (see Tips, left)	45 mL
2 tbsp	water	30 mL
¼ cup	raw cashews	60 mL
¼ cup	walnuts	60 mL
¼ cup	raw whole almonds	60 mL
3 tbsp	raw shelled hemp seeds	45 mL
2 tsp	sesame seeds	10 mL
Pinch	fine sea salt	Pinch

1. In a food processor fitted with the metal blade, process dates, cacao powder, agave nectar and water until smooth. Add cashews, walnuts, almonds, hemp seeds, sesame seeds and salt. Process until the ingredients come together to form a sticky mass, stopping the motor once and scraping down the sides of the work bowl.

2. Transfer to a cutting board. Using your hands, press out the mixture until it is 1 inch (2.5 cm) thick and shape into a square about 6 inches (15 cm) long. Cut into 9 bars, each approximately 3 inches (7.5 cm) long and 1 inch (2.5 cm) wide. Place on a platter or baking sheet lined with parchment paper and refrigerate for one hour to set. Serve immediately or cover and refrigerate for up to 2 weeks.

Variations

Various kinds of nuts and seeds can be substituted in the same quantities. For example, you may substitute chia seeds for the sesame seeds. If you have Brazil nuts on hand, try substituting them for the cashews. By experimenting, you may find a combination that suits you to a tee.

Buckwheat Toast

This crunchy favorite is great served as a breakfast side with a healthy scoop of almond butter. It's also just perfect on its own.

Makes 8 slices

Tips

To soak the buckwheat for this recipe, combine 4 cups (1 L) groats and 8 cups (2 L) water. Cover and set aside for 2 hours, changing the water every 30 minutes. Drain, discarding soaking water. Rinse under cold running water until the water runs clear.

When dehydrating raw breads, you have options in terms of the texture produced. For crispier, firm bread, dehydrate until all the moisture has been removed. This will make storage easier — because it doesn't contain moisture, it can't spoil. For softer, more chewy bread, retain moisture in the middle of the bread by reducing the dehydrating time. Make sure to store breads that contain moisture in the refrigerator. Because they contain water, bacteria have the potential to grow.

When spreading out raw breads or crackers on a dehydrator sheet, keep a small bowl of room-temperature water off to the side. Use this to wet your hands intermittently to prevent the dough from sticking to your hands.

- **Electric food dehydrator**

4 cups	buckwheat groats, soaked (see Tips, left)	1 L
¼ cup	filtered water	60 mL
2 tbsp	cold-pressed (extra virgin) olive oil	30 mL
1 tsp	nutritional yeast	5 mL
1 tsp	fine sea salt	5 mL
½ cup	ground flax seeds	125 mL
2 tbsp	sesame seeds	30 mL

1. In a food processor fitted with the metal blade, in batches, as necessary, process soaked buckwheat, water, olive oil, nutritional yeast and salt until smooth, stopping the motor once and scraping down the sides of the work bowl once, adding more water 1 tbsp (15 mL) at a time, if necessary, to facilitate purée. Transfer to a bowl.

2. Add flax seeds and sesame seeds and stir well. Set aside for 10 to 15 minutes, until the flax absorbs the liquid and swells up.

3. Transfer to nonstick dehydrator sheets. Using the palm of your hand, spread the dough evenly in a thin layer approximately ½ inch (1 cm) thick. Cut into 8 pieces. Dehydrate at 105°F (41°C) for 10 to 12 hours or until bread is firm enough to handle.

4. Flip bread onto mesh sheets and dehydrate at 105°F (41°C) for 5 to 6 hours or until dry and crisp like toast. Serve warm or allow to cool. Transfer to an airtight container and store at room temperature for up to 5 days.

Banana Pecan French Toast

This take on classic French toast will be your new favorite raw breakfast dish. It takes very little time to prepare and even less to consume. I particularly enjoy eating this with Caramel Sauce (page 369).

Makes 16 slices

Tips

To soak the pecans for this recipe, combine 1 cup (250 mL) pecans with 2 cups (500 mL) water. Cover and set aside for 30 minutes. Drain and rinse under cold running water.

When making raw food recipes, your juices should always be freshly pressed or squeezed. If freshly pressed apple juice is not available, look for pure apple juice (not from concentrate) with no sugar added.

When spreading out raw breads or crackers on a dehydrator sheet, keep a small bowl of room-temperature water off to the side. Use this to wet your hands intermittently to prevent the dough from sticking to your hands.

- **Electric food dehydrator**

1 cup	pecans, soaked (see Tips, left)	250 mL
3 cups	chopped bananas	750 mL
¼ cup	(approx.) freshly squeezed orange juice	60 mL
¼ cup	apple juice (see Tips, left)	60 mL
¼ cup	raw agave nectar	60 mL
2 tsp	ground cinnamon	10 mL
Pinch	fine sea salt	Pinch
2 cups	ground flax seeds	500 mL
	Filtered water, optional	

1. In a blender, combine bananas, soaked pecans, orange juice, apple juice, agave nectar, cinnamon and salt. Blend at high speed until smooth, gradually adding a little more orange juice to help blend, if necessary.
2. Transfer to a deep bowl. Stir in flax seeds and, using your hands, work until the mixture is the consistency of bread dough. If the dough is too firm, add more orange juice, 1 tbsp (15 mL) at a time, until desired consistency has been reached.
3. Transfer the dough onto a nonstick dehydrator sheet and, using the palm of your hand, spread it evenly in a layer approximately ¾ inch (2 cm) thick. Use a small knife to cut the dough into 16 equal slices. Dehydrate at 105°F (41°C) for 8 to 10 hours or until dry enough to handle. Flip slices onto a mesh sheet and dehydrate at 105°F (41°C) for 3 to 4 hours or until firm on the outside and soft in the middle. Serve warm or allow to cool. Transfer to an airtight container and refrigerate for up to 2 weeks. Before serving, place on a nonstick dehydrator sheet and reheat at 105°F (41°C) for 30 minutes to warm.

Variation

Omit the pecans and increase the ground flax seeds to 3 cups (750 mL). Add 1 cup (250 mL) water to the blender. This will give you a nut-free version of the French toast, which is a good way to limit the amount of fat or calories in your diet and also accommodate people who have nut allergies.

Pear and Walnut Pancakes

Soft and fluffy, these pancakes are very easy to create and even easier to eat. I enjoy them with Blueberry Date Syrup (page 22) and a side of Eggplant Bacon (page 41).

Makes 8 pancakes

Tips

To soak the walnuts for this recipe, combine in a bowl with 3 cups (750 mL) water. Cover and set aside for 30 minutes. Drain, discarding soaking liquid, and rinse under cold running water until the water runs clear.

Although I have called for vanilla extract for convenience, in my opinion, the best-tasting and healthiest form of vanilla is seeds that come directly from the pod. They are easy to use — split the pod lengthwise down the middle with a paring knife and, using the back of the knife, scrape the seeds away from you in one clean motion. Do not discard the pods; use them to infuse flavor into liquids such as nut milks and agave nectar, or your favorite spirit.

When making this recipe, it is important not to let the pancakes become too dehydrated; otherwise you will be left with crackers. Check on them every hour or two to make sure they do not become dry. The humidity level in the room and the ripeness of the fruit can play a role in the amount of dehydrating time they will need.

- **Electric food dehydrator**

1½ cups	walnuts, soaked (see Tips, left)	375 mL
3 cups	chopped pears	750 mL
¼ cup	filtered water	60 mL
1	banana	1
3 tbsp	raw agave nectar	45 mL
1 tbsp	melted coconut oil (see Tips, page 40)	15 mL
2 tsp	raw vanilla extract or ½ tsp (2 mL) vanilla seeds (see Tips, left)	10 mL
Pinch	ground cinnamon	Pinch
Pinch	fine sea salt	Pinch
½ cup	ground flax seeds	125 mL

1. In a blender, combine walnuts, pears and water. Blend at high speed until smooth. Add banana, agave nectar, coconut oil, vanilla, cinnamon and sea salt. Blend at high speed until smooth.

2. Transfer to a bowl. Add flax seeds and stir well. Set aside for 15 minutes to allow the flax to absorb some liquid and swell.

3. Using a ladle, scoop out 8 equal portions of batter and arrange evenly on a nonstick dehydrator sheet, leaving plenty of space between scoops. Using your hands, shape into thin rounds. Dehydrate at 105°F (41°C) for 4 to 5 hours or until firm enough to flip. Flip onto a mesh sheet and dehydrate for 2 to 3 hours or until the centers of the pancakes are no longer wet. Serve warm or allow to cool. Transfer to an airtight container and refrigerate for up to 2 weeks. To serve, place on a nonstick dehydrator sheet and reheat in the dehydrator at 105°F (41°C) for 20 to 30 minutes or until warmed through.

Variation

If walnuts are not available, substitute an equal amount of raw cashews, soaked in water for 30 minutes.

Almond Banana Crêpes

Thin and light, these classic takes on the French specialty are absolutely delicious. They require very little time to prepare and can be stored in an airtight container at room temperature for up to two weeks. I like to drizzle them with Chocolate Sauce (page 369) or top them with a heaping pile of Macerated Berries (page 331) and a dollop of Cashew Whipped Cream (page 367).

Makes 8 to 10 crêpes

Tip

To make almond flour, place whole raw almonds in a food processor fitted with the metal blade and process until they become flour-like in consistency. The key is to process them long enough so no large pieces of almond remain, without overprocessing. When processed for too long, the fats will begin to break down and you will start to get something similar to almond butter. When creating almond flour from scratch, 1 cup (250 mL) whole almonds will yield ¾ cup (175 mL) almond flour.

- **Electric food dehydrator**

4 cups	chopped bananas	1 L
3 tbsp	filtered water	45 mL
2 tbsp	raw agave nectar (see Tips, page 35)	30 mL
1 tsp	raw vanilla extract or ¼ tsp (1 mL) vanilla seeds (see Tips, page 38)	5 mL
Pinch	ground cinnamon	Pinch
Pinch	fine sea salt	Pinch
½ cup	almond flour (see Tip, left)	125 mL
2 tbsp	ground flax seeds	30 mL

1. In a food processor fitted with the metal blade, process bananas, water, agave nectar, vanilla, cinnamon and salt until smooth.

2. Transfer to a bowl. Stir in almond flour and ground flax seeds until well incorporated. Set aside for 15 minutes so the flax can absorb some of the liquid and swell.

3. Using a ladle, scoop out 8 to 10 equal portions of batter and arrange evenly on a nonstick dehydrator sheet, leaving plenty of space between scoops. Using the back of the ladle, flatten each portion to ¼ inch (0.5 cm) thick.

4. Dehydrate at 105°F (41°C) for 3 to 4 hours or until firm enough to remove from the sheet without sticking. Flip the crêpes onto the mesh sheet and dehydrate at 105°F (41°C) for 1 to 2 hours or until the middle of each crêpe is no longer wet. Allow to cool, then transfer to an airtight container. Store at room temperature for up to 2 weeks.

Banana Coconut Hotcakes

These little cakes contain only five ingredients but are full of healthy fats as well as potassium — and they are addictive. I love eating them on their own or with a healthy dollop of Caramel Sauce (page 36).

Makes 12 to 15 hotcakes

Tips

To ripen bananas quickly, place them in a paper bag with an uncut apple and tightly fold over the end of the bag. The apple will emit ethylene gas, which will help to speed ripening. Place the bag in a warm, dry area until the bananas are ripe.

Use unsweetened medium-shredded unsulfured coconut. Not only is this type of coconut nutritionally beneficial, the medium shred size will help the hotcakes hold together during the drying process.

Coconut oil is solid at room temperature. It has a melting temperature of 76°F (24°C), so it is easy to liquefy. To melt it, place near a source of heat. If you have a dehydrator, you can place the required amount of coconut oil in it in a shallow bowl at 100°F (38°C) for 5 to 6 minutes, until melted. If you do not have a dehydrator, place a shallow glass bowl over a pot of simmering water.

4 cups	chopped bananas	1 L
1 cup	dried shredded coconut (see Tips, left)	250 mL
3 tbsp	melted coconut oil (see Tips, left)	45 mL
¼ cup	raw agave nectar	60 mL
1 tsp	ground cinnamon	5 mL

1. In a food processor fitted with the metal blade, process bananas, coconut, coconut oil, agave nectar and cinnamon until smooth.

2. Using a ladle, scoop out 12 to 15 equal portions of batter, each approximately 2 inches (5 cm) in diameter and ¾ inch (2 cm) thick, and arrange evenly on a nonstick dehydrator sheet, leaving plenty of space between scoops. Dehydrate at 105°F (41°C) for 4 to 5 hours or until firm enough to remove from the sheet without sticking. Flip onto a mesh sheet and dehydrate for 1 to 2 hours or until barely moist but still soft throughout. Remove from the dehydrator and allow to cool. Store in the refrigerator in an airtight container for up to 2 weeks.

Eggplant Bacon

These crispy eggplant strips are delicious. Combine them with Buckwheat Toast (page 36), Sunflower Seed Miso Butter (page 20), sliced tomatoes and lettuce for the perfect raw BLT.

Makes 40 strips

Tips

Sometimes eggplant can have a slightly bitter taste, which "sweating" remedies. Sprinkle eggplant slices with a little sea salt and place over a colander. Set aside for 30 to 45 minutes, until eggplant releases its moisture. Pat slices dry with paper towels.

While wheat-free tamari is not raw, it is gluten-free. The raw alternative for tamari, nama shoyu, does contain gluten. If you are following a completely raw diet and can tolerate gluten, by all means substitute an equal quantity of nama shoyu.

When purchasing extra virgin olive oil, make sure the label says "cold-pressed." Some olive oils are extracted using a centrifuge system, which spins the olives at a very high rate. This heats the olives and the resulting oil, depriving it of its raw status.

- **Electric food dehydrator**
- **Mandoline**

1	medium eggplant (about 12 oz/375 g)	1
¼ cup	cold-pressed (extra virgin) olive oil	60 mL
3 tbsp	raw agave nectar	45 mL
2 tbsp	wheat-free tamari (see Tips, left)	30 mL
1 tbsp	filtered water	15 mL
2 tsp	chipotle chile powder	10 mL

1. Cut a thin slice from each end of the eggplant. Using a mandoline or a sharp knife, slice the eggplant lengthwise into strips ½ inch (1 cm) thick. Place in a shallow baking dish.

2. In a small bowl, whisk together olive oil, agave nectar, tamari, water and chipotle powder. Pour over eggplant strips and toss gently (eggplant can tear easily) to ensure even coating. Set aside to marinate for 30 minutes.

3. Lay marinated strips on a nonstick dehydrator sheet (you may need more than one, depending upon the kind of dehydrator you have) and dehydrate at 105°F (41°C) for 12 to 15 hours or until crispy. Allow to cool and store in an airtight container at room temperature for up to 2 weeks. If the eggplant picks up moisture from the air, return it to the dehydrator at 105°F (41°C) for 30 to 45 minutes to crisp it up again.

Variation

For a Southwest version of eggplant bacon, try whisking in 1 tbsp (15 mL) Mexican-style chile powder blend, 1 tsp (5 mL) ground cumin and ¼ tsp (1 mL) lemon juice.

Cashew, Mushroom and Red Pepper Scramble

This recipe, a rich and satisfying blend of protein, vitamins and minerals, is especially nutritious if you use high-quality nutritional yeast. Serve this with Eggplant Bacon (page 41) and Buckwheat Toast (page 36) for a great special-occasion breakfast.

Makes 4 portions

Tips

To soak the cashews for this recipe, place in a bowl and cover with 6 cups (1.5 L) water. Cover and set aside for 30 minutes. Drain, discarding soaking water, and rinse under cold running water until the water runs clear.

To clean mushrooms, use a damp cloth to brush off any dirt from the surface. Never clean mushrooms with water. Mushrooms are like a sponge — they will absorb the water and turn gray.

While wheat-free tamari is not raw, it is gluten-free. The raw alternative for tamari, nama shoyu, does contain gluten. If you are following a completely raw diet and can tolerate gluten, by all means substitute an equal quantity of nama shoyu.

Nutritional yeast is used in vegan and raw food diets mainly because it is a source of vitamin B_{12}. It is pasteurized, so technically it does not qualify as a raw food. However, in addition to the necessary nutrients, it adds a deep umami-like flavor to many dishes.

3 cups	raw cashews, soaked (see Tips, left)	750 mL
1/2 cup	sliced, trimmed small white mushrooms	125 mL
2 tbsp	wheat-free tamari (see Tips, left)	30 mL
1 tsp	flax oil	5 mL
1/2 cup	chopped red bell pepper	125 mL
1/4 cup	nutritional yeast (see Tips, left)	60 mL
2 tsp	freshly squeezed lemon juice	10 mL
1 tbsp	chopped fresh thyme leaves	15 mL
1 tsp	fine sea salt	5 mL

1. In a bowl, toss together mushrooms, tamari and flax oil. Set aside to marinate for 10 minutes.
2. Meanwhile, in a food processor fitted with the metal blade, process red pepper, nutritional yeast, lemon juice, thyme and salt until mixture is smooth and no visible pieces of red pepper remain. Add soaked cashews and process until smooth, stopping the motor and scraping down the sides of the work bowl as necessary. Add to marinated mushrooms and stir well.

Variation

For a more extravagant version of this dish, try using a mixture of rare and wild mushrooms in place of the button mushrooms. I like using king oyster, shiitake and chanterelle mushrooms.

Smoothies, Juices and Other Drinks

Water is fundamental to human life — our cells consist mostly of water. So it's not surprising that water plays a significant role in a successful raw food diet. Not only do we drink water, but fruits and vegetables contain water, and it is their liquid component that enables us to easily transform these foods into refreshing and nutritious drinks.

Smoothies, freshly made juices and other drinks made from nutritious whole foods are one way to consume the nutrients you need to keep you healthy. Drinking smoothies is one of the tricks for getting more raw, unprocessed foods into your diet. Smoothies, which are made in a blender, are quick and easy to prepare. They can be made from ingredients such as dairy-alternative "milks," leafy greens or fresh or frozen berries that you're likely to have on hand.

When making smoothies, you start with a liquid base such as a nut milk, fruit juice or water. Typical fruit and vegetable ingredients include berries, apples, pears, kale and celery. Nutritional balance is easily achieved by including ingredients such as hemp or flax seeds or a spoonful or so of a nut or seed butter, which adds healthy fats and protein to the drink and also helps to create a creamy texture. To sweeten smoothies, add one or two pitted dates and/or banana. Not only do these fruits add body, they provide added nutrients, including fiber. In fact, smoothies differ from juices precisely because they contain fiber. Just be aware that fiber can make the drink very thick if you don't add enough liquid.

Because they do not contain fiber, juices are an extremely concentrated source of vitamins, minerals and phytonutrients. The absence of fiber means that your body can assimilate the nutrients more quickly. When you drink freshly made juice, your body doesn't need to burn energy to digest fiber, so it has time to relax, detoxifying and cleansing itself.

I've included recipes for nut milks because making your own nut milk means you control the ingredients — you know exactly what it contains. There is no added salt, sugar or hidden emulsifiers. You create a product that is raw and unpasteurized and a fraction of the cost of prepared versions.

And to help you extend your consumption of nutritious raw foods into your social life, I've included several recipes for "mocktails" — delicious non-alcoholic drinks made with fruits and vegetables. I've also included four recipes for nut milks. In addition to being refreshing beverages that can be consumed on their own when chilled, nut milks form the basis for many recipes in this book, especially smoothies and soups.

Almond Milk

Almond milk is a refreshing creation that addresses one of the most common allergens in the world — dairy products. Although lower in protein, almond milk contains the phytochemicals found in almonds as well as trace amounts of potassium, magnesium, manganese, phosphorus and B vitamins. This recipe is very simple to make and, after soaking the almonds, takes no time at all. Use this in smoothies and soups or as a refreshing pick-me-up any time of the day. If you are feeling a bit peckish or having a slight slump, a glass of cold almond milk will provide instant energy.

Makes 4 cups (1 L)

Tips

To soak the almonds for this recipe, place in a bowl and add 2 cups (500 mL) filtered water. Cover and set aside for at least 30 minutes or up to 12 hours. If you are soaking the nuts at room temperature, change the water every 3 hours (if they are refrigerated, this step isn't necessary). When the soaking time has been completed, drain, discard the soaking water and rinse under cold running water until the water runs clear.

The leftover almond pulp can be refrigerated in a covered container for up to 3 days. If you own a dehydrator you can use it to make almond flour. Spread the pulp on a nonstick dehydrator sheet and dehydrate at 105°F (41°C) for 5 to 6 hours or until dry and crisp. Cool and transfer to an airtight container. Keep at room temperature for up to 2 weeks.

Always make sure to use filtered or pure spring water to make nut milks, as well as other raw food recipes.

- **Nut milk bag or cheesecloth (see page 13)**

1 cup	whole raw almonds, soaked (see Tips, left)	250 mL
4 cups	filtered water (see Tips, left)	1 L

1. In a blender, combine almonds and water. Blend at high speed for 30 to 60 seconds or until the liquid becomes milky white and no visible pieces of almond remain.
2. Pour into a nut milk bag placed over a pitcher, large enough to accommodate the liquid, and strain. Starting at the top of the bag and using your hands, squeeze in a downward direction to extract the remaining milk (for cheesecloth instructions, see page 14). Cover and refrigerate the milk for up to 3 days. Discard the pulp or save for another use (see Tips, left.)

Variation

Sweetened Almond Milk: After straining, return milk to the blender and add a chopped pitted date, a dash of raw vanilla extract and a pinch of sea salt. Blend until smooth.

Cashew Milk

This version of raw non-dairy milk is a little higher in fat than some others, which makes it well suited for uses such as adding to coffee and tea. It is also a great base for smoothies such as Almond Butter and Jelly Smoothie (page 53), Cake Batter Smoothie (page 53) and Chocolate Raspberry Mint Ice (page 56). I also like it as a base for soups, among other uses.

Makes 4 cups (1 L)

Tip

To soak the cashews for this recipe, place in a bowl and add 2 cups (500 mL) filtered water. Cover and set aside for at least 30 minutes or up to 12 hours. If you are soaking the nuts at room temperature, change the water every 3 hours (if they are refrigerated, this step isn't necessary). When the soaking time has been completed, drain, discard the soaking water and rinse under cold running water until the water runs clear.

- **Nut milk bag or cheesecloth (see page 13)**

1 cup	raw cashews, soaked (see Tip, left)	250 mL
4 cups	filtered water	1 L

1. In a blender, combine soaked cashews and water. Blend at high speed for 30 to 45 seconds or until liquid becomes milky white and no visible pieces of cashew remain.

2. Pour into a nut milk bag placed over a pitcher, large enough to accommodate the liquid, and strain. Starting at the top of the bag and using your hands, squeeze in a downward direction to extract the remaining milk (for cheesecloth instructions, see page 14). Cover and refrigerate the milk for up to 3 days. Discard the pulp.

Variations

Extra-Creamy Cashew Milk: Use 2 cups (500 mL) drained soaked cashews to 4 cups (1 L) water.

Cashews are naturally slightly sweet, but if you prefer a sweeter result, add 1 tbsp (15 mL) raw agave nectar after straining.

Hemp Milk

Hemp has a very distinctive flavor, and raw milk made from hemp seeds has a nuttier flavor than most. Hemp milk, like the seeds it is made from, is rich in omega-3 fats. I like to use hemp milk on cereal, in smoothies or simply as a drink.

Makes 4 cups (1 L)

Tip

Shelled hemp seeds are soft and small enough to make straining unnecessary. However, if you prefer, strain the milk through a nut milk bag. Starting at the top of the bag, use your hands to squeeze in a downward direction to extract the milk. Discard the solids.

4 cups	filtered water	1 L
3 tbsp	raw shelled hemp seeds	45 mL

1. In a blender, combine water and hemp seeds. Blend at high speed for 30 to 45 seconds or until the liquid becomes milky white and no visible pieces of hemp seeds remain. Transfer to a pitcher, cover and refrigerate for up to 3 days.

Variation

Cinnamon-Strawberry Hemp Milk: After processing the hemp milk, add ½ cup (125 mL) chopped hulled strawberries and 2 tsp (10 mL) ground cinnamon. Blend at high speed until smooth.

Coconut Milk

Coconut milk is higher in fat than other raw milks, which makes it perfect for adding to tea and other warm beverages.

Makes 4 cups (1 L)

Tips

To soak the coconut for this recipe, place in a bowl and add 2 cups (500 mL) water. Cover and set aside for 30 minutes. Drain and rinse under cold running water until the water runs clear.

After refrigeration, a small layer of fat will form at the top of the container. Simply stir this fat back into the liquid, using a small whisk or fork, before drinking.

• **Nut milk bag or cheesecloth (see page 13)**

1 cup	unsweetened dried shredded coconut, soaked (see Tips, page 40)	250 mL
4 cups	filtered water	1 L
Pinch	fine sea salt	Pinch

1. In a blender, combine water, coconut and salt. Blend at high speed for 1 minute or until the liquid becomes milky white and no visible pieces of coconut remain.
2. Pour into a nut milk bag placed over a pitcher, large enough to accommodate the liquid, and strain as for Cashew Milk (page 46).

Variation

Strawberry Chocolate Coconut Milk: After straining the coconut milk, return it to the blender. Add ½ cup (125 mL) chopped hulled strawberries, 3 tbsp (45 mL) agave nectar and 2 tbsp (30 mL) cacao powder and blend again until smooth.

Cinnamon Toast Crunch Smoothie

This drink makes a great breakfast on the go. Nutrient-dense and filling, it should keep you satisfied well into the lunch hour.

Makes 1½ cups (375 mL)

Tips

This makes enough for one generous serving. Double the recipe if you want more.

When transitioning to a raw food diet, for convenience you can substitute store-bought prepared nut milks for homemade versions. Although they have been pasteurized, they are a good way to begin incorporating dairy alternatives into your diet. While not as nutrient-dense as the raw versions, they have a longer shelf life and can be stored unrefrigerated until opened.

1 cup	Almond Milk (page 45)	250 mL
2 tbsp	almond butter	30 mL
1	banana	1
2	chopped pitted dates	2
1 tbsp	chopped gingerroot	15 mL
2 tsp	ground cinnamon	10 mL

1. In a blender, combine almond milk, almond butter, banana, dates, ginger and cinnamon. Blend at high speed until smooth. Serve immediately.

Variations

For a lighter version, use only 1 tbsp (15 mL) almond butter. This makes a great midday snack.

Experiment using different nut butters and/or ground spices to achieve flavor combinations that suit your palate. I love pumpkin seed butter and a pinch of ground cloves as substitutes for the almond butter and cinnamon. Nut and/or seed butters have complex flavors; it's fun to explore combining them with various spices.

Eat Your Greens Smoothie

Here is the perfect solution for days when you feel the need to increase your consumption of greens but don't have time to make Perfect Green Juice (page 18).

Makes 1½ cups (375 mL)

Tips

This makes enough for one generous serving. Double the recipe if you want more.

For the best results, make sure your mango is perfectly ripe and the greens are beautifully crisp.

Before chopping the kale, remove the long stem that runs up through the leaf almost to the top of the plant. Use only the leafy green parts.

1 cup	Hemp Milk (page 47)	250 mL
½ cup	chopped peeled mango	125 mL
½ cup	chopped trimmed kale	125 mL
¼ cup	chopped romaine lettuce	60 mL
¼ cup	chopped parsley leaves	60 mL
1	banana	1
1	chopped pitted date	1

1. In a blender, combine hemp milk, mango, kale, lettuce, parsley, banana and date. Blend at high speed until smooth.

Variations

Substitute an equal quantity of chopped papaya or pear for the mango.

Substitute an equal quantity of arugula, spinach or mustard greens for the lettuce.

Substitute cilantro leaves for the parsley.

Orange Cream Smoothie

This smoothie is a take on the Creamsicles that you enjoyed as a kid.

Makes 2 cups (500 mL)

Tip

If you prefer, use ½ tsp (2 mL) vanilla seeds instead of the vanilla extract.

½ cup	Almond Milk (page 45)	125 mL
½ cup	freshly squeezed orange juice	125 mL
1	banana	1
2	chopped pitted dates	2
2 tsp	raw vanilla extract (see Tip, left)	5 mL
Dash	raw agave nectar	Dash

1. In a blender, combine almond milk, orange juice, banana, dates, vanilla and agave nectar. Blend at high speed until smooth. Serve immediately.

Variations

Substitute Hemp Milk (page 47) or Coconut Milk (page 47) for the Almond Milk.

Apple Pie Smoothie

If you have risk factors for Type 2 diabetes, beginning your day with this delicious smoothie will get you off to a particularly good start. Studies show that cinnamon can help to control blood sugar levels, and it is also a potent antioxidant.

Makes 2 cups (500 mL)

Tips

If you don't have coconut butter, substitute 2 tbsp (30 mL) melted coconut oil (see Tips, page 40).

Use high-quality organic cinnamon. You will get the freshest flavor by grinding whole cinnamon sticks in a spice grinder.

1 cup	Almond Milk (page 45)	250 mL
½ cup	chopped peeled, cored apple	125 mL
1 tbsp	coconut butter (see Tips, left)	15 mL
1 tsp	ground cinnamon	5 mL
3 tbsp	filtered water	45 mL
1	chopped pitted date	1
Pinch	ground cloves	Pinch

1. In a blender, combine almond milk, apple, coconut butter and cinnamon. Blend at high speed until smooth. Add water, date and cloves. Blend at high speed until smooth. Serve immediately.

Banana Cream Pie Smoothie

This smoothie is light, fluffy and soft, just like the dessert it takes its name from. The trick to making this truly delicious is to use bananas that are overripe.

Makes 1½ cups (375 mL)

Tip

Substitute ¼ cup (60 mL) melted coconut oil for the coconut butter. Coconut oil is solid at room temperature (see Tips, page 40 for melting instructions.)

1 cup	Almond Milk (page 45)	250 mL
2	bananas	2
3 tbsp	coconut butter (see Tips, left)	45 mL
2	chopped pitted dates	2
½ tsp	raw vanilla extract	2 mL
Dash	raw agave nectar	Dash

1. In a blender, combine almond milk, bananas, coconut butter, dates, vanilla and agave nectar. Blend at high speed until smooth.

Variation

If young Thai coconuts are available, substitute the shredded flesh of two (approximately 1 cup/250 mL) for the coconut butter. Young Thai coconuts are green; their flesh is very soft and easily blends into a creamy consistency. Because they are young, they contain a lot of water and yield only ½ to ¾ cup (125 to 175 mL) flesh per coconut.

Lemon Meringue Smoothie

This delicious smoothie is tart yet slightly sweet. It is detoxifying and alkalizing because lemon juice buffers acidity.

Makes 1½ cups (375 mL)

Tip

When purchasing citrus fruit, always buy organic, as they are some of the most heavily chemically treated crops (see page 10).

1 cup	Hemp Milk (page 47)	250 mL
¼ cup	freshly squeezed lemon juice	60 mL
1	banana	1
2 tbsp	Date Paste (page 80)	30 mL
2 tsp	raw vanilla extract or ½ tsp (2 mL) vanilla seeds	10 mL
1 tsp	raw agave nectar	5 mL

1. In a blender, combine hemp milk, lemon juice, banana, date paste, vanilla and agave nectar. Blend at high speed until smooth.

Variation

Substitute the juice of Meyer lemons for regular lemons — they are slightly sweeter.

Coconut Cardamom Smoothie

This smoothie can be served slightly warm around holiday time for a perfectly spiced, nutritionally dense treat. Use freshly ground cardamom for the best results.

Makes 1½ cups (375 mL)

Tip

To grind cardamom seeds, split open the pod, extract the seeds and use a spice grinder or mortar and pestle to grind them into a fine powder. You can also use the back of a small sauté pan, applying pressure on a surface such as a cutting board.

1 cup	Coconut Milk (page 47)	250 mL
1	banana	1
1	chopped pitted date	1
2 tbsp	coconut butter (see Tips, page 31)	30 mL
1 tbsp	raw agave nectar	15 mL
1 tsp	ground cardamom (see Tip, left)	5 mL
Pinch	fine sea salt	Pinch

1. In a blender, combine coconut milk, banana, date, coconut butter, agave nectar, cardamom and salt. Blend at high speed until smooth. Serve immediately.

Spiced Almond Thai Smoothie

> In Thai cooking the flavor profiles are built around sweet, salty, hot and sour. This smoothie is a delicious blend of such flavors that will excite your taste buds.

Makes 1½ cups (375 mL)

Tip

Remember to balance flavors proportionately in any recipe. For example, if using lime juice (sour), it is a good idea to add something sweet (such as agave nectar) to balance the acidity. If something salty is included, a nutrient-dense fat will help to mask the saltiness.

1 cup	Almond Milk (page 45)	250 mL
3 tbsp	almond butter	45 mL
2 tbsp	raw agave nectar (see Tips, page 35)	30 mL
2 tbsp	raw shelled hemp seeds	30 mL
½ tsp	freshly squeezed lime juice	2 mL
½ tsp	ground coriander seeds	2 mL
1	fresh wild lime leaf (see Tips, page 193)	1
¼ tsp	freshly grated gingerroot (see Tips, page 133)	1 mL
Pinch	fine sea salt	Pinch
Pinch	ground cayenne pepper	Pinch

1. In a blender, combine almond milk, almond butter, agave nectar, hemp seeds, lime juice, coriander, lime leaf, ginger, salt and cayenne. Blend at high speed until smooth.

Avocado Vanilla Smoothie

> This light yet creamy smoothie takes just two minutes to make and will leave you feeling satisfied for hours. The healthy fats in the avocado will be used for energy.

Makes 1½ cups (375 mL)

Tip

When following a strictly raw food diet, make sure to purchase vanilla extract that has been processed using a cold extraction method. Some vanilla beans are put into an oven after being harvested, so if you're using vanilla beans, make sure to look for those that have been sun-dried and are labeled "raw."

1 cup	Hemp Milk (page 47)	250 mL
½	small avocado (see Tips, page 81)	½
2	chopped pitted dates	2
2 tsp	raw agave nectar	10 mL
2 tsp	raw vanilla extract or ½ tsp (2 mL) raw vanilla seeds (see Tips, left)	10 mL

1. In a blender, combine hemp milk, avocado, dates, agave nectar and vanilla. Blend at high speed until smooth. Serve immediately.

Cake Batter Smoothie

Here's a smoothie that is so rich, creamy and delicious, you'll think you've licked the wooden spoon that scraped out the mixing bowl.

Makes 2 cups (500 mL)

Tips

To use the meat of an orange, place it on a cutting board and remove a bit of the skin from the top and bottom to create flat surfaces. This will reveal the thickness of the pith. Using a sharp knife, with a downward motion remove the skin and the pith. Shave off any remaining bits of pith, then cut between the membranes to produce wedges of pure citrus flesh, which are called suprêmes.

Substitute ¼ tsp (1 mL) vanilla seeds for the extract.

1 cup	Cashew Milk (page 46)	250 mL
½	small avocado	½
¼ cup	chopped orange segments (see Tips, left)	60 mL
¼ cup	Date Paste (page 80)	60 mL
1	banana	1
1 tsp	raw agave nectar	5 mL
1 tsp	freshly squeezed lemon juice	5 mL
1 tsp	raw vanilla extract (see Tips, left)	2 mL
Pinch	fine sea salt	Pinch

1. In a blender, combine cashew milk, avocado, orange, date paste, banana, agave nectar, lemon juice, vanilla and salt. Blend at high speed until smooth. Serve immediately.

Variations

Substitute Hemp Milk for the Cashew Milk and an equal quantity of chopped banana for the avocado.

Substitute ¼ cup (60 mL) fresh orange juice and a pitted date for the chopped orange.

Almond Butter and Jelly Smoothie

This smoothie is a delicious take on the classic peanut butter and jelly sandwich.

Makes 2 cups (500 mL)

Tip

I've used almond butter in place of peanut butter because so many people have peanut allergies. Use another nut or seed butter to suit your taste.

1 cup	Cashew Milk (page 46)	250 mL
¼ cup	almond butter	60 mL
5	strawberries	5
5	raspberries	5
½ cup	chopped banana	125 mL
¼ cup	seedless red grapes	60 mL
2 tbsp	raw agave nectar (see Tips, page 35)	30 mL

1. In a blender, combine cashew milk, almond butter, strawberries, raspberries, banana, grapes and agave nectar. Blend at high speed until smooth. Serve immediately.

Tropical Mango Smoothie

This smoothie is perfect for the warmer months, when your body is craving lighter foods. It is also an easy way consume four servings of fruit within a matter of minutes.

Makes 2 cups (500 mL)

Tip

I like to keep frozen organic berries on hand to help sweeten smoothies and make them cold. When your favorite fruit is in season, purchase it in bulk and freeze some to use in smoothies throughout the year.

1 cup	Almond Milk (page 45)	250 mL
½ cup	chopped peeled mango (see Tip, page 154)	125 mL
½ cup	chopped peeled papaya	125 mL
¼ cup	chopped pear	60 mL
1	banana	1
2	strawberries	2

1. In a blender, combine almond milk, mango, papaya, pear, banana and strawberries. Blend at high speed until smooth. Serve immediately.

Variations

Substitute various kinds of fleshy fruit for the mango and papaya. Watermelon and cantaloupe work equally well, as do honeydew melon and orange segments.

Just Peachy Blueberry Picnic

This smoothie is a wonderful summertime treat when peaches are in season and perfectly ripe. The addition of ginger is a delicious touch.

Makes 2 cups (500 mL)

Tips

To remove the stone from a peach, slice around the middle with a paring knife, cutting the peach into two equal halves. If the fruit is ripe the stone will come out easily with your fingers.

When any stone fruits such as peaches become ripe, store them in the refrigerator. This stops the ripening process and they will keep for up to a week.

½ cup	Hemp Milk (page 47)	125 mL
1	large peach, peeled	1
½ cup	blueberries	125 mL
1 tbsp	chopped gingerroot	15 mL
1 tsp	freshly squeezed lemon juice	5 mL

1. In a blender, combine hemp milk, peach, blueberries, ginger and lemon juice. Blend at high speed until smooth. Serve immediately.

Variations

Substitute an equal quantity of blackberries or brambleberries for the blueberries.

Substitute a nectarine for the peach.

Substitute Almond Milk (page 45) for the Hemp Milk.

The Antioxidizer

I like to describe this drink as the Fountain of Youth in a glass, because it contains an abundance of ingredients that are high in antioxidants.

Makes 1½ cups (375 mL)

Tip

Raw chocolate (cacao) is loaded with antioxidants. It is very high in polyphenols, a class of phytonutrients that have been shown to benefit the cardiovascular system. They help to lower blood pressure and reduce LDL ("bad cholesterol") oxidation, an integral part of atherosclerosis, and they also help to prevent blood cells from clumping.

1 cup	Hemp Milk (page 47)	250 mL
¼ cup	chopped trimmed kale	60 mL
8	blueberries	8
1	banana	1
2	chopped pitted dates	2
1 tbsp	raw cacao powder	15 mL
2 tsp	raw shelled hemp seeds	10 mL

1. In a blender, combine hemp milk, kale, blueberries, banana, dates, cacao powder and hemp seeds. Blend at high speed until smooth. Serve immediately.

Variations

Substitute Almond Milk for the Hemp Milk.

Substitute chopped arugula, spinach or chard for the kale.

Sweet Green Drink

This drink is a great way to get greens into your body. It is smooth, clean and fruity.

Makes 2½ cups (625 mL)

Tip

Before chopping the kale, remove the long stem that runs up through the leaf almost to the top. Use only the leafy green parts.

1 cup	Almond Milk (page 45)	250 mL
½ cup	chopped trimmed kale (see Tip, left)	125 mL
¼ cup	baby spinach	60 mL
¼ cup	chopped pear	60 mL
1	leaf romaine lettuce	1
2	chopped pitted dates	2
1	banana	1

1. In a blender, combine almond milk, kale, spinach, pear, lettuce, dates and banana. Blend at high speed until smooth. Serve immediately.

Variations

Substitute chard, arugula or collard greens for the kale and red leaf lettuce or baby bok choy for the romaine lettuce.

Chocolate Raspberry Mint Ice

Raspberries and cooling mint, combined with just a kick of chocolate, make this slightly tart drink particularly refreshing. It is a fabulous afternoon pick-me-up.

Makes 1½ cups (375 mL)

Tips

This recipe uses standard-size ice cubes. If your ice cubes are smaller, use a larger quantity. Depending on their size, you may need as many as 12.

Keep raw cacao powder in an airtight container away from light and heat, which will destroy its nutrients in addition to making the powder stale.

1 cup	Cashew Milk (page 46)	250 mL
6	ice cubes (see Tips, left)	6
¼ cup	raspberries	60 mL
2 tbsp	raw cacao powder (see Tips, page 55)	30 mL
2 tbsp	raw agave nectar	30 mL
¼ cup	fresh mint leaves	60 mL

1. In a blender, combine cashew milk and half of the ice cubes. Blend at medium speed until ice is finely chopped, about 30 seconds. Add remaining ice cubes, raspberries, cacao powder, agave nectar and mint. Blend at medium speed for 30 seconds (you want to retain some texture from the ice, so do not blend until completely smooth).

Variations

Substitute a dash of peppermint extract for the mint.

Substitute Almond Milk for the Cashew Milk.

Cacao Strawberry Smoothie

This rich and decadent smoothie is perfect any time of the day.

Makes 2 cups (500 mL)

Tips

Like all nuts, hazelnuts, also known as filberts, provide vitamin E, fiber, magnesium and B vitamins. They are also a great source of valuable antioxidants.

Using cashews will produce a creamier smoothie.

1 cup	Almond Milk (page 45)	250 mL
¼ cup	whole raw hazelnuts or cashews	60 mL
10 to 15	strawberries	10 to 15
3	chopped pitted dates	3
1	banana	1
2 tbsp	raw cacao powder	30 mL

1. In a blender, combine almond milk, hazelnuts, strawberries, dates, banana and cacao powder. Blend at high speed until smooth. Serve immediately.

Variations

This recipe works with all berries. I enjoy replacing the strawberries with ½ cup (125 mL) blueberries and blackberries and adding a pinch of cinnamon.

Pear and Almond Smoothie

I love drinking this for a midday snack. Although this drink is delicious on its own, it also makes a great accompaniment for Simple Marinated Kale Salad (page 142).

Makes 1½ cups (375 mL)

Tip

The best place to purchase almond butter is in bulk food stores, as it can be quite pricey when purchased in small quantities. When purchasing nut butters, try to make sure they are raw and organic. Find a favorite brand or source and stick with it.

1 cup	Almond Milk (page 45)	250 mL
½ cup	chopped pear	125 mL
1	chopped pitted date	1
2 tbsp	almond butter	30 mL
1 tsp	raw vanilla extract or ¼ tsp (1 mL) vanilla seeds	5 mL
½ tsp	ground cinnamon	2 mL

1. In a blender, combine almond milk, pear, date, almond butter, vanilla and cinnamon. Blend at high speed until smooth. Serve immediately.

Variations

Replace the almond butter with ¼ cup (60 mL) raw whole almonds.

Chocolate Pear and Almond Smoothie: Substitute the cinnamon with 2 tbsp (30 mL) raw cacao powder and add 1 tbsp (15 mL) raw agave nectar.

Blueberry, Date, Fig and Carob Elixir

This thick, creamy and rich drink is bursting with antioxidants and heart-healthy fats. I enjoy this when my body needs a quick pick-me-up.

Makes 1½ cups (375 mL)

Tips

To soak the dates and figs, cover with 1 cup (250 mL) water. Set aside for 30 minutes. Drain, discarding water.

Substitute ¼ tsp (1 mL) vanilla seeds for the extract.

3	chopped dried pitted dates, soaked (see Tips, left)	3
3	chopped dried figs, soaked	3
1 cup	blueberries	250 mL
1 cup	Almond Milk (page 45)	250 mL
¼ cup	freshly squeezed orange juice	60 mL
2 tbsp	carob powder	30 mL
1 tsp	raw vanilla extract	5 mL

1. In a blender, combine soaked dates and figs, blueberries, almond milk, orange juice, carob powder and vanilla. Blend at high speed until smooth.

Chocolate Cherry Delight

This smoothie is so full of deep, rich chocolate flavor you won't believe it's good for you. Cherries are particularly high in antioxidants such as anthocyanins.

Makes 2 cups (500 mL)

Tip

For this smoothie, use dark red cherries. To remove the pits, place each cherry on a cutting board and gently push down on it with the butt end of a chef's knife.

1 cup	Hemp Milk (page 47)	250 mL
½ cup	pitted cherries (see Tips, left)	125 mL
1	banana	1
3 tbsp	raw cacao powder (see Tips, page 35)	45 mL
2 tbsp	raw shelled hemp seeds	30 mL
1 tbsp	raw agave nectar	15 mL

1. In a blender, combine hemp milk, cherries, banana, cacao powder, hemp seeds and agave nectar. Blend at high speed until smooth.

Nutty Vanilla Smoothie

This rich and creamy blend of nuts and nut milk is so addictive and good for you that I promise you will be making it time and time again.

Makes 2 cups (500 mL)

Tips

To soak the nuts for this recipe, place them in a bowl with 1½ cups (375 mL) water and set aside for 30 minutes. Drain, discarding water. Rinse under cold running water until the water runs clear.

When blending this smoothie, make sure to process long enough for the nuts to become completely puréed and creamy.

Walnuts contain more omega-3 fatty acids than other nuts, almonds are higher in calcium, and pecans are highly antioxidant.

¼ cup	walnuts, soaked (see Tips, left)	60 mL
¼ cup	almonds, soaked	60 mL
¼ cup	pecans, soaked	60 mL
1 cup	Almond Milk (page 45)	250 mL
¼ cup	coconut water (see Tips, page 21)	60 mL
2 tbsp	raw agave nectar	30 mL
2 tbsp	raw vanilla extract or 2 tsp (10 mL) vanilla seeds	30 mL

1. In a blender, combine soaked walnuts, almonds and pecans, almond milk, coconut water, agave nectar and vanilla. Blend at high speed until smooth (see Tips, left). Serve immediately.

Variations

Replace any of the nuts with ¼ cup (60 mL) soaked cashews or Brazil nuts. Be aware that Brazil nuts will not purée to a smooth consistency because they are so dense.

The Gardener

This smoothie is so delicious you would never know it is good for you. Don't let the green color scare you — it is sweet and flavorful.

Makes 2 cups (500 mL)

Tip

Cilantro, like all herbs and spices, contains an abundance of phytonutrients with antioxidant properties. Early research suggests that it may help with digestion, ease bloating and relieve gas.

1 cup	Almond Milk (page 45)	250 mL
½	bunch fresh cilantro leaves	½
¼	bunch fresh parsley leaves	¼
¼ cup	fresh basil leaves	60 mL
2	leaves romaine lettuce	2
1	banana	1
¼ cup	chopped pineapple	60 mL

1. In a blender, combine almond milk, cilantro, parsley, basil, lettuce, banana and pineapple. Blend at high speed until smooth. Serve immediately.

Cinnamon Pineapple Creamsicle

This sweet, tasty treat is full of flavors that will make you remember the days when you went running for the ice cream truck when you heard its bell.

Makes 2 cups (500 mL)

Tip

Coconut butter is a blend of coconut oil and coconut meat. It is high in healthy fats and adds creaminess to smoothies and sauces. Don't confuse it with coconut oil, as they are different. However, in this recipe, you can substitute 2 tbsp (30 mL) coconut oil for the coconut butter; because the coconut butter is denser, you need twice as much oil to compensate.

½ cup	Cashew Milk (page 46)	125 mL
⅓ cup	freshly squeezed orange juice	75 mL
1 cup	chopped pineapple	250 mL
1	banana	1
1 tbsp	coconut butter (see Tip, left)	15 mL
1 tsp	ground cinnamon	5 mL
2 tsp	raw vanilla extract or ½ tsp (2 mL) vanilla seeds	10 mL

1. In a blender, combine cashew milk, orange juice, pineapple, banana, coconut butter, cinnamon and vanilla. Blend at high speed until smooth. Serve immediately.

Variation

Substitute Almond Milk for the Cashew Milk.

Purple Pomegranate Smoothie

This smoothie is sweet and full of flavor. Thanks to the berries and pomegranate seeds, it is also loaded with antioxidants.

Makes 1½ cups (375 mL)

Tip

Organic berries are some of nature's most nutrient-dense fruits. The combination of berries and pomegranate seeds in this recipe makes it very high in antioxidants — a Fountain of Youth in a glass.

1 cup	Almond Milk (page 45)	250 mL
½ cup	pomegranate seeds	125 mL
½ cup	blueberries	125 mL
¼ cup	blackberries	60 mL
1	banana	1
2	chopped pitted dates	2

1. In a blender, combine almond milk, pomegranate seeds, blueberries, blackberries, banana and dates. Blend at high speed until smooth. Serve immediately.

Variations

Substitute any dairy-free milk or 1 cup (250 mL) filtered water and 2 to 3 tbsp (30 to 45 mL) raw shelled hemp seeds for the almond milk.

Thank You Berry Much Smoothie

This cold, delicious smoothie is loaded with vitamin C. If you keep berries in the freezer, this is quick and easy to make.

Makes 2 cups (500 mL)

Tip

Buy organic frozen berries in bulk and keep them in your freezer to use as needed. Adding frozen berries to your smoothie will have the same effect as using ice. Frozen berries are generally cheaper when you purchase them in larger quantities. They can be stored for up to six months in an airtight container.

1 cup	freshly squeezed orange juice	250 mL
6	strawberries	6
10	blueberries	10
4	blackberries	4
4	raspberries	4
1	banana	1
1	chopped pitted date	1

1. In a blender, combine orange juice, strawberries, blueberries, blackberries, raspberries, banana and date. Blend at high speed until smooth. Serve immediately.

Variations

Try using gooseberries or brambleberries or even cranberries as a substitute for one of the berries. If using a less sweet fruit, add 1 to 2 tbsp (15 to 30 mL) raw agave nectar or ¼ cup (60 mL) Date Paste (page 80).

Juice in a Blender

This cold, fruity drink is part smoothie and part juice. Because it's not as filling as a smoothie, it is particularly nice on a hot day when your body is craving lighter foods.

Makes 2 cups (500 mL)

Tip

If your blender won't chop ice, put the ice cubes in a plastic bag, place on a cutting board and smash with a rolling pin until crushed. Add along with the other ingredients.

½ cup	freshly squeezed orange juice	125 mL
2	ice cubes (see Tip, left)	2
½ cup	chopped apple	125 mL
½ cup	seedless grapes (yellow, green or red)	125 mL
¼ cup	chopped pineapple	60 mL

1. In a blender, combine orange juice and ice. Blend at medium speed until ice is chopped. Add apple, grapes and pineapple. Blend at high speed until smooth. Serve immediately.

Variations

Substitute other freshly squeezed juices, such as mango, pomegranate or blueberry, for the orange.

Substitute cantaloupe, honeydew or another soft melon for the pineapple.

Strawberry Kiwi Smoothie

Serve this luscious smoothie at the height of the summer months, when strawberries and kiwis are in season.

Makes 2 cups (500 mL)

Tip

To extract the flesh from kiwifruit, using a paring knife, remove a small amount of skin from the bottom. Carefully insert a small spoon (a grapefruit spoon is ideal) between the flesh and the skin and rotate it until the skin becomes loose. Scoop out the flesh.

1 cup	freshly squeezed orange juice	250 mL
2	kiwifruit, peel removed	2
1	banana	1
8 to 10	strawberries	8 to 10
1 tsp	raw agave nectar	5 mL
1 tsp	raw vanilla extract (see Tips, page 38) or ¼ tsp (1 mL) vanilla seeds	5 mL

1. In a blender, combine orange juice, kiwis, banana, strawberries, agave nectar and vanilla. Blend at high speed until smooth. Serve immediately.

Variation

Substitute 2 tbsp (30 mL) Date Paste (page 80) for the agave nectar.

Blueberry Lemon Elixir

This drink is detoxifying and, with the addition of ginger, anti-inflammatory.

Makes 1 cup (250 mL)

½ cup	filtered water	125 mL
½ cup	blueberries	125 mL
¼ cup	freshly squeezed lemon juice	60 mL
3 tbsp	raw agave nectar (see Tips, page 63)	45 mL
2 tsp	chopped gingerroot	10 mL

Tip

If you don't have raw agave nectar, substitute 3 tbsp (45 mL) Date Paste (page 80) in this recipe. Date paste is delicious and nutritious and makes a very effective sweetener.

1. In a blender, combine water, blueberries, lemon juice, agave nectar and gingerroot. Blend at high speed until smooth.

Sesame and Orange Elixir

I call this an elixir because it contains an abundance of nutrients.

Makes 2 cups (500 mL)

1½ cups	freshly squeezed orange juice	375 mL
½	banana	½
¼ cup	sesame seeds	60 mL
1 tsp	ground cinnamon	5 mL

Tip

Sesame seeds provide calcium, magnesium, phosphorus and protein and a small amount of potassium. Alkali-forming foods such as fruits, vegetables, nuts and seeds may, over the long term, help to maintain bone density. These foods also provide other bone-building minerals such as boron, zinc, vitamin K_1, omega-3 fats and lycopene.

1. In a blender, combine orange juice, banana, sesame seeds and cinnamon. Blend at high speed until smooth. Serve immediately.

Pink Grapefruit and Melon Slush

> This ice-cold drink is just like a slushie, with a difference — this version has no refined sugars or hidden ingredients. It is made from fresh fruit, including fat-burning grapefruit.

Makes 1½ cups (375 mL)

Tips

Grapefruit juice provides potassium, vitamin C and phytonutrients such as polyphenols, among other compounds.

If your blender won't chop ice, put the ice cubes in a plastic bag, place on a cutting board and smash with a rolling pin until crushed. Add along with the other ingredients.

½ cup	freshly squeezed pink grapefruit juice	125 mL
3	large ice cubes, divided (see Tips, left)	3
1 cup	chopped melon	250 mL
2 tbsp	raw agave nectar	30 mL

1. In a blender, combine grapefruit juice and half of the ice. Blend at medium speed until ice is chopped. Add melon and agave nectar and remaining ice and blend at high speed until chunky but not completely smooth (you want the ice to retain some texture). Serve immediately.

Variations

Use cantaloupe, honeydew or any other soft melon. If you are using watermelon, increase the amount to 1½ cups (375 mL) because of its high water content.

Spicy Cinnamon Lemonade

> This special lemonade is both sweet and tart, slightly spicy and delicious.

Makes 4 cups (1 L)

Tips

When purchasing agave nectar, be sure to look for products labeled "raw." If you have concerns, ask your purveyor.

If your blender won't chop ice, put the ice cubes in a plastic bag, place on a cutting board and smash with a rolling pin until crushed. Add along with the other ingredients.

2 cups	freshly squeezed lemon juice (about 8 lemons)	500 mL
1 cup	filtered water	250 mL
¾ cup	raw agave nectar (see Tips, left)	175 mL
3	large ice cubes	3
1 tbsp	ground cinnamon	15 mL
½ tsp	cayenne pepper	2 mL

1. In a blender, combine lemon juice, water, agave nectar, ice cubes, cinnamon and cayenne pepper. Blend at high speed until ice is chopped. Serve immediately.

The Fat-Burner

Although this drink may have some bitter undertones, the healthy effects of the grapefruit and cranberries make it a wonderful detoxifier.

Makes 1½ cups (375 mL)

Tips

To separate grapefruit segments, follow the instructions for segmenting an orange on page 67.

If you find this smoothie too bitter, add 2 tbsp (30 mL) raw agave nectar.

Kelp powder is made from dried seaweed. It adds a salty taste to foods and is a source of the mineral iodine, which promotes a healthy thyroid.

2 cups	chopped grapefruit segments (see Tips, left)	500 mL
½ cup	chopped orange segments	250 mL
¼ cup	cranberries	60 mL
¼ cup	water	60 mL
2 tbsp	flax oil	30 mL
1 tbsp	freshly squeezed lemon juice	15 mL
½ tsp	kelp powder (see Tips, left)	2 mL
Pinch	cayenne pepper	Pinch
Pinch	ground turmeric	Pinch

1. In a blender, combine grapefruit, orange, cranberries, water, flax oil, lemon juice, kelp powder, cayenne and turmeric. Blend at high speed until smooth. Serve immediately.

Blue Sunset Smoothie

Not only is this smoothie antioxidant-rich, the hemp seeds provide as much as 10 grams of complete protein. It is also easily digestible because the beneficial bacteria in the kombucha promote a healthy digestive system. This is a great morning drink.

Makes 1½ cups (375 mL)

Tip

Kombucha is a fermented tea that aids in digestion and provides your gut with beneficial bacteria. It is available in the refrigerated section of natural foods stores and well-stocked supermarkets. If you don't have kombucha, substitute 1 cup (250 mL) filtered water and 1 tsp (5 mL) apple cider vinegar.

1 cup	kombucha (see Tip, left)	250 mL
1	small banana	1
¼ cup	blueberries	60 mL
2 tbsp	raw shelled hemp seeds	30 mL

1. In a blender, combine kombucha, banana, blueberries and hemp seeds. Blend at high speed until smooth. Serve immediately.

Choco-Hemp-aholic

This velvety smooth chocolate smoothie provides iron, antioxidants and protein. The trick to making it rich is to use ripe bananas and high-quality cacao powder. This makes a great pick-me-up or midday snack.

Makes 2 cups (500 mL)

Tip

To ripen bananas quickly, place them in a paper bag with an uncut apple and tightly fold over the end of the bag. The apple will emit ethylene gas, which will help to speed ripening. Place the bag in a warm, dry area until the bananas are ripe.

1 cup	filtered water	250 mL
1	banana	1
2	pitted dates	2
3 tbsp	raw shelled hemp seeds	45 mL
2 tbsp	raw cacao powder	30 mL

1. In a blender, combine water, banana, dates, hemp seeds and cacao powder. Blend at high speed until smooth.

Bodybuilder Smoothie

This smoothie is the perfect drink for post-workout recovery. The hemp seeds provide complete protein to help build muscle mass and the coconut water supplies electrolytes, which replace the salts and sugars lost in exercise. Coconut water is also a good source of potassium, which helps to build cellular structure.

Makes 2 cups (500 mL)

Tip

If hemp seeds are not available, try adding a scoop of your favorite protein powder — I prefer hemp or sprouted brown rice protein. I like to add them to smoothies to provide additional protein (not all are raw, so read the labels). They are available in natural foods stores and well-stocked supermarkets.

1 cup	coconut water (see Tip, page 21)	250 mL
1/4 cup	freshly squeezed orange juice	60 mL
1/4 cup	blueberries	60 mL
1/4 cup	chopped pineapple	60 mL
1/4 cup	raw shelled hemp seeds (see Tip, left)	60 mL
1	banana	1

1. In a blender, combine coconut water, orange juice, blueberries, pineapple, hemp seeds and banana. Blend at high speed until smooth. Serve immediately.

Electrifying Electrolyte Drink

This is a great post-workout drink because it replenishes the body with natural sugars and electrolytes lost through perspiration. It is a particularly good source of the mineral potassium.

Makes 1½ cups (375 mL)

Tip

If you are using fresh coconut water in this recipe, purchase a white coconut, also known as a young Thai coconut. A brown coconut is mature and will contain no water, although the meat — unlike the meat from a young coconut, which resembles jelly — is ideal for shredding.

1 cup	coconut water (see Tip, left)	250 mL
2 tbsp	cool green tea	30 mL
1	banana	1
8	blueberries	8

1. In a blender, combine coconut water, green tea, banana and blueberries. Blend at high speed until smooth. Serve immediately.

Green Apple Elixir

This sweet-and-savory drink is great for replenishing electrolytes. It is very refreshing and makes a good post-workout drink in place of water.

Makes 2 cups (500 mL)

Tip

The outer stalks of celery can be tough and fibrous. For best results, peel the stalk with a vegetable peeler. Save the peel to make soups, sauces or stocks.

½ cup	coconut water	125 mL
3 tbsp	freshly squeezed lemon juice	45 mL
4	Granny Smith apples, quartered and cored	4
1	large stalk celery, peeled (see Tip, left)	1
¼ cup	parsley leaves	60 mL
1 tsp	chopped gingerroot	5 mL

1. In a blender, combine coconut water, lemon juice, apples, celery, parsley and ginger. Blend at high speed until smooth. Serve immediately.

Variations

Replace the parsley with an equal quantity of cilantro.

Although coconut water is optimal, you may use filtered water if none is available.

Daterade

Made with coconut water, this simple drink is a great electrolyte replacer. It's ideal after a workout because it enables you to avoid those sugar-loaded athletic drinks.

Makes 2 cups (500 mL)

Tip

To soak the dates for this recipe, place in a bowl and add 2 cups (500 mL) water. Cover and set aside for 1 hour. Drain, discarding liquid.

10 to 12	pitted Medjool dates, soaked and chopped (see Tip, left)	10 to 12
2 cups	coconut water (see Tip, page 21)	500 mL

1. In a blender, combine coconut water and soaked dates. Blend at high speed until smooth. Serve immediately.

The Kitchen Sink

This smoothie contains everything but the kitchen sink. It will keep you feeling full for hours and give you enough energy to run a marathon.

Makes 2½ cups (625 mL)

Tip

To use the meat of an orange, place it on a cutting board and remove a bit of the skin from the top and bottom of the orange to create flat surfaces. This will reveal the thickness of the pith. Using a sharp knife with a downward motion, remove the skin and the pith. Shave off any remaining bits of pith, then cut between the membranes to produce wedges of pure citrus flesh, which are called suprêmes.

1 cup	coconut water	250 mL
½ cup	packed baby spinach	125 mL
¼ cup	chopped baby bok choy	60 mL
¼ cup	chopped pineapple	60 mL
¼ cup	chopped orange segments (see Tip, left)	60 mL
3	strawberries	3
5	blueberries	5
1 tbsp	raw shelled hemp seeds	15 mL

1. In a blender, combine coconut water, spinach, bok choy, pineapple, orange, strawberries, blueberries and hemp seeds. Blend at high speed until smooth. Serve immediately.

Variations

Substitute an equal quantity of kale for the bok choy and/or arugula for the spinach.

In season, add half a peach, chopped, to this smoothie.

Beta-Carotene Burst

This juice is rich in beta-carotene, which your body converts into vitamin A, an especially important nutrient for your eyes.

Makes 2 cups (500 mL)

Tip

Whole vegetables such as carrots can go through the juicer as long as they will fit through the feed tube. Make sure you don't jam the machine by trying to put too much through at one time, and always use the proper tool to push foods through.

- **Juicer**

8 to 10	medium carrots, sliced if necessary, divided	8 to 10
2	apples, quartered, divided	2
1	leaf romaine lettuce	1
1 tsp	freshly squeezed lemon juice	5 mL

1. In a juicer, process 1 apple, 4 carrots and the lettuce. Add remaining apples and carrots. Add lemon juice through the feed tube. Whisk and divide between two glasses. Serve immediately.

Variation

Substitute 3 slices of sweet potato, each approximately 1 inch (2.5 cm) in diameter, for three of the carrots. This will produce a luscious starchy juice that is also high in beta-carotene.

Pink Sunset Juice

This juice is a perfect aid in maintaining weight loss, because the grapefruit juice helps your body to burn fat. It is a unique blend of fruit and vegetable juices that you wouldn't normally think to combine, but they merge into a tasty surprise.

Makes 1½ cups (375 mL)

Tips

I don't recommend using a juicer to juice the grapefruit because that quantity of pith would make the juice bitter.

Studies show that grapefruit helps to prevent fat from accumulating in the abdominal region, a condition known as metabolic syndrome, which can be a precursor to diabetes.

- **Juicer**

1	pink grapefruit (see Tips, left)	1
2	carrots, sliced if necessary	2
2	apples, quartered	2

1. Cut the grapefruit in half and juice using a manual citrus juicer.

2. In a juicer, process carrots and apples. Combine with the grapefruit juice and whisk well. Serve immediately.

Variations

Substitute 2 pears for the apples.

If you prefer, omit the apples and substitute 4 to 6 carrots.

Gingery Carrot Love Juice

Although this juice contains just carrots and ginger, to me it tastes like ice cream. I love drinking this on a warm summer day.

Makes 1½ cups (375 mL)

Tip

Carrots are extremely high in beta-carotene, a carotenoid, which your body converts to vitamin A. Because smoking and drinking alcohol reduce the levels of beta-carotene in the blood, consuming adequate amounts of this nutrient is recommended if you consume alcohol on a regular basis and/or smoke tobacco.

- **Juicer**

10 to 12	carrots, sliced if necessary, divided	10 to 12
1	piece (1 inch/2.5 cm) gingerroot, skin on	1

1. In a juicer, process 3 carrots and the ginger. Process remaining carrots. Whisk and divide into two glasses, if desired.

Variations

Add a sliced apple if you like a little more sweetness.

Adjust the quantity of ginger to suit your taste.

Carrot and Apple Lemonade

This drink is tart and refreshing. It provides an abundance of nutrients and is especially high in beta-carotene, which is protective against cancer. An effective antioxidant, beta-carotene is particularly beneficial for eye health.

Makes 2 cups (500 mL)

Tip

To get the maximum yield from citrus, allow the fruit to sit at room temperature for 30 minutes before juicing. Once it is at room temperature, use the palm of your hand to roll it on the counter to release the juices before slicing and squeezing.

- **Juicer**

4 to 6	carrots, sliced if necessary, divided	4 to 6
2	apples, quartered, divided	2
½	lemon, skin on, cut in wedges, divided	½
3 tbsp	raw agave nectar	45 mL
Pinch	ground cinnamon	Pinch

1. In a juicer, process 1 carrot, followed by 1 apple quarter and 1 piece of lemon. Repeat until all the carrots, apples and lemon have been juiced.
2. Transfer to a container and whisk in the agave nectar and cinnamon. Serve immediately or cover and refrigerate for up to 2 days.

Lemon Ginger Cayenne Cold Fighter

This warm drink is perfect when you have a scratchy throat or feel a cold coming on.

Makes 1 cup (250 mL)

Tip

To heat the water for this recipe, bring to a boil. Remove from heat and set aside to cool slightly, for 2 to 3 minutes. This will ensure that the water is below 105°F (41°C) and won't destroy any of the enzymes in the other ingredients.

¾ cup	warm filtered water (see Tip, left)	175 mL
3 tbsp	freshly squeezed lemon juice	45 mL
1	piece (1 inch/2.5 cm) gingeroot, puréed (see Tips, page 133)	1
¼ tsp	cayenne pepper	1 mL

1. In a large cup, combine water, lemon juice, puréed ginger and cayenne. Whisk and serve immediately.

Iron-Builder Juice

This deep red juice provides both iron and folic acid, which studies show protects against colon cancer.

Makes 1½ cups (375 mL)

Tips

Bunched beets contain beet greens, which are the leaves attached to fresh (not storage) beets. They are a fabulous dark green.

After juicing you will be left with pulp. Save the pulp — it can easily be turned into raw crackers. Just be sure to remove the seeds from produce, such as the apple in this recipe, before juicing.

- **Juicer**

3	large red beets, sliced, divided	3
4	medium carrots, sliced, divided	4
½	bunch Swiss chard or beet greens, divided (see Tips, left)	½
1	small apple, sliced, divided	1

1. In a juicer, process one-quarter of the beets, 1 carrot, one-quarter of the chard and one-quarter of the apple. Repeat until all the vegetables have been juiced. Whisk well and serve immediately.

Variations

Substitute 1 head of romaine lettuce or 1 bunch spinach or arugula for the chard.

Grasshopper Juice

This juice is packed full of vitamins, minerals and other nutrients. It is perfect for a midday pick-me-up when blood sugar levels begin to drop.

Makes 2 cups (500 mL)

Tip

Use any kind of green sprouts, such as sunflower, pea, broccoli or radish sprouts, in this recipe. Take care to wash sprouts especially thoroughly before consuming them, as they are dense and can be a haven for bacteria. Look for sprouts in natural foods stores or well-stocked supermarkets.

- **Juicer**

2	medium apples, quartered, divided	2
1	bunch kale, divided	1
½	cucumber, cut into 4 pieces, divided	½
4	stalks celery, divided	4
¼ cup	sprouts (see Tip, left)	60 mL

1. In a juicer, process half an apple, one-quarter of the kale, 1 piece cucumber, 1 stalk celery and 1 tbsp (15 mL) of the sprouts. Repeat three times. Whisk and serve immediately.

Variations

Substitute 2 pears for the apples and/or an equal quantity of another leafy green for the kale.

Green Juice Detox

This juice is loaded with chlorophyll, which is a powerful antioxidant.

Makes 1 cup (250 mL)

Tip

When juicing vegetables that contain lower amounts of water, such as kale, follow them through the juicer with vegetables or fruits, such as cucumber, that are higher in water. Sometimes the liquid from less juicy vegetables gets left in the gears of the juicer. Following with a vegetable with high water content helps to flush it out.

- **Juicer**

2	bunches kale, divided	2
2	cucumbers, sliced, divided	2
6	stalks celery, divided	6
¼	bunch parsley	¼
¼	lemon, skin on	¼

1. In a juicer, process 1 bunch kale, 3 stalks celery, 1 cucumber and the parsley and lemon. Repeat with remaining kale, celery and cucumber. Whisk and serve immediately.

Green Tea Metabolizer

> This lemony blend is perfect for anyone who wants to reduce sugar intake.

Makes 1½ cups (375 mL)

Tip

Green tea contains three major components that may help people lose weight. Caffeine, theanine and catechins are reputed to prevent fat from being stored in the body and to raise the metabolic rate, which helps burn existing fat.

½ cup	warm filtered water (see Tip, page 70)	125 mL
½ tsp	matcha green tea powder	2 mL
1	English cucumber, sliced	1
4	celery stalks	4
2	leaves romaine lettuce	2
½	lemon, skin on	½

1. In a large cup, combine warm water and green tea powder. Set aside to steep for 5 minutes.
2. In a juicer, process cucumber, celery, lettuce and lemon. Add to the steeped tea, whisk and serve immediately.

Variation

If matcha powder is not available, substitute ½ cup (125 mL) steeped regular green tea.

Bitter Detoxifier

> If you're really keen on the benefits of raw food, try this juice. The bitterness takes some time to get used to, but it is very good for you. The dark green leafy vegetables contain potassium, lutein, beta-carotene and vitamin K_1.

Makes 1 cup (250 mL)

Tip

The more often you consume bitter greens, the more your body will accept them. If you're a "newbie," try using 2 juiced apples and half the quantity of dandelion greens. Gradually decrease the quantity of apples and increase the quantity of bitter greens to suit your taste.

- Juicer

1	bunch dandelion greens	1
½	bunch kale	½
½	English cucumber, sliced	½
4	leaves romaine lettuce	4
¼	bunch parsley	¼
¼	lemon, skin on, sliced	¼
1	apple, sliced, optional	1

1. In a juicer, process half of each of the ingredients: dandelion greens, kale, cucumber, lettuce, parsley, lemon and apple, if using. Repeat. Whisk and serve immediately.

Variation

Substitute 1 bunch kale and ½ bunch Swiss chard for the dandelion greens.

Mint and Lemon Greenie

This drink is a great detox tea that is high in chlorophyll. I like to steep it and drink it warm or refrigerate it and serve with a few ice cubes.

Tips

If you do not have loose-leaf green tea, use a green tea bag.

If you find this drink a little harsh, add 2 tbsp (30 mL) raw agave nectar to sweeten.

I also like to add 1 tsp (5 mL) puréed ginger to give the drink even stronger detoxifying properties.

1 cup	filtered water	250 mL
2 tbsp	freshly squeezed lemon juice	30 mL
2 tbsp	torn mint leaves	30 mL
1 tsp	green tea leaves	5 mL
6	kale leaves	6

1. In a pot, bring water to a boil. Remove from heat. Add lemon juice, mint and tea leaves. Set aside to steep for 5 minutes. Strain. If desired, refrigerate for 1 hour, until chilled.
2. In a juicer, process kale. Add kale juice to the steeped tea. Whisk well and serve immediately.

Nog Me Up

This take on holiday eggnog is rich and perfectly spiced. It is sure to be a crowd-pleaser. Although raw, it has all the creaminess and flavor of the traditional version.

Makes 2 cups (500 mL)

Tips

To soak the almonds for this recipe, place in a bowl and add ½ cup (125 mL) water. Cover and set aside for 30 minutes. Drain, discarding soaking water. Rinse under cold running water until the water runs clear.

Because nutmeg loses it flavor and becomes bitter when ground, it is best to freshly grate it for use.

¼ cup	whole raw almonds, soaked (see Tips, left)	60 mL
1½ cups	Almond Milk (page 45)	375 mL
¼ cup	Date Paste (page 80)	60 mL
1 tbsp	raw agave nectar	15 mL
1 tsp	raw vanilla extract or ¼ tsp (1 mL) vanilla seeds	5 mL
1 tsp	ground cinnamon	5 mL
Pinch	freshly grated ground nutmeg	Pinch
Pinch	ground cloves	Pinch
	Raw agave nectar, optional	

1. In a blender, combine almond milk, soaked almonds, date paste, agave nectar, vanilla, cinnamon, nutmeg and cloves. Blend at high speed until smooth. Taste. If drink is not sweet enough for you, add 1 to 2 tsp (5 to 10 mL) agave nectar, and blend again. Serve immediately.

Pineapple Piña Colada

This rich and creamy drink is full of healthy fats and sweet pineapple. If I'm not serving this as a mocktail, I like to add a scoop of my favorite protein powder.

Makes 1½ cups (375 mL)

Tip

Coconut butter is a blend of coconut oil and coconut meat that is high in healthy fats and adds creaminess to smoothies and sauces. It is available in the nut butter section of natural foods stores or well-stocked supermarkets. Don't confuse it with coconut oil, because they are different.

1 cup	Coconut Milk (page 47)	250 mL
½ cup	chopped pineapple	125 mL
3 tbsp	coconut butter (see Tip, left)	45 mL
1	banana	1
1	chopped pitted Medjool date	1

1. In a blender, combine coconut milk, pineapple, coconut butter, banana and date. Blend at high speed until smooth.

Variations

Substitute an equal quantity of Almond Milk (page 45) or Cashew Milk (page 46) for the Coconut Milk.

For added protein, add 2 tbsp (30 mL) raw shelled hemp seeds.

Grapefruit, Spirulina and Blackberry Frozen Martini

This refreshing drink is perfect for the warmer months. It can be served to dinner-party company and also makes a tasty afternoon snack or morning energy drink.

Makes 1½ cups (375 mL)

Tip

Spirulina is a blue-green alga that has many healthful properties. It has trace amounts of vitamins and minerals and is a source of phytonutrients with antioxidant properties; it is also thought to be extremely detoxifying. Spirulina can be found in the natural foods section of well-stocked grocery stores.

½ cup	freshly squeezed grapefruit juice	125 mL
3	large ice cubes, divided (see Tips, page 63)	3
½ cup	frozen blackberries	125 mL
1 tsp	raw shelled hemp seeds	5 mL
1 tsp	spirulina powder (see Tip, left)	5 mL

1. In a blender, combine grapefruit juice and half the ice cubes. Blend at medium speed for 10 seconds. Add remaining ice and blend at medium speed for 10 seconds. Add the frozen blackberries, hemp seeds and spirulina powder and blend at medium speed until the ice and berries are still chunky and the texture is slushy. Serve immediately.

Frozen Strawberry and Orange Daiquiri

> You may be drinking this instead of a daiquiri, but this icy-cold treat provides more than your recommended daily intake of vitamin C.

Makes 1½ cups (375 mL)

Tips

Using frozen berries makes your smoothie cold without the addition of ice. Buying frozen berries in bulk is quite cost-effective.

If you do not have any almond milk, substitute ¼ cup (60 mL) filtered water and 3 tbsp (45 mL) hemp seeds.

¾ cup	freshly squeezed orange juice	175 mL
¼ cup	Almond Milk (page 45)	60 mL
1 cup	frozen strawberries	250 mL
1	banana	1
¼ cup	chopped orange segments (see Tip, page 67)	60 mL
1 tsp	raw vanilla extract or ¼ tsp (1 mL) vanilla seeds	5 mL

1. In a blender, combine orange juice, almond milk, frozen strawberries, banana, orange and vanilla. Blend at high speed until smooth. Serve immediately.

Blissful Bloody Mary

> This take on a classic Bloody Mary contains high amounts of cancer-fighting lycopene, among other nutrients. To serve it as a mocktail, add a celery stick stirrer and serve over ice. It also makes a very refreshing pick-me-up at any time of the day.

Makes 2 cups (500 mL)

Tips

The outer stalks of celery can be tough and fibrous. For best results, peel the stalk with a vegetable peeler. Save the peel to make soups, sauces or stocks.

While wheat-free tamari is not raw, it is gluten-free. The raw alternative for tamari, nama shoyu, does contain gluten.

2 cups	chopped tomatoes	500 mL
1 cup	chopped celery (see Tips, left)	250 mL
¼ cup	chopped seeded red bell pepper	60 mL
¼ cup	parsley leaves	60 mL
2 tbsp	wheat-free tamari (see Tips, left)	30 mL
1 tsp	celery seeds	5 mL
1 tsp	apple cider vinegar	5 mL

1. In a blender, combine tomatoes, celery, bell pepper, parsley, tamari, celery seeds and vinegar. Blend at high speed until smooth. Serve immediately.

Summer Sangria

This tantalizing summer drink is a perfect blend of ripe fruit juices. Enjoy its standout flavors on their own or add an equal quantity of your favorite full-bodied red wine.

Makes 5 cups (1.25 L)

Tips

Sparkling grape juice has been pasteurized. If you're following a strictly raw diet, substitute an equal quantity of sparkling water.

Garnish this drink with some fresh orange and apple slices and some fresh berries. I also like to float a few lemon and grapefruit slices to balance the sweetness.

2 cups	freshly squeezed orange juice	500 mL
1 cup	sparkling water	250 mL
1 cup	sparkling grape juice (see Tips, left)	250 mL
½ cup	freshly pressed apple juice	125 mL
¼ cup	freshly pressed pear juice	60 mL
2 tbsp	freshly squeezed lemon juice	30 mL
2 tbsp	raw agave nectar	30 mL

1. In a pitcher, mix together orange juice, sparkling water, grape, apple and pear juices, lemon juice and agave nectar. Refrigerate for 1 hour.

Variation

For another great mocktail, put 2½ cups (625 mL) sangria in a blender and add 1 cup (250 mL) chopped peaches. The fiber in the peaches gives the drink a little body and the peaches add a beautiful summer flavor.

Making Crackers from Pulp

You can make crackers from leftover juicer pulp (both vegetable and fruit pulp work). In a food processor fitted with the metal blade, process 1 cup (250 mL) juicer pulp, ¼ cup (60 mL) cold-pressed olive oil and a pinch of fine sea salt until smooth. Add ½ cup (125 mL) ground flax seeds and pulse to blend. Using a rubber spatula, spread on a nonstick dehydrator sheet. Dehydrate at 105°F (41°C) for 10 to 12 hours, until crispy. Break into crackers and store in an airtight container for up to 2 weeks.

Dips and Spreads

The accompaniments are much of what makes raw food so appealing. I love a raw bread or cracker, but what would either one be without something to dip it into or spread on top?

In raw cuisine, dips and spreads almost always serve as a source of protein or healthy fats. They can be extremely simple or intricate. I like to make a few different raw dips at a time and keep them in the fridge. Whenever I'm feeling peckish, all it takes is some celery or carrot sticks and I can enjoy a delicious and nutritious snack.

Tomatillo and Chia Seed Salsa

The chia seeds in this recipe provide omega-3 fatty acids, which have many health benefits. I like to serve this tangy salsa as a side with dishes that have strong Southwest flavors, such as Bursting Burritos (page 250), or as a quick midday snack.

Makes 2 cups (500 mL)

Tips

Tomatillos resemble small green tomatoes. They come wrapped in a husk, which needs to be removed before using. They are quite tart but very tasty.

Two tablespoons (30 mL) of chia seeds provide about 7 grams of alpha-linolenic acid (ALA), a type of omega-3 fat that is the essential fatty acid — without it, we could not survive. It is called essential because our bodies are unable to make it and must obtain it from food. Good sources of ALA include flax seeds, chia seeds, walnuts and walnut oil. Research has demonstrated ALA's ability to reduce chronic inflammation and other risk factors for diabetes, heart disease and stroke. It is estimated that North Americans get an average of about 1.5 grams of ALA per day, while some experts recommend intakes of 2.3 to 3 grams per day. Reaching this goal is easy if you include ALA-rich foods as part of your daily diet.

1½ cups	diced tomatillos (see Tips, left)	375 mL
¼ cup	chopped cilantro leaves	60 mL
2 tbsp	chia seeds	30 mL
1 tbsp	freshly squeezed lemon juice	15 mL
2 tsp	cold-pressed (extra virgin) olive oil	10 mL
½ tsp	fine sea salt	2 mL

1. In a bowl, combine tomatillos, cilantro, chia seeds, lemon juice, olive oil and salt. Toss well. Cover and set aside for 10 minutes to allow the chia seeds to swell, which will add texture and body to the salsa. Serve immediately or cover and refrigerate for up to 2 days.

Variation

Substitute an equal quantity of fresh tomatoes for the tomatillos.

Date Paste

This is a very versatile recipe. I love using it as a dip for sliced apples, but it is also a rich whole-food sweetener that makes a perfect alternative to refined sugar. It can be used as a replacement for agave nectar in many recipes and is a great finish for many raw desserts.

Makes 1 cup (250 mL)

Tips

To soak the dates for this recipe, place in a bowl and add 2 cups (500 mL) water. Cover and set aside for 20 minutes. Drain, discarding soaking water.

10	chopped pitted dates, soaked (see Tips, left)	10
1 cup	filtered water	250 mL

1. In a food processor fitted with the metal blade, process soaked dates and water until smooth. Use immediately or transfer to an airtight container and refrigerate for up to one week.

Variation

For a sweeter paste, substitute the water with freshly squeezed orange juice, or use half of each.

Hemp Basil Bruschetta

A light and refreshing mix of fresh garlic, basil pesto, juicy tomatoes and protein-packed hemp seeds makes this a delicious snack anytime.

Makes 2 cups (500 mL)

Tip

Always use a very sharp knife when cutting tomatoes and before chopping, remove the core. Insert the tip of a paring knife into the stem end and turn the tomato while holding the knife steady. Remove and discard the core.

1½ cups	diced tomatoes	375 mL
3 tbsp	raw shelled hemp seeds	45 mL
3 tbsp	Basil, Spinach and Walnut Pesto (page 186; see Variation, below)	45 mL
2 tbsp	finely diced red onion	30 mL
1 tsp	cold-pressed (extra virgin) olive oil	5 mL
¼ tsp	fine sea salt	1 mL
4	pieces Zucchini Hemp Bread (page 324)	4

1. In a bowl, combine tomatoes, hemp seeds, pesto, onion, olive oil and salt. Toss to combine. Spoon liberally over bread and serve immediately.

Variation

If you do not have pesto, substitute with 2 cloves minced garlic and ¼ cup (60 mL) fresh basil leaves cut in chiffonade style. To chiffonade basil, stack whole leaves in a neat pile and roll into a tight cylinder. Using a sharp chef's knife, slice as thinly as possible into strips.

Perfect Guacamole

This simple, classic dip is one of the best flavor combinations possible, as well as being very nutritious. It is fabulous with Corn and Carrot Nachos (page 325) or Bursting Burritos (page 250).

Makes 3 cups (750 mL)

Tips

The key is not to purée the avocado but to retain its texture so the guacamole is somewhat chunky.

To remove the pit from an avocado, use a paring knife to remove the nib at the top. Insert the blade of the knife where the nib was and turn the avocado from top to bottom to cut it in half lengthwise. Twist the two halves apart. Stick the knife into the pit and with one motion turn it 90 degrees. As you twist the knife, pull out the pit.

3	medium avocados	3
¼ cup	freshly squeezed lemon juice	60 mL
2 tbsp	finely diced red onion	30 mL
3	cloves garlic, minced	3
1 tsp	fine sea salt	15 mL
Pinch	freshly ground black pepper	Pinch

1. In a bowl, combine avocados, lemon juice, onion, garlic, salt and pepper. Using a wire whisk, fork or potato masher, mix until the avocado is crushed and the ingredients are evenly distributed. Serve immediately or cover and refrigerate for up to 3 days.

Variations

There are many variations of guacamole. Play around to see what suits your taste buds best. I sometimes like to add ¼ cup (60 mL) chopped cilantro leaves, 2 tbsp (30 mL) chopped tomatoes and a pinch of cayenne pepper or some minced fresh chile pepper for some heat.

Avocado Spinach Dip

This creamy dip is delightful. It is sure to fool any dedicated dairy-lovers — they won't believe it doesn't contain cream cheese, mascarpone or heavy cream. The key to making it perfect is to use perfectly ripe avocados. I like to serve this with fresh veggies as dippers, or even as a dressing on light salad greens.

Makes 4 cups (1 L)

Tips

Spinach contains about 90 percent water. When cooking or marinating spinach, a good amount of the water will come out of it. Make sure to drain off the excess moisture before adding it to your recipe; otherwise it will affect the end result.

To ripen avocados more quickly, place them in a brown paper bag or wrap them in newspaper along with a tomato or apple. The gases from the fruit will penetrate the avocado and help to speed up the ripening. If your avocado is ripe and won't be consumed within a day or two, place it in the coolest part of your refrigerator. This will lengthen its life by up to a week or more. Once an avocado has been removed from the fridge, do not put it back — it will turn black.

2 cups	chopped spinach leaves	500 mL
½ cup	cold-pressed (extra virgin) olive oil, divided	125 mL
¼ cup	freshly squeezed lemon juice	60 mL
2 tbsp	nutritional yeast (see Tips, page 83)	30 mL
3	cloves garlic, minced	3
2 tsp	fine sea salt, divided	10 mL
2	small avocados, chopped (about 2 cups/500 mL)	2
3 tbsp	chopped red onion	45 mL

1. In a bowl, toss spinach, ¼ cup (60 mL) olive oil, lemon juice, nutritional yeast, garlic and 1 tsp (5 mL) salt. Set aside for 30 minutes to soften. Once it is soft, drain the spinach.

2. In a food processor fitted with the metal blade, process marinated spinach for 30 seconds, until broken down. Add avocados and onion and process until smooth. With the motor running, slowly add remaining olive oil through the feed tube, until mixture is creamy. Add remaining salt and pulse to blend.

Olive Oil

Although extra virgin olive oil should, by definition, be cold-pressed, it is worth checking the label. Some olive oils are extracted using a centrifuge system, which spins the olives at a very high rate. This heats the olives and the resulting oil, depriving it of its raw status.

Cashew Spinach Dip

This dip is rich and delicious and reminiscent of spinach dips you might find at your local pub. Serve it with carrot and/or celery sticks or Buckwheat, Sunflower and Almond Breadsticks (page 320), which are a perfect match for dipping. I also like to serve this as a sandwich between two crispy romaine lettuce leaves.

Makes 3 cups (750 mL)

Tips

To soak the cashews for this recipe, place them in a bowl and cover with 4 cups (1 L) water. Cover and set aside for 30 minutes. Drain, discarding soaking water, and rinse under cold running water until the water runs clear.

Nutritional yeast is used in vegan and raw food diets mainly because it is a source of vitamin B_{12}. It is pasteurized, so technically it does not qualify as a raw food. However, in addition to necessary nutrients, it adds a deep, umami-like flavor to many dishes.

To extract the maximum amount of juice from a lemon, make sure it is at room temperature. Rolling the lemon around on the counter while pressing lightly with the palm of your hand also helps by releasing juice from the flesh.

2 cups	raw cashews, soaked (see Tips, left)	500 mL
6 tbsp	freshly squeezed lemon juice, divided	90 mL
3 tbsp	nutritional yeast (see Tips, left)	45 mL
1/4 cup	chopped red onion	60 mL
10	cloves garlic	10
1 tbsp	fine sea salt, divided	15 mL
Pinch	freshly ground black pepper	Pinch
3 cups	chopped spinach leaves	750 mL
1 tbsp	cold-pressed (extra virgin) olive oil	15 mL
1/4 cup	cold-pressed hemp oil	60 mL

1. In a food processor fitted with the metal blade, pulse 1/4 cup (60 mL) lemon juice, nutritional yeast, onion, garlic, 2 tsp (10 mL) salt and pepper, until chopped and blended. Add soaked cashews and process until smooth, stopping the motor once and scraping down the sides of the bowl.

2. In a bowl, toss spinach, olive oil, remaining 2 tbsp (30 mL) lemon juice and remaining 1 tsp (5 mL) salt. Add to food processor and process until smooth, stopping the motor once and scraping down the sides of the bowl. With the motor running, slowly add the hemp oil through the feed tube, processing until mixture is smooth and creamy. Transfer to a bowl and serve immediately or cover and refrigerate for up to 3 days.

Variation

For a lower-fat and lower-calorie version of this recipe, substitute 2 1/2 cups (625 mL) sunflower seeds for the cashews. Add 1/4 tsp (1 mL) freshly ground nutmeg along with the spinach.

Cucumber Raita

Raita is a specialty of Indian cuisine, where it is used as a cooling agent to balance spicy dishes. I like to use this savory blend as a spread for raw sandwiches instead of mayonnaise. It is particularly delicious with Zucchini Hemp Bread (page 324).

Makes 2½ cups (625 mL)

Tips

To soak the pine nuts for this recipe, combine with 3 cups (750 mL) water. Cover and set aside for 1 hour. Drain, discarding soaking water. Rinse under cold running water until the water runs clear.

Use the large holes of a box grater to shred the cucumber. If you prefer, you can also use your food processor, fitted with the shredding blade.

2 cups	raw pine nuts, soaked (see Tips, left)	500 mL
½ cup	filtered water	125 mL
3 tbsp	freshly squeezed lemon juice	45 mL
3 tbsp	chopped cilantro leaves	45 mL
2 tbsp	chopped green onion, white part with a bit of green	30 mL
1 tsp	ground cumin	5 mL
1 tsp	chopped gingerroot	5 mL
½ tsp	ground coriander	2 mL
½ tsp	fine sea salt	2 mL
½ cup	shredded cucumber (about ½ cucumber; see Tips, left)	125 mL

1. In a food processor fitted with the metal blade, process soaked pine nuts and water until smooth and blended. Add lemon juice, cilantro, green onion, cumin, ginger, coriander and salt and pulse several times to blend. Transfer to a serving bowl. Add cucumber and stir well. Chill for at least 30 minutes before serving.

Variation

Substitute 2 cups (500 mL) soaked cashews for the pine nuts and add 1 tsp (5 mL) apple cider vinegar along with the lemon juice.

Adzuki and Sea Veggie Dip

Although these beans need to soak for a long time, this dip is out-of-this-world delicious. It contains sea vegetables, which provide iodine, a mineral the body has a tough time getting from other sources.

Makes 3 cups (750 mL)

Tips

Adzuki beans have a very hard exterior shell, which takes a long time to soften through soaking. To soak the beans for this recipe, combine with 3 cups (750 mL) water. Cover and set aside for 48 hours in the refrigerator, changing the water every 12 hours. Drain, discarding soaking water. Rinse under cold running water until the water runs clear.

Adzuki beans are a good source of protein and are high in fiber, potassium, magnesium and phosphorus. Because of their high fiber content, they may, like other legumes, help you feel full longer.

Nori, a deep purple alga, and dulse, a red seaweed, are often referred to as sea vegetables. They are among the best sources of natural iodine and also contain an appreciable amount of potassium. Iodine is essential for the proper functioning of the thyroid gland, which produces hormones needed for growth, development, reproduction and a healthy metabolism.

1 cup	dried adzuki beans, soaked (see Tips, left)	250 mL
½ cup	chopped celery	125 mL
¼ cup	freshly squeezed lemon juice	60 mL
2 tbsp	chopped gingerroot	30 mL
2 tsp	sesame oil (untoasted) (see Tips, page 171)	10 mL
1 tsp	fine sea salt	5 mL
½ cup	chopped nori sheets (about 4)	125 mL
2 tsp	dried dulse flakes	10 mL
¼ cup	cold-pressed hemp oil	60 mL

1. In a food processor fitted with the metal blade, process celery, lemon juice, ginger, sesame oil and salt until smooth. Add nori and dulse and process until blended. Add soaked adzuki beans and process for 3 minutes, stopping the motor once and scraping down the sides of the work bowl.
2. With the motor running, slowly add the hemp oil through the feed tube and process until smoothly blended.

Curried Sunflower Dip

This dip is a rich, aromatic blend of protein, healing spices and fiber. It can be used as a spread for Buckwheat and Sunflower Seed Pizza Crust (page 326) or as a dip with some chunky vegetables such as carrot sticks, broccoli florets or cucumber slices.

Makes 3 cups (750 mL)

Tips

To soak the sunflower seeds for this recipe, combine with 3 cups (750 mL) water. Cover and set aside for 30 minutes. Drain, discarding water and any shells or unwanted particles. Rinse under cold running water until the water runs clear.

Research supports ginger's ability to reduce inflammation, much like low-dose analgesics such as ibuprofen.

2 cups	raw sunflower seeds, soaked (see Tips, left)	500 mL
3 tbsp	chopped white onion (about 1/4 small)	45 mL
2 tbsp	raisins	30 mL
1 tbsp	chopped gingerroot	15 mL
1 tbsp	curry powder	15 mL
2 tsp	ground cumin	10 mL
1/2 tsp	ground coriander	2 mL
Pinch	turmeric	Pinch
1 tsp	fine sea salt	5 mL
3 tbsp	freshly squeezed lemon juice	45 mL
1/2 cup	chopped cilantro leaves	125 mL

1. In a food processor fitted with the metal blade, process onion, raisins, ginger, curry powder, cumin, coriander, turmeric, salt and lemon juice until smooth. Add soaked sunflower seeds and process for 3 minutes, stopping the motor once or twice and scraping down the sides of the work bowl. Add cilantro and pulse for 20 to 30 seconds or until combined.

Variations

Substitute 2 cups (500 mL) soaked cashews for the sunflower seeds.

If you crave a spicy kick, add 1/4 cup (60 mL) chopped jalapeño pepper in Step 1.

Creamy Coconut Curried Sunflower Dip: Add 1/4 cup (60 mL) coconut butter in Step 1, plus an additional pinch of sea salt.

Spicy Cashew Mayonnaise

This heavenly spread is scrumptious served in a variety of different ways. I like spreading it on Zucchini Hemp Bread (page 324), topped with some fresh avocado slices, or as a dressing on Simple Marinated Kale Salad (page 142).

Makes 2 cups (500 mL)

Tips

To soak the cashews for this recipe, cover with 2 cups (500 mL) water. Cover and set aside for 30 minutes. Drain, discarding water, and rinse under cold running water until the water runs clear.

Coconut oil is solid at room temperature. It has a melting temperature of 76°F (24°C), so it is easy to liquefy. If you have a dehydrator, place the required amount in a shallow dish and warm at 105°F (41°C) for 15 minutes or until melted. If you do not have a dehydrator, place in a shallow glass bowl over a pot of simmering water.

If you don't have a high-powered blender, use a food processor fitted with the metal blade to make this spread, although the end result will not be as creamy.

1 cup	raw cashews, soaked (see Tips, left)	250 mL
1	clove garlic	1
$\frac{1}{2}$ cup	filtered water	125 mL
$\frac{1}{4}$ cup	melted coconut oil (see Tips, left)	60 mL
3 tbsp	cold-pressed (extra virgin) olive oil	45 mL
$\frac{1}{2}$ tsp	dry mustard powder	2 mL
$\frac{1}{2}$ tsp	fine sea salt	2 mL
$\frac{1}{4}$ tsp	cayenne pepper	1 mL

1. In a high-powered blender (see Tips, left) at high speed, blend soaked cashews, garlic, water, coconut oil, olive oil, mustard powder, salt and cayenne until smooth and creamy. Transfer to a serving bowl. Cover and refrigerate for up to 5 days.

Variations

You can vary the oils in this recipe to suit your taste or what you have on hand. Substitute $\frac{1}{2}$ cup (125 mL) olive oil for the olive and coconut oils. You could also use $\frac{1}{4}$ cup (60 mL) each olive and flax oils or olive and hemp oils. Always make sure to use half and half; otherwise the strong flavor of the seed oil will overpower the mayo.

Lemon Hemp Dill Mayo

> This simple sauce is delicious and versatile. Spread it on Zucchini Hemp Bread (page 324) or Herbed Pumpkin Seed Flatbread (page 321) or enjoy it as a dressing for light, crisp greens. This makes a large quantity, but you can halve it if desired.

Yields 4 cups (1 L)

Tips

To soak the hemp seeds for this recipe, add 2 cups (500 mL) water. Set aside for 30 minutes. Drain and discard water.

If you don't have a high-powered blender, you can make this and the following recipe in a food processor fitted with the metal blade, although the result will not be quite as creamy.

1½ cups	raw shelled hemp seeds, soaked (see Tips, left)	375 mL
1 cup	filtered water	250 mL
1 cup	cold-pressed (extra virgin) olive oil	250 mL
¼ cup	freshly squeezed lemon juice	60 mL
3	cloves garlic	3
2 tbsp	dried dill weed	30 mL
1 tbsp	fine sea salt	15 mL

1. In a high-powered blender (see Tips, left), combine soaked hemp seeds, water, olive oil, lemon juice, garlic, dill and salt. Blend at high speed until smooth and creamy. Transfer to an airtight container and refrigerate for up to 5 days.

Sun-Dried Tomato Hemp Mayonnaise

> This easy-to-make sauce can replace store-bought mayonnaise. It is a great dip for crudités and is fabulous spread on Zucchini Hemp Bread (page 324).

Makes 2½ cups (625 mL)

Tips

To soak the hemp seeds for this recipe, cover with 1 cup (250 mL) water. Set aside for 30 minutes. Drain and discard any remaining water.

To rehydrate the tomatoes for this recipe, cover with 1 cup (250 mL) water. Set aside for 30 minutes. Drain and discard soaking water.

½ cup	raw shelled hemp seeds, soaked (see Tips, left)	125 mL
¼ cup	dry-packed sun-dried tomatoes, soaked (see Tips, left)	60 mL
1 cup	cold-pressed (extra virgin) olive oil	250 mL
3 tbsp	freshly squeezed lemon juice	45 mL
2 tbsp	filtered water	30 mL
1 tsp	apple cider vinegar	5 mL
¼ tsp	fine sea salt	1 mL

1. In a high-powered blender (see Tips, above), combine olive oil, soaked hemp seeds, rehydrated tomatoes, lemon juice, water, vinegar and salt. Blend at high speed until smooth. Transfer to a bowl and serve immediately or cover and refrigerate for up to 5 days.

Hemp Avocado Mayonnaise

This mayonnaise has only five ingredients and can be made in less than five minutes. It is delicious as a spread or as a dip for cut-up vegetables.

Makes 1 cup (250 mL)

Tips

Because it contains puréed avocado, this mayonnaise will begin to turn brown (oxidize) fairly quickly. It should be used as soon as possible after preparation.

Always keep high-quality oils away from sunlight and heat, which encourage the healthy fatty acids to deteriorate, diminishing nutrition.

1	large avocado	1
2 tbsp	filtered water	30 mL
2 tsp	freshly squeezed lemon juice	10 mL
½ tsp	fine sea salt	2 mL
½ cup	cold-pressed hemp oil	125 mL

1. In a blender, combine avocado, water, lemon juice and salt until smooth. Remove the lid and, with the motor running, slowly drizzle the hemp oil over the purée, processing until the mixture is smooth and creamy. Transfer to a bowl and serve immediately.

Variations

Use this recipe as a basic avocado mayonnaise and vary the herbs and spices to suit your taste.

Curry Avocado Mayonnaise: Add 1 tsp (5 mL) curry powder, ½ tsp (2 mL) ground cumin and a pinch each of ground turmeric and cayenne pepper.

Fresh Herb Avocado Mayonnaise: Add ¼ cup (60 mL) chopped parsley, 1 tbsp (15 mL) chopped fresh thyme, 2 tsp (10 mL) chopped chives and 1 tsp (10 mL) chopped fresh rosemary.

Creamy Baba Ghanouj

This classic Middle Eastern eggplant concoction makes a perfect dip for raw veggies. It is also delicious spread on Zucchini Hemp Bread (page 324).

Makes 3 cups (750 mL)

Tips

To sweat the eggplant for this recipe, sprinkle with 1 tsp (5 mL) sea salt, toss well and set aside in a colander for 30 minutes. The eggplant will release droplets of liquid. Rinse well in fresh cold water and, using your hands, squeeze out the excess moisture.

In many recipes that call for olive oil, it can be substituted with another high-quality oil such as flax, hemp or pumpkin seed oil. The only factor to consider — so long as you are using good-quality cold-pressed oils — is the flavor profile you are trying to achieve.

- **Electric food dehydrator**

2 cups	chopped peeled eggplant (about 1 medium), sweated (see Tips, left)	500 mL
¼ cup	cold-pressed (extra virgin) olive oil, divided	60 mL
2 tbsp	wheat-free tamari (see Tips, page 102)	30 mL
2 tsp	freshly ground black pepper	10 mL
¼ cup	freshly squeezed lemon juice	60 mL
3 tbsp	filtered water	45 mL
2	cloves garlic, minced	2
¼ cup	tahini	60 mL
2 tbsp	chopped fresh thyme leaves	30 mL

1. In a bowl, combine eggplant, 2 tbsp (30 mL) olive oil, tamari and pepper. Transfer to a nonstick dehydrator sheet and spread evenly. Dehydrate at 115°F (46°C) for 30 to 45 minutes or until mixture is slightly soft.

2. In a food processor fitted with the metal blade, process dried eggplant, remaining 2 tbsp (30 mL) olive oil, lemon juice, water and garlic until smooth, stopping the motor once to scrape down the sides of the work bowl (you don't want any pieces of vegetable remaining). Add tahini and thyme and pulse to blend. Serve immediately or cover and refrigerate for up to 3 days. You may need to add a little more oil or water depending on the density of the eggplant. If the mixture seems thin, add 2 to 3 tbsp (30 to 45 mL) olive oil and pulse 2 or 3 times to blend.

Variations

Substitute the olive oil with flax oil or hemp oil, or use equal parts olive and hemp oils to maintain a neutral flavor.

Olive and Parsley Tapenade

This savory dip is great with carrot or celery sticks. It can also be used as a salad topper or a spread in sandwiches.

Makes 1 cup (250 mL)

Tips

You may use any type of olive in this recipe, but I prefer salty kalamata olives. I also like to use a mixture of 1/2 cup (125 mL) green olives and 1/2 cup (125 mL) black olives.

Parsley is especially rich in the antioxidant apigenin, which helps other antioxidants do their work.

2 cups	coarsely chopped flat-leaf (Italian) parsley leaves	500 mL
1 cup	pitted black or green olives (see Tips, left)	250 mL
3	cloves garlic	3
1 tbsp	raw shelled hemp seeds	15 mL
1/2 cup	cold-pressed (extra virgin) olive oil	125 mL
1 tbsp	freshly squeezed lemon juice	15 mL

1. In a food processor fitted with the metal blade, pulse parsley, olives, garlic, hemp seeds, olive oil and lemon juice until slightly broken down and blended but not paste-like. You want to retain the texture of the olives and the parsley. Serve immediately or cover and refrigerate for up to 5 days.

Creamy Cashew Tzatziki

This garlicky dip is perfect with Buckwheat Sunflower and Almond Breadsticks (page 320). It also makes a luscious topping for Cauliflower Rice (page 274). To turn it into a tasty falafel, spread tzatziki liberally over a crisp romaine lettuce leaf; top with a second leaf and wrap around a Lemon and Cilantro Falafel (page 225).

Makes 3 1/2 cups (825 mL)

Tips

To soak the cashews for this recipe, cover with 3 cups (750 mL) water. Set aside for 30 minutes. Drain, discarding soaking water. Rinse under cold running water until the water runs clear.

If you don't have a high-powered blender, you can make this recipe in a food processor fitted with the metal blade.

2 cups	raw cashews, soaked (see Tips, left)	500 mL
3/4 cup	filtered water	175 mL
1/4 cup	freshly squeezed lemon juice	60 mL
1/2 tsp	fine sea salt	2 mL
1/2 cup	shredded cucumber	125 mL
6 to 8	cloves garlic, minced	6 to 8
1 tbsp	dried dill weed or 1/4 cup (60 mL) chopped fresh dill fronds	15 mL

1. In a high-powered blender (see Tips, left), combine soaked cashews, water, lemon juice and salt. Blend at high speed until smooth. Transfer to a bowl.
2. Add cucumber, garlic and dill and stir well. Serve immediately or cover and refrigerate for up to 5 days.

Pumpkin Seed Chimichurri

This South American–inspired dip bursts on your tongue with flavor. In addition to being a great dip for veggies such as leaves of romaine hearts, it makes a fabulous chunky dressing for salad.

Makes 1½ cups (375 mL)

Tips

To soak the pumpkin seeds for this recipe, combine with 2 cups (500 mL) water in a bowl. Cover and set aside for 30 minutes. Drain, rinse and discard any remaining water.

Pumpkin seeds provide an impressive array of nutrients. They contain healthy polyunsaturated and monounsaturated fats, protein, fiber, iron, magnesium, potassium, zinc, manganese, thiamine (vitamin B$_1$) and vitamin E — not bad for the seeds of a common squash.

Parsley comes in two different varieties: flat-leaf (also called Italian parsley) and curly. Both are very good for you. Flat-leaf parsley has more flavor when it is left in a roughly chopped state.

1 cup	raw pumpkin seeds, soaked (see Tips, left)	250 mL
3 tbsp	freshly squeezed lemon juice	45 mL
3 tbsp	cold-pressed (extra virgin) olive oil	45 mL
1 tbsp	apple cider vinegar	15 mL
2 tbsp	chopped gingerroot	30 mL
3	cloves garlic	3
1 tbsp	chili powder	15 mL
1 tsp	ground cumin	5 mL
½ tsp	sea salt	2 mL
Pinch	cayenne pepper	Pinch
1 cup	chopped cilantro leaves	250 mL
½ cup	chopped flat-leaf (Italian) parsley leaves	125 mL
3 tbsp	(approx.) filtered water, optional	45 mL

1. In a food processor fitted with the metal blade, process lemon juice, olive oil, vinegar, ginger, garlic, chili powder, cumin, salt and cayenne until smooth. Using a rubber spatula, scrape down the sides of the work bowl.

2. Add cilantro, parsley and soaked pumpkin seeds and pulse just until mixture is chopped and blended (you want the result to be a bit chunky, not smooth). If the mixture seems dry, add water through the feed tube in increments of 1 tbsp (15 mL) and pulse to integrate. Serve immediately or cover and refrigerate for up to 5 days.

Variations

Substitute 1½ cups (375 mL) sunflower seeds or ¾ cup (175 mL) almonds for the pumpkin seeds in this recipe. Soak either for 30 minutes in 2 cups (500 mL) water. Cover and set aside. Drain and discard any remaining water.

Pumpkin Seed "Refried Beans"

Just like the real thing, this take on traditional Mexican refried beans is packed full of iron and protein. Spread it on Soft-Shell Tortillas (page 328) or enjoy it as a snack on its own. This recipe really helped me while I was transitioning to a raw diet, because I found the texture and flavors very familiar.

Makes 4 cups (1 L)

Tips

To soak the pumpkin seeds for this recipe, combine with 6 cups (1. 25 L) water. Cover and set aside for 30 minutes. Drain, discarding water.

Ounce for ounce, pumpkin seeds are one of the best plant sources of iron. Make sure to include a source of vitamin C — such as citrus juice, cilantro or parsley — when consuming plant-based iron, as this will help your body to absorb the mineral. With that in mind, I like to serve this dip with Herb Citrus Vinaigrette (page 166) or even a squeeze of fresh lemon juice.

3 cups	raw pumpkin seeds, soaked (see Tips, left)	750 mL
1 cup	chopped seeded red bell pepper	250 mL
¼ cup	chopped red onion (about ½ small)	60 mL
¼ cup	chopped parsley leaves	60 mL
3	cloves garlic	3
2 tbsp	chili powder	30 mL
2 tbsp	ground cumin	30 mL
¼ cup	cold-pressed (extra virgin) olive oil	60 mL
½ cup	freshly squeezed lemon juice	125 mL
1 tsp	fine sea salt	5 mL
1 cup	(approx.) filtered water	250 mL

1. In a food processor fitted with the metal blade, process bell pepper, onion, parsley, garlic, chili powder, cumin, olive oil, lemon juice and salt until smooth. Stop the motor once and scrape down the sides of the bowl.
2. Add soaked pumpkin seeds and process until smooth. With the motor running, add water through the feed tube in a steady stream until a soft, pâté-like consistency is achieved. Serve immediately or cover and refrigerate for up to 5 days.

Variations

Substitute an equal quantity of raw sunflower seeds or almonds, soaked as per the instructions above, for the pumpkin seeds.

Raw Chickpea Hummus

This living-food version of the classic dip is sure to make you wonder how you ever enjoyed the store-bought version. The trick to making this dip is soaking the chickpeas long enough that they become soft. I like to serve hummus with fresh vegetables such as celery or carrot sticks or some crisp romaine lettuce leaves. A real treat is to accompany it with Buckwheat, Sunflower and Almond Breadsticks (page 320), which you can make if you are lucky enough to own a food dehydrator.

Makes 4 cups (1 L)

Tips

To soak the chickpeas for this recipe, place in a bowl and add 3 cups (750 mL) water. Cover and set aside for 10 hours, changing the water every 3 hours. Drain, discarding water, and rinse under cold running water until the water runs clear. If you are soaking the chickpeas overnight, change the water and place them in the refrigerator when you go to bed, to prevent them from becoming sour. In the refrigerator they will need to be soaked for at least 12 hours but the water won't need to be changed; cold temperatures retard the soaking process.

Dried chickpeas will double in size when soaked. For example, 1 cup (250 mL) dried chickpeas will produce 2 cups (500 mL) soaked chickpeas.

1 cup	dried chickpeas, soaked (see Tips, left)	500 mL
½ cup	chopped seeded red bell pepper	125 mL
¼ cup	freshly squeezed lemon juice	60 mL
2	cloves garlic	2
2 tsp	ground cumin	10 mL
1 tsp	fine sea salt	5 mL
¼ cup	tahini	60 mL
¾ cup	cold-pressed (extra virgin) olive oil (see page 82)	175 mL

1. In a food processor fitted with the metal blade, pulse bell pepper, lemon juice, garlic, cumin and salt. Using a rubber spatula, scrape down the sides of the bowl and pulse again until finely chopped and blended.

2. Add soaked chickpeas and process until chunky, stopping the motor once and scraping down the sides of the work bowl. Add tahini and process until smooth.

3. With the motor running, add olive oil through the feed tube in a slow, steady stream, processing until creamy. Spoon into a serving bowl and serve immediately or cover and refrigerate for up to 3 days.

Variation

Replace the red pepper and cumin with ½ cup (125 mL) chopped celery, 2 tsp (10 mL) dried dill weed and 1 tsp (5 mL) chopped gingerroot.

Sunflower-Sage Mock Chicken Salad

This raw food variation on traditional chicken salad is loaded with flavor. It's delicious simply scooped onto celery or carrot sticks and it's also a great sandwich filling with Zucchini Hemp Bread (page 324) or as a garnish for Sun-Dried Tomato and Carrot Burgers (page 220). It also makes a fine protein-packed topper for a green salad.

Makes 2½ cups (625 mL)

Tips

To soak the sunflower seeds for this recipe, place in a bowl and add 4 cups (1 L) water. Cover and set aside for 1 hour. Drain, discarding water and any shells or unwanted particles. Rinse under cold running water until the water runs clear.

Look for dried rubbed sage leaves in the spice section of well-stocked supermarkets.

2 cups	raw sunflower seeds, soaked (see Tips, left)	500 mL
3 tbsp	freshly squeezed lemon juice	45 mL
1 tbsp	dried rubbed sage leaves (see Tips, left)	15 mL
3	cloves garlic	3
2 tsp	fine sea salt	10 mL
¼ cup	filtered water	60 mL

1. In a food processor fitted with the metal blade, pulse lemon juice, sage, garlic and salt, until chopped and blended. Add soaked sunflower seeds and process until smooth and blended. With the motor running, gradually add water through the feed tube. Taste and adjust seasoning, adding more salt if necessary. Transfer to a container, cover and refrigerate for up to 3 days.

Variations

For a richer, more extravagant taste, substitute an equal quantity of soaked cashews for the sunflower seeds.

Add 1 tbsp (15 mL) chopped fresh dill and ¼ cup (60 mL) chopped red bell pepper.

Sweet Chili and Pecan Pâté

This pâté is packed with nutrition and very simple to prepare. I love it as a dip with fresh veggie sticks, served with a side of Sour Cream and Onion Kale Chips (page 298). Since this makes a fairly large quantity, it is a perfect dish to take to a potluck.

Makes 4½ cups (1.1 L)

Tips

To soak the pecans and sunflower seeds for this recipe, place in a bowl with 6 cups (1.5 L) water. Cover and set aside for 30 minutes. Drain, discarding any remaining water and any shells or unwanted particles. Rinse under cold running water until the water runs clear.

When processing, be aware that you want the final product to be free of any visible pieces of nuts or seeds. Adding a little water in the final step helps the blade to properly purée the mixture.

Pecans, like all tree nuts, contain potassium, manganese, phosphorus, vitamin E and magnesium and also provide protein.

3 cups	raw pecans, soaked (see Tips, left)	750 mL
½ cup	raw sunflower seeds, soaked	125 mL
¼ cup	chopped cilantro leaves	60 mL
3	cloves garlic	3
1 tbsp	chili powder	15 mL
1 tsp	sea salt	5 mL
½ tsp	freshly squeezed lemon juice	2 mL
½ cup	Date Paste (page 80)	125 mL
¼ cup	water, optional	60 mL

1. In a food processor fitted with the metal blade, pulse cilantro, garlic, chili powder, salt and lemon juice, until chopped and blended. Stop the motor and scrape down the sides of the work bowl. Add date paste and process until smooth. Scrape down the sides of the work bowl.

2. Add soaked pecans and sunflower seeds and process until smooth and blended, stopping the motor and scraping down the sides of the work bowl, if necessary. If the mixture is not smooth enough, turn on the machine and drizzle the water thorough the feed tube as needed (see Tips, left). When smooth, transfer to an airtight container, cover and refrigerate for up to 4 days.

Lemon-Ginger-Dill Sunflower Seed Pâté

Here's a light and flavorful dip that makes a perfect pairing with carrot or celery sticks or even spicy vegetables such as radishes. It also makes a great salad topper and is awesome rolled between sheets of nori to make raw sushi.

Makes 3 cups (750 mL)

Tips

To soak the sunflower seeds for this recipe, place in a bowl and add 3 cups (750 mL) water. Cover and set aside for 30 minutes. Drain, discarding water and any shells or unwanted particles. Rinse under cold running water until the water runs clear.

When using a food processor to make dips, raw pâtés or sauces, make sure to stop it once or twice and scrape down the sides of the work bowl, using a rubber spatula. This will ensure that the ingredients are evenly incorporated and that there won't be any chunks of food in the finished product.

2 cups	raw sunflower seeds, soaked (see Tips, left)	500 mL
¼ cup	chopped celery	60 mL
¼ cup	freshly squeezed lemon juice	60 mL
¼ cup	chopped fresh dill fronds	60 mL
2 tbsp	chopped gingerroot	30 mL
1 tsp	fine sea salt	5 mL

1. In a food processor fitted with the metal blade, process celery, lemon juice, dill, ginger and salt until smooth and blended, stopping the motor once to scrape down the sides of the work bowl. Add soaked sunflower seeds and process until smooth. Transfer to a serving bowl and serve immediately or cover and refrigerate for up to 4 days.

Variations

Substitute 2 cups (500 mL) raw cashews for the sunflower seeds. They need to be soaked for 30 minutes as well.

I like to use different spices when making pâtés or dips. Be adventurous and see what flavor combinations you can come up with for this recipe. One of my favorites is ½ cup (125 mL) chopped tomato, 2 tbsp (30 mL) dried basil and 4 garlic cloves in place of the celery, dill weed and ginger.

Mung Bean Pâté

This creamy and delicious pâté is a great way to curb your protein cravings. I love eating it as a "sandwich" between two crisp lettuce leaves with a few slices of tomato and red onion. If you're just transitioning to a raw food diet, try it as a spread on warm slices of your favorite crusty bread.

Makes 3 cups (750 mL)

Tips

To soak the mung beans for this recipe, place them in a bowl and cover with 3 cups (750 mL) water. Cover and set aside for 8 hours, changing the water every 3 hours. If you are soaking the beans overnight, place them in the fridge before you go to bed. They will need to be soaked for at least 10 hours, but the water won't need to be changed — cold temperatures retard the process. Drain, discarding the water, and rinse under cold running water until the water runs clear.

When making a dip in a food processor, add the flavoring components of the recipe first. This ensures that they are thoroughly broken down and well integrated into the final product.

1 cup	dried mung beans, soaked (see Tips, left)	250 mL
½ cup	chopped celery	125 mL
¼ cup	chopped red bell pepper	60 mL
¼ cup	freshly squeezed lemon juice	60 mL
2 tbsp	chopped gingerroot	30 mL
1 tsp	dried dill weed	5 mL
1 tsp	fine sea salt	5 mL
¼ cup	tahini	60 mL
½ cup	cold-pressed hemp oil	125 mL

1. In a food processor fitted with the metal blade, process celery, red pepper, lemon juice, ginger, dill and salt, until chopped and blended. Add soaked mung beans and process for 2 to 3 minutes, until the beans are broken down and combined with the other ingredients. Stop the motor and scrape down the sides of the work bowl. Add tahini and process for 2 minutes until smooth.
2. With the motor running, add hemp oil through the feed tube in a slow, steady stream until mixture becomes smooth and soft. Transfer to an airtight container and refrigerate for up to 5 days.

Variation

This recipe will work using any soaked legume or seed. Instead of the mung beans, try substituting 2 cups (500 mL) pumpkin seeds, soaked for 30 minutes.

Creamy Red Pepper and Celery Pâté

This recipe is nutrient-dense and packed with flavor. It is very easy to prepare and makes a perfect midday snack. I enjoy eating it like a dip, using carrot and celery sticks and other raw veggies to scoop it up.

Makes 3 cups (750 mL)

Tips

To soak the walnuts for this recipe, combine with 3 cups (750 mL) water. Cover and set aside for 1 hour. Drain, discarding water. Rinse under cold running water until the water runs clear.

If you have time, always try to soak nuts and seeds before eating them. Nuts, seeds and whole grains contain compounds known as anti-nutrients, which bind minerals until they are needed to fuel growth. Soaking nuts and seeds stimulates the growth phase, which neutralizes their enzyme inhibitors. When this happens, proteins and vitamins are synthesized and minerals are released. By soaking nuts and seeds before consuming them, you increase the amount of protein, vitamins and minerals that your body can absorb from them.

2 cups	walnut pieces soaked (see Tips, left)	500 mL
½ cup	chopped celery	125 mL
½ cup	chopped red bell pepper	125 mL
¼ cup	freshly squeezed lemon juice	60 mL
¼ cup	nutritional yeast (see Tip, page 124)	60 mL
1 tbsp	ground cumin	15 mL
1 tsp	fine sea salt	5 mL
2	cloves garlic	2
¼ cup	cold-pressed flax oil	60 mL

1. In a food processor fitted with the metal blade, process celery, red pepper, lemon juice, nutritional yeast, cumin, salt and garlic, until no large pieces of vegetable remain, stopping the motor once and scraping down the sides of the work bowl. Add soaked walnuts and process for 2 to 3 minutes, until walnuts are broken down and mixture is smooth, stopping the motor once and scraping down the sides of the work bowl.

2. With the motor running, slowly add flax oil through the feed tube until mixture is smooth and creamy. Transfer to an airtight container and refrigerate for up to 5 days.

Variation

For a spicy curry-flavored dip, instead of 1 tbsp (15 mL) ground cumin, substitute 1 tbsp (15 mL) curry powder, 1 tsp (5 mL) ground cumin and a pinch each of ground turmeric and cayenne.

Herbed Mushroom and Walnut Pâté

This earthy pâté is a perfect blend of fresh herbs, juicy mushrooms and dense walnuts. I love eating it with some crispy French Onion Flax Crackers (page 319) and glass of cold Almond Milk (page 45).

Makes 3 cups (750 mL)

Tips

To soak the walnuts for this recipe, combine with 2 cups (500 mL) water in a bowl. Cover and set aside for 30 minutes. Drain, discarding soaking water, and rinse under cold running water until the water runs clear.

Never clean mushrooms by washing them in running water, or they will become gray and soggy. Use a damp towel to lightly brush the surface. This will remove any dirt.

While wheat-free tamari is not raw, it is gluten-free. The raw alternative for tamari, nama shoyu, does contain gluten. If you are following a completely raw diet and can tolerate gluten, by all means substitute an equal quantity of nama shoyu.

1 cup	walnut pieces, soaked (see Tips, left)	250 mL
3 cups	sliced assorted mushrooms	750 mL
3 tbsp	cold-pressed (extra virgin) olive oil	45 mL
2 tbsp	wheat-free tamari (see Tips, left)	30 mL
2 tbsp	chopped fresh thyme, divided	30 mL
Pinch	fine sea salt	Pinch
3 tbsp	chopped white onion (about ¼ small)	45 mL
3 tbsp	chopped celery (about 1 stalk)	45 mL
2	cloves garlic	2
2 tbsp	nutritional yeast	30 mL
2 tbsp	cold-pressed hemp oil	30 mL
2 tbsp	filtered water	30 mL

1. In a bowl, toss mushrooms, olive oil, tamari, 1 tbsp (15 mL) chopped thyme and salt. Set aside to marinate for 15 minutes.

2. In a food processor fitted with the metal blade, process onion, celery, garlic, nutritional yeast, hemp oil, water and remaining thyme until smooth. Add marinated mushrooms and process until smooth. Add soaked walnuts and process until smooth and creamy. Serve immediately or cover and refrigerate for up to 4 days.

Variations

Use your favorite mushrooms to make this recipe. I love using a mixture of cremini, portobello, oyster and button mushrooms. When using meatier mushrooms such as portobellos, make sure to slice them thinly so they have a chance to absorb the marinade and soften. If you are having trouble getting the mushrooms to soften, after combining them with the marinade ingredients, spread them out on a nonstick dehydrator sheet and dehydrate at 105°F (41°C) for 20 to 30 minutes.

Almond Mock Tuna Pâté

I call this "mock tuna" because the dill, lemon and celery remind me of the taste of conventional tuna salad. It is great served as a snack or as a dip for fresh carrot or celery sticks; you can also scoop it up with crispy romaine lettuce leaves. This makes a great main dish as well, spooned onto a collard leaf with some fresh tomato slices and topped with Spicy Cashew Mayonnaise (page 87).

Makes 2 cups (500 mL)

Tips

To soak the almonds for this recipe, place them in a bowl and add 4 cups (1 L) water. Cover and set aside for 30 minutes. Drain and discard any remaining water. Rinse under cold running water until the water runs clear.

The outer stalks of celery can be tough and fibrous. For best results, peel the stalk with a vegetable peeler. Save the peel to make soups, sauces or stocks.

When you are working with raw food recipes that use soaked nuts or seeds, be aware that the results won't be consistent every time. The amount of moisture or humidity in the air and how long the nuts or seeds are soaked will influence the result. That's why, when making a purée, it's a good idea to have a little water on hand to blend in at the end. Better to add less liquid at the outset than to have too much, which will produce a mushy result. You can always add liquid at the end, but it can't be removed once it's integrated into the recipe.

2 cups 500 mL	whole raw almonds, soaked (see Tips, left)	
¼ cup	chopped celery (see Tips, left)	60 mL
¼ cup	chopped fresh dill fronds	60 mL
2	cloves garlic	2
¼ cup	freshly squeezed lemon juice	60 mL
1 tsp	fine sea salt	5 mL
¼ cup	(approx.) water, optional	60 mL

1. In a food processor fitted with the metal blade, process celery, dill, garlic, lemon juice and salt until smooth. Add soaked almonds and process for 3 minutes. Using a rubber spatula, scrape down the sides of the bowl. If the result is too thick for your liking, add water in 1 tbsp (15 mL) increments, pulsing to blend, until desired consistency is achieved.

Variations

Substitute 3 cups (750 mL) sunflower seeds for the almonds. Cover and soak in 4 cups (1 L) water for 30 minutes and continue as above.

If you prefer, substitute ¼ cup (60 mL) hemp oil for the optional water. This will give a richer taste.

If you do not have fresh dill, substitute 2 tbsp (30 mL) dried dill weed.

Herbed Mushroom Duxelles

This dip is a take on a classic French stuffing. It is delicious served with Buckwheat, Sunflower and Almond Breadsticks (page 320), but if you would like something more convenient, fresh cauliflower and broccoli florets are wonderful too.

Makes 3 cups (750 mL)

Tips

Never clean mushrooms by washing them in running water, or they will become gray and soggy. Use a damp towel to lightly brush the surface. This will remove any dirt.

While wheat-free tamari is not raw, it is gluten-free. The raw alternative for tamari, nama shoyu, does contain gluten. If you are following a completely raw diet and can tolerate gluten, by all means substitute an equal quantity of nama shoyu.

- **Electric food dehydrator**

2 cups	sliced white mushrooms	500 mL
1 cup	sliced shiitake mushrooms	250 mL
1 cup	sliced oyster mushrooms	250 mL
¼ cup	cold-pressed (extra virgin) olive oil	60 mL
1 tsp	fine sea salt	5 mL
3 tbsp	wheat-free tamari (see Tips, left)	45 mL
2 tbsp	chopped fresh thyme leaves	30 mL

1. In a bowl, toss together white, shiitake and oyster mushrooms, olive oil, salt and tamari. Ladle onto a nonstick dehydrator sheet and spread evenly. Dehydrate at 115°F (46°C) for 45 to 60 minutes or until mushrooms appear sautéed.

2. Transfer mushrooms to a food processor fitted with the metal blade. Add thyme and process until smooth. Transfer to a serving bowl and serve immediately or cover and refrigerate for up to 4 days.

Variation

Use any kind of mushrooms for this recipe. If using portobello mushrooms, which are denser than other varieties, increase the amount of olive oil and tamari to compensate.

Red Pepper, Dill and Cashew Ricotta

This raw "cheese" is a perfect blend of red pepper, creamy cashews and spices. It is very versatile. Use it as a dairy replacement on dishes such as pizza and lasagna. It also makes a delicious dip for fresh vegetables.

Makes 6 cups (1.5 L)

Tips

To soak the cashews for this recipe, place in a bowl and add 12 cups (3 L) water. Cover and set aside for 30 minutes. Drain, discarding soaking water, and rinse under cold running water until the water runs clear.

I use both a food processor and a blender in this recipe to create two different textures, which mimics traditional ricotta cheese. The food processor creates a slightly chunky texture while the blender makes a smooth purée.

If you have a high-powered blender, use it to make this cheese — the purée will be smoother and creamier than if made in a regular blender.

6 cups	raw cashews, soaked, divided (see Tips, left)	1.5 L
1 cup	chopped red bell pepper	250 mL
1 cup	filtered water, divided	250 mL
½ cup	freshly squeezed lemon juice, divided	125 mL
2 tbsp	dried dill weed	30 mL
1 tbsp	nutritional yeast	15 mL
4	cloves garlic	4
1 tbsp	fine sea salt, divided	15 mL

1. In a food processor fitted with the metal blade, process red pepper, ¼ cup (60 mL) water, ¼ cup (60 mL) lemon juice, dill, nutritional yeast, garlic and 2 tsp (10 mL) salt, until smooth. Add half the soaked cashews and process until smooth, stopping the motor and scraping down the sides of the work bowl as necessary. Transfer to a bowl and set aside.

2. In a blender (see Tips, left), combine remaining soaked cashews and remaining water, lemon juice and salt. Blend at high speed until smooth and creamy. Add to red pepper mixture and, using a rubber spatula, gently fold together. Serve immediately or store in an airtight container in the refrigerator for up to 4 days.

Variation

Substitute ¼ cup (60 mL) chopped fresh dill fronds for the dried dill weed.

Cashew Scallion Cream Cheese

This take on traditional cream cheese is rich and spreadable. Use it virtually anytime you want a spread. It's great on Buckwheat Toast (page 36) or Cinnamon Raisin Flax Bagels (page 33). I also like to use it as a replacement for store-bought hummus, as a dip for carrot sticks and broccoli florets.

Makes 2½ cups (625 mL)

Tips

To soak the cashews for this recipe, place in a bowl and cover with 4 cups (1 L) water. Cover and set aside for 30 minutes. Drain, discarding soaking water, and rinse under cold running water until the water runs clear.

I like to keep cashews soaking in my fridge for up to three days, submerged in water and covered. You will need to change the water 1 to 2 times daily to prevent the cashews from becoming sour or fermenting. Presoaked cashews are handy to have on hand because in a matter of minutes you can make Cashew Whipped Cream (page 367) or Cashew Milk (page 46).

This recipe was tested in a high-powered blender (see page 106). If you do not have one, follow the same method using a food processor fitted with the metal blade.

2 cups	raw cashews, soaked (see Tips, left)	500 mL
1 cup	chopped green onions, white and green parts, divided	250 mL
¼ cup	filtered water	60 mL
1 tbsp	freshly squeezed lemon juice	15 mL
1 tsp	fine sea salt	5 mL

1. In a high-powered blender (see Tips, left) at high speed, blend ½ cup (125 mL) green onions, water, lemon juice and salt, until smooth. Add soaked cashews and blend at high speed until smooth, stopping the motor once and stirring the mixture with a rubber spatula. Transfer to a serving bowl and stir in remaining ½ cup (125 mL) green onions. Serve immediately or cover and refrigerate for up to 3 days.

Variations

This recipe can be enhanced with a variety of herbs and spices or seasonings. For instance, try substituting parsley leaves for half of the green onion and adding a clove of garlic.

For a Thai-inspired version, in Step 1, add 1 tbsp (15 mL) raw agave nectar, 1 tsp (5 mL) ground coriander seeds, 1 tsp (5 mL) finely chopped gingerroot and ½ tsp (2 mL) apple cider vinegar.

Cashew Feta Cheese

I love to serve this on romaine lettuce leaves or on Greek Kale Salad (page 143).

Makes 2¼ cups (550 mL)

Tip

Always store dried herbs in an airtight container, away from light and heat, to maintain shelf life and freshness.

2 cups	raw cashews	500 mL
¼ cup	cold-pressed (extra virgin) olive oil	60 mL
2 tbsp	dried oregano	30 mL
1 tsp	fine sea salt	5 mL

1. In a food processor fitted with the metal blade, pulse cashews until slightly broken down. Add olive oil, oregano and salt and process until well combined. (You want to retain some of the texture of the cashews so the mixture resembles feta cheese.) Serve immediately or cover and refrigerate for up to 7 days.

Variations

You can substitute an equal quantity of flax oil, hemp oil or pumpkin seed oil for the olive oil.

Cashew Cheddar Cheese

This sauce provides the mouth feel of traditional Cheddar cheese. Try using it as a spread on a bed of lettuce topped with Walnut Portobello Burgers (page 219) and a dollop of Sun-Dried Tomato Ketchup (page 198).

Makes 4 cups (1 L)

Tip

To soak the cashews for this recipe, place them in a bowl and add 4 cups (1 L) water. Cover and set aside for 30 minutes. Drain, discarding soaking water. Rinse under cold running water until the water runs clear.

2½ cups	raw cashews, soaked (see Tip, left)	625 mL
1 cup	water	250 mL
½ cup	nutritional yeast (see Tips, page 119)	125 mL
2 tbsp	freshly squeezed lemon juice	30 mL
1 tsp	turmeric	5 mL
1 tsp	fine sea salt	5 mL

1. In a food processor fitted with the metal blade, process water, nutritional yeast, lemon juice, turmeric and salt until incorporated. Add soaked cashews and process until smooth, stopping the motor once to scrape down the sides of the work bowl. Transfer to a bowl, cover and refrigerate for up to 4 days.

Variation

For a Southwest spin, add 1 tbsp (15 mL) ground cumin and 1 tsp (5 mL) chili powder. If you are craving a little more spice, add 1 tsp (5 mL) chipotle pepper powder.

Macadamia Mozzarella

This creamy sauce, which on occasion makes a wonderful substitute for cheese, is perfect spread on raw pizza topped with Red Pepper Basil Marinara Sauce (page 184) and some chopped fresh kale. I also love this over a bed of crispy lettuce and fresh vegetables, finished with a squeeze of fresh lemon juice.

Makes 2 cups (500 mL)

Tips

To soak the macadamia nuts for this recipe, place in a bowl and cover with 2 cups (500 mL) water. Cover and set aside for 1 hour. Drain, discarding liquid. Rinse under cold running water until the water runs clear.

Macadamia nuts are so deliciously creamy and contain so many good fats, there is no guilt in enjoying them.

If you have a high-powered blender, use it to make this sauce.

1 cup	raw macadamia nuts, soaked (see Tips, left)	250 mL
¼ cup	filtered water	60 mL
¼ cup	cold-pressed (extra virgin) olive oil	60 mL
3 tbsp	nutritional yeast	45 mL
1	clove garlic	1
½ tsp	fine sea salt	2 mL

1. In a food processor fitted with the metal blade, process soaked macadamia nuts, water, olive oil, nutritional yeast, garlic and salt. Transfer to a bowl. Serve immediately or cover and refrigerate for up to 4 days.

The High-Powered Blender

If you have transitioned to a raw food diet, a high-powered blender is one of the most useful pieces of equipment to have. The powerful motor and multipurpose design mean it can perform many more tasks than a conventional blender. High-powered blenders can transform whole heads of green vegetables and whole fruits into smooth purées and also turn nuts into cream sauces. With a regular blender the texture is never as creamy and smooth.

Soups

Few words connote comfort more than soup. For most of us, the sound of that evocative word conjures up images of a warm bowl of puréed potato and leek soup or chunky black bean soup with corn and peppers. Although raw food soups are not served piping hot, they are as delicious as their cooked counterparts. Because raw soups do not rely on heavy ingredients such as dairy or meat-based stocks, they must derive their flavors from spices, herbs, a variety of acids, such as vinegars and citrus juices, and healthy fats. When brought together thoughtfully, these robust ingredients quickly combine to create mouth-watering soups.

The key to creating great raw soups is understanding the components and how they work together. Most raw soups are puréed in a food processor, a blender or, if you are lucky enough to have one, a high-powered blender. Puréeing breaks down the cell walls of the produce and amalgamates the ingredients to create a smooth-textured result. Marinating raw ingredients is another technique that simulates some of the features of cooked food. It helps to create the mouth feel associated with food that has been slightly cooked or steamed.

All raw soups, obviously, contain liquid. Water, fresh juices and nut milks are common. The liquid may also be derived from juiced vegetables, wheat-free tamari or even unpasteurized miso. Raw soups usually also contain healthy fats such as avocado, tahini, nut or seed butters or soaked nuts, which add creaminess, a particularly appealing feature in traditional soups. Herbs or spices add flavor, zest and freshness. All raw soups have some form of salt or an ingredient such as sea vegetables that brings a salty flavor to the dish. They also contain some form of acid, such as fresh lemon or lime juice or vinegar.

Raw soups are among the most delicious recipes provided by a raw food diet. The combination of flavors and textures, as well as their nutritional content, will compel you to create them time and time again. Some of my personal favorites from this book include Cauliflower Gumbo (page 119), Corn and Red Pepper Chowder (page 121) and Creamy Hemp and Broccoli Chowder (page 122). For some simple yet elegant lighter soups, try Brown Rice Miso Broth (page 135), Thai Coconut Soup (page 134) or Lemon, Cucumber and Dill Soup (page 116).

Summer Gazpacho

This is a nice light soup that can be served as a starter or side or even as a main dish. It also makes a great snack — keep some in the fridge and dip a spoon into it throughout the day. It takes only minutes to prepare.

Makes 6 cups (1.5 L)

Tips

Once it is diced, toss the avocado with a little lemon juice to prevent it from oxidizing and turning brown.

The outer stalks of celery can be tough and fibrous. For best results, peel the stalk with a vegetable peeler. Save the peel to make soups, sauces or stocks.

4 cups	chopped tomatoes, divided	1 L
1 cup	chopped seeded red bell pepper, divided	250 mL
½ cup	chopped fresh basil leaves	125 mL
4	chopped pitted dates	4
1	clove garlic	1
½ tsp	fine sea salt	2 mL
½ cup	filtered water	125 mL
¼ cup	cold-pressed (extra virgin) olive oil (see page 82)	60 mL
¼ cup	freshly squeezed lemon juice	60 mL
½ cup	finely diced celery (see Tips, left)	125 mL
¼ cup	diced avocado (½ small avocado)	60 mL
2 tbsp	raw shelled hemp seeds	30 mL

1. In a food processor fitted with the metal blade, process 3 cups (750 mL) chopped tomatoes, ¾ cup (175 mL) chopped red pepper, basil, dates, garlic, salt, water, olive oil and lemon juice until smooth and blended. Transfer to a bowl.

2. Stir in celery, avocado, hemp seeds and remaining tomatoes and bell pepper. Serve immediately or refrigerate in an airtight container for up to 3 days.

Variations

Complete Step 1, then vary the vegetables you add to suit your taste. For instance, I like to add diced yellow, green or orange peppers instead of the remaining tomatoes and bell pepper, plus ½ tsp (2 mL) celery salt and a pinch each of cayenne pepper and dried oregano. Minced seeded jalapeño is nice too, instead of the cayenne.

Fruit Gazpacho

This sweet, refreshing soup is full of flavor and light on the calories. I really enjoy it with a glass of Mint and Lemon Greenie (page 73).

Makes 4 cups (1 L)

Tip

You may use any blend of frozen fruit in this recipe. I also like using blackberries, gooseberries or cherries. When making this soup, make sure to use at least 2 cups (500 mL) frozen berries to give the soup body.

2 cups	chopped hulled strawberries	500 mL
1 cup	frozen raspberries (see Tip, left)	250 mL
1 cup	frozen blueberries	250 mL
1 cup	chopped kiwifruit	250 mL
1 cup	coconut water (see Tips, page 21)	250 mL
¼ cup	freshly squeezed lime juice	60 mL
¼ cup	fresh mint leaves	60 mL
Pinch	fine sea salt	Pinch

1. In a food processor fitted with the metal blade, pulse strawberries, raspberries, blueberries and kiwi until chopped and broken down (it is important to keep the texture at this point). Add coconut water, lime juice, mint and salt. Pulse to combine. Serve immediately or cover and refrigerate for up to 3 days.

Cream of Celery Soup

This creamy take on a classic French favorite is full of flavor. I love it topped with a dollop of Cashew Cheddar Cheese (page 105) and some thinly sliced fresh basil.

Makes 3 cups (750 mL)

Tip

Although unpasteurized miso is not 100 percent raw, it is often used in raw food diets because it is fermented, which provides healthy bacteria to aid digestion. Brown rice miso is gluten-free and also contains vitamin B_{12}.

- **Juicer**

2 cups	chopped celery	500 mL
½ cup	chopped avocado	125 mL
2 tsp	unpasteurized brown rice miso	10 mL
2 cups	celery juice (about 15 stalks)	500 mL
2 tsp	freshly squeezed lemon juice	10 mL
1 tsp	raw agave nectar	5 mL

1. In a food processor fitted with the metal blade, process celery, avocado, miso, celery juice, lemon juice and agave nectar until smooth and creamy. Serve immediately or cover and refrigerate for up to 3 days.

Variation

Substitute an additional 2 cups (500 mL) freshly pressed celery juice for the chopped celery. Add an additional ½ cup (125 mL) chopped avocado.

Creamy Portobello Mushroom Soup

This soup may be served warm (see Variations, below), which makes it perfect for those chilly nights when you need something to make you feel cozy.

Makes 5 cups (1.25 L)

Tips

To soak the cashews for this recipe, place in a bowl and cover with 2 cups (500 mL) water. Cover and set aside for 30 minutes. Drain, discarding soaking water, and rinse under cold running water until the water runs clear.

Make sure to add any liquid from the portobello mushrooms to the blender in Step 3.

Portobello mushroom stems may be used in any recipe. However, make sure to trim the bottom of the stem. Chop the remainder and use just like the cap.

1 cup	raw cashews, soaked (see Tips, left)	250 mL
4 cups	chopped portobello mushrooms	1 L
2 tbsp	cold-pressed (extra virgin) olive oil	30 mL
3 tbsp	wheat-free tamari	45 mL
4 cups	Cashew Milk (page 46), divided	1 L
2 tbsp	nutritional yeast (see Tips, page 119)	30 mL
1 tbsp	chopped fresh thyme leaves	15 mL
½ tsp	fine sea salt	2 mL
Pinch	freshly ground black pepper	Pinch

1. In a bowl, toss together mushrooms, olive oil and tamari. Set aside for 10 to 15 minutes, until softened.
2. In a blender, combine 2 cups (500 mL) cashew milk, soaked cashews, nutritional yeast, thyme, salt and pepper. Blend at high speed until smooth and creamy.
3. Add marinated mushrooms, with liquid, and process until smooth. Transfer to a bowl and stir in remaining 2 cups (500 mL) cashew milk. Serve immediately or cover and refrigerate for up to 3 days.

Variations

Try using different varieties of mushrooms. I like the combination of 2 cups (500 mL) shiitake mushrooms, 1 cup (250 mL) button mushrooms and 1 cup (250 mL) cremini mushrooms.

If you prefer a hot, non-creamy soup, substitute an equal quantity of water for the cashew milk in Step 2. Bring to a boil and remove from heat. Set aside for a few minutes, then complete the recipe.

Spicy Carrot and Ginger Soup

A beautifully aromatic soup that is sweet, spicy and light. Among other nutrients, the carrots provide beta-carotene, which your body makes into vitamin A.

Makes 3 cups (750 mL)

Tips

If you don't have a high-powered blender, you can make this recipe in a food processor fitted with the metal blade, although the result will not be quite as creamy. A high-powered blender will make the carrots and sesame seeds much smoother than the results you can achieve using a food processor.

To remove the skin from gingerroot with the least amount of waste, use the edge of a teaspoon. With a brushing motion, scrape off the skin to reveal the yellow root.

When purchasing agave nectar, be sure to look for products labeled "raw." Most of the agave nectar on the market has been heated to a high temperature and does not qualify as raw food. If you have concerns, ask your purveyor.

1 cup	chopped carrots (about 2 small)	250 mL
2 tbsp	white sesame seeds	30 mL
1 tbsp	chopped gingerroot (see Tips, left)	15 mL
1 tsp	fine sea salt	5 mL
1/4 tsp	cayenne pepper	1 mL
2 1/2 cups	filtered water	625 mL
1 tbsp	raw agave nectar (see Tips, left)	15 mL

1. In a high-powered blender (see Tips, left), combine carrots, sesame seeds, ginger, salt, cayenne, water and agave nectar. Blend at high speed until smooth. Serve immediately or cover and refrigerate for up to 3 days.

Variations

If you prefer a creamier texture, add 1/4 cup (60 mL) chopped avocado.

If you don't have raw agave nectar, substitute 1/4 cup (60 mL) Date Paste (page 80) in this recipe. Date paste is delicious and nutritious and makes a very effective sweetener.

If you don't like spicy foods, omit the cayenne and add 1 tsp (5 mL) ground cumin and 1/2 tsp (2 mL) ground cinnamon. This will give the soup a slightly Moroccan flavor profile. Substituting date paste for the agave nectar will strengthen this effect.

Red Pepper and Tomato Bisque

This soup is a velvety blend of tomato, red pepper and avocado. It is so deliciously creamy that you will want to make it time and time again.

Makes 4 cups (1 L)

Tip

The outer stalks of celery can be tough and fibrous. For best results, peel the stalk with a vegetable peeler. Save the peel to make soups, sauces or stocks.

2 cups	chopped tomatoes	500 mL
1 cup	chopped seeded red bell pepper	250 mL
1/4 cup	chopped celery (see Tip, left)	60 mL
1/4 cup	chopped avocado (1/2 small)	60 mL
1/2 tsp	fine sea salt	2 mL
1/2 tsp	dried basil	2 mL
1/4 cup	filtered water	60 mL
3 tbsp	cold-pressed (extra virgin) olive oil	45 mL

1. In a blender, combine tomatoes, red pepper, celery, avocado, salt, basil, water and olive oil. Blend at high speed until smooth and creamy. Serve immediately or cover and refrigerate for up to 3 days.

Variations

If you like spicy food, add 1/2 tsp (2 mL) cayenne or even a chopped fresh chile pepper.

Substitute 1/4 cup (60 mL) soaked cashews for the avocado. Place cashews in a bowl, cover with 1/2 cup (125 mL) water and set aside to soak for 30 minutes. Drain and rinse under cold running water until the water runs clear.

French Onion Soup

This light and flavorful soup is perfect for those days when it is cold outside.

Makes 4 cups (1 L)

Tip

Although unpasteurized miso is not 100 percent raw, it is often used in raw food diets because it is fermented, which provides healthy bacteria to aid digestion. Brown rice miso is gluten-free and also contains vitamin B_{12}.

3½ cups	hot filtered water, divided	825 mL
⅓ cup	unpasteurized brown rice miso	75 mL
2 tbsp	wheat-free tamari (see Tips, page 102)	30 mL
1 tbsp	raw agave nectar	15 mL
2 tsp	chopped fresh thyme leaves	10 mL
½ tsp	apple cider vinegar	2 mL
1	clove garlic	1
½ cup	Caramelized Onions (page 292)	125 mL

1. In a food processor fitted with the metal blade, process 2 cups (500 mL) water, miso, tamari, agave nectar, thyme, vinegar and garlic until smooth.
2. Transfer to a bowl and stir in caramelized onions and remaining water. Serve immediately.

Creamy Green Pea and Mint Soup

This soup is a take on the classic green pea soup, which is usually finished with heavy cream. It is delicious on its own or topped with a large dollop of Cashew Sour Cream (page 204).

Makes 4 cups (1 L)

Tips

To soak the cashews for this recipe, place in a bowl and cover with ½ cup (125 mL) water. Cover and set aside for 30 minutes. Drain, discarding soaking water, and rinse under cold running water until the water runs clear.

If your blender is not large enough to accommodate this much liquid, add half the almond milk and blend. Transfer to a bowl and stir in the remainder of the almond milk.

¼ cup	raw cashews, soaked (see Tips, left)	60 mL
3 cups	Almond Milk (page 45)	750 mL
3 tbsp	freshly squeezed lemon juice	45 mL
2 cups	fresh green peas	500 mL
¼ cup	fresh mint leaves	60 mL
1	clove garlic	1
1 tsp	fine sea salt	5 mL

1. In a blender (see Tips, left), combine soaked cashews, almond milk, lemon juice, green peas, mint, garlic and salt. Blend at high speed until smooth. Serve immediately or cover and refrigerate for up to 3 days.

Variation

You may substitute Cashew Milk (page 46) or even water if you do not have almond milk on hand. But keep in mind that nut milks add a richness to soup that you cannot get from water.

Pesto Soup

This soup is simply delicious. I love the way the fresh flavors play off against each other to create a creamy yet healthy soup.

Makes 4 cups (1 L)

Tip

The avocado will begin to oxidize once exposed to the air, so for maximum enjoyment, eat this soup as soon as it is prepared.

2½ cups	chopped spinach leaves (1 large bunch)	625 mL
½	small avocado	½
3 tbsp	Basil, Spinach and Walnut Pesto (page 186) or Variations, below	45 mL
1 tsp	fine sea salt	5 mL
2 cups	filtered water	500 mL
1½ tbsp	freshly squeezed lemon juice	22 mL

1. In a blender, combine spinach, avocado, pesto, salt, water and lemon juice. Blend at high speed until smooth. Serve immediately or cover and refrigerate for up to 2 days.

Variations

If you do not have Basil, Spinach and Walnut Pesto on hand, substitute ¼ cup (60 mL) walnuts and 3 cloves garlic.

For a different flavor profile, substitute the lemon juice with 3 tbsp (45 mL) orange juice and the garlic with 1 tbsp (15 mL) chopped fresh ginger.

Lemon, Cucumber and Dill Soup

This light, summery soup makes a perfect snack or starter for a meal. I love to top it with a dollop of Cashew Sour Cream (page 204).

Makes 3 cups (750 mL)

Tip

In many recipes that call for olive oil, it can be substituted with another high-quality oil such as flax, hemp or pumpkin seed oil. The only factor to consider — so long as you are using good-quality cold-pressed oils — is the flavor profile you are trying to achieve.

2 cups	chopped peeled, seeded cucumber	500 mL
1/2 cup	chopped romaine lettuce (4 to 5 leaves)	125 mL
1/4 cup	filtered water	60 mL
1/4 cup	chopped fresh dill fronds	60 mL
1	clove garlic	1
3 tbsp	freshly squeezed lemon juice	45 mL
2 tbsp	cold-pressed (extra virgin) olive oil	30 mL
1/2 tsp	fine sea salt	2 mL
	Cashew Sour Cream (page 204), optional	

1. In a food processor fitted with the metal blade, process cucumber, lettuce, water, dill, garlic, lemon juice, olive oil and salt until smooth. Transfer to a bowl. Cover and refrigerate until chilled, at least 1 hour or up to 3 hours. Serve garnished with a dollop of Cashew Sour Cream, if using, and additional dill.

Variations

Replace the romaine lettuce with 1/4 cup (60 mL) chopped baby arugula or 1/2 cup (125 mL) chopped baby spinach.

For a creamier version of this soup, add 1/2 cup (125 mL) chopped avocado before puréeing.

Cream of Spinach Soup

This creamy, rich and flavorful soup is a velvety smooth purée of fresh vegetables and seasonings. The deep flavor of the spinach balanced by the slightly floral celery will create beautiful music on your tongue.

Makes 4 cups (1 L)

Tips

To soak the cashews for this recipe, place in a bowl and cover with 1 cup (250 mL) water. Cover and set aside for 30 minutes. Drain, discarding soaking water, and rinse under cold running water until the water runs clear.

If the spinach won't fit into your blender, divide it in half and blend with the remaining ingredients in two increments.

- **Juicer**

½ cup	raw cashews, soaked (see Tips, left)	125 mL
8 cups	chopped spinach leaves	2 L
½ cup	chopped tomato	125 mL
2	cloves garlic	2
1 tsp	fine sea salt	5 mL
1 cup	filtered water	250 mL
½ cup	celery juice (about 4 stalks)	125 mL
1 tbsp	freshly squeezed lemon juice	15 mL

1. In a blender, combine soaked cashews, spinach, tomato, garlic, salt, water, celery juice and lemon juice. Blend at high speed until smooth and creamy. Serve immediately or cover and refrigerate for up to 3 days.

Variations

Substitute ½ cup (125 mL) chopped avocado for the cashews. It will produce the same creamy texture. If you are using avocado, don't keep this soup for longer than 2 days in the refrigerator.

Substitute 2 cups (500 mL) baby arugula or a mixture of chard and kale for 2 cups (500 mL) of the chopped spinach.

Zesty Spinach, Avocado and Lime Soup

This is a great soup to enjoy during the summer months. The tangy lime flavor and the lightness of the spinach are a perfect hot-weather combination. I like to serve this slightly chilled with a side of Simple Marinated Kale Salad (page 142).

Makes 2 cups (500 mL)

Tips

Dulse is a red seaweed. It is one of the best sources of natural iodine, which helps to keep your thyroid healthy. Look for it in well-stocked grocery stores, where it can be found in dried form in a shaker-type bottle. It has a salty flavor and makes a great substitute for salt in soups and sauces.

This soup can be stored for up to two days. However, it is best consumed when just made, because it contains avocado, which begins to oxidize once exposed to air.

2½ cups	chopped spinach leaves	625 mL
1½ cups	filtered water	375 mL
3 tbsp	freshly squeezed lime juice	45 mL
½	medium avocado	½
2	cloves garlic	2
1 tsp	dried dulse flakes (see Tips, left)	5 mL
¼ tsp	fine sea salt	1 mL
Pinch	cayenne pepper	Pinch

1. In a blender, combine spinach, water, lime juice, avocado, garlic, dulse, salt and cayenne. Blend at high speed until smooth. Serve immediately or cover and refrigerate for up to 2 days (see Tips, left).

Variations

Try using chard, kale or any other dark green leafy vegetable in place of the spinach.

Add herbs or spices such as cumin, basil or oregano to suit your taste.

Cauliflower Gumbo

This soup is a rich and hearty take on a classic specialty from the American South. One trick to successfully executing this soup is to cut the cauliflower into uniform pieces, which helps to ensure a smooth purée.

Tips

To soak the sun-dried tomatoes for this recipe, place in a bowl and add 1 cup (250 mL) water. Cover and set aside for 30 minutes. Drain and discard any remaining water.

Nutritional yeast is used mainly in vegan and raw food diets because it is a source of vitamin B_{12}. It is pasteurized, so technically it does not qualify as a raw food. However, in addition to necessary nutrients, it adds a deep, umami-like flavor to many dishes.

- **Electric food dehydrator**

3 tbsp	dry-packed sun-dried tomatoes, soaked (see Tips, left)	45 mL
2½ cups	cauliflower florets, divided	625 mL
¼ cup	cold-pressed (extra virgin) olive oil, divided	60 mL
2 tsp	fine sea salt, divided	10 mL
2 cups	Cashew Milk (page 46)	500 mL
½ cup	nutritional yeast (see Tips, left)	125 mL
2 tsp	freshly squeezed lemon juice	10 mL
1 tsp	chili powder	5 mL
1 tbsp	chopped fresh thyme leaves	15 mL
1 tbsp	chopped parsley leaves	15 mL

1. In a mixing bowl, toss cauliflower with 2 tbsp (30 mL) olive oil and 1 tsp (5 mL) salt. Place on a nonstick dehydrator sheet and dehydrate at 105°F (41°C) for 30 to 40 minutes or until slightly softened.

2. In a food processor fitted with the metal blade, pulse 2 cups (500 mL) of the softened cauliflower, cashew milk, nutritional yeast, lemon juice, chili powder, soaked sun-dried tomatoes and remaining olive oil and salt until slightly broken down but not completely puréed, about 30 seconds. Transfer to a bowl and stir in remaining cauliflower, along with thyme and parsley. Taste for seasoning and serve immediately or cover and refrigerate for up to 3 days.

Variations

Substitute Almond Milk (page 45) for the Cashew Milk.

Substitute other chopped fresh green herbs for the parsley and thyme. I like using ½ tsp (2 mL) chopped fresh rosemary and ½ tsp (2 mL) chopped fresh sage leaves.

Salad in a Soup

This soup is a light green delight full of chlorophyll and energy-giving greens. It is great with a piece of Zucchini Hemp Bread (page 324).

Makes 4 cups (1 L)

Tips

The outer stalks of celery can be tough and fibrous. For best results, peel the stalk with a vegetable peeler. Save the peel to make soups, sauces or stocks.

Flax oil is made from ground flax seeds. It is particularly high in omega-3 fatty acids, which makes it very perishable — be sure to store it in the refrigerator. You can use this nutritious oil in virtually any raw food recipe that calls for oil.

When purchasing agave nectar, be sure to look for products labeled "raw." Most of the agave nectar on the market has been heated to a high temperature and does not qualify as raw food. If you have concerns, ask your purveyor.

To keep salad greens fresh, remove them from the packaging as soon as you get them home and wash under cool water. Wrap in paper towels or in a clean, damp tea towel and store in the bottom part of your fridge.

2 cups	filtered water	500 mL
1 cup	chopped romaine lettuce	250 mL
1 cup	baby spinach	250 mL
½ cup	packed coarsely chopped arugula	125 mL
½ cup	chopped red or green leaf lettuce	125 mL
¼ cup	chopped celery (see Tips, left)	60 mL
1	clove garlic	1
¼ cup	cold-pressed flax oil (see Tips, left)	60 mL
3 tbsp	freshly squeezed lemon juice	45 mL
2 tbsp	raw agave nectar (see Tips, left)	30 mL
1 tsp	fine sea salt	5 mL

1. In a food processor fitted with the metal blade, process water, romaine lettuce, spinach, arugula and leaf lettuce until smooth. Add celery, garlic, flax oil, lemon juice, agave nectar and salt and process until smooth. Serve immediately or cover and refrigerate for up to 2 days.

Variations

This recipe will work using any combination of salad greens in the same measurements. I like lola rosa lettuce, chard or even kale. Because greens are often gritty, make sure they are thoroughly washed and free of grit before processing. Swishing them around in a basin of lukewarm water, then rinsing under cold running water, usually does the trick.

Corn and Red Pepper Chowder

This rich and luxurious take on traditional chowder is fabulously creamy. I love making it when fresh corn is in season.

Makes 4 cups (1 L)

Tips

To soak the cashews for this soup, place in a bowl and cover with 1 cup (250 mL) water. Cover and set aside for 30 minutes. Drain, discarding soaking water, and rinse under cold running water until the water runs clear.

To remove kernels from a cob of corn, stand the cob up on its flat end. Using a chef's knife in a downward motion, gently strip away the kernels, making sure not to remove too much of the starchy white body of the cob, which will not purée smoothly.

If fresh dill is not available, use 2 tsp (10 mL) dried dill weed.

Substitute the red bell peppers with orange or yellow bell peppers in the same quantity.

½ cup	raw cashews, soaked (see Tips, left)	125 mL
2½ cups	freshly shucked corn kernels, divided (3 to 4 cobs; see Tips, left)	625 mL
2 cups	Cashew Milk (page 46)	500 mL
1 cup	chopped red bell pepper, divided	250 mL
¼ cup	cold-pressed hemp oil	60 mL
3 tbsp	chopped fresh dill fronds, divided	45 mL
1 tsp	fine sea salt	5 mL

1. In a blender, combine soaked cashews, 2 cups (500 mL) corn, cashew milk, ¾ cup (175 mL) bell pepper, hemp oil, 2 tbsp (30 mL) dill and salt. Blend at high speed until smooth and creamy.
2. Transfer to a bowl and add remaining corn, bell pepper and dill. Stir well. Serve immediately or cover and refrigerate for up to 3 days.

Creamy Hemp and Broccoli Chowder

This soup is surprisingly filling, rich and hearty. I love the way the flavors of the nutritional yeast and the broccoli interplay.

Tips

To soak the hemp seeds for this recipe, place in a bowl and add 2 cups (500 mL) water. Cover and set aside for 30 minutes. Drain, discarding soaking water. Rinse under cold running water until the water runs clear.

Nutritional yeast is used in vegan and raw food diets mainly because it is a source of vitamin B_{12}. It is pasteurized, so technically it does not qualify as a raw food. However, in addition to necessary nutrients, it adds a deep, umami-like flavor to many dishes.

Make sure not to blend the soup too much in Step 2. You want the broccoli and hemp seeds to be broken down but not completely puréed.

- **Electric food dehydrator**

1 cup	raw shelled hemp seeds, soaked (see Tips, left)	250 mL
2½ cups	broccoli florets	625 mL
¼ cup	cold-pressed (extra virgin) olive oil, divided	60 mL
2 tsp	freshly squeezed lemon juice, divided	10 mL
1 tbsp	fine sea salt, divided	15 mL
3 cups	Cashew Milk (page 46)	750 mL
¾ cup	nutritional yeast (see Tips, left)	175 mL
1 tbsp	chopped fresh thyme leaves	15 mL
2	cloves garlic	2

1. In a bowl, toss together broccoli, 1 tbsp (15 mL) olive oil, 1 tsp (5 mL) lemon juice and 1 tsp (5 mL) salt. Transfer to a nonstick dehydrator sheet and dehydrate at 105°F (41°C) for 30 minutes or until slightly softened.

2. In a blender, combine cashew milk, nutritional yeast, thyme, garlic and remaining olive oil, lemon juice and salt. Blend at high speed until smooth. Add softened broccoli and soaked hemp seeds and pulse until slightly broken down but not puréed. Serve immediately or cover and refrigerate for up to 3 days.

Garden Veggie Soup

A delicious blend of summer vegetables in a light tomato basil broth, this soup is the perfect reason to eat your veggies.

Makes 4 cups (1 L)

Tips

To soak the sun-dried tomatoes for this recipe, place in a bowl and cover with 1 cup (250 mL) water. Cover and set aside for 30 minutes. Drain and discard any remaining water.

If you have a high-powered blender (see page 106), use it to make this soup. It will be smoother and creamier than when made in a regular blender.

Whenever you measure fresh herbs such as basil, make sure to press them firmly into the measuring cup to ensure exact measurement.

The outer stalks of celery can be tough and fibrous. For best results, peel the stalk with a vegetable peeler. Save the peel to make soups, sauces or stocks.

¼ cup	dry-packed sun-dried tomatoes, soaked (see Tips, left)	60 mL
3 cups	chopped tomatoes, divided	750 mL
3 tbsp	freshly squeezed lemon juice, divided	45 mL
1 tbsp	cold-pressed (extra virgin) olive oil	15 mL
1 tsp	fine sea salt, divided	5 mL
2	cloves garlic	2
2 cups	chopped spinach leaves	500 mL
½ cup	packed fresh basil leaves	125 mL
¼ cup	chopped cauliflower florets	60 mL
¼ cup	chopped carrot	60 mL
¼ cup	chopped celery (see Tips, left)	60 mL

1. In a food processor fitted with the metal blade, process 2 cups (500 mL) chopped tomatoes, 2 tbsp (30 mL) lemon juice, soaked sun-dried tomatoes, olive oil, garlic and ½ tsp (2 mL) salt until smooth. Transfer to a bowl.

2. Add remaining chopped tomatoes, lemon juice and salt to food processor, along with cauliflower, carrot and celery, and process until smooth. Add to sun-dried tomato mixture. Stir well and serve immediately. Cover and refrigerate any leftovers for up to 3 days.

Avgolemeno Soup

This take on the classic Greek soup is a perfect blend of sweetness and tart lemon flavor, plus just the right amount of creaminess.

Makes 3½ cups (875 mL)

Tips

Nutritional yeast is used in vegan and raw food diets mainly because it is a source of vitamin B_{12}. It is pasteurized, so technically it does not qualify as a raw food. However, in addition to necessary nutrients, it adds a deep, umami-like flavor to many dishes.

If you have a high-powered blender, use it to make this soup. It will be smoother and creamier than when made in a regular blender.

2 cups	Cashew Milk (page 46)	500 mL
½ cup	freshly squeezed lemon juice	125 mL
1 tbsp	raw agave nectar	15 mL
½ cup	chopped avocado	125 mL
2 tbsp	nutritional yeast (see Tips, left)	30 mL
1 tsp	fine sea salt	5 mL
¼ tsp	ground turmeric	1 mL
¼ cup	chopped parsley leaves	60 mL
1 tbsp	torn mint leaves	15 mL
¼ cup	Cauliflower Rice (page 274)	60 mL

1. In a food processor fitted with the metal blade, process cashew milk, lemon juice, agave nectar, avocado, nutritional yeast, salt and turmeric until smooth and creamy. Transfer to a bowl. Add parsley, mint leaves and Cauliflower Rice. Serve immediately or cover and refrigerate for up to 2 days.

Variation

Instead of the avocado, substitute ½ cup (125 mL) cashews soaked in 1 cup (250 mL) water for 30 minutes, then drained and rinsed under cold running water. This will create the same creamy consistency.

Sprouted Lentil and Spinach Soup

If you're trying to increase the amount of protein you consume, this flavorful soup is a good start. The key is to have perfectly sprouted lentils to make the texture right. You will need to start sprouting the lentils at least two days before you want to make the soup.

Makes 4 cups (1 L)

Tips

To sprout the lentils for this recipe, soak in 2 cups (500 mL) water at room temperature for 24 hours, changing the water every 3 hours. Transfer to a colander and rinse under cold running water. Place the colander over a bowl and set aside in a dry area of your kitchen. Rinse the lentils every 2 to 3 hours to keep them damp but not moist. Before going to bed, rinse the lentils and place a damp cloth overtop. In the morning, rinse again. Repeat this process for 2 days, until tails approximately 1/4 inch (0.5 cm) long have sprouted from the lentils. Rinse and drain. The lentils are now ready for use in your recipe, or you can cover them and refrigerate for up to a week.

To soak the sun-dried tomatoes for this recipe, place in a bowl and add 1 cup (250 mL) water. Cover and set aside for 30 minutes. Drain, discarding any remaining water.

1/2 cup	green lentils, sprouted (see Tips, left)	125 mL
1/4 cup	dry-packed sun-dried tomatoes, soaked (see Tips, left)	60 mL
2 cups	baby spinach	500 mL
1/4 cup	cold-pressed (extra virgin) olive oil, divided	60 mL
1/4 cup	freshly squeezed lemon juice, divided	60 mL
1 tsp	fine sea salt	5 mL
2 cups	chopped tomatoes	500 mL
1 cup	filtered water	250 mL
1 tsp	wheat-free tamari	5 mL
1	clove garlic	1
1/2 tsp	dried oregano	2 mL
1/4 tsp	dried basil	1 mL

1. In a bowl, toss together the spinach, 1 tbsp (15 mL) olive oil, 1 tbsp (15 mL) lemon juice and the salt. Set aside to marinate for 15 to 20 minutes.

2. In a food processor fitted with the metal blade, process chopped tomatoes, water, tamari, garlic, oregano, basil, soaked sun-dried tomatoes and remaining lemon juice and olive oil until smooth and no large pieces remain.

3. Add marinated spinach and sprouted lentils and process for 10 to 15 seconds or until the soup is slightly puréed but still retains some texture. Serve immediately or cover and refrigerate for up to 2 days.

Variations

You can substitute the sprouted lentils with an equal quantity of any sprouted legume, such as chickpeas or mung beans. Follow the same instructions as for sprouting lentils.

If baby spinach is not available, substitute 1 1/2 cups (375 mL) spinach leaves. Mature spinach will create a deeper flavor, which is why you need less. If using mature spinach, make sure to rinse it well, as it generally contains a large amount of grit.

Living Hemp Consommé

I like to make this soup when I am craving a light and aromatic broth-style soup. It makes a perfect starter for a more elaborate meal or a great light pick-me-up. This blend of fresh vegetable and fruit juices pairs well with Bursting Burritos (page 250) and Simple Marinated Kale Salad (page 142).

Makes 4 cups (1 L)

Tips

Use freshly made juices for this recipe. When juicing, make sure to have your ingredients prepared ahead of time. This will speed up the process and make it much easier to put the produce through the machine.

While wheat-free tamari is not raw, it is gluten-free. The raw alternative for tamari, nama shoyu, does contain gluten. If you are following a completely raw diet and can tolerate gluten, by all means substitute an equal quantity of nama shoyu.

- **Juicer**

1 cup	carrot juice	250 mL
½ cup	celery juice	125 mL
½ cup	kale juice	125 mL
½ cup	beet juice	125 mL
¼ cup	apple juice	60 mL
1 tbsp	freshly squeezed lemon juice	15 mL
½ cup	water	125 mL
½ cup	chopped tomatoes	125 mL
2 tbsp	raw shelled hemp seeds	30 mL
2 tbsp	wheat-free tamari (see Tips, left)	30 mL
½ tsp	raw agave nectar	2 mL
¼ tsp	apple cider vinegar	1 mL

1. In a blender, combine carrot, celery, kale, beet, apple and lemon juices, water, tomatoes, hemp seeds, tamari, agave nectar and vinegar. Blend at high speed until smooth. Strain through a fine-mesh sieve. Cover and refrigerate for at least 30 minutes or up to 3 days.

Curried Butternut Squash and Mango Soup

This rich and aromatic soup is deliciously different. I love to top each serving with a dollop of Cashew Sour Cream (page 204).

Makes 4 cups (1 L)

Tips

Shredding the squash before processing helps to ensure it blends evenly. The best way to shred the squash for this recipe is to use the shredding blade of your food processor or the large holes on a box grater.

If you have a high-powered blender, use it to make this soup. It will be smoother and creamier than when made in a regular blender.

2 cups	shredded butternut squash (see Tips, left)	500 mL
1 cup	Almond Milk (page 45)	250 mL
¾ cup	chopped mango	175 mL
¼ cup	chopped avocado	60 mL
1 tbsp	curry powder	15 mL
2 tsp	freshly squeezed lemon juice	10 mL
1 tsp	ground cumin	5 mL
½ tsp	fine sea salt	2 mL
¼ tsp	turmeric	1 mL

1. In a blender, combine squash, almond milk, mango, avocado, curry powder, lemon juice, cumin, salt and turmeric. Blend at high speed until smooth and creamy. Serve immediately or transfer to a bowl, cover and refrigerate for up to 3 days.

Variation

For a slightly sweeter flavor, add ½ tsp (2 mL) ground cinnamon and a pinch each of freshly grated nutmeg and ground cloves.

Cumin-Spiked Sweet Potato Soup

This creamy soup is a delicious blend of aromatic cumin and hearty sweet potato. I like to finish it with a drizzle of Spirulina, Lemon and Ginger Hemp Oil (page 203).

Makes 4 cups (1 L)

Tips

To soak the cashews for this recipe, place in a bowl and add ½ cup (125 mL) water. Cover and set aside for 30 minutes. Drain, discarding soaking water, and rinse under cold running water until the water runs clear.

Shredding the sweet potato before processing it helps to ensure it blends evenly. The best way to shred the sweet potato for this recipe is to use the shredding blade of your food processor or the large holes of a box grater.

Use freshly made juices for this recipe. When juicing, make sure to have your ingredients prepared ahead of time. This will speed up the process and make it much easier to put the produce through the machine.

If you have a high-powered blender, use it to make this soup. It will be smoother and creamier than when made in a regular blender.

- **Juicer**

¼ cup	raw cashews, soaked (see Tips, left)	60 mL
2 cups	shredded sweet potato (about 2 medium; see Tips, left)	500 mL
1 cup	carrot juice	250 mL
¾ cup	apple juice	175 mL
½ cup	filtered water	125 mL
1 tbsp	cold-pressed (extra virgin) olive oil	15 mL
1 tbsp	ground cumin	15 mL
½ tsp	fine sea salt	2 mL

1. In a blender (see Tips, left), combine sweet potato, carrot juice, apple juice and water. Blend at high speed until smooth. Add soaked cashews, olive oil, cumin and salt and blend until smooth and creamy. Transfer to a bowl and serve immediately or cover and refrigerate for up to 3 days.

Variation

Replace the cumin with ½ tsp (2 mL) cinnamon and a pinch each of ground nutmeg, allspice and ground cloves.

Pear and Pumpkin Porridge (page 25)

Morning Energy Bars (page 35)

Cinnamon Pineapple Creamsicle Smoothies (page 59)

Raw Chickpea Hummus (page 94) and Hemp Avocado Mayonnaise (page 89)

Spicy Carrot and Ginger Soup (page 112)

Lemon, Cucumber and Dill Soup (page 116)

Kale Waldorf Salad (page 144)

Mango, Jicama, Pumpkin Seed and Fresh Herb Salad (page 154)

Sesame, Hemp and Carrot Slaw (page 162)

Moroccan Chickpea Stew (page 226)

Mexican Corn Tortilla Soup

This soup is a thick, rich blend of traditional Mexican flavors. I like to enjoy a big bowl garnished with chopped chives and a dollop of Cashew Sour Cream (page 204).

Makes 3 cups (750 mL)

Tip

Chili powder blends are a mixture of herbs and spices, and some are much hotter than others. Taste yours before adding it to this recipe to make sure it isn't too spicy to suit your palate.

1 cup	chopped seeded red bell pepper (about 1 small)	250 mL
¾ cup	cilantro leaves (½ bunch)	175 mL
2 tbsp	ground cumin	30 mL
1 tbsp	chili powder (see Tip, left)	15 mL
1	clove garlic	1
½ tsp	fine sea salt	2 mL
2 cups	filtered water	500 mL
1 tbsp	freshly squeezed lemon juice	15 mL
1 tbsp	orange juice	15 mL
1½ cups	Corn and Carrot Nachos (page 325)	375 mL
½	avocado	½

1. In a blender, combine bell pepper, cilantro, cumin, chili powder, garlic, salt, water and lemon and orange juices. Blend at high speed until smooth. Add nachos and avocado and blend at high speed until smooth. Serve immediately or cover and refrigerate for up to 3 days.

Variations

Substitute any fresh green herb for the cilantro. An equal quantity of flat-leaf parsley, fresh basil leaves or even fresh dill would work well in this recipe.

If you like heat, add a pinch of cayenne pepper, 1 tsp (5 mL) dried red pepper flakes or dried chipotle chile powder to taste.

Smoked Tomato and Jalapeño Soup

This chunky, spicy soup has great southwestern flavor. It is delicious served with a few Corn and Carrot Nachos (page 325) and topped with a dollop of Cashew Sour Cream (page 204).

Makes 4 cups (1 L)

Tips

To soak the sun-dried tomatoes for this recipe, place in a bowl and add 1 cup (250 mL) water. Cover and set aside to soak for 30 minutes. Drain and discard any remaining water.

Whenever you use a food processor to make dips, pâtés, soups or sauces, stop it once or twice and scrape down the sides of the work bowl, using a rubber spatula. This will help to ensure that all the ingredients are evenly incorporated and that no large pieces of food will be in the finished product.

Substitute an equal quantity of cold-pressed pumpkin seed, flaxseed, olive or sunflower oil for the hemp oil.

¼ cup	dry-packed sun-dried tomatoes, soaked (see Tips, left)	60 mL
3 cups	chopped tomatoes	750 mL
¼ cup	chopped jalapeño peppers	60 mL
2	cloves garlic	2
2 tbsp	filtered water	30 mL
2 tbsp	freshly squeezed lemon juice	30 mL
3 tbsp	cold-pressed hemp oil (see Tips, left)	45 mL
2 tsp	ground cumin	10 mL
1 tsp	chili powder	5 mL
1 tsp	smoked sweet paprika	5 mL
1 tsp	fine sea salt	5 mL

1. In a food processor fitted with the metal blade, process chopped tomatoes, jalapeño and garlic for 2 minutes or until no large pieces remain. Scrape down the sides of the work bowl.

2. Add soaked sun-dried tomatoes, water, lemon juice, hemp oil, cumin, chili powder, smoked paprika and salt. Process for 2 to 3 minutes or until smooth. Serve immediately or cover and refrigerate for up to 3 days.

Variations

I like heat in my soups, so I also add ½ tsp (2 mL) cayenne pepper in Step 2.

If you do not have smoked paprika, substitute a dried chipotle pepper ground in a spice grinder or chipotle chile powder to taste.

Jicama, Corn, Quinoa and Lime Hot Pot

> This chunky soup is best served fresh out of the blender, with a side of Pumpkin Seed "Refried Beans" (page 93). You will need to soak the quinoa for this recipe one day in advance.

Makes 4 cups (1 L)

Tips

To sprout the quinoa for this recipe, place in a bowl and add 2 cups (500 mL) water. Cover and set aside to soak for 6 hours, changing the water once. Drain, rinse and discard any remaining water. Transfer to a colander and rinse under cold running water. Place the colander over a bowl and set aside for 24 hours, rinsing the quinoa every 2 to 3 hours to keep it damp but not moist. Before going to bed, rinse the quinoa and place a damp cloth overtop. In the morning, rinse again. Continue to rinse quinoa every 2 to 3 hours until tails approximately ¼ inch (0.5 cm) long have sprouted. This will take 24 to 30 hours in total. The quinoa is now ready for use in your recipe, or you can cover it and refrigerate for up to one week.

Jicama tastes like a cross between an apple, celery and a potato. It is native to Mexico and is very versatile, with a pleasantly crunchy texture that is perfect in many dishes.

If lime juice is not available, use an equal quantity of lemon juice and add 1 fresh wild lime leaf (also known as "Kaffir" lime leaf) in Step 1.

¼ cup	quinoa, sprouted (see Tips, left)	125 mL
2 cups	Cashew Milk (page 46)	500 mL
1 cup	chopped jicama (see Tips, left)	250 mL
1 cup	fresh corn kernels	250 mL
½ cup	chopped red bell pepper	125 mL
3 tbsp	freshly squeezed lime juice (see Tips, left)	45 mL
2 tsp	ground cumin	10 mL
1 tsp	fine sea salt	5 mL
½ tsp	chili powder	2 mL
1	clove garlic	1
Pinch	cayenne pepper	Pinch
½ cup	chopped cilantro	125 mL

1. In a blender, combine cashew milk, jicama, corn, bell pepper, lime juice, cumin, sea salt, chili powder, garlic and cayenne. Blend at medium speed for 30 seconds, until slightly broken down but still chunky. Add sprouted quinoa and blend at medium speed for 10 seconds to slightly break down the seeds.
2. Transfer to a bowl and garnish with cilantro. Serve immediately.

Dashi Broth

Dashi is a traditional broth made from slowly simmered water with sea vegetables and seasonings. This raw version is great because it contains trace minerals from the dulse, including iodine, which is great for keeping your thyroid healthy.

Makes 1¼ cups (300 mL)

Tip

This recipe pairs well with other dishes that contain sea vegetables such as kelp, kombu, wakame or arame. To make a lovely soup, I reconstitute dried seaweed by covering it with twice its volume of warm water and setting it aside for 15 minutes, then draining. I then place the seaweed in a bowl and add some chopped green onion, sesame seeds and a good-sized portion of dashi broth.

1 cup	filtered water	250 mL
¼ cup	wheat-free tamari (see Tips, page 126)	60 mL
2½ tbsp	raw agave nectar	37 mL
1½ tbsp	dulse powder	22 mL
1 tbsp	apple cider vinegar	15 mL

1. In a blender, combine water, tamari, agave nectar, dulse powder and vinegar. Blend at high speed until combined. Transfer to an airtight container, cover and refrigerate for up to a week.

Variations

Substitute 1 tbsp (15 mL) kelp powder for the dulse.

Place the dashi broth in a shallow dish and dehydrate at 105°F (41°C) for 2 to 3 hours to concentrate the flavors and to warm slightly. This is a good way to serve a dish slightly warm and to bring out the intense, bright flavors of the broth.

Spicy Asian Sweet-and-Sour Broth with Vegetable Strips

This delicious soup melds the flavors of sweet and sour. Paired with the fresh vegetables, it provides tantalizing textures and a robust kick of spice.

Makes 3 cups (750 mL)

Tips

To purée gingerroot, use a fine, sharp-toothed grater, such as those made by Microplane.

If you like spice, add a bit more cayenne.

Agave nectar is a sap that is extracted at low temperature from the piña, or center of the agave plant. When purchasing agave nectar, be sure to look for products labeled "raw." Most of the agave nectar on the market has been heated to a high temperature and does not qualify as raw food. If you have concerns, ask your purveyor.

Before slicing the kale, remove the long stem that runs up through the leaf almost to the top of the plant. Use only the leafy green parts.

2 cups	filtered water	500 mL
3 tbsp	raw agave nectar (see Tips, left)	45 mL
2 tbsp	apple cider vinegar	30 mL
1 tbsp	freshly squeezed lemon juice	15 mL
¼ tsp	dulse flakes	1 mL
¼ tsp	puréed gingerroot (see Tips, left)	1 mL
⅛ tsp	cayenne pepper	0.5 mL
½ cup	thinly sliced kale (see Tips, left)	125 mL
½ cup	shredded carrot	125 mL
¼ cup	thinly sliced celery (see Tips, page 123)	60 mL
3 tbsp	sliced green onion, green part only	45 mL

1. In a blender, combine water, agave nectar, vinegar, lemon juice, dulse, ginger and cayenne. Blend at high speed until combined. Transfer to a bowl.
2. Stir in kale, carrot, celery and green onion. Cover and refrigerate for 1 hour, until slightly chilled, or up to 2 days. If refrigerated, before serving, let stand at room temperature for 30 minutes to allow flavors to bloom.

Thai Coconut Soup

This soup is a refreshing burst of flavors. I enjoy making it when I get a craving for a taste of Thailand. The coconut water provides a perfect blend of hydrating electrolytes.

Makes 3 cups (750 mL)

Tips

If you are using a fresh coconut, it is impossible to predict how much water it will contain. To be safe, have some canned coconut water on hand to ensure that you have enough to make this recipe. If you're purchasing coconut water, look for high-quality products that don't contain additives or preservatives. Many prepared coconut waters contain added sugar and other ingredients.

Coconut water is nature's electrolyte replacer. It is full of naturally occurring salts and sugars, which help to regulate many bodily functions. It is also a great source of potassium.

1½ cups	coconut water (see Tips, left)	375 mL
¼ cup	dried shredded coconut	60 mL
½ cup	chopped tomato	125 mL
½ cup	fresh basil leaves	125 mL
¼ cup	fresh cilantro leaves	60 mL
3 tbsp	freshly squeezed lime juice	45 mL
2 tbsp	raw agave nectar	30 mL
2 tbsp	cold-pressed (extra virgin) olive oil	30 mL
1 tsp	chopped gingerroot	5 mL
1	clove garlic	1
½ tsp	fine sea salt	2 mL
¼ cup	thinly sliced seeded red bell pepper	60 mL
¼ cup	thinly sliced green onions, green part only	60 mL
1 tbsp	raw shelled hemp seeds	15 mL

1. In a blender, combine coconut water, shredded coconut, tomato, basil, cilantro, lime juice, agave nectar, olive oil, ginger, garlic and salt. Blend at high speed until smooth. Transfer to a bowl. Stir in bell pepper, green onions and hemp seeds. Serve immediately or cover and refrigerate for up to 3 days.

Brown Rice Miso Broth

This perfectly seasoned broth is a great base to which you can add various thinly sliced vegetables such as kale, carrots, celery or mushrooms. The trick is to use the highest-quality unpasteurized miso paste you can find.

Makes 4 cups (1 L)

Tips

Although unpasteurized miso paste is not 100 percent raw, it is often used in raw food diets because it is fermented, which provides healthy bacteria to aid digestion. Brown rice miso is gluten-free and also contains vitamin B_{12}.

The miso will leave a bit of sediment behind. If you want a clear broth, strain it through a fine-mesh sieve to remove all the particles.

4 cups	hot water	1 L
½ cup	unpasteurized brown rice miso paste (see Tips, left)	125 mL
2 tsp	dried dulse flakes	10 mL
¼ cup	finely sliced green onion, white and green parts	60 mL

1. In a deep bowl, whisk water and miso until paste completely dissolves. Stir in dulse and green onion. Serve immediately.

Variation

I like to add some soaked lentils (see page 256) to this soup for an added dose of protein, along with ¼ cup (60 mL) each shredded celery, carrot and red bell pepper.

Sweet-and-Sour Broth with Kelp Noodles

This light and spicy broth is fat-free. With the addition of kelp noodles it is full of life-giving minerals and other nutrients.

Makes 4 cups (1 L)

Tips

To purée gingerroot, use a fine, sharp-toothed grater, such as those made by Microplane.

Kelp noodles are available at natural foods stores. For this recipe, use them directly from the package or, if you prefer, substitute an equal quantity of Marinated Kelp Noodles (page 243).

Dulse is a red seaweed. It is one of the best sources of natural iodine, which helps to keep your thyroid healthy. Look for it in well-stocked grocery stores, where it can be found in dried form in a shaker-type bottle. It has a salty flavor and makes a great substitute for salt in soups and sauces.

Store dried seaweeds such as dulse in an airtight container away from heat and moisture. This will extend their shelf life, as well as keeping the flavor fresher and preserving their nutrients.

3 cups	filtered water	750 mL
½ cup	raw agave nectar	125 mL
¼ cup	apple cider vinegar	60 mL
2 tbsp	freshly squeezed lemon juice	30 mL
2 tbsp	wheat-free tamari	30 mL
½ tsp	puréed gingerroot (see Tips, left)	2 mL
¼ tsp	dried dulse flakes	1 mL
¾ cup	kelp noodles (see Tips, left)	175 mL

1. In a blender, combine water, agave nectar, vinegar, lemon juice, tamari, ginger and dulse. Blend at high speed until smooth. Transfer to a bowl and stir in the noodles. Serve immediately or cover and refrigerate for up to 3 days.

Variation

If you do not have kelp noodles, soak ¼ cup (60 mL) each arame and wakame in 1 cup (250 mL) warm water for 15 minutes. Drain and add to the puréed soup with a little Simple Marinated Kale Salad (page 142). Wakame and arame are types of seaweed. They typically come in dried form and need to be reconstituted in warm water before using.

Salads and Dressings

When we hear the words "raw food," we almost automatically think of salad. Salads are an important part of a raw food diet — but not just any salads. You really need to focus on making sure they are nutrient-dense. For instance, while you may enjoy a traditional salad of iceberg lettuce with tomato slices, cucumbers and French dressing, if that's all you're having for a meal, it will not provide enough nutrients to help you sustain a busy lifestyle. You need a salad that is packed with nutrients. Start with nourishing greens such as kale, arugula, spinach, bok choy, cabbage or chard. Adding wholesome ingredients such as avocado, carrots, beets, hemp seeds, pumpkin seeds or cashews, to name just a few, will help to ensure that you feel satiated. It will also provide your body with the nutrition it needs.

You can also make a salad more healthful by paying attention to the dressing. I like to use a high-powered blender to make dressings because it allows me to add ingredients such as spinach or kale. If you have transitioned to a raw food diet, a high-powered blender is one of the most useful pieces of equipment to have (see page 106).

A typical salad dressing is made from refined oil, vinegar, refined salt and refined sugar. If you are using a store-bought version, it is also likely to contain preservatives. You can immediately improve the nutritional profile of any salad by making a dressing based on a heart-healthy cold-pressed organic oil. Healthy oils range from extra virgin olive oil to cold-pressed nut and seed oils such as walnut, hemp and flax. Use a blender to add tasty and nutritious ingredients such as avocado, miso, fresh herbs, seeds or nuts. If you like a hint of sweetness, you don't need to resort to refined sugar. Ingredients such as dates or raw agave nectar will do the trick, while also adding nutrients. Use unrefined fine sea salt or seaweed to add a salty flavor.

Poured over a bed of greens or a more substantial mix of vegetables, healthy dressings can dramatically improve the nutrient profile of any salad while helping to fill you up to keep you feeling satisfied throughout the day.

The Big Salad

This salad is a beautiful big bowl of crisp romaine lettuce and healthy dark greens, finished with your favorite vegetables. Consider it a blank canvas on which to create your masterpiece salads. The combination of shredded carrot and beet mixed with tomato wedges, cucumber and avocado provides the perfect base for any mix of fresh lettuces and your favorite dressing.

Tips

Virtually any dressing works well on this salad. My favorite is Herb Citrus Vinaigrette (page 166), but I also enjoy Lemon Poppy Seed Dressing (page 175) or Sun-Dried Tomato French Dressing (page 170).

Before chopping the kale, remove the long stem that runs up through the leaf almost to the top of the plant. Use only the leafy green parts.

When chopping lettuce for a salad, make sure to cut bite-sized pieces, about 1 inch (2.5 cm) square. Dressing spills are more likely to occur with larger pieces.

2 cups	chopped romaine lettuce (see Tips, left)	500 mL
1 cup	chopped trimmed kale	250 mL
1/4 cup	shredded carrot (about 1 small)	60 mL
1/4 cup	shredded beet (about 1/2 small)	60 mL
1/4 cup	dressing (see Tips, left)	60 mL
1/2 cup	tomato wedges (about 1 small)	125 mL
1/4 cup	sliced cucumber (about 1/2 small)	60 mL
1/4 cup	sliced avocado (about 1/2 small)	60 mL
1/4 cup	Raw Chickpea Hummus (page 94)	60 mL

1. In a serving bowl, toss together romaine lettuce, kale, carrot, beet and dressing. Arrange tomato wedges, cucumber and avocado slices and hummus overtop. Serve immediately.

Variations

Substitute Lemon-Ginger-Dill Sunflower Seed Pâté (page 97) for the hummus and/or 3 tbsp (45 mL) Perfect Guacamole (page 81) for the avocado.

For an additional boost of protein, add 2 tbsp (30 mL) raw shelled hemp seeds.

Wilted Spinach Salad

This simple salad is a wonderful dish that can be served on its own or used as a base for nutritious toppings such as Perfect Guacamole (page 81), Raw Chickpea Hummus (page 94) or Sweet Chili and Pecan Pâté (page 96).

Makes 1 main-course or 2 side salads

Tips

You may substitute the lemon juice with an equal quantity of lime juice.

If you use baby spinach to make this recipe, use twice as much because it is lighter and less dense.

6 cups	chopped spinach leaves (see Tips, left)	1.5 L
½ cup	cold-pressed (extra virgin) olive oil	125 mL
¼ cup	freshly squeezed lemon juice	60 mL
1 tsp	fine sea salt	5 mL

1. In a bowl, toss together spinach, olive oil, lemon juice and salt until well combined. Set aside for 15 minutes, until spinach wilts. Serve immediately or transfer to an airtight container and refrigerate for up to 2 days.

Softened Broccoli

This simple salad is a great way to eat broccoli in its raw form, because it has the mouth feel of being lightly steamed. The marinade is a perfect balance of lemon juice, olive oil and salt. It provides a delicate flavor that tastes delicious.

Makes 1 main-course or 2 side salads

Tip

If you prefer, use some of the broccoli stems in this recipe. Trim away the tough outside layer (approximately ½ inch/1 cm) and slice thinly. Substitute for a portion of the florets.

3 cups	broccoli florets, stems removed	750 mL
3 tbsp	cold pressed (extra virgin) olive oil	45 mL
2 tbsp	freshly squeezed lemon juice	30 mL
1 tsp	fine sea salt	5 mL

1. In a bowl, toss together broccoli, olive oil, lemon juice and salt. Mix well and set aside to soften for 15 minutes. Serve immediately or transfer to an airtight container and refrigerate for up to 3 days.

Mega-Green Hemp Bowl

Here's an easy way to add nutritious green vegetables to your diet. This salad takes very little time to prepare and for convenience can be made ahead and refrigerated for up to two days. It is delicious with many of the dressings in this book. My favorites include Creamy Sunflower Seed Dressing (page 178), Greek Hemp Dressing (page 167) and Spicy Miso Dressing (page 174). This salad is also good with a large dollop of Red Pepper, Dill and Cashew Ricotta (page 103) or Perfect Guacamole (page 81).

Makes 1 main-course or 2 side salads

Tips

Kale, a form of cabbage, belongs to a group of vegetables called crucifers, which also includes arugula, chard, cauliflower, radishes, broccoli and Brussels sprouts. Crucifers contain cancer-fighting phytochemicals. These cancer fighters are very susceptible to high temperatures and are water-soluble, which means their nutritional benefit is maximized when they are eaten raw. Dark leafy greens such as kale and Swiss chard also contain appreciable amounts of calcium and magnesium.

Before chopping the kale, remove the long stem that runs up through the leaf almost to the top of the plant. Use only the leafy green parts.

2 cups	chopped spinach leaves	500 mL
1 cup	thinly sliced kale (see Tip, left)	250 mL
1 cup	thinly sliced chard	250 mL
½ cup	arugula	125 mL
3 tbsp	raw shelled hemp seeds	45 mL
½ cup	cold-pressed hemp oil	125 mL
¼ cup	freshly squeezed lemon juice	60 mL
1 tsp	fine sea salt	5 mL

1. In a bowl, toss spinach, kale, chard, arugula and hemp seeds. Add hemp oil, lemon juice and salt and toss well. Set aside for 15 minutes to soften the greens. Serve immediately or transfer to an airtight container and refrigerate for up to 2 days.

Bitter Greens Bowl

This combination of greens perfectly balances bitter and sweet flavors. I like to pair this salad with dressings that are a bit sweet, such as Sweet Onion and Teriyaki Dressing (page 176) or Raspberry Hazelnut Dressing (page 175).

(page 176)

Makes 1 main-course or 2 side salads

Tips

Substitute an equal quantity of spinach for the escarole or dandelion greens.

Agave nectar is a sap that is extracted at low temperatures from the piña, or center, of the agave plant. When purchasing agave nectar, look for products labeled "raw."

1 cup	thinly sliced dandelion greens	250 mL
1 cup	chopped escarole	250 mL
½ cup	chopped radicchio	125 mL
½ cup	chopped endive	125 mL
½ cup	frisée	125 mL
½ cup	cold-pressed flax oil	125 mL
¼ cup	freshly squeezed lemon juice	60 mL
3 tbsp	raw agave nectar (see Tips, left)	45 mL
1 tsp	fine sea salt	5 mL

1. In a bowl, toss dandelion greens, escarole, radicchio, endive and frisée. Add flax oil, lemon juice, agave nectar and salt and mix well. Set aside for 15 minutes to soften. Serve immediately or transfer to an airtight container and refrigerate for up to 2 days.

Simple Marinated Kale Salad

This is an easy way to marinate kale, which is often referred to as a "superfood." It is good on its own or with most of the dressings in this book, including Creamy Sunflower Seed Dressing (page 178) and Strawberry, Mango and Basil Dressing (page 172). For a quick hit of protein, sprinkle some hemp seeds overtop.

Makes 1 main-course or 2 side salads

Tips

Before chopping the kale, remove the long stem that runs up through the leaf. Use only the leafy green parts.

Cut the kale very thinly, to expose as much surface area as possible to the marinade.

2 cups	thinly sliced kale (see Tips, left)	500 mL
¼ cup	cold-pressed (extra virgin) olive oil	60 mL
2 tbsp	freshly squeezed lemon juice	30 mL
1 tsp	fine sea salt	5 mL

1. In a bowl, toss together kale, olive oil, lemon juice and salt. Set aside for 10 minutes to soften. Serve immediately or transfer to an airtight container and refrigerate for up to 3 days. Before serving, toss with dressing, if desired.

Variation

Substitute ¼ cup (60 mL) flax oil for the olive oil and 2 tsp (10 mL) apple cider vinegar for the lemon juice.

Greek Kale Salad

This delicious salad has all the components of a traditional Greek salad, but it's made with nutrient-dense kale and explodes in the mouth with flavor. This salad takes a bit of work to make but the flavors are sensational and the end result is well worth the effort.

Makes 2 main-course or 4 side salads

Tips

Before chopping the kale, remove the long stem that runs up through the leaf almost to the top of the plant. Use only the leafy green parts.

You can purchase olives with the pits already removed. Although they cost a little more money, they are worth it if you are worried about swallowing a pit or biting into one and chipping a tooth.

4 cups	thinly sliced trimmed kale (see Tips, left)	1 L
1 tbsp	cold-pressed (extra virgin) olive oil	15 mL
2 tsp	freshly squeezed lemon juice	10 mL
1 tsp	fine sea salt	5 mL
½ cup	Lemon Avocado Dressing (page 177)	125 mL
1 cup	thinly sliced tomato wedges	250 mL
½ cup	sliced cucumber	125 mL
¼ cup	thinly sliced red onion	60 mL
¼ cup	diced red bell pepper	60 mL
¼ cup	pitted kalamata olives (see Tips, left)	60 mL
½ cup	Cashew Feta Cheese (page 105), divided	125 mL

1. In a bowl, toss kale, olive oil, lemon juice and salt. Set aside to marinate for 10 to 15 minutes, until softened.
2. Add Lemon Avocado Dressing and toss to coat evenly. Add tomato wedges, cucumber, onion, bell pepper, olives and ¼ cup (60 mL) cashew cheese and toss to coat. Transfer to a serving bowl and garnish with remaining cashew cheese. Serve immediately or cover and refrigerate for up to 2 days.

Variations

Replace the kale with chopped romaine lettuce. Omit the olive oil, lemon juice and salt and skip Step 1.

You may replace the kalamata olives with your favorite type of black olive.

Kale Waldorf Salad

This version of the classic American salad replaces iceberg lettuce with heart-healthy kale and the mayonnaise with a delicious oil-free blended dressing. The key is to cut the kale very finely to allow it to soften properly.

Makes 1 to 2 main-course or 3 side salads

Tips

To soak the cashews for this recipe, place in a bowl and add ½ cup (125 mL) water. Cover and set aside for 20 minutes. Drain, discarding soaking water, and rinse under cold running water until the water runs clear.

Before chopping the kale, remove the long stem that runs up through the leaf almost to the top of the plant. Use only the leafy green parts.

¼ cup	raw cashews, soaked (see Tips, left)	60 mL
2 cups	thinly sliced trimmed kale (see Tips, left)	500 mL
2 tbsp	cold-pressed (extra virgin) olive oil	30 mL
¼ cup	freshly squeezed lemon juice, divided	60 mL
1 tbsp	apple cider vinegar, divided	15 mL
2 tsp	fine sea salt, divided	10 mL
1 cup	thinly sliced tart apple, divided	250 mL
½ cup	thinly sliced celery, divided	125 mL
½ cup	filtered water	125 mL
½ cup	walnuts, halves or pieces	125 mL
¼ cup	raisins	60 mL

1. In a bowl, toss together kale, olive oil, 2 tsp (10 mL) lemon juice, 1 tsp (5 mL) cider vinegar and 1 tsp (5 mL) salt. Set aside to soften for 10 minutes. Transfer to a serving dish.

2. In a blender, combine ½ cup (125 mL) apple, ¼ cup (60 mL) celery, water, soaked cashews and remaining lemon juice, vinegar and salt. Blend at high speed until smooth and creamy. Pour over softened kale. Add walnuts, raisins and remaining apple and celery and toss. Set aside to marinate for 5 minutes. Serve immediately.

Variations

Over the years I've made many different versions of this salad. I like to make it using chopped dried fruit such as prunes, dried apricots or dried cranberries instead of the raisins.

In addition to walnuts I add ¼ cup (60 mL) whole raw almonds to increase the protein and calcium content.

Collard Cobb Salad

The classic Cobb salad is traditionally made with iceberg lettuce. This version, which qualifies as a special-occasion salad, is much more nutritious and, in my opinion, delicious. It takes a bit of work and planning because some of the ingredients, such as Eggplant Bacon, need to be made well ahead of time, but it is worth the effort. You can double or triple the quantity to suit your needs.

Makes 2 main-course salads

Tips

To soak the cashews for this recipe, place in a bowl and cover with ½ cup (125 mL) water. Cover and set aside for 30 minutes. Drain, discarding soaking water, and rinse under cold running water until the water runs clear.

To trim the collard greens for this recipe, lay them flat on a cutting board and use a paring knife to trim the center spine away from each leaf. You will be left with two green strips. Slice these thickly.

Dehydrated foods such as Eggplant Bacon will be crispy when they first come out of the dehydrator and will remain crispy if stored in an airtight container. Once they are exposed to the outside air, they will begin to pick up moisture and can become soft. To make them crispy again, place them back in the dehydrator for 3 to 4 hours.

2 cups	thickly sliced trimmed collard greens (about ½ bunch)	500 mL
3 tbsp	cold-pressed (extra virgin) olive oil	45 mL
2 tsp	freshly squeezed lemon juice	10 mL
½ tsp	fine sea salt	2 mL
½ cup	Eggplant Bacon (page 41), crumbled	125 mL
½ cup	No-Egg Salad (page 150)	125 mL
½ cup	Walnut Mince (page 293)	125 mL
1	small avocado, cubed	1
½ cup	chopped tomato	125 mL
¼ cup	raw shelled hemp seeds	60 mL

Dressing

3 tbsp	raw cashews, soaked (see Tips, left)	45 mL
½ cup	cold-pressed hemp oil	125 mL
¼ cup	chopped cilantro leaves	60 mL
3 tbsp	chopped green onion, white part with a bit of green	45 mL
3 tbsp	apple cider vinegar	45 mL
2 tsp	freshly squeezed lemon juice	10 mL
1 tsp	dried dill weed	5 mL
½ tsp	mustard powder	2 mL
1 tsp	fine sea salt	5 mL

1. In a bowl, toss together collard greens, olive oil, lemon juice and salt. Set aside to marinate for 10 minutes, until softened.

2. Arrange the greens on a platter or serving plate. Arrange Eggplant Bacon, No-Egg Salad, Walnut Mince, avocado, chopped tomato and hemp seeds evenly overtop.

3. *Dressing:* In a blender, combine hemp oil, cilantro, green onion, vinegar, lemon juice, dill, mustard, salt and soaked cashews. Blend at high speed until smooth and creamy. Pour evenly over salad.

Spicy Wilted Watercress Salad

This salad is very simple to prepare and is sure to become an instant favorite. The contrasting flavors and textures of the watercress, red pepper and sesame seeds are particularly appealing. Slightly dehydrating the watercress changes the texture, creating a steamed effect, which intensifies its flavor.

Makes 2 side salads

Tips

To prepare the watercress for this recipe, place on a cutting board and trim approximately ½ inch (1 cm) of the stems off each bunch.

A dehydrator is a great tool for softening leafy greens. Make sure to allow enough time for the greens to soften up but not so much that they become crispy. The lemon juice, oil and salt also contribute to the softening. The key to maintaining even softening of greens is to ensure that all pieces are cut to the same size.

- **Electric food dehydrator**

3 cups	trimmed watercress (about 2 large bunches)	750 mL
½ cup	finely sliced red bell pepper (about ½ medium)	125 mL
¼ cup	sesame seeds	60 mL
3 tbsp	freshly squeezed lemon juice	45 mL
2 tbsp	cold-pressed (extra virgin) olive oil	15 mL
½ tsp	ground cumin	2 mL
¼ tsp	fine sea salt	1 mL
¼ tsp	turmeric	1 mL
¼ tsp	cayenne pepper	1 mL

1. In a bowl, toss together watercress, red pepper, sesame seeds, lemon juice, olive oil, cumin, salt, turmeric and cayenne, until coated. Place on a nonstick dehydrator sheet and spread evenly. Dehydrate at 105°F (41°C) for 25 to 30 minutes or until watercress is slightly wilted and takes on the appearance of being lightly steamed. Serve immediately.

Variation

Make this recipe using virtually any soft leafy green. I like using a combination of 1 cup (250 mL) baby spinach, 1 cup (250 mL) watercress and 1 cup (250 mL) dandelion greens.

Spicy Grapefruit and Chard Salad

This simple salad can be made ahead of time and stored in the refrigerator for up to three days. The subtle flavors of the leafy greens, tart grapefruit and slightly sweet red peppers marry perfectly on the tongue. Dehydrating the greens creates the mouth feel of their being slightly steamed (see Tips, page 146).

Makes 1 main-course or 2 side salads

Tip

A chard leaf has a long, thick vein running through its center. When working with chard, keep the soft vein at the top of the leaf intact. However, as you move toward the bottom (stem end) of the leaf, the vein becomes larger and tougher and needs to be removed. Lay the leaf flat on a cutting board and use a paring knife to remove the thick part of the vein and discard. For this recipe, slice the remaining leafy green part into thin strips.

- **Electric food dehydrator**

2 cups	thinly sliced trimmed Swiss chard (see Tip, left)	500 mL
3 tbsp	cold-pressed (extra virgin) olive oil	45 mL
2 tsp	freshly squeezed lemon juice	10 mL
1/4 tsp	fine sea salt	1 mL
1/2 cup	grapefruit segments (about 1/2 medium) (see Tips, page 152)	125 mL
1/4 cup	finely sliced red bell pepper	60 mL
1 tbsp	sesame seeds	15 mL
1/4 cup	Spicy Red Pepper Flax Oil (page 203)	60 mL

1. In a bowl, toss chard, olive oil, lemon juice and salt. Transfer to a nonstick dehydrator sheet and spread evenly. Dehydrate at 105°F (41°C) for 15 to 20 minutes or until slightly softened.

2. Transfer to a bowl. Add grapefruit, red pepper, sesame seeds and Spicy Red Pepper Flax Oil. Toss well. Serve immediately or cover and refrigerate for up to 3 days.

Variations

This recipe will work using virtually any soft green. Kale, baby bok choy, arugula, mustard greens or dandelion greens can be substituted for the chard.

Substitute an equal quantity of any other seed or finely chopped nuts for the sesame seeds.

Arugula and Spinach Salad with Candied Pecans

> This salad is a take on classic flavor pairings from French cuisine. The upside to this version is that it contains no refined sugars and no hidden unhealthy oils.

Makes 4 side salads

Tips

If you are cutting fruits such as apples or pears ahead of time, be aware that they will oxidize (turn brown) unless treated with acid. To prevent the apple from oxidizing, after shredding, place in a bowl of water with 1 to 2 tbsp (30 to 45 mL) freshly squeezed lemon juice. Drain well before adding to the salad.

When purchasing agave nectar, be sure to look for products labeled "raw." Most of the agave nectar on the market has been heated to a high temperature and does not qualify as raw food. If you have concerns, ask your purveyor.

2 cups	baby arugula	500 mL
2 cups	baby spinach	500 mL
½ cup	shredded apple (about ½ small)	125 mL
¼ cup	cold-pressed hazelnut oil	60 mL
3 tbsp	apple cider vinegar	45 mL
½ tsp	fine sea salt, divided	2 mL
½ cup	pecans	125 mL
2 tbsp	freshly squeezed orange juice	30 mL
¼ cup	raw agave nectar (see Tips, left)	60 mL

1. In a serving bowl, toss arugula, spinach, apple, hazelnut oil, vinegar and ¼ tsp (1 mL) salt. Set aside.
2. In a separate bowl, toss pecans, orange juice, agave nectar and remaining salt. Add to greens, toss and serve.

Variations

Substitute an equal quantity of shredded pear for the apple.

I use hazelnut oil because it pairs well with the pecans in this recipe. You can use an equal quantity of cold-pressed (extra virgin) olive oil to replace it.

Endive, Mushroom and Walnut Salad

This full-flavored salad is rich and meaty. I like to serve it alongside a plate of fresh greens such as crispy romaine hearts or Simple Marinated Kale Salad (page 142).

Makes 2 side salads

Tips

While wheat-free tamari is not raw, it is gluten-free. The raw alternative for tamari, nama shoyu, does contain gluten. If you are following a completely raw diet and can tolerate gluten, by all means substitute an equal quantity of nama shoyu.

Endives have a mildly bitter flavor and are best served as soon as possible after they are pulled apart, to prevent oxidation.

1 cup	sliced trimmed button mushrooms	250 mL
3 tbsp	cold-pressed hemp oil	45 mL
2 tbsp	wheat-free tamari (see Tips, left)	30 mL
½ tsp	fine sea salt	2 mL
3 cups	torn Belgian endive leaves (about 2 large)	750 mL
2 tsp	freshly squeezed lemon juice	10 mL
½ cup	chopped walnuts	125 mL
¼ cup	Cashew Sour Cream (page 204)	60 mL
¼ cup	fresh tarragon leaves, roughly chopped	60 mL

1. In a bowl, toss mushrooms, hemp oil, tamari and salt. Set aside for 10 minutes to soften the mushrooms.
2. Meanwhile, in a serving bowl, combine endive leaves and lemon juice. Toss. Add walnuts and set aside.
3. Add Cashew Sour Cream to mushroom mixture and toss to coat. Add to endive mixture along with the tarragon. Toss well and serve.

Variations

For a nut-free version of this salad, substitute ¼ cup (60 mL) raw shelled hemp seeds for the walnuts.

Substitute 3 tbsp (45 mL) Herb Citrus Vinaigrette (page 166) or Greek Hemp Dressing (page 167) for the Cashew Sour Cream.

No-Egg Salad

This recipe tastes and looks like the real thing, the one your mama used to make back when you were a kid. The turmeric gives it a yellow color that makes it resemble traditional egg salad. I enjoy this between two leaves of crisp romaine lettuce or on a piece of Zucchini Hemp Bread (page 324).

Makes 2 cups (500 mL)

Tip

To soak the cashews for this recipe, place in a bowl and add 3 cups (750 mL) water. Cover and set aside for 20 minutes. Drain, discarding soaking water, and rinse under cold running water until the water runs clear.

1½ cups	raw cashews, soaked (see Tip, left)	375 mL
¼ cup	freshly squeezed lemon juice	60 mL
¼ cup	filtered water	60 mL
¼ cup	chopped celery	60 mL
1 tbsp	dried dill weed	15 mL
1 tsp	fine sea salt	5 mL
½ tsp	turmeric	2 mL
1	clove garlic	1
¼ cup	Spicy Cashew Mayonnaise (page 87)	60 mL
¼ cup	finely diced red onion	60 mL

1. In a food processor fitted with the metal blade, process lemon juice, water, celery, dill, salt, turmeric and garlic until smooth.
2. Add soaked cashews and process for 3 minutes. Using a rubber spatula, scrape down the sides of the work bowl. Process for 1 to 2 minutes or until all the pieces of cashew have been puréed.
3. Transfer to a bowl and stir in Spicy Cashew Mayonnaise and red onion. Serve immediately or cover and refrigerate for up to 3 days.

Variation

For a lower-cal and more convenient version of this salad, substitute ¼ cup (60 mL) cold-pressed (extra virgin) olive oil for the Spicy Cashew Mayonnaise. Add slowly through the feed tube during Step 2, after the cashews have been puréed.

Taco Salad

This salad is sure to be a crowd-pleaser with its crisp romaine, crunchy corn chips and creamy guacamole. I love serving it as an appetizer to launch a Southwest-themed dinner. It's a bit of work but well worth it as a special-occasion dish. Increase the quantity to suit your needs.

Makes 2 main-course salads

Tip

When cutting lettuce, always make sure to use a very sharp, dry knife. A dull blade will initiate the process of oxidization. If the lettuce gets wet, the water will cause the exposed cell walls to oxidize more quickly than if it were dry.

4 cups	chopped romaine lettuce	1 L
1/2	medium avocado, cubed	1/2
1/2 cup	chopped tomato	125 mL
1/4 cup	finely diced red onion	60 mL
1/4 cup	chopped cilantro leaves	60 mL
1 tbsp	freshly squeezed lemon juice	15 mL
1	clove garlic, minced	1
2 tsp	ground cumin	10 mL
1 tsp	chili powder	5 mL
1/2 cup	Corn and Carrot Nachos (page 325)	125 mL
1/4 cup	Walnut Mince (page 293)	60 mL
1/4 cup	Cashew Sour Cream (page 204)	60 mL

1. In a bowl, toss together lettuce, avocado, tomato, onion, cilantro, lemon juice, garlic, cumin, chili powder, nachos, Walnut Mince and Cashew Sour Cream until well incorporated. Serve immediately.

Variations

You can make an even more celebratory version of this dish by substituting 1/2 cup (125 mL) Perfect Guacamole (page 81) for the avocado, lemon juice and garlic.

If you really feel like gilding the lily, substitute 1/4 cup (60 mL) Tomatillo and Chia Seed Salsa (page 79) for the tomato, red onion and cilantro.

Softened Fennel, Grapefruit and Parsley Salad

This tart and fresh-tasting salad is perfect on its own or paired with some simply cut crisp romaine lettuce.

Makes 4 side salads

Tips

To shave the fennel for this recipe, slice the bulb lengthwise through the middle. Remove core and green fronds from the top. Using a mandoline, slice fennel approximately 1/4 inch (0.5 cm) thick.

To segment a grapefruit, place it on a cutting board and remove a bit of skin from the top and bottom to create a flat surface. This will reveal the thickness of the pith. Using a sharp knife in a downward motion, remove the skin and the pith. Shave off any remaining bits of pith, then take a small knife and cut in between the half-moon segments of fruit, one at a time. Ease out each segment with your knife until all have been removed.

- **Electric food dehydrator**
- **Mandoline**

2 cups	shaved fennel (about 1 large or 2 small bulbs; see Tips, left)	500 mL
1 tbsp	cold-pressed olive or flax oil	15 mL
2 tsp	freshly squeezed lemon juice	10 mL
2 tsp	raw agave nectar	10 mL
1/2 tsp	fine sea salt	2 mL
	Coarsely chopped romaine lettuce, optional	
1/2 cup	grapefruit segments (see Tips, left)	125 mL
1/2 cup	chopped parsley leaves	125 mL

1. In a bowl, toss fennel, olive oil, lemon juice, agave nectar and salt. Spread evenly over a nonstick dehydrator sheet and dehydrate at 105°F (41°C) for 45 minutes or until slightly softened.

2. If using, line a serving bowl or deep platter with romaine lettuce. Add fennel, making sure to include any liquids from the dehydrator tray. Add grapefruit and parsley and toss to coat.

Variations

Try using various types of healthy oils in this recipe to marinate the fennel. I like pumpkin seed oil with this flavor combination.

Substitute an equal quantity of orange segments for the grapefruit (see Tips, page 153).

Mixed Citrus, Hemp and Mint Salad

This salad is a delicious balance of sweet citrus, fresh mint, rich flax oil and soft hemp seeds. The combination of textures and flavors pairs well with a glass of fresh juice such as Perfect Green Juice (page 18) or Iron-Builder Juice (page 70).

Makes 4 side salads

Tips

To prepare the citrus for this recipe, place each fruit on a cutting board and remove a bit of skin from the top and bottom to create a flat surface. This will reveal the thickness of the pith. Using a sharp knife in a downward motion, remove the skin and the pith. Shave off any remaining bits of pith, then cut between the membranes to produce wedges of pure citrus flesh, which are segments.

Hemp seeds are considered to be a complete protein, meaning they contain all eight essential amino acids. One tablespoon (15 mL) of raw shelled hemp seeds provides up to 5 grams of protein and appreciable amounts of vitamins B_1 (thiamine) and B_6 (pyridoxine), folate, phosphorus, magnesium, zinc and manganese. Two tablespoons (30 mL) of hemp seeds essentially meets your daily requirement for omega-3 fatty acids.

1 cup	cubed orange segments (about 1 small)	250 mL
½ cup	cubed grapefruit segments (about ½ small)	125 mL
¼ cup	cubed lemon segments (about ½ small)	60 mL
½ cup	torn fresh mint leaves	125 mL
¼ cup	raw shelled hemp seeds (see Tips, left)	60 mL
2 tbsp	cold-pressed flax oil	30 mL
1 tbsp	raw agave nectar	15 mL
Pinch	fine sea salt	Pinch

1. In a serving bowl, toss orange, grapefruit, lemon, mint, hemp seeds, flax oil, agave nectar and salt. Cover and set aside to macerate for 20 minutes. Serve immediately or cover and refrigerate for up to 2 days.

Variation

To transform this salad into a brunch dish, add ¼ cup (60 mL) chopped peeled apple and 2 tbsp (30 mL) freshly chopped flat-leaf parsley. Toss well.

Mango, Jicama, Pumpkin Seed and Fresh Herb Salad

This light yet intense salad is bursting with fresh summer flavors and interesting textures. It is sure to impress your guests at a dinner party or Saturday afternoon picnic.

Tips

To peel and chop a mango, cut a small slice from the top and bottom of the fruit to make flat ends. Using a vegetable peeler, carefully peel away the skin. Stand mango upright on a cutting board. Using a chef's knife, run the blade through the flesh, taking approximately three slices from each of the four sides. When you are close to the stone, use a paring knife to remove any remaining flesh from around the middle.

Pumpkin seeds provide an impressive array of nutrients. They contain healthy poly- and monounsaturated fats, protein, fiber, iron, magnesium, potassium, zinc, manganese, thiamine (vitamin B_1) and vitamin E — not bad for the seeds of a common squash.

2 cups	sliced peeled jicama	500 mL
1 cup	sliced peeled mango	250 mL
1/2 cup	raw pumpkin seeds	125 mL
2 tbsp	freshly squeezed lime juice	30 mL
2 tbsp	cold-pressed (extra virgin) olive oil	30 mL
1/4 cup	chopped parsley leaves	60 mL
1/4 cup	chopped cilantro leaves	60 mL
1/4 cup	chopped basil leaves	60 mL
Pinch	fine sea salt	Pinch

1. In a serving bowl, toss jicama, mango, pumpkin seeds, lime juice and olive oil until evenly coated. Set aside to macerate for 15 minutes. Add parsley, cilantro, basil and salt and toss gently. Serve immediately or cover and refrigerate for up to 3 days.

Variation

Substitute the jicama with 1 cup (250 mL) thinly sliced apple, 1 cup (250 mL) thinly sliced pear and 2 tbsp (30 mL) sesame seeds.

Avocado and Cucumber Salad

This light and creamy side salad will play games with your taste buds. I like to serve this over crisp romaine lettuce leaves or baby spinach.

Tip

Do not chop the parsley too finely for this recipe. You want it to be a main ingredient in this salad, as opposed to a side note. Similarly, by keeping the avocado and cucumber chunky, you ensure a salad-like result. If the ingredients were diced it would be more like a salsa.

2 cups	cubed (1 inch/2.5 cm) avocado (about 3 medium)	500 mL
1 cup	cubed (1 inch/2.5 cm) peeled seeded cucumber (about $\frac{1}{2}$ large)	250 mL
$\frac{1}{3}$ cup	coarsely chopped flat-leaf parsley leaves	75 mL
3 tbsp	cold-pressed flax oil	45 mL
2 tbsp	freshly squeezed lemon or lime juice	30 mL
$1\frac{1}{2}$ tsp	fine sea salt	7 mL
Pinch	freshly ground black pepper	Pinch

1. In a serving bowl, toss avocado, cucumber, parsley, flax oil, lemon juice, salt and freshly ground pepper, until well coated. Serve immediately.

Variations

Add $\frac{1}{2}$ cup (125 mL) chopped tomatoes.

Replace the parsley with an equal quantity of coarsely chopped cilantro leaves and add 1 tsp (5 mL) chili powder and $\frac{1}{2}$ tsp (2 mL) ground cumin to give this salad a southwestern spin.

"Roasted" Red Pepper and Eggplant Salad

This rustic, hearty salad is a take on a classic Italian side dish. The recipe does take some time to prepare but in the end it is worth it.

Makes 4 side salads

Tips

To make this recipe, you'll need a dehydrator with adjustable racks that can be spaced apart so the peppers can stand upright.

Be sure to start the peppers well ahead of time. "Roasting" them overnight is very time-efficient. Once that is done, the rest of the recipe takes only 30 minutes from start to finish.

After the peppers have been roasted, you can use them immediately or cover and refrigerate for up to 5 days.

When purchasing extra virgin olive oil, make sure the label says "cold-pressed." Some olive oils are extracted using a centrifuge system, which spins the olives at a very high speed. This heats them and the resulting oil, depriving it of its raw status.

- **Electric food dehydrator**

4	medium red bell peppers (see Tips, left)	4
¼ cup	cold-pressed (extra virgin) olive oil, divided	60 mL
1 tbsp	fine sea salt, divided	15 mL
8	slices eggplant, cut lengthwise, 1 inch (2.5 cm) thick	8
¼ cup	thinly sliced fresh basil leaves (about 1 bunch)	60 mL
2 tbsp	apple cider vinegar	30 mL
1 tbsp	raw agave nectar	15 mL

1. In a bowl, toss red peppers, 2 tbsp (30 mL) olive oil and 1 tsp (5 mL) salt. Arrange evenly on a nonstick dehydrator sheet and dehydrate at 105°F (41°C) for 10 to 12 hours or until the skin starts to appear shriveled and looks as if it will slide off easily. Transfer to a bowl, cover tightly with plastic wrap and set aside until the skins blister, about 20 minutes. Using a sharp knife, lift off skins and discard. Slice peppers in strips about ½ inch (1 cm) wide and set aside.

2. Lay eggplant slices flat on a cutting board and sprinkle both sides with 1 tsp (5 mL) salt. Stack the slices on top of each other and place on a flat surface such as a baking sheet. Put a weight on top (a foil-wrapped brick works well) and set aside for 20 to 30 minutes, until the eggplant emits liquid. Rinse under cold running water and cut into strips approximately ½ inch (1 cm) wide.

3. In a serving bowl, combine eggplant, red peppers, basil, vinegar, agave nectar and remaining olive oil and salt. Serve immediately or transfer to an airtight container and refrigerate for up to 3 days.

Variations

Toss the softened eggplant and peppers in a thick, rich dressing such as Creamy Sunflower Seed Dressing (page 178). Or serve them over a bed of baby arugula, tossed with Cashew Feta Cheese (page 105) and garnished with Almond Parmesan Cheese (page 204).

Antipasto Salad

> This appetizer salad is sweet, tangy and rich. It is a wonderful starter for any meal.

Tips

Use the smallest mushrooms you can find. If they are larger, cut them into quarters.

To slice the eggplant for this recipe, cut off a lengthwise strip approximately ½ inch (1 cm) thick. Slice crosswise into thin strips. Repeat, if necessary.

Marinating vegetables in something acidic (which helps to break down the cell walls) along with salt (to draw out the moisture) and some fat (which acts as a conductor) makes them soft without applying heat. To facilitate this process, cut the vegetables finely so the marinade can penetrate all the way through.

1 cup	trimmed small button mushrooms (see Tips, left)	250 mL
⅔ cup	cold-pressed (extra virgin) olive oil, divided	150 mL
1 tbsp	chopped fresh thyme	15 mL
2 tsp	wheat-free tamari	10 mL
2 tsp	fine sea salt, divided	10 mL
½ cup	thinly sliced zucchini	125 mL
1 tsp	chopped fresh rosemary	5 mL
2 tbsp	water	30 mL
1 tbsp	brown rice miso paste	15 mL
1 tsp	apple cider vinegar	5 mL
1 tsp	raw agave nectar	5 mL
½ cup	thinly sliced eggplant (see Tips, left)	125 mL
½ cup	thinly sliced red bell pepper	125 mL
3 tbsp	thinly sliced fresh basil leaves	45 mL
1 tbsp	raw shelled hemp seeds	15 mL
1 cup	frisée or radicchio leaves (see Variation, below)	250 mL

1. In a serving bowl, toss together mushrooms, 2 tbsp (30 mL) olive oil, thyme, tamari and ½ tsp (2 mL) salt. Set aside for 15 to 20 minutes, until softened.
2. Meanwhile, in a separate bowl, toss zucchini with 2 tbsp (30 mL) olive oil, rosemary and ½ tsp (2 mL) salt. Set aside for 10 to 15 minutes, until softened.
3. In another bowl, combine 2 tbsp (30 mL) olive oil, water, miso, vinegar and agave nectar. Add eggplant and toss until coated. Set aside for 10 to 15 minutes, until softened.
4. In another bowl, toss red pepper, 2 tbsp (30 mL) olive oil, basil, hemp seeds and ½ tsp (2 mL) salt. Set aside.
5. When vegetables have finished marinating, add zucchini, eggplant and red pepper mixtures to mushrooms. Add frisée and remaining 2 tbsp (30 mL) olive oil and ½ tsp (2 mL) of salt. Toss well and serve.

Variation

For something a little different, try substituting the frisée or radicchio with a bitter lettuce such as escarole or Belgian endive, which stand up to the strong flavors.

Jicama Potato Salad

> This salad is a light, crisp take on the classic potato salad. It is made with jicama, a vegetable with a high water content to nourish your cells.

Tips

Jicama, which tastes like a blend of potato, celery and apple, is a beautifully crisp and mildly sweet vegetable. I like to shred it and add it to my favorite green salad for extra crunch.

The outer stalks of celery can be tough and fibrous. For best results, peel the stalk with a vegetable peeler. Save the peel to make soups, sauces or stocks.

Nutritional yeast is used in vegan and raw food diets mainly because it is a source of vitamin B_{12}. It is pasteurized, so technically it does not qualify as a raw food. However, in addition to necessary nutrients, it adds a deep, umami-like flavor to many dishes.

3 cups	diced peeled jicama (1 large or 2 small), divided	750 mL
½ cup	chopped celery, divided (see Tips, left)	125 mL
3 tbsp	freshly squeezed lemon juice	45 mL
2 tbsp	nutritional yeast (see Tips, left)	30 mL
2 tbsp	cold-pressed (extra virgin) olive oil	30 mL
2 tsp	fine sea salt	10 mL
1 tsp	dried dill weed	5 mL
1 tsp	sweet paprika	5 mL
¼ cup	chopped green onion, green parts only	60 mL

1. In a food processor fitted with the metal blade, process 2 cups (500 mL) jicama, ¼ cup (60 mL) celery, lemon juice, nutritional yeast, olive oil, salt, dill and paprika until smooth, stopping the motor once and scraping down the sides of the bowl.
2. Transfer to a serving bowl and stir in remaining 1 cup (250 mL) diced jicama and the green onion. Serve immediately.

Variations

For a creamer version of this salad, process only 1 cup (250 mL) of the jicama in Step 1. Stir in ½ cup (125 mL) Spicy Cashew Mayonnaise (page 87) in Step 2. Omit the cayenne pepper in the mayonnaise if you don't want the salad to be spicy.

I like to add ¼ cup (60 mL) chopped pickles and a bit of finely diced red onion to this salad. When purchasing pickles, look for ones that have not been heated or pasteurized but are fermented and organic.

Shredded Heaven Salad

This rich, dark green salad is full of nutrition from the kale and collard greens, which are nutritionally dense. The dressing contains many flavors that pair well with the greens.

Makes 1 main-course or 2 side salads

Tips

One trick when making this recipe is to cut the greens thinly to ensure that they become soft when marinated.

Using a high-powered blender to make the dressing ensures that it becomes very creamy and the carrots are properly blended.

Kale and collard leaves have a long, thick vein that runs through the center. When working with these vegetables, keep the soft vein at the top of the leaf intact. However, as you move toward the bottom (stem end) of the leaf, the vein becomes larger and tougher and needs to be removed. Lay the leaf flat on a cutting board, use a paring knife to remove the thick part of the vein and discard. For this recipe, slice the remaining leafy green part into thin strips.

2 cups	thinly sliced trimmed kale (see Tips, left)	500 mL
1 cup	thinly sliced trimmed collard greens	250 mL
3 tbsp	cold-pressed flax oil	45 mL
2 tsp	freshly squeezed lemon juice	10 mL
½ tsp	fine sea salt	2 mL
½ cup	shredded carrot	125 mL
¼ cup	shredded beet	60 mL
2 tbsp	sesame seeds	30 mL
1 tbsp	raw shelled hemp seeds	15 mL
2 tsp	chopped green onion, white part with a bit of green	10 mL
½ cup	Chinese Five-Spice Carrot, Coconut and Ginger Dressing (page 171)	125 mL

1. In a bowl, toss kale, collard greens, flax oil, lemon juice and salt. Set aside for 10 minutes to soften.
2. Add carrot, beet, sesame seeds, hemp seeds and green onion and mix well. Add dressing and toss until well coated. Serve immediately.

Variations

This recipe will work equally well using only collard greens or only kale. I also like to add ¼ cup (60 mL) broccoli florets in Step 1.

Substitute pumpkin, sunflower or black sesame seeds for the hemp and sesame seeds. For a little more protein, add ¼ cup (60 mL) whole raw cashews along with the seeds.

Lentil and Spinach Salad

This is a great salad that can be enjoyed any time of the day. I like to pair it with a large scoop of Perfect Guacamole (page 81).

(page 81)

Makes 3 side salads

Tips

To soak the lentils for this recipe, place in a bowl and add 3 cups (750 mL) water. Cover and set aside for 8 hours, changing the water once. Drain, discarding liquid, and rinse under cold running water until the water runs clear.

Before eating dried lentils, chickpeas and quinoa raw, make sure to soak them long enough that they become soft, to enable the body to break them down more easily.

1 cup	dried green lentils, soaked (see Tips, left)	250 mL
2 cups	baby spinach	500 mL
3 tbsp	cold-pressed (extra virgin) olive oil	45 mL
3 tbsp	freshly squeezed lemon juice, divided	45 mL
½ tsp	fine sea salt	2 mL
¼ cup	chopped tomato	60 mL
2 tbsp	finely diced red onion	30 mL
2 tbsp	nutritional yeast	30 mL
2 tbsp	cold-pressed hemp oil	30 mL
1 tbsp	dried basil	15 mL
Pinch	fine sea salt	Pinch

1. In a bowl, toss together spinach, olive oil, 2 tbsp (30 mL) lemon juice and salt. Set aside for 10 minutes to soften spinach.
2. In another bowl, toss tomato, onion, nutritional yeast, hemp oil, basil, salt, remaining lemon juice and soaked lentils. Add to marinated spinach and toss well. Set aside for at least 10 minutes or up to 2 hours before serving. Serve immediately or transfer to an airtight container and refrigerate for up to 3 days.

Creamy Chickpea Salad

This protein-rich salad is delicious smothered in avocado and slices of tomato and served between two crisp romaine lettuce leaves like a sandwich.

Makes 4 to 5 side salads

Tips

To soak the chickpeas for this recipe, combine with 4 cups (1 L) water. Cover and set aside for 3 hours. Drain, discarding soaking water. Rinse under cold running water until the water runs clear.

To soak the cashews for this recipe, combine with ½ cup (125 mL) water. Cover and set aside for 30 minutes. Drain, discarding soaking water, and rinse under cold running water until the water runs clear.

The outer stalks of celery can be tough and fibrous. For best results, peel the stalk with a vegetable peeler. Save the peel to make soups, sauces or stocks.

2 cups	dried chickpeas, soaked (see Tips, left)	500 mL
¼ cup	raw cashews, soaked (see Tips, left)	60 mL
½ cup	freshly squeezed lemon juice	125 mL
2 tbsp	nutritional yeast	30 mL
¼ cup	filtered water	60 mL
½ tsp	fine sea salt	2 mL
1 tsp	dried dill weed	5 mL
¼ cup	cold-pressed (extra virgin) olive oil	60 mL
¼ cup	diced red bell pepper	60 mL
¼ cup	diced celery (see Tips, left)	60 mL
¼ cup	finely diced cucumber	60 mL
¼ cup	chopped parsley leaves	60 mL
2 tbsp	finely diced red onion	30 mL

1. In a food processor fitted with the metal blade, process soaked chickpeas, lemon juice, nutritional yeast water and salt until chickpeas are broken down and the mixture is somewhat smooth. Using a rubber spatula, scrape down the sides of the work bowl. Add soaked cashews and dill weed. Process until smooth, stopping the motor and scraping down the sides of the work bowl as necessary.

2. With the motor running, slowly add the olive oil through the feed tube to form an emulsion. Transfer to a serving bowl. Add red pepper, celery, cucumber, parsley and onion and mix well. Serve immediately.

Variation

For a creamier version of this salad, add ¼ cup (60 mL) Hemp Avocado Mayonnaise (page 89) along with the red pepper.

Sesame, Hemp and Carrot Slaw

This take on classic coleslaw has virtually all the same flavors and textures but is much more nutritious, because the healthy fats in the hemp seeds and hemp oil are much better for you than those contained in generic store-bought mayonnaise. This can serve as a crunchy addition on top of a green salad or as a meal on its own. It also makes a great side for main courses such as Walnut Portobello Burgers (page 219) or a pizza made with Buckwheat and Sunflower Seed Pizza Crust (page 326).

Makes 2 main-course or 4 side salads

Tips

Be sure to zest your lemon before juicing. For this quantity of zest you will need 2 to 3 lemons.

Hemp oil provides omega fatty acids, which your body needs. It has a good balance of omega-3 and omega-6 essential fatty acids and also provides omega-9 fatty acids and a small amount of vitamin E.

Hemp seeds are considered a complete protein, meaning they contain all eight essential amino acids. One tablespoon (15 mL) of raw shelled hemp seeds provides up to 5 grams of protein and appreciable amounts of vitamins B_1 (thiamine) and B_6 (pyridoxine), folate, phosphorus, magnesium, zinc and manganese. Two tablespoons (30 mL) of hemp seeds essentially meets your daily requirement for omega-3 fatty acids.

- **Box grater or food processor fitted with the shredding blade**

3 cups	shredded carrots	750 mL
1 cup	shredded red cabbage	250 mL
¼ cup	cold-pressed hemp oil	60 mL
3 tbsp	freshly squeezed lemon juice (see Tips, left)	45 mL
½ tsp	fine sea salt	2 mL
¼ cup	chopped parsley leaves	60 mL
3 tbsp	sesame seeds	45 mL
3 tbsp	raw shelled hemp seeds	45 mL
2 tbsp	caraway seeds	30 mL
2 tbsp	finely grated lemon zest	30 mL

1. In a bowl, toss together carrots, red cabbage, hemp oil, lemon juice and salt. Set aside for 15 to 20 minutes, until softened.

2. Add parsley, sesame, hemp and caraway seeds and lemon zest and toss well. Taste for seasoning, adding more salt if necessary. Serve immediately.

Variation

You can give this slaw an Asian spin by substituting rice wine vinegar for the lemon juice and sesame oil for the hemp oil. Add a sprinkle of dried dulse flakes.

Sun-Dried Tomato, Red Onion and Parsley Slaw

I like to eat this delicious salad on its own or over a big bowl of Cauliflower Rice (page 274) generously sprinkled with hemp seeds.

Makes 4 side salads

Tips

To soak the sun-dried tomatoes for this recipe, place them in a bowl and cover with 2 cups (500 mL) water. Cover and set aside for 20 minutes. Drain and discard soaking water.

To make perfect onion slices, cut a small slice from each end. Peel away the skin and cut the onion in half lengthwise. Place halves on a cutting board and, using a chef's knife, slice lengthwise into thin equal pieces.

Simple recipes, such as this, that contain healthy fats such as hemp or flax oil are a great way to get nutrition into your body with little preparation. Because healthy oils are labeled as fats, some people don't realize that, although high in calories, used in moderation they are actually good for you.

½ cup	dry-packed sun-dried tomatoes, soaked, drained and finely diced (see Tips, left)	125 mL
¾ cup	coarsely chopped flat-leaf parsley leaves	175 mL
2 tbsp	finely grated lemon zest	30 mL
½	small red onion, thinly sliced (see Tips, left)	½
2	cloves garlic, minced	2
¼ cup	cold-pressed hemp or flax oil	60 mL
2 tbsp	apple cider vinegar	30 mL
1 tbsp	freshly squeezed lemon juice	15 mL
1 tbsp	raw agave nectar	15 mL
½ tsp	fine sea salt	2 mL

1. In a bowl, toss together sun-dried tomatoes, parsley and lemon zest. Set aside.
2. In a separate bowl, toss onion, garlic, hemp oil, vinegar, lemon juice, agave nectar and salt. Set aside for 10 minutes to soften. Add to sun-dried tomato mixture and toss well. Serve immediately or transfer to an airtight container and refrigerate for up to 3 days.

Variation

Try this recipe with the addition of ½ cup (125 mL) fresh basil leaves and 2 tbsp (30 mL) chopped fresh thyme leaves.

Creamy Sweet Potato, Parsnip and Caraway Slaw

> This slaw is so good you will want to have it for lunch every day. The key is to shred the root vegetables thinly enough so they can soften.

Makes 2 side salads

Tip

When purchasing extra virgin olive oil, make sure the label says "cold-pressed." Some olive oils are extracted using a centrifuge system, which spins the olives at a very high rate. This heats the olives and the resulting oil, depriving it of its raw status.

1 cup	shredded sweet potato	250 mL
½ cup	shredded parsnip	125 mL
3 tbsp	cold-pressed (extra virgin) olive oil	45 mL
2 tbsp	freshly squeezed lemon juice	30 mL
½ tsp	fine sea salt	2 mL
½ cup	Cashew Sour Cream (page 204)	125 mL
2 tsp	caraway seeds	10 mL

1. In a bowl, toss together sweet potatoes, parsnips, olive oil, lemon juice and salt, until well coated. Set aside for 10 minutes to soften.
2. Add Cashew Sour Cream and caraway seeds, toss well and serve immediately.

Lemon and Hemp Vinaigrette

> This flavorful dressing is perfect over fresh organic baby greens and also pairs well with Simple Marinated Kale Salad (page 142) and Mega-Green Hemp Bowl (page 141).

Makes 2 cups (500 mL)

Tip

Hemp oil provides omega fatty acids, which your body needs. It has a good balance of omega-3 and omega-6 essential fatty acids and also provides omega-9 fatty acids and a small amount of vitamin E.

1 cup	cold-pressed hemp oil	250 mL
¾ cup	freshly squeezed lemon juice	175 mL
¼ cup	filtered water	60 mL
¼ cup	raw shelled hemp seeds	60 mL
1 tsp	dried oregano	5 mL
¼ tsp	fine sea salt	1 mL

1. In a blender, combine hemp oil, lemon juice, water, hemp seeds, oregano and salt. Blend at high speed until smooth. Serve immediately or cover and refrigerate for up to 5 days.

Variation

If you are transitioning to a raw food diet, substitute 1 tbsp (15 mL) Dijon mustard for the hemp seeds. Although not completely raw, it is a great way to help emulsify dressings without adding many calories.

Lemony Shredded Beet and Carrot Cream Slaw

This is a deliciously creamy yet light slaw. The rich cashew cream and refreshing lemon juice are perfect balances for each other, and I love how the caraway seeds complement the lemon. I enjoy this with Portobello Carpaccio (page 270) or Moussaka (page 228), among other recipes.

Makes 4 side salads

Tip

Flax oil provides healthy omega-3 fats, which are essential for overall health and well-being. They help to reduce inflammation and other risk factors for diabetes, heart disease and stroke, among other benefits.

- Box grater or food processor fitted with the metal blade

2 cups	shredded beets	500 mL
1 cup	shredded carrots	250 mL
1/4 cup	freshly squeezed lemon juice	60 mL
2 tbsp	cold-pressed flax oil	30 mL
1 tsp	fine sea salt	5 mL
1 tbsp	caraway seeds	15 mL
1/2 cup	Cashew Sour Cream (page 204)	125 mL

1. In a bowl, toss beets, carrots, lemon juice, flax oil, salt and caraway seeds, until evenly coated. Set aside to marinate for 10 to 15 minutes, until softened.
2. Add Cashew Sour Cream and toss well. Set aside for at least 5 minutes or up to 1 hour to allow vegetables absorb some of the flavor from the cashew cream. Serve immediately.

Variation

Substitute 1/4 cup (60 mL) chopped cilantro leaves, 2 tsp (10 mL) ground cumin and 1 tsp (5 mL) chili powder for the caraway seeds.

Herb Citrus Vinaigrette

This dressing is light and refreshing. It is perfect with a simple green salad topped with organic cherry tomatoes and a sprinkling of seeds.

Makes 3 cups (750 mL)

Tip

To get the maximum yield from citrus fruit, allow it to sit at room temperature for 30 minutes before juicing. Once it is at room temperature, roll it on the counter while pressing lightly with the palm of your hand, to release the juices before squeezing.

1 cup	cold-pressed (extra virgin) olive oil	250 mL
¼ cup	freshly squeezed lemon juice	60 mL
¼ cup	freshly squeezed orange juice	60 mL
¼ cup	freshly squeezed grapefruit juice	60 mL
½ cup	chopped parsley leaves	125 mL
½ cup	packed basil leaves	125 mL
3 tbsp	chopped fresh oregano leaves	45 mL
¼ tsp	fine sea salt	1 mL
Dash	raw agave nectar	Dash

1. In a blender, combine olive oil, lemon juice, orange juice, grapefruit juice, parsley, basil, oregano, salt and agave nectar. Blend at high speed until smooth. Serve immediately or cover and refrigerate for up to 5 days.

Variation

To put an Asian spin on this dressing, substitute an equal quantity of cilantro leaves for the parsley and add 1 tsp (5 mL) sesame oil.

Sweet Sesame Orange Vinaigrette

This dressing is perfect for a simple light salad of crisp, fresh romaine or baby spinach. I would add a garnish of black or white sesame seeds, orange segments and some fresh herbs.

Makes 1½ cups (375 mL)

Tip

To soak the sesame seeds, combine with ½ cup (125 mL) water. Cover and set aside for 30 minutes. Drain, discarding water. Rinse under cold running water until the water runs clear.

¼ cup	sesame seeds, soaked (see Tip, left)	60 mL
¾ cup	freshly squeezed orange juice	175 mL
½ cup	cold-pressed hemp oil	125 mL
2 tbsp	freshly squeezed lemon juice	30 mL
2 tbsp	raw agave nectar	30 mL
1 tsp	fine sea salt	5 mL

1. In a blender, combine soaked sesame seeds, orange juice, hemp oil, lemon juice, agave nectar and salt. Blend at high speed until smooth. Serve immediately or cover and refrigerate for up to 5 days.

Detox Vinaigrette

I love this cleansing dressing served simply over a mix of fresh spring lettuces such as baby spinach, radicchio, frisée and romaine, tossed with some chopped avocado and sliced bell peppers.

Makes 1½ cups (375 mL)

Tips

This dressing has a fairly strong lemon flavor. If you prefer a more neutral taste, add ¼ cup (60 mL) extra virgin olive oil and 2 tbsp (30 mL) agave nectar.

Substitute the dulse flakes with 1 tsp (5 mL) kelp powder.

¾ cup	cold-pressed flax oil	175 mL
¼ cup	freshly squeezed lemon juice	60 mL
½ tsp	finely grated lemon zest	2 mL
2 tsp	chopped gingerroot	10 mL
½ tsp	dried dulse flakes	2 mL
¼ tsp	fine sea salt	1 mL
Dash	cayenne pepper	Dash

1. In a blender, combine flax oil, lemon juice, lemon zest, ginger, dulse, salt and cayenne. Blend at high speed until smooth. Serve immediately or cover and refrigerate for up to 5 days.

Greek Hemp Dressing

This dressing is tangy and full of flavor. It pairs perfectly with Greek Kale Salad (page 143), but it is also very nice tossed with crisp lettuce, kalamata olives, cucumber slices and tomato wedges. For a finishing touch, add some Cashew Feta Cheese (page 105).

Makes 2 cups (500 mL)

Tips

To soak the hemp seeds for this recipe, combine with 1 cup (250 mL) water. Cover and set aside for 20 minutes. Drain, discarding water. Rinse under cold running water until the water runs clear.

For convenience, substitute ¼ cup (60 mL) hemp butter for the soaked hemp seeds.

½ cup	raw shelled hemp seeds, soaked (see Tips, left)	125 mL
½ cup	cold-pressed (extra virgin) olive oil	125 mL
¼ cup	cold-pressed hemp oil	60 mL
¾ cup	freshly squeezed lemon juice	175 mL
3 tbsp	filtered water	45 mL
2 tbsp	dried oregano	30 mL
1 tsp	fine sea salt	5 mL

1. In a blender, combined soaked hemp seeds, olive oil, hemp oil, lemon juice, water, oregano and salt. Blend at high speed until smooth. Serve immediately or cover and refrigerate for up to 5 days.

Flax and Hemp Italian Dressing

This tangy and flavor-packed dressing is perfect over fresh, crisp lettuce or as a marinade for sliced vegetables. Use high-quality dried herbs for the most flavor.

Makes 2 cups (500 mL)

Tips

Raw agave nectar is a sap that is extracted at low temperatures from the piña, or center, of the agave plant, which is native to Mexico. When purchasing agave nectar, be sure to look for products labeled "raw." Most of the agave nectar on the market has been heated to a high temperature and does not qualify as raw food. If you have concerns, ask your purveyor.

When purchasing dried herbs, try to buy organic versions. Always store dried herbs in an airtight container in a cool, dry place away from light.

½ cup	cold-pressed flax oil	125 mL
½ cup	freshly squeezed lemon juice	125 mL
¼ cup	apple cider vinegar	60 mL
¼ cup	filtered water	60 mL
3 tbsp	raw agave nectar (see Tips, left)	45 mL
1	clove garlic	1
1 tsp	fine sea salt	5 mL
½ tsp	dried oregano	2 mL
½ tsp	dried basil	2 mL
¼ tsp	fennel seeds	1 mL
¼ tsp	dried dill weed	1 mL
Pinch	freshly ground black pepper	Pinch
¼ cup	chopped red bell pepper	60 mL
¼ cup	chopped carrot	60 mL
3 tbsp	raw shelled hemp seeds	45 mL

1. In a blender, combine flax oil, lemon juice, vinegar, water, agave nectar, garlic, salt, oregano, basil, fennel seeds, dill and black pepper. Blend at high speed until smooth.

2. Add red pepper, carrot and hemp seeds and blend at medium to low speed (depending on how powerful your blender is) until no large pieces remain but mixture is not entirely smooth (you want the dressing to retain some texture). Serve immediately or cover and refrigerate for up to 5 days.

Variations

To increase the fiber in this dressing, substitute the agave nectar with ¼ cup (60 mL) Date Paste (page 80).

Substitute various kinds of vegetables for the carrot and red pepper. I particularly like the combination of ¼ cup (60 mL) chopped cauliflower and ¼ cup (60 mL) chopped green or yellow pepper.

"Roasted" Garlic, Hemp and Parsley Dressing

Although more work than most, this dressing is well worth it. Providing protein and essential fatty acids, it is perfect paired with nut-based foods, because it holds up to strong flavors. I enjoy it tossed with simple greens, served as a side dish alongside Walnut Portobello Burgers (page 219), Herbed Hemp and Cashew Gnocchi Carbonara (page 242) or Garlic, Spinach and Mushroom Tarts (page 216).

Makes 1 cup (250 mL)

Tip

To store hemp seeds, place them in an airtight container and refrigerate. This will prevent the fats from turning rancid. Hemp seeds can also be frozen for up to 6 months. They are extremely high in protein, containing up to 5 grams per tablespoon (15 mL).

- **Electric food dehydrator**

15 to 20	cloves garlic, peeled	15 to 20
3 tbsp	cold-pressed (extra virgin) olive oil	45 mL
2 cups	chopped flat-leaf parsley	500 mL
½ cup	cold-pressed hemp oil	125 mL
¼ cup	freshly squeezed lemon juice	60 mL
¼ cup	raw shelled hemp seeds	60 mL
½ tsp	fine sea salt	2 mL
¼ tsp	sweet paprika	1 mL
¼ cup	(approx.) filtered water	60 mL

1. In a shallow dish, combine garlic and olive oil. Toss well. Place in dehydrator, and spread evenly. Dehydrate at 105°F (41°C) for 10 to 12 hours or until brown (it should resemble traditional roasted garlic).

2. In a blender, combine "roasted" garlic, parsley, hemp oil, lemon juice, hemp seeds, salt and paprika. Blend at high speed until smooth.

3. Scrape down the sides of the blender jar. With the motor running, slowly add enough water through the opening in the lid to create a creamy dressing. Serve immediately or cover and refrigerate for up to 5 days.

Variations

Substitute ¼ cup (60 mL) freshly squeezed lime juice, 1 tbsp (15 mL) chopped gingerroot and 1 tsp (5 mL) ground coriander for the parsley and lemon juice.

Substitute an equal quantity of sesame seeds, soaked in ½ cup (125 mL) water for 20 minutes, for the hemp seeds. Drain and discard the soaking water and rinse under cold running water.

Sun-Dried Tomato French Dressing

This dressing is thick, rich and tangy. I love it over crisp romaine lettuce with fresh cherry tomatoes or slathered on Zucchini Hemp Bread (page 324). It also makes a great dip for carrot and celery sticks.

Makes 2 cups (500 mL)

Tips

To soak the sun-dried tomatoes for this recipe, place in a bowl and add 1 cup (250 mL) water. Cover and set aside for 20 minutes. Drain and discard any remaining water.

To soak the dates for this recipe, place them in a bowl and cover with ½ cup (125 mL) water. Cover and set aside for 20 minutes. Drain and rinse, discarding soaking water.

When purchasing sun-dried tomatoes, buy those that are dry rather than packed in oil. That allows you to control both the kind and quantity of oil you consume. Soak the tomatoes in room-temperature water for 20 to 30 minutes to make them soft again.

¼ cup	dry-packed sun-dried tomatoes, soaked (see Tips, left)	60 mL
3	chopped pitted Medjool dates, soaked	3
1½ cups	cold-pressed (extra virgin) olive oil	375 mL
¼ cup	apple cider vinegar	60 mL
2 tsp	wheat-free tamari	10 mL
2	cloves garlic	2
½ tsp	dried basil	2 mL
½ tsp	dried oregano	2 mL
½ tsp	mustard powder	2 mL
½ tsp	freshly ground black pepper	2 mL

1. In a blender, combine olive oil, vinegar, tamari, garlic, basil, oregano, mustard, pepper and soaked sun-dried tomatoes and dates. Blend at high speed until smooth. Serve immediately or cover and refrigerate for up to 5 days.

Variations

Substitute 3 tbsp (45 mL) raw agave nectar for the dates.

Substitute 2 tbsp (30 mL) dry-packed sun-dried tomatoes for the amount called for and add 2 tbsp (30 mL) goji berries and 2 Medjool dates. Soak the tomatoes, goji berries and dates in 1 cup (250 mL) water for 20 minutes. Drain and discard any remaining water. Blend as above.

Chinese Five-Spice Carrot, Coconut and Ginger Dressing

This pleasantly spiced and slightly sweet dressing works particularly well with strongly flavored green vegetables such as thinly sliced collard or dandelion greens or escarole. The strong flavors of the dressing can stand up to the greens. I particularly enjoy it with Simple Marinated Kale Salad (page 142).

Makes 3½ cups (825 mL)

Tips

If you don't have Chinese five-spice powder, substitute this quantity with ½ tsp (2 mL) ground cinnamon, ¼ tsp (1 mL) fennel seeds and a pinch each of ground cloves, ground star anise and freshly ground black pepper.

When following a completely raw food diet, look for sesame oil that is untoasted and completely unrefined. It will be labeled "cold-pressed."

If you don't have a high-powered blender, you can make this dressing in a food processor fitted with the metal blade, although the result will be not quite as creamy.

Coconut butter is a blend of coconut oil and coconut meat. You can find it in natural foods stores next to the coconut oil. In this recipe you may substitute an equal quantity of coconut oil, but the dressing will not be as rich or creamy.

2 cups	chopped carrots	500 mL
¾ cup	filtered water	175 mL
¼ cup	wheat-free tamari	60 mL
¼ cup	sesame oil, untoasted (see Tips, left), or cold-pressed (extra virgin) olive oil (see page 82)	60 mL
3 tbsp	coconut butter	45 mL
2 tbsp	chopped gingerroot	30 mL
1 tbsp	Chinese five-spice powder (see Tips, left)	15 mL
Pinch	cayenne pepper	Pinch

1. In a high-powered blender (see Tips, left), combine carrots, water, tamari, sesame oil, coconut butter, ginger, Chinese five-spice and cayenne. Blend at high speed until creamy and smooth. (You may need to stop the blender once at the beginning to scrape down the sides of the container.) Serve immediately or cover and refrigerate for up to 3 days.

Grapefruit and Blueberry Dressing

This dressing is best enjoyed on some crisp romaine lettuce tossed with organic blueberries and hemp seeds.

Makes 1 cup (250 mL)

Tips

Flax oil is extremely sensitive to heat and should be stored in the refrigerator. Otherwise it will quickly become rancid.

If the taste of the grapefruit juice is too strong, use ¼ cup (60 mL) each orange and grapefruit juice.

½ cup	freshly squeezed grapefruit juice (see Tips, left)	125 mL
½ cup	cold-pressed flax oil (see Tips, left)	125 mL
½ cup	blueberries	125 mL
2 tbsp	freshly squeezed lemon juice	30 mL
1 tbsp	raw agave nectar	15 mL
½ tsp	fine sea salt	2 mL

1. In a blender, combine grapefruit juice, flax oil, blueberries, lemon juice, agave nectar and salt. Blend at high speed until smooth. Serve immediately or cover and refrigerate for up to 3 days.

Variation

Substitute the flax oil with an equal quantity of either hemp or cold-pressed (extra virgin) olive oil.

Strawberry, Mango and Basil Dressing

This light and summery dressing is perfect over bitter greens such as dandelion greens, radicchio or endive. Finish the salad with a sprinkling of raw pecans.

Makes 1½ cups (375 mL)

Tips

To store basil leaves, rinse well in cool water to remove any dirt and dry in a salad spinner. Wrap in slightly damp paper towels and refrigerate for up to one week.

If you do not have fresh basil, substitute 2 tsp (10 mL) dried basil.

1½ cups	chopped mango (about 2 large)	375 mL
1 cup	hulled strawberries, chopped	250 mL
½ cup	cold-pressed (extra virgin) olive oil	125 mL
¼ cup	packed basil leaves	60 mL
3 tbsp	freshly squeezed lemon juice	45 mL
2 tbsp	apple cider vinegar	30 mL
1 tbsp	raw shelled hemp seeds	15 mL
½ tsp	fine sea salt	2 mL

1. In a blender, combine strawberries, olive oil, basil, lemon juice, vinegar, hemp seeds and salt. Blend at high speed until smooth. Serve immediately or cover and refrigerate for up to 3 days.

Green Destiny Dressing

This dressing is creamy and delicious. I love it over baby arugula tossed with yellow grape tomatoes and a healthy dollop of Cashew Feta Cheese (page 105).

(page 105)

Makes 1½ cups (375 mL)

Tips

Kale comes in many different forms. The most common, green kale, is widely available. Black kale, which is also called dinosaur kale or lacinato kale, is reputed to be the most nutrient-dense.

Tahini, or sesame seed paste/butter, has a wonderful creamy texture and provides calcium, phosphorus, vitamin E and mono- and polyunsaturated fats.

¾ cup	cold-pressed (extra virgin) olive oil	175 mL
¼ cup	freshly squeezed lemon juice	60 mL
½ cup	spinach leaves	125 mL
¼ cup	chopped trimmed kale	60 mL
2 tbsp	tahini (see Tips, left)	30 mL
1 tbsp	raw shelled hemp seeds	15 mL
1	clove garlic	1
1 tsp	fine sea salt	5 mL
1 tsp	dried oregano	5 mL
¼ cup	filtered water, optional	60 mL

1. In a blender, combine olive oil, lemon juice, spinach and kale. Blend at high speed until smooth.
2. Add tahini, hemp seeds, garlic, salt and oregano and blend at high speed until smooth. If the dressing is too thick, add water to achieve the desired consistency. Serve immediately or cover and refrigerate for up to 3 days.

Variations

Substitute kale with other dark leafy greens such as mustard greens or dandelion greens. If using dandelion greens, which are quite bitter, add 1 to 2 tbsp (30 to 45 mL) raw agave nectar.

If you do not have dried oregano, substitute an equal quantity of dried basil or ground cumin or 3 tbsp (45 mL) chopped fresh parsley.

Spicy Miso Dressing

This dressing is one of my favorites, served over a simple seaweed salad (see Tip, below).

Makes 1½ cups (375 mL)

Tip

To make a simple seaweed salad, soak dried seaweed in warm water for 10 to 15 minutes or until soft. Drain, rinse under cold running water and toss with enough of this dressing to coat. Sprinkle with black sesame seeds for a finishing touch.

¾ cup	brown rice miso (see Tips, page 188)	175 mL
¼ cup	sesame oil, untoasted (see Tips, page 171)	60 mL
½ cup	filtered water	125 mL
3 tbsp	freshly squeezed lemon juice	45 mL
1 tbsp	raw agave nectar	15 mL
1 tsp	cayenne pepper	5 mL
1 tsp	chopped gingerroot	5 mL

1. In a blender, combine miso, sesame oil, water, lemon juice, agave nectar, cayenne and ginger. Blend at high speed until smooth. Serve immediately or cover and refrigerate for up to 5 days.

Variation

Substitute 2 tbsp (30 mL) chopped jalapeño peppers and ¼ cup (60 mL) chopped cilantro for the cayenne pepper.

Southwest Cilantro Dressing

This creamy dressing is packed with flavor. It is great served on Simple Marinated Kale Salad (page 142) or even just crisp romaine lettuce.

Makes 2 cups (500 mL)

Tip

To soak the pumpkin seeds for this recipe, place in a bowl and add 1 cup (250 mL) water. Cover and set aside for 20 minutes. Drain and rinse under cold running water.

¼ cup	raw pumpkin seeds, soaked (see Tip, left)	60 mL
½ cup	cold-pressed (extra virgin) olive oil	125 mL
½ cup	freshly squeezed lemon juice	125 mL
½ cup	chopped red bell pepper	125 mL
½ cup	chopped cilantro leaves	125 mL
3 tbsp	tahini	45 mL
1 tbsp	ground cumin	15 mL
2 tsp	chili powder	10 mL
1 tsp	fine sea salt	5 mL
Pinch	cayenne pepper	Pinch

1. In a blender, combine all the ingredients. Blend at high speed until smooth. Serve immediately or cover and refrigerate for up to 3 days.

Lemon Poppy Seed Dressing

This dressing is light and tangy. The poppy seeds pop in your mouth, providing a pleasant texture. This is great recipe for the summer months, served on a salad that contains fresh fruit and seeds.

Makes 1½ cups (375 mL)

Tip

To soak the cashews for this recipe, cover with 1 cup (250 mL) water. Set aside for 30 minutes. Drain, discarding soaking water, and rinse under cold running water until the water runs clear.

½ cup	raw cashews, soaked (see Tip, left)	125 mL
¾ cup	cold-pressed (extra virgin) olive oil	175 mL
¼ cup	filtered water	60 mL
3 tbsp	freshly squeezed lemon juice	45 mL
2 tbsp	raw agave nectar	30 mL
½ tsp	fine sea salt	2 mL
2 tbsp	poppy seeds	30 mL

1. In a blender, combine olive oil, water, lemon juice, agave nectar, salt and soaked cashews. Blend at high speed until smooth. Transfer to a container and stir in poppy seeds. Serve immediately or cover and refrigerate for up to 5 days.

Variations

Substitute 2 tbsp (30 mL) apple cider vinegar for the lemon juice.

For a bolder poppy seed flavor, blend 1 tbsp (15 mL) of the poppy seeds with the rest of the ingredients, then stir in the remainder.

Raspberry Hazelnut Dressing

This blend of fresh raspberries and hazelnuts is perfect in any light salad.

Makes 1 cup (250 mL)

Tip

To soak the hazelnuts for this recipe, place in a bowl and add 1 cup (250 mL) water. Cover and set aside for 30 minutes. Drain. Rinse under cold running water until the water runs clear.

¼ cup	hazelnuts, soaked (see Tip, left)	60 mL
1 cup	fresh raspberries	250 mL
½ cup	cold-pressed (extra virgin) olive oil	125 mL
¼ cup	freshly squeezed lemon juice	60 mL
2 tbsp	raw agave nectar	30 mL
1 tbsp	filtered water	15 mL
Pinch	fine sea salt	Pinch

1. In a blender, combine raspberries, olive oil, lemon juice, agave nectar, water, salt and soaked hazelnuts. Blend at high speed until smooth. Serve immediately or cover and refrigerate for up to 3 days.

Sweet Onion Teriyaki Dressing

This sweet and tangy dressing is great served on a myriad of raw food sandwiches, salads or wraps. It provides the taste and texture of good mass-market onion and teriyaki dressings without high-fructose corn syrup or refined sugars.

Makes 2 cups (500 mL)

Tip

While wheat-free tamari is not raw, it is gluten-free. The raw alternative for tamari, nama shoyu, does contain gluten. If you are following a completely raw diet and can tolerate gluten, by all means substitute an equal quantity of nama shoyu.

¾ cup	cold-pressed (extra virgin) olive oil	175 mL
¼ cup	filtered water	60 mL
¼ cup	freshly squeezed lemon juice	60 mL
¼ cup	wheat-free tamari (see Tip, left)	60 mL
¼ cup	raw agave nectar	60 mL
1 tsp	chopped gingerroot (see Tips, below)	5 mL
1	clove garlic	1
¼ cup	Caramelized Onions (page 292)	60 mL

1. In a blender, combine olive oil, water, lemon juice, tamari, agave nectar, ginger and garlic. Blend at high speed until smooth.
2. Transfer to a container and stir in caramelized onions. Serve immediately or cover and refrigerate for up to 5 days.

Orange and Basil Miso Dressing

Here's a light and refreshing dressing that is great on any green salad. The refreshing flavors make it perfect for the warmer-weather months.

Makes 2 cups (500 mL)

Tips

To remove the skin from fresh gingerroot with the least amount of waste, use the edge of a teaspoon. With a brushing motion, scrape off the skin to reveal the yellow root.

Substitute the olive oil with either hemp or flaxseed oil.

Substitute fresh cilantro, chives or flat-leaf parsley for the basil.

1 cup	filtered water	250 mL
¾ cup	freshly squeezed orange juice	175 mL
¼ cup	unpasteurized brown rice miso paste	60 mL
¼ cup	fresh basil leaves	60 mL
3 tbsp	cold-pressed (extra virgin) olive oil	45 mL
1 tbsp	chopped gingerroot (see Tips, left)	15 mL
¼ tsp	fine sea salt	1 mL

1. In a blender, combine water, orange juice, miso, basil, olive oil, ginger and salt. Blend at high speed until smooth. Use immediately or cover and refrigerate for up to 5 days.

Sesame Carrot Ginger Dressing

This dressing is completely oil-free yet packed with flavor. I like to serve it with a mixture of fresh greens that includes arugula, romaine lettuce and baby spinach.

Makes 4½ cups (1.1 L)

Tips

I specify a high-powered blender for this recipe because it will ensure that the carrots, sesame seeds and ginger become as smooth and creamy as possible. If you do not have a high-powered blender, use a regular blender on the highest setting, although the result will not be quite as creamy.

One key to a successful result is to chop the carrots very finely before adding them to the blender.

4 cups	filtered water	1 L
⅔ cup	apple cider vinegar	150 mL
⅓ cup	wheat-free tamari (see Tips, page 176)	75 mL
3 tbsp	raw agave nectar	45 mL
4 cups	finely chopped peeled carrots (see Tips, left)	1 L
¼ cup	sesame seeds	60 mL
2 tbsp	chopped gingerroot (see Tips, page 176)	30 mL

1. In a high-powered blender, combine water, vinegar, tamari, agave nectar, carrots, sesame seeds and ginger. Blend at high speed until smooth. Serve immediately or cover and refrigerate for up to 3 days.

Variations

For a creamier version of this recipe, replace the sesame seeds with an equal quantity of hemp seeds.

Add 2 tsp (10 mL) untoasted sesame oil for a true Asian flavor.

Lemon Avocado Dressing

The addition of oregano makes this reminiscent of a creamy Greek-style dressing. I like to serve it over crisp romaine lettuce, avocado slices and juicy tomato wedges.

Makes 3 cups (750 mL)

Tip

Substitute 1 tsp (5 mL) each of chopped fresh thyme, rosemary and sage for the oregano to create a creamy herb-spiked avocado dressing.

2 cups	filtered water	500 mL
⅔ cup	freshly squeezed lemon juice	150 mL
⅓ cup	cold-pressed (extra virgin) olive oil	75 mL
½	medium avocado, chopped	½
3	cloves garlic	3
2 tbsp	dried oregano	30 mL
1 tsp	fine sea salt	5 mL

1. In a blender, combine water, lemon juice, olive oil, avocado, garlic, oregano and salt. Blend at high speed until smooth. Serve immediately or cover and refrigerate for up to 3 days.

Creamy Sunflower Seed Dressing

This dressing, which can substitute for a classic Caesar salad dressing, is free of added oil. However, it is also very high in flavor. To make a raw Caesar-type salad, serve it over some crispy romaine lettuce and diced tomatoes. Top with Almond Parmesan Cheese (page 204) and Eggplant Bacon (page 41).

Makes 3½ cups (875 mL)

Tips

To soak the sunflower seeds for this recipe, place in a bowl and add 2 cups (500 mL) water. Cover and set aside for 30 minutes. Drain, discarding water and any shells or unwanted particles. Rinse under cold running water until the water runs clear.

Although it is not necessary to refrigerate nutritional yeast, make sure to store it in an airtight container away from light. This will extend its shelf life, help to retain its B vitamins and keep the flavor more robust.

Traditional Caesar dressings contain anchovies, which add saltiness and the flavor of the ocean. When a recipe calls for anchovies, dried seaweed powder or flakes are usually a good substitute.

1 cup	raw sunflower seeds, soaked (see Tips, left)	250 mL
2 cups	filtered water	500 mL
¼ cup	freshly squeezed lemon juice	60 mL
2 tsp	apple cider vinegar	10 mL
2 tsp	nutritional yeast (see Tips, left)	10 mL
1 tsp	fine sea salt	5 mL
1 tsp	dried dulse flakes	5 mL
3 to 4	cloves garlic	3 to 4
2	pitted dates	2

1. In a blender, combine soaked sunflower seeds, water, lemon juice, vinegar, nutritional yeast, salt, dulse, garlic and dates. Blend at high speed until smooth. Serve immediately or cover and refrigerate for up to 3 days.

Variations

The combination of 1 cup (250 mL) soaked sunflower seeds and 2 cups (500 mL) water can be a base for a dressing to which various flavors can be added. For instance, substitute ¼ cup (60 mL) chopped parsley leaves, 3 tbsp (45 mL) freshly squeezed lemon juice, 2 cloves minced garlic, 1 tbsp (15 mL) ground cumin, 1 tsp (5 mL) chili powder and a dash of cayenne pepper for the dulse, nutritional yeast and quantity of garlic suggested.

Substitute an equal quantity of soaked cashews for the sunflower seeds and add 1 tbsp (15 mL) nutritional yeast.

Creamy Coconut Russian Dressing

This creamy version of the classic Russian dressing is perfect tossed with crisp romaine and a few cherry tomatoes. It also makes a great spread on sandwiches.

Makes 1½ cups (375 mL)

Tips

To soak the sun-dried tomatoes for this recipe, place in a bowl and add 1 cup (250 mL) water. Cover and set aside for 20 minutes. Drain and rinse.

To soak the dates for this recipe, place them in a bowl and cover with ½ cup (125 mL) water. Cover and set aside for 20 minutes. Drain and rinse.

Coconut butter is the meat from the coconut blended with the oil. It is usually available in natural foods stores, next to the coconut oil. If you do not have access to coconut butter, substitute ¼ cup (60 mL) coconut oil.

If you are transitioning to a raw diet, substitute ¼ cup (60 mL) chopped pickles such as gherkins, which have been pasteurized, for the cucumber.

¼ cup	dry-packed sun-dried tomatoes, soaked (see Tips, left)	60 mL
2	chopped, pitted Medjool dates, soaked	2
½ cup	cold-pressed (extra virgin) olive oil	125 mL
¼ cup	filtered water	60 mL
¼ cup	freshly squeezed lemon juice	60 mL
¼ cup	chopped tomato	60 mL
3 tbsp	coconut butter (see Tips, left)	45 mL
3 tbsp	chopped green onion, white part with a bit of green	45 mL
2 tbsp	apple cider vinegar	30 mL
1 tsp	celery seeds	5 mL
1 tsp	fine sea salt	5 mL
½ tsp	dry mustard	2 mL
¼ cup	finely diced cucumber	60 mL

1. In a blender, combine olive oil, water, lemon juice, chopped tomato and soaked sun-dried tomatoes. Blend at high speed until smooth and no large pieces of tomato remain.

2. Add coconut butter, green onion, vinegar, celery seeds, salt, mustard and soaked dates. Blend at high speed until smooth and creamy. Transfer to a container and fold in cucumber. Serve immediately or cover and refrigerate for up to 3 days.

Green Delight Dressing

> This dressing is a perfect blend of creamy avocado and fresh greens. The bright flavors of lemon and dill will make your taste buds dance.

Makes 2 cups (500 mL)

Tip

Kale belongs to a group of vegetables called crucifers, which also includes arugula, cauliflower, radishes, broccoli and Brussels sprouts. Crucifers contain cancer-fighting phytochemicals. These cancer fighters are very susceptible to high temperatures and are water-soluble, which means their nutritional benefit is maximized when they are eaten raw. Dark green leafy greens such as kale also contain appreciable amounts of calcium and magnesium.

1½ cups	water	375 mL
½ cup	freshly squeezed lemon juice	125 mL
¼ cup	cold-pressed (extra virgin) olive oil	60 mL
1	small avocado	1
¼	bunch parsley leaves	¼
2	kale leaves, trimmed (see Tips, page 159)	2
2	garlic cloves	2
1 tbsp	dried dill weed	15 mL
½ tsp	fine sea salt	2 mL

1. Blend water, lemon juice, olive oil, avocado, parsley, kale, garlic, dill and salt at high speed until smooth.

Variations

Substitute ½ cup (125 mL) baby spinach or ¼ cup (60 mL) each baby spinach and arugula for the kale.

Substitute ¼ cup (60 mL) fresh dill weed for the dried.

Spirulina Tahini Ginger Cream

> This creamy and zesty dressing is great with dark leafy greens. I particularly enjoy it with Softened Broccoli (page 140) or Simple Marinated Kale Salad (page 142).

Makes 1½ cups (375 mL)

Tip

Tahini is wonderful for making velvety dressings and sauces, because of its ability to easily create creamy textures.

½ cup	filtered water	125 mL
½ cup	tahini	125 mL
¼ cup	freshly squeezed lemon juice	60 mL
1 tbsp	chopped gingerroot	15 mL
½ tsp	fine sea salt	2 mL
½ tsp	spirulina powder	2 mL
Pinch	kelp powder or dried dulse flakes	Pinch

1. In a blender, combine water, tahini, lemon juice, ginger, salt, spirulina and kelp powder. Blend at high speed until smooth. Serve immediately or cover and refrigerate for up to 3 days.

Sauces and Condiments

Sauces and condiments are an important component of a raw food diet. Without them, many dishes would just be sliced vegetables with nuts or seeds sprinkled overtop. Some sauces play a specific role in dishes, working in a scientific way to soften foods or make them easier to digest. Others are there to tweak the flavor of a finished dish and/or add valuable nutrients, rounding out the nutritional profile.

Many of the sauces in this book reflect international cuisine. Some contain an abundance of spice, some are sweet and others qualify as rich and delicious. But all work to make meals more interesting and enjoyable.

Herbed Avocado Purée

I love this simple sauce as a garnish for salads. If I'm having a dinner party, I often put it in a squeeze bottle and use it to make a design on the plates.

Makes 1 cup (250 mL)

Tip

Because it contains avocado, this sauce will oxidize quickly, so try to use it up the same day it is made. If you are storing it, press plastic wrap directly onto the surface before refrigerating and store for up to one day.

1	small avocado, chopped	1
¼	bunch fresh parsley leaves	¼
¼	bunch fresh cilantro leaves	¼
¼ cup	packed basil leaves	60 mL
¼ cup	packed fresh mint leaves	60 mL
3 tbsp	filtered water	45 mL
2 tbsp	freshly squeezed lemon juice	30 mL
½ tsp	fine sea salt	2 mL

1. In a food processor, process ingredients until smooth. Transfer to a serving bowl (see Tip, left).

Variation

Substitute 1 tbsp (15 mL) chopped fresh sage leaves, 2 tsp (10 mL) chopped fresh rosemary and 1 clove garlic for the cilantro, basil and mint.

Arrabbiata Sauce

This rich, spicy tomato sauce is very versatile. Use it any way you would use a classic pasta sauce, but with a raw food base.

Makes 4 cups (1 L)

Tips

To soak the sun-dried tomatoes for this recipe, combine with 2 cups (500 mL) warm water. Set aside for 30 minutes. Drain, discarding liquid.

If you have a high-powered blender, use it to make this sauce.

½ cup	dry-packed sun-dried tomatoes, soaked (see Tips, left)	125 mL
3 cups	chopped tomatoes, divided	750 mL
¼ cup	cold-pressed (extra virgin) olive oil	60 mL
2 tbsp	freshly squeezed lemon juice	30 mL
2	cloves garlic	2
2 tsp	dried chile flakes	10 mL
1 tsp	nutritional yeast	5 mL
¼ cup	finely sliced fresh basil leaves	60 mL

1. In a food processor fitted with the metal blade, process soaked sun-dried tomatoes, 2 cups (500 mL) chopped tomatoes, olive oil, lemon juice, garlic, chile flakes and nutritional yeast until smooth. Transfer to a bowl. Stir in remaining chopped tomatoes and the fresh basil. Serve immediately or cover and refrigerate for up to 4 days.

Red Pepper Basil Marinara Sauce

> Toss this rich tomato sauce with Zucchini Noodles (page 244) or use as a base for Buckwheat and Sunflower Seed Pizza Crust (page 326).

Makes about 8 cups (2 L)

Tips

Substitute ¼ cup (60 mL) packed fresh basil leaves for the dried basil.

If you have a high-powered blender, use it to make this sauce.

½ cup	dry-packed sun-dried tomatoes, soaked (see Tips, below)	125 mL
2 cups	chopped tomatoes	500 mL
1 cup	chopped seeded red bell pepper	250 mL
1 cup	cold-pressed (extra virgin) olive oil	250 mL
¼ cup	filtered water	60 mL
1 tbsp	nutritional yeast	15 mL
1 tbsp	dried basil	15 mL
½ tbsp	fine sea salt	7 mL

1. In a blender, combine ingredients. Blend at high speed until smooth. Serve immediately or cover and refrigerate for up to 3 days.

Tomato Basil Marinara Sauce

> This light, fresh tomato sauce is best made in the summer months, when local field-grown tomatoes and fresh basil are at their peak.

Makes 6 cups (1.5 L)

Tips

To soak the sun-dried tomatoes for this recipe, combine with 2 cups (500 mL) warm water. Set aside for 20 minutes. Drain, discarding liquid.

Any tomato variety works well in this recipe.

If fresh basil is not available, use 1 tbsp (15 mL) dried basil.

½ cup	dry-packed sun-dried tomatoes, soaked (see Tips, left)	125 mL
¼ cup	cold-pressed (extra virgin) olive oil	60 mL
3 tbsp	freshly squeezed lemon juice	45 mL
5	cloves garlic	5
1 tsp	fine sea salt	5 mL
½ cup	fresh basil leaves	125 mL
1 tsp	cayenne pepper, optional	5 mL
3 cups	chopped tomatoes	750 mL

1. In a food processor fitted with the metal blade, process olive oil, lemon juice, garlic and salt until blended. Scrape down the sides of the work bowl. Add soaked sun-dried tomatoes, basil and cayenne, if using, and process until smooth. Add fresh tomatoes and pulse until finely chopped and blended (do not process until smooth; you want to maintain some of the texture of the fresh tomatoes). Serve immediately or cover and refrigerate for up to 3 days.

Tomato and Pumpkin Seed Basil Marinara

This recipe makes a light and refreshing chunky tomato sauce with slightly crunchy pumpkin seeds. This sauce, which is great over Zucchini Noodles (page 244) finished with Almond Parmesan Cheese (page 204), does double duty as a dip for celery sticks or scooped up with crispy romaine lettuce leaves.

Makes 4 cups (1 L)

Tips

To soak the pumpkin seeds for this recipe, combine with 1 cup (250 mL) water. Cover and set aside for 30 minutes. Drain, discarding water. Rinse under cold running water until the water runs clear.

To soak the sun-dried tomatoes for this recipe, combine with 1 cup (500 mL) warm water. Set aside for 30 minutes. Drain, discarding liquid.

Nuts and seeds are in their dormant state when they are totally raw. When you soak them in filtered water, you bring them back to life. Soaking also makes nuts and seeds more digestible and enables their nutrients to be more easily absorbed. If you have time, it's always wise to soak nuts and seeds before consuming them.

½ cup	raw pumpkin seeds, soaked (see Tips, left)	125 mL
¼ cup	dry-packed sun-dried tomatoes, soaked (see Tips, left)	60 mL
¼ cup	cold-pressed (extra virgin) olive oil	60 mL
¼ cup	packed basil leaves	60 mL
2 tbsp	freshly squeezed lemon juice	30 mL
3	cloves garlic	3
1 tsp	sea salt	5 mL
3 cups	chopped fresh tomatoes	750 mL

1. In a food processor fitted with the metal blade, process olive oil, basil, lemon juice, garlic and salt until smooth (you do not want to have any pieces of garlic).
2. Add fresh tomatoes and process until puréed. Add soaked pumpkin seeds and sun-dried tomatoes and process for 2 to 3 minutes or until all ingredients are well combined, stopping the motor halfway through and scraping down the sides of the work bowl. Serve immediately or cover and refrigerate for up to 3 days.

Variation

Add ¼ cup (60 mL) Almond Parmesan Cheese (page 204) along with the soaked pumpkin seeds for a slightly richer sauce with more protein.

Basil, Spinach and Walnut Pesto

> This rich green sauce makes a great topping for Zucchini Noodles (page 244). For added nutrition, scatter some raw shelled hemp seeds overtop. This pesto also makes a tasty dip with any raw bread.

Makes 2 cups (500 mL)

Tips

Flax oil provides healthy omega-3 fats, which are essential for overall health and well-being. They help to reduce inflammation and other risk factors for diabetes, heart disease and stroke, among other benefits.

If flax oil is not available, try using hemp oil, olive oil, avocado oil or hazelnut oil.

¼ cup	freshly squeezed lemon juice	60 mL
3	cloves garlic	3
2 tsp	fine sea salt	10 mL
1 tsp	freshly ground black pepper	5 mL
1 cup	fresh basil leaves	250 mL
4 cups	chopped spinach leaves	1 L
½ cup	chopped walnut halves or pieces	125 mL
¼ cup	cold-pressed flax oil	60 mL

1. In a food processor fitted with the metal blade, process lemon juice, garlic, salt and pepper until no large pieces of garlic remain. Add basil, spinach and walnuts and process until smooth.
2. With the motor running, gradually add flax oil through the feed tube, until blended. Transfer to a bowl and serve immediately or cover and refrigerate for up to 3 days.

Basil and Spinach Cream Sauce

> I love this sauce at the height of summer, when fresh basil and spinach are in season. The creamy texture lends itself very well to many different raw food applications. It is great over raw pastas such as Zucchini Noodles (page 244) or as a cream sauce for Jicama Perogies (page 260). I also like to use it as a dressing for salads.

Makes 1½ cups (375 mL)

Tips

To soak the cashews and pine nuts for this recipe, cover with 2 cups (500 mL) water. Set aside for 30 minutes. Drain, discarding water. Rinse until the water runs clear.

If you have a high-powered blender, use it to make this sauce.

¼ cup	raw cashews, soaked (see Tips, left)	60 mL
¼ cup	raw pine nuts, soaked	60 mL
½ cup	packed basil leaves or 1 tbsp (15 mL) dried basil	125 mL
½ cup	coarsely chopped spinach	125 mL
1	clove garlic	1
½ tsp	fine sea salt	2 mL
¼ cup	water	60 mL
3 tbsp	freshly squeezed lemon juice	45 mL

1. In a food processor fitted with the metal blade, process soaked cashews and pine nuts, basil, spinach, garlic, salt, water and lemon juice until smooth. Transfer to a bowl. Serve immediately or cover and refrigerate for up to 3 days.

Herbed Pumpkin Seed and Hemp Oil Pesto

This sauce is wonderful in the warmer months, when your body is craving greener and lighter foods. It is perfect served with Zucchini Noodles (page 244), and I love to spoon it onto Sun-Dried Tomato and Carrot Burgers (page 220) in place of ketchup. It also does double duty as a dressing on simple mixed greens.

Makes 2 cups (500 mL)

Tip

To soak the pumpkin seeds for this recipe, place in a bowl and add 1 cup (250 mL) water. Cover and set aside for 30 minutes. Drain, discarding any remaining water. Rinse under cold running water until the water runs clear.

½ cup	raw pumpkin seeds, soaked (see Tip, left)	125 mL
¼ cup	freshly squeezed lemon juice	60 mL
4	cloves garlic	4
½ tsp	fine sea salt	2 mL
1 cup	packed basil leaves	250 mL
¾ cup	parsley leaves	175 mL
¾ cup	cilantro leaves	175 mL
½ cup	cold-pressed hemp oil	125 mL

1. In a food processor fitted with the metal blade, process lemon juice, garlic and salt until no large pieces of garlic remain, stopping the motor and scraping down the sides of the work bowl if necessary. Add basil, parsley and cilantro and process just until the herbs are chopped. Scrape down the sides of the work bowl and process for 10 to 15 seconds, until herbs are finely and uniformly chopped.

2. Add soaked pumpkin seeds and process until incorporated. With the motor running, slowly add hemp oil through the feed tube, until mixture is smoothly blended. Season with additional salt to taste. Serve immediately or cover and refrigerate for up to 5 days.

Variation

For a spicy Southwest spin, substitute an additional 1 cup (250 mL) cilantro leaves for the basil and ½ cup (125 mL) walnuts for the pumpkin seeds. Add 2 tbsp (30 mL) chopped jalapeño pepper, 1 tbsp (15 mL) ground cumin and 2 tsp (10 mL) chili powder, processing with the lemon juice in Step 1.

Cashew Alfredo Sauce

I love the deep, rich flavor and texture of this creamy sauce. It is pairs perfectly with Zucchini Noodles (page 244) topped with Almond Parmesan Cheese (page 204). I also love to use it as a spread on crisp stalks of celery or fresh romaine lettuce leaves.

Makes 3 cups (750 mL)

2 cups	raw cashews, soaked (see Tips, left)	500 mL
3/4 cup	filtered water	175 mL
3 tbsp	nutritional yeast (see Tips, page 189)	45 mL
2 tbsp	cold-pressed (extra virgin) olive oil or flax oil	30 mL
1 tbsp	brown rice miso (see Tips, left)	15 mL
1 tbsp	freshly squeezed lemon juice	15 mL
1	clove garlic	1
1 tsp	fine sea salt	5 mL

1. In a blender, combine soaked cashews, water, nutritional yeast, olive oil, miso, lemon juice, garlic and salt. Blend at high speed until smooth. Transfer to a bowl and serve immediately or cover and refrigerate for up to 3 days.

Variation

Instead of the cashews, substitute 1 cup (250 mL) macadamia nuts soaked in 2 cups (500 mL) water for 30 minutes, drained and rinsed, and an additional 1/4 cup (60 mL) olive or flax oil.

Tips

To soak the cashews for this recipe, place in a bowl and add 4 cups (1 L) water. Cover and set aside for 30 minutes. Drain, discarding any remaining water. Rinse under cold running water until the water runs clear.

Cashews provide protein, copper, zinc, phosphorus, potassium and magnesium and are a source of healthy monounsaturated fat.

Although unpasteurized miso is not 100 percent raw, it is often used in raw food diets because it is fermented, which provides healthy bacteria to aid digestion. Brown rice miso is gluten-free and also contains vitamin B$_{12}$.

If you have a high-powered blender, use it to make this sauce. It will be smoother and creamier than when made in a regular blender.

Cashew and Cauliflower Hollandaise

This take on the classic French sauce will provide a good amount of protein. I love serving it for breakfast over Buckwheat Toast (page 36) with a side of Eggplant Bacon (page 41). It is also delicious with Zucchini Noodles (page 244) tossed with some sliced tomatoes and olives.

Makes 2 cups (500 mL)

Tips

To soak the cashews for this recipe, combine in a bowl with 2 cups (500 mL) water. Cover and set aside for 30 minutes. Drain, discarding any remaining water. Rinse under cold running water until the water runs clear.

Nutritional yeast is used in vegan and raw food diets mainly because it is a source of vitamin B_{12}. It is pasteurized, so technically it does not qualify as a raw food. However, in addition to necessary nutrients, it adds a deep, umami-like flavor to many dishes.

If you have a high-powered blender, use it to make this sauce. It will be smoother and creamier than when made in a regular blender.

1 cup	raw cashews, soaked (see Tips, left)	250 mL
½ cup	chopped cauliflower florets (about ¼ small cauliflower)	125 mL
½ cup	filtered water	125 mL
¼ cup	cold-pressed (extra virgin) olive oil	60 mL
¼ cup	nutritional yeast (see Tips, left)	60 mL
3 tbsp	freshly squeezed lemon juice	45 mL
1 tbsp	apple cider vinegar	15 mL
1 tsp	ground turmeric	5 mL
½ tsp	fine sea salt	2 mL

1. In a blender, combine soaked cashews, cauliflower, water, olive oil, nutritional yeast, lemon juice, vinegar, turmeric and salt. Blend at high speed until smooth. Transfer to a bowl and serve immediately or cover and refrigerate for up to 4 days.

Chermoula Sauce

Based on a traditional North African herb and spice blend, this sauce is packed full of flavor as well as nutrition. I like to use this as a table condiment for salads and soups. A few dollops makes a great finish for Red Beet Carpaccio (page 271). If you don't like a lot of heat, it makes a great substitute for hot sauce. I also like to use it as a filling, sandwiched between two crisp lettuce leaves, with some sliced avocado and fresh tomato wedges.

Makes 2 cups (500 mL)

Tips

To yield the maximum amount of juice from a lemon, make sure it is at room temperature. Rolling the lemon around on counter, pressing lightly with the palm of your hand, also helps by releasing juice from the flesh.

When using a food processor to make dips, pâtés or sauces, you should stop it once or twice and scrape down the sides of the bowl with a rubber spatula. This helps to ensure that all of the ingredients are evenly incorporated and that no large pieces remain in the finished product.

1 cup	chopped cilantro leaves	250 mL
1 cup	chopped parsley leaves	250 mL
¼ cup	chopped green onions, white and green parts	60 mL
7	cloves garlic	7
2 tbsp	chili powder	30 mL
2 tbsp	ground cumin	30 mL
1 tbsp	smoked sweet paprika	15 mL
1 tbsp	raw agave nectar	15 mL
2 tsp	finely grated lemon zest	10 mL
1 tsp	dried chile flakes	5 mL
1 tsp	ground cinnamon	5 mL
1 tsp	fine sea salt	5 mL
1 cup	freshly squeezed lemon juice	250 mL
Pinch	cayenne pepper	Pinch
½ cup	cold-pressed (extra virgin) olive oil	125 mL

1. In a food processor fitted with the metal blade, process cilantro, parsley, green onions, garlic, chili powder, cumin, paprika, agave nectar, lemon zest, chile flakes, cinnamon, salt, lemon juice and cayenne for 2 to 3 minutes or until a chunky paste has formed, stopping the motor and scraping down the sides of the work bowl once or twice. With the motor running, gradually add olive oil through the feed tube until a thick paste forms. Transfer to a bowl and serve immediately or cover and refrigerate for up to 3 days.

Sweet-and-Sour Thai Almond Butter Sauce

This delectable sauce is a perfect balance of sweet, sour, salty and slightly hot. It goes well with Marinated Kelp Noodles (page 243), Zucchini Noodles (page 244) or any other raw pasta.

Makes 4½ cups (1.1 L)

Tips

The best place to purchase almond butter is bulk food stores, as it can be quite pricey when purchased in small quantities. When purchasing nut butters, make sure they are raw and organic. Find a favorite brand or source and stick with it.

To remove the skin from fresh gingerroot with the least amount of waste, use the edge of a teaspoon. With a brushing motion, scrape off the skin to reveal the yellow root.

To purée gingerroot, use a fine, sharp-toothed grater, such as those made by Microplane.

When purchasing agave nectar, be sure to look for products labeled "raw." Most of the agave nectar on the market has been heated to a high temperature and does not qualify as raw food. If you have concerns, ask your purveyor.

2 cups	almond butter (see Tips, left)	500 mL
4	garlic cloves	4
2 tsp	puréed gingerroot (see Tips, left)	10 mL
1 tsp	fine sea salt	5 mL
¼ tsp	cayenne pepper	1 mL
1 cup	water	250 mL
1 cup	apple cider vinegar	250 mL
½ cup	raw agave nectar	125 mL

1. In a food processor fitted with the metal blade, process almond butter, garlic, ginger, salt, cayenne, water, vinegar and agave nectar. Transfer to a bowl. Use immediately or cover and refrigerate for up to 5 days.

Variation

For a more exotic version of this sauce, add 1 tsp (5 mL) ground coriander, 1 fresh wild ("Kaffir") lime leaf and a pinch of turmeric.

Yellow Coconut Curry Sauce

This smooth and rich curry sauce is as delicious as virtually any traditional yellow curry, but with none of the hidden unhealthy fats found in refined oils. It is slightly spicy and great served on cold nights when the body is craving warmth. I like to toss it with Zucchini Noodles (page 244) served over a bed of Cauliflower Rice (page 274), accompanied by Simple Marinated Kale Salad (page 142) sprinkled with hemp seeds.

Yields 4 cups (1 L)

Tips

To soak the cashews for this recipe, place in a bowl and add 2 cups (500 mL) water. Cover and set aside for 20 minutes. Drain, discarding any remaining water. Rinse under cold running water until water runs clear.

Coconut butter is a blend of coconut oil and coconut meat that is high in healthy fats and adds creaminess to smoothies and sauces. It is available in the nut butter section of natural foods stores or well-stocked supermarkets. Don't confuse it with coconut oil, because they are different.

If coconut butter is not available, substitute 3 tbsp (45 mL) dried shredded coconut.

Depending on the curry powder you use, this recipe may pack a punch. Add 2 tbsp (30 mL) and try a taste, then add more if you prefer.

All curry powders are not the same. If you have access to a good Asian market, it's worth a trip to stock up on high-quality spices. It will make a world of difference to the flavor of Asian-style sauces.

1 cup	raw cashews, soaked (see Tips, left)	250 mL
2 cups	water	500 mL
¼ cup	chopped tomato	60 mL
3 tbsp	coconut butter (see Tips, left)	45 mL
2 to 3 tbsp	curry powder (see Tips, left)	30 to 45 mL
1 tbsp	ground cumin	15 mL
1 tbsp	chopped gingerroot	15 mL
2	cloves garlic	2
1	wild lime leaf (see Tips, page 193)	1
2 tsp	fine sea salt	10 mL
1 tsp	freshly squeezed lemon juice	5 mL

1. In a blender, combine soaked cashews, water, tomato, coconut butter, curry powder, cumin, ginger, garlic, lime leaf, salt and lemon juice. Blend at high speed until smooth. Serve immediately or cover and refrigerate for up to 3 days.

Discarding Soaking Water

When working with soaked nuts and seeds, always make sure to discard the water that you soak them in. Bits of dirt or other contaminants may get into the soaking water, and you don't want to consume those. Use fresh filtered water to blend with the nuts and/or seeds to create a purée.

Lo Mein "Stir-Fry" Sauce

This sauce is light and low in calories, yet full of spicy flavor. It is perfect served with Zucchini Noodles (page 244), Marinated Kelp Noodles (page 243) or Simple Marinated Kale Salad (page 142).

Makes 4 cups (1 L)

Tips

The outer stalks of celery can be tough and fibrous. For best results, peel the stalk with a vegetable peeler. Save the peel to make soups, sauces or stocks.

To purée gingerroot, use a fine, sharp-toothed grater, such as those made by Microplane.

Wild lime leaves, often called "Kaffir" lime leaves, are the leaves of a small Asian lime tree. Look for them in Asian markets.

5 cups	chopped celery (see Tips, left)	1.25 L
1 tbsp	chopped jalapeño pepper	15 mL
1 tbsp	puréed gingerroot (see Tips, left)	15 mL
1	fresh wild lime leaf	1
1 tsp	sea salt	5 mL
¼ cup	cold-pressed (extra virgin) olive oil	60 mL
3 tbsp	freshly squeezed lemon juice	45 mL
3 tbsp	water	45 mL
1 tbsp	raw agave nectar	15 mL

1. In a food processor fitted with the metal blade, process celery, jalapeño, ginger, lime leaf, salt, olive oil, lemon juice, water and agave nectar until smooth. Transfer to a bowl. Serve immediately or cover and refrigerate for up to 3 days.

Variation

For a spicier version of this sauce, substitute an equal quantity of small red or green Thai chiles for the jalapeño pepper.

Spicy Pad Thai Sauce

This sauce is full of flavor and a source of protein, which is provided by the hemp seeds. I like pairing it with Simple Marinated Kale Salad (page 142) and some Zucchini Noodles (page 244). A topping of Chili Cumin Almonds (page 301) makes the perfect finish.

Yields 4 cups (1 L)

Tips

To soak the hemp seeds for this recipe, place in a bowl and cover with 4 cups (1 L) water. Cover and set aside for 30 minutes. Drain, discarding soaking water. Rinse under cold running water until the water runs clear.

If you prefer, substitute 2 cups (500 mL) hemp butter for the hemp seeds in this recipe.

To purée gingerroot, use a fine, sharp-toothed grater, such as those made by Microplane.

2½ cups	raw shelled hemp seeds, soaked (see Tips, left)	625 mL
1 cup	filtered water	250 mL
¼ cup	freshly squeezed lemon juice	60 mL
2 tbsp	raw agave nectar	30 mL
2 tbsp	puréed gingerroot (see Tips, left)	30 mL
1 tbsp	fine sea salt	15 mL
2 tsp	cayenne pepper	10 mL
1 tsp	ground cumin	5 mL
4	pitted dates	4

1. In a food processor fitted with the metal blade, process soaked hemp seeds, water, lemon juice, agave nectar, ginger, salt, cayenne, cumin and dates until smooth. Transfer to a bowl. Serve immediately or cover and refrigerate for up to 5 days.

Variation

If you are not a fan of spicy food, substitute 1 tbsp (15 mL) chopped jalapeño pepper for the cayenne. It will produce a much milder yet flavorful heat.

Miso Mushroom Gravy

This perfect blend of earthy mushrooms and nutritious miso is delicious as well as good for you. I like to serve this over Walnut Portobello Burgers (page 219), Meatloaf (page 254) or Sunflower Date Salisbury Steak (page 253).

Makes 1 cup (250 mL)

Tips

If you do not have brown rice miso, substitute an equal quantity of red miso or light miso, or an additional 2 tsp (10 mL) wheat-free tamari. However, be aware that unpasteurized brown rice miso is the closest form to being raw; it also doesn't contain gluten.

If you have a high-powered blender, use it to make this sauce.

2 cups	thinly sliced button mushrooms, divided	500 mL
½ cup	cold-pressed (extra virgin) olive oil, divided	125 mL
2 tsp	wheat-free tamari, divided	10 mL
1 tbsp	brown rice miso (see Tips, left)	15 mL
1	clove garlic	1
½ cup	water	175 mL
1 tbsp	chopped fresh thyme	15 mL

1. In a bowl, toss 1 cup (250 mL) sliced mushrooms with 2 tbsp (30 mL) olive oil and 1 tsp (5 mL) tamari. Set aside for 15 minutes to soften.
2. In a blender, combine remaining 1 cup (250 mL) mushrooms, olive oil and tamari, miso, garlic and water. Blend at high speed until smooth. Add to the reserved sliced mushrooms and stir in thyme. Serve immediately or cover and refrigerate for up to 3 days.

Wasabi Cream

This spicy cream sauce is perfect over Zucchini Noodles (page 244) garnished with freshly grated carrot and finished with a splash of sesame oil.

Makes 1 cup (250 mL)

Tips

To soak the cashews for this recipe, cover with 1 cup (250 mL) water. Set aside for 30 minutes. Drain, discarding soaking liquid. Rinse until the water runs clear.

If you have a high-powered blender, use it to make this sauce.

½ cup	raw cashews, soaked (see Tips, left)	125 mL
3 tbsp	filtered water	45 mL
3 tbsp	wheat-free tamari	45 mL
2 tbsp	wasabi powder	30 mL
1 tbsp	chopped gingerroot	15 mL
1 tsp	dried dulse flakes	5 mL

1. In a blender, combine soaked cashews, water, tamari, wasabi, ginger and dulse. Blend at high speed until smooth. Transfer to a bowl and serve immediately or cover and refrigerate for up to 3 days.

Miso Glaze Sauce

This sauce is a delicious blend of salty fermented miso and sweet agave nectar. I like to use this as a sauce on Walnut Portobello Burgers (page 219).

Makes 1 cup (250 mL)

Tip

Eating fermented foods such as miso can help to keep you healthy. Fermentation introduces healthy bacteria and lactic acid to the digestive tract, increasing the digestibility of some foods. Fermented foods also stimulate the immune system and support the absorption of nutrients.

½ cup	water	125 mL
¼ cup	brown rice miso (see Tip, left)	60 mL
3 tbsp	raw agave nectar	45 mL
1 tbsp	cold-pressed (extra virgin) olive oil	15 mL
1 tsp	apple cider vinegar	5 mL

1. In a blender, combine water, miso, agave nectar, olive oil and vinegar. Blend at high speed until smooth. Serve immediately or transfer to an airtight container, cover and refrigerate for up to 5 days.

Living Hot Sauce

Use this as a table condiment or as an addition to savory salad dressing or sauce recipes in this book, such as Red Pepper Basil Marinara Sauce (page 184).

Makes 3 cups (750 mL)

Tips

Increase the cayenne to as much as 1 tbsp (15 mL). If you like things less spicy, try using as little as ¼ tsp (1 mL).

Capsaicin, the heat source in chile peppers, possesses anti-inflammatory properties that may benefit health conditions involving low-grade inflammation, such as heart disease, arthritis and diabetes.

If you have a high-powered blender, use it to make this sauce.

½ cup	chopped red bell pepper	125 mL
½ cup	chopped jalapeño peppers	125 mL
3 tbsp	filtered water	45 mL
2 tbsp	apple cider vinegar	30 mL
1 tbsp	raw agave nectar	15 mL
2 tsp	cayenne pepper (see Tips, left)	10 mL
¼ tsp	fine sea salt	1 mL

1. In a food processor, process bell and jalapeño peppers, water, vinegar, agave nectar, cayenne and salt until smooth. Transfer to a container and serve immediately or cover and refrigerate for up to 3 days.

Variations

If you prefer a spicier sauce, substitute an equal quantity of Thai bird's-eye chiles for the jalapeños. If you prefer a milder version, omit 1 tsp (5 mL) of the cayenne pepper.

Piri-Piri Sauce

This spicy Portuguese sauce is a welcome addition to any meal. It is a great table condiment and also makes a nice addition to dips or spreads, such as Red Pepper, Dill and Cashew Ricotta (page 103) or Pumpkin Seed "Refried Beans" (page 93).

Makes ½ cup (125 mL)

Tip

When working with chile peppers, it is a good idea to use gloves. The essential oils found in the seeds and pith of the chile will stay on your hands and burn if you touch sensitive parts of your face such as your eyes.

¼ cup	cold-pressed (extra virgin) olive or flax oil	60 mL
¼ cup	chopped red chile peppers, stems removed (see Tip, left) or ½ tsp (2 mL) cayenne pepper	60 mL
1 tbsp	sweet paprika	15 mL
1 tbsp	chopped parsley leaves	15 mL
1	clove garlic	1
½ tsp	fine sea salt	2 mL

1. In a blender, combine olive oil, chiles, paprika, parsley, garlic and salt. Blend until smooth. Transfer to an airtight container, cover and refrigerate for up to 3 days.

My Favorite Hot Sauce

This tomato-based hot sauce is a perfect blend of hot and tangy. Used like ketchup, it provides a spicy kick to many dishes.

Makes ¾ cup (175 mL)

Tips

To soak the sun-dried tomatoes and dates for this recipe, cover with 1 cup (250 mL) water. Set aside for 30 minutes. Drain, discarding soaking water.

Substitute 3 tbsp (45 mL) chopped jalapeño peppers for the cayenne. If you like spice, substitute 3 tbsp (45 mL) chopped habanero chiles — they are one of the hottest chile peppers in the world.

¼ cup	dry-packed sun-dried tomatoes, soaked (see Tips, left)	60 mL
2	chopped pitted Medjool dates, soaked	2
¼ cup	filtered water	60 mL
3 tbsp	coconut oil	45 mL
2 tbsp	raw agave nectar	30 mL
2 tbsp	apple cider vinegar	30 mL
1 tbsp	freshly squeezed lemon juice	15 mL
2 tsp	cayenne pepper	10 mL
1	clove garlic	1
½ tsp	fine sea salt	2 mL

1. In a blender, combine soaked sun-dried tomatoes and dates, water, coconut oil, agave nectar, vinegar, lemon juice, cayenne, garlic and salt. Blend at high speed until smooth. Transfer to an airtight container or glass jar and refrigerate for up to 3 days.

Spicy Harissa Sauce

This North African-influenced hot sauce is packed full of flavor and nutrition. I like using it on salads or as a final finish to sauces topping raw pasta dishes.

Makes 1 cup (250 mL)

Tips

Cayenne pepper is pure ground dried cayenne chile peppers. It is very hot and should be used in moderation.

Capsaicin has been shown to improve digestive health and reduce the tendency for blood cells to clump (platelet aggregation), which helps to improve circulation and may reduce the risk for stroke.

2 cups	chopped red bell peppers	500 mL
¼ cup	cold-pressed (extra virgin) olive oil	60 mL
2 tbsp	freshly squeezed lemon juice	30 mL
1 tbsp	raw agave nectar	15 mL
1	clove garlic	1
½ tsp	caraway seeds	2 mL
½ tsp	ground coriander	2 mL
½ tsp	cayenne pepper (see Tips, left) or ¼ cup (60 mL) chopped jalapeño peppers	2 mL
¼ tsp	fine sea salt	1 mL

1. In a food processor fitted with the metal blade, process red peppers, olive oil, lemon juice, agave nectar, garlic, caraway seeds, coriander, cayenne and salt until smooth. Transfer to an airtight container or glass jar and refrigerate for up to 3 days.

Sun-Dried Tomato Ketchup

This raw ketchup recipe is so close to the real thing you won't be able to believe it is free of refined sugars and preservatives and completely uncooked.

Makes 2 cups (500 mL)

Tip

To soak the sun-dried tomatoes, dates and raisins for this recipe, cover with 2 cups (500 mL) water. Set aside for 30 minutes. Drain and rinse, reserving soaking water. Use 1 cup (250 mL) reserved soaking water to make the ketchup. If you do not have enough, add filtered water as required.

1 cup	dry-packed sun-dried tomatoes, soaked (see Tip, left)	250 mL
3	chopped pitted Medjool dates, soaked	3
2 tbsp	raisins, soaked	30 mL
1 cup	reserved soaking water (see Tip, left)	250 mL
2 tbsp	apple cider vinegar	30 mL

1. In a blender, preferably a high-powered one, combine soaked sun-dried tomatoes, dates and raisins, water and vinegar. Blend at high speed until smooth. Transfer to an airtight container and refrigerate for up to 5 days.

Variation

Substitute the raisins with 3 tbsp (45 mL) raw agave nectar and an additional Medjool date.

Sun-Dried Tomato Barbecue Sauce

This tangy sauce makes a delectable replacement for traditional sugar-laden barbecue sauces. It pairs well with raw food recipes where barbecuing would be the traditional method of preparation, such as mock burgers or meat. I like to serve this with Walnut Portobello Burgers (page 219) or Sun-Dried Tomato and Carrot Burgers (page 220), or as a dip for Eggplant Bacon (page 41).

Makes 2½ cups (625 mL)

Tips

To soak the sun-dried tomatoes for this recipe, place in a bowl and add 2 cups (500 mL) water. Cover and set aside for 30 minutes. Drain, discarding any remaining water.

When purchasing agave nectar, be sure to look for products labeled "raw." Most of the agave nectar on the market has been heated to a high temperature and does not qualify as raw food. If you have concerns, ask your purveyor.

If you have a high-powered blender, use it to make this sauce. With a regular blender, the texture is never as creamy and smooth.

1 cup	dry-packed sun-dried tomatoes, soaked (see Tips, left)	250 mL
1 cup	filtered water	250 mL
¼ cup	apple cider vinegar	60 mL
¼ cup	raw agave nectar (see Tips, left)	60 mL
3 tbsp	chopped green onion, green and white parts	45 mL
3 tbsp	cold-pressed (extra virgin) olive oil	45 mL
2 tbsp	freshly squeezed lemon juice	30 mL
1 tbsp	wheat-free tamari	15 mL
½ tsp	fine sea salt	2 mL
½ tsp	smoked sweet paprika, optional	2 mL
Pinch	cayenne pepper	Pinch

1. In a blender, combine soaked sun-dried tomatoes, water, vinegar, agave nectar, green onion, olive oil, lemon juice, tamari, salt, paprika, if using, and cayenne. Blend at high speed until smooth. Transfer to an airtight container or glass jar and refrigerate for up to 4 days.

Cocktail Sauce

This classic sauce, traditionally served as an accompaniment to shrimp, has a divine flavor, thanks in part to the fresh horseradish.

Makes 1½ cups (375 mL)

Tip

While wheat-free tamari is not raw, it is gluten-free. The raw alternative, nama shoyu, contains gluten. If you are following a completely raw diet, by all means substitute an equal quantity of nama shoyu.

1 cup	Sun-Dried Tomato Ketchup (page 198)	250 mL
¼ cup	freshly grated horseradish	60 mL
1 tbsp	wheat-free tamari (see Tip, left)	15 mL
1 tbsp	apple cider vinegar	15 mL

1. In a bowl, combine ingredients. Stir well. Set aside for 30 to 45 minutes. Transfer to an airtight container and refrigerate for up to 5 days.

Variation

Substitute the ketchup with ½ cup (125 mL) sun-dried tomatoes, 3 tbsp (45 mL) raisins and 4 pitted dates, soaked in 2 cups (500 mL) warm water for 30 minutes and drained. Add a dash of agave.

Raw Vegan Worcestershire Sauce

This sweet and tangy sauce has a perfect balance of sweet, sour, salty and spicy. I like to use it with dishes that contain mushrooms, or ingredients that can stand up to intense flavors. It is also great on Parsnip "Fried Rice" (page 275).

Makes 1 cup (250 mL)

Tip

Use tamarind that comes in a block, not the paste. To soak the tamarind, break off a piece about 2 inches (5 cm) wide and soak in 1 cup (250 mL) warm water for 1 hour. Drain and transfer to a food processor or a blender. Add ½ cup (125 mL) warm water and process until smooth. Transfer to a fine-mesh strainer and press pulp through, discarding solids.

¼ cup	tamarind, soaked (see Tip, left)	60 mL
¼ cup	filtered water	60 mL
¼ cup	chopped tomato	60 mL
3 tbsp	freshly squeezed orange juice	45 mL
2 tsp	freshly squeezed lime juice	10 mL
1	clove garlic	1
¼ tsp	ground allspice	1 mL
¼ tsp	ground cinnamon	1 mL

1. In a food processor fitted with the metal blade, process soaked tamarind, water, tomato, orange juice, lime juice, garlic, allspice and cinnamon until smooth. Transfer to an airtight container. Serve immediately or cover and refrigerate for up to 7 days.

Raw Mustard

Once you've tried this creamy raw mustard, you will never want to use mustard from a jar again. Use it any way you would use prepared mustard. I particularly enjoy it served on a Walnut Portobello Burger (page 219) or any raw sandwich. To gild the lily, add Eggplant Bacon (page 41) and some slices of fresh tomato.

Makes 1½ cups (375 mL)

Tips

To soak the mustard seeds for this recipe, place in a bowl and add 1 cup (250 mL) water. Cover and set aside for 30 minutes. Drain, discarding soaking water. Rinse under cold running water until the water runs clear.

To soak the dates for this recipe, place in a bowl and add 1 cup (250 mL) water. Cover and set aside for 30 minutes. Drain, discarding any remaining water.

Mustard seeds are spicy by nature. The longer you allow them to sit after they have been ground, the less spicy they become. I like to use yellow mustard seeds, as they have less of a kick. Brown mustard seeds are spicier than the yellow ones.

½ cup	mustard seeds, soaked (see Tips, left)	125 mL
4	chopped pitted Medjool dates, soaked (see Tips, left)	4
½ cup	cold-pressed flax or extra virgin olive oil	125 mL
¼ cup	freshly squeezed lemon juice	60 mL
1 tsp	fine sea salt	5 mL

1. In a blender, combine soaked mustard seeds and dates, flax oil, lemon juice and salt until smooth and creamy. Serve immediately or transfer to an airtight container and refrigerate for up to 7 days.

Variations

Instead of the oil in this recipe, substitute ¼ cup (60 mL) cashews soaked in 1 cup (250 mL) water for 30 minutes, then drained and rinsed, plus 3 tbsp (45 mL) filtered water. Purée before adding remaining ingredients.

Substitute 3 tbsp (45 mL) raw agave nectar for the dates.

If you have a high-powered blender, use it to make this mustard. It will be smoother and creamier than when made in a regular blender.

Red Pepper Mole Sauce

This sweet yet savory sauce is a perfect blend of chocolate and spice. Traditionally moles are cooked, but I often make this sauce when I do dinners with Mexican flavors. Try serving it with Bursting Burritos (page 250), Taco Salad (page 151) or Cauliflower Rice (page 274). Finish with a dollop of Cashew Sour Cream (page 204).

Makes 1 cup (250 mL)

Tips

To make this recipe, you'll need a dehydrator with moveable racks that can be adjusted so the peppers can stand upright.

Be sure to start the recipe well in advance, as the peppers need to be dehydrated for up to 10 hours.

Placing the softened and slightly warm peppers in a bowl and covering with plastic wrap allows steam to be trapped in the bowl, which blisters the skins of the peppers, helping to facilitate their removal.

Dehydrating the peppers brings out a layer of concentrated flavor that cannot be achieved with raw red peppers. If you do not have a dehydrator, you can use 2 cups (500 mL) chopped red peppers instead, but be aware that the flavor will not be as intense.

- **Electric food dehydrator (see Tips, left)**

3	red bell peppers	3
1 tbsp	olive oil	15 mL
1 tsp	sea salt, divided	5 mL
3 tbsp	melted coconut oil (see Tips, page 252)	45 mL
2 tbsp	raw cacao powder	30 mL
2 tsp	raw agave nectar	10 mL
½ tsp	ground cumin	2 mL
¼ tsp	ground coriander	1 mL
Pinch	cayenne pepper	Pinch

1. In a bowl, toss bell peppers, olive oil and ½ tsp (2 mL) salt. Arrange evenly on a nonstick dehydrator sheet. Dehydrate at 105°F (41°C) for 8 to 10 hours or until soft. Transfer to a bowl, cover with plastic and set aside for 20 minutes, until skin blisters.

2. Using a paring knife, gently remove the skin, membranes and seeds from the peppers. Place the flesh in a blender and add coconut oil, cacao powder, agave nectar, cumin, coriander, cayenne and remaining salt. Blend until smooth. Transfer to a serving bowl. Serve immediately or cover and refrigerate for up to 3 days.

Spicy Red Pepper Flax Oil

This flavorful oil can be used for a variety of applications. Being a chef, I like to use it as a garnish on the plate. It also makes a great addition to many dishes and can even stand in as a raw hot sauce to be sprinkled over a dish.

Makes 1 cup (250 mL)

Tips

This recipe is a great way to get healthy fats into your diet.

Flax oil contains a high amount of omega-3 fatty acids, which among other benefits help to regulate mood.

2 cups	chopped red bell pepper	250 mL
1/4 cup	cold-pressed flax oil	60 mL
1/2 tsp	freshly squeezed lemon juice	2 mL
1/4 tsp	fine sea salt	1 mL
1 tsp	cayenne pepper	5 mL

1. In a food processor, process ingredients until smooth, stopping the motor once or twice and scraping down the sides of the work bowl. Serve immediately or cover and refrigerate for up to 3 days.

Variation

Substitute 2 tbsp (30 mL) chopped jalapeño pepper for the cayenne.

Spirulina, Lemon and Ginger Hemp Oil

This simple recipe has many different uses. I like to drizzle it on soups, such as Corn and Red Pepper Chowder (page 121) or Cauliflower Gumbo (page 119).

Makes 1 cup (250 mL)

Tip

Simple recipes, such as this, that contain healthy fats such as hemp or flax oil are a great way to get nutrition into your body with little preparation. Because healthy oils are labeled as fats, some people don't realize that, although high in calories, when used in moderation they are actually good for you.

3/4 cup	cold-pressed hemp oil	175 mL
1 tbsp	finely grated lemon zest	15 mL
1/4 cup	freshly squeezed lemon juice	60 mL
2 tbsp	chopped gingerroot	30 mL
1 tsp	spirulina powder	5 mL

1. In a blender, combine hemp oil, lemon zest and juice, ginger and spirulina. Blend at high speed until smooth. Refrigerate for up to 3 days.

Variation

Lemon, Garlic and Thyme Flax Oil: Blend 1/2 cup (125 mL) flax oil with 2 tbsp (30 mL) freshly squeezed lemon juice, 1 tbsp (15 mL) lemon zest, 1 tbsp (15 mL) chopped fresh thyme leaves, 2 cloves garlic and 1/2 tsp (2 mL) sea salt.

Cashew Sour Cream

You will be surprised at how creamy and rich this non-dairy version of sour cream is. It is a perfect finish for many recipes in this book.

Makes 3 cups (750 mL)

2 cups	raw cashews, soaked (see Tips, left)	500 mL
¾ cup	filtered water	175 mL
⅓ cup	freshly squeezed lemon juice	75 mL
2 tbsp	apple cider vinegar (see Tips, left)	30 mL
1 tsp	fine sea salt	5 mL

Tips

To soak the cashews for this recipe, cover with 4 cups (1 L) water. Set aside for 30 minutes. Drain, discarding soaking water. Rinse under cold running water until water runs clear.

Apple cider vinegar is a healthy addition to your diet. Be sure to use versions containing the "mother." Because they are fermented, they add healthy bacteria to your gut.

1. In a blender, preferably a high-powered one, combine soaked cashews, water, lemon juice, vinegar and salt. Blend at high speed until smooth. Transfer to an airtight container and refrigerate for up to 5 days.

Variations

Use this basic recipe to build upon and create other sauces. I like to add 2 tbsp (30 mL) rehydrated sun-dried tomatoes, 1 tsp (5 mL) smoked paprika and ½ tsp (2 mL) chili powder to create a smoky tomato cashew cream.

Almond Parmesan Cheese

This light alternative to dairy cheese is rich, delicious and so pleasantly salty. The nutritional yeast provides the deep umami flavor traditionally associated with Parmesan. I like to have it on hand as a finish for many dishes.

Makes 2 cups (500 mL)

2 cups	whole raw almonds	500 mL
½ cup	nutritional yeast (see Tips, page 189)	125 mL
1 tsp	fine sea salt	5 mL

Tips

When processing almonds in a food processor, make sure not to overprocess. This will split the oils from the protein and cause clumping.

1. In a food processor, process ingredients until no large pieces of almonds remain. The mixture should be light and fluffy and contain no visible pieces. Use immediately or refrigerate for up to one month.

Variations

Substitute an equal quantity of walnuts for the almonds.

After the ingredients have been processed, add a chopped fresh herb such as thyme, parsley, chives, sage or rosemary and pulse a couple of times to blend.

Sesame Tartar Sauce

This creamy yet light sauce works equally as well as a salad dressing or as an accompaniment to many raw food dishes.

Makes 1½ cups (375 mL)

Tips

Tahini is a sesame seed paste. It has a wonderful creamy texture and provides calcium, phosphorus, vitamin E and both mono- and polyunsaturated fats.

If your sauce seems thin after processing, add 2 tbsp (30 mL) tahini and pulse to blend.

½ cup	tahini (see Tips, left)	125 mL
½ cup	filtered water	125 mL
3 tbsp	freshly squeezed lemon juice	45 mL
2 tbsp	chopped fresh dill	30 mL
1	clove garlic	1
½ tsp	fine sea salt	2 mL
¼ cup	chopped cucumber	60 mL
2 tbsp	chopped red onion	30 mL
2 tbsp	sesame seeds	30 mL

1. In a food processor fitted with the metal blade, process tahini, water, lemon juice, dill, garlic and salt until smooth and creamy. Transfer to a bowl and stir in the cucumber, onion and sesame seeds. Serve immediately or cover and refrigerate for up to 5 days.

Black Olive Relish

This delectable sauce is sweet and salty. I love serving it as a garnish over salad. It also balances the fat in dishes such as Cashew Alfredo Sauce (page 188).

Makes ½ cup (125 mL)

Tip

"Relish" is a term for a condiment that is both sweet and sour. I like to make different forms of relish using ingredients that compliment a dish. The key is find the right balance of sweet and sour.

1 cup	pitted black olives	250 mL
3 tbsp	raw agave nectar	45 mL
2 tbsp	apple cider vinegar	30 mL
1 tbsp	chopped red onion	15 mL
1	clove garlic	1

1. In a food processor fitted with the metal blade, pulse olives until slightly broken down. Add agave nectar, vinegar, onion and garlic and process until smooth, stopping the motor and scraping down the sides of the work bowl as necessary. Transfer to a bowl and serve immediately or cover and refrigerate for up to 5 days.

Variation

To add crispness and create a slightly watery texture, add ¼ cup (60 mL) chopped cucumber along with the onion.

Caramelized Onion and Cherry Tomato Relish

This sweet and tangy sauce is a perfect match for richer dishes that require a bit of acidity. I like serving this with Chickpea and Zucchini Fritters (page 284) or Sweet Potato and Zucchini Mac 'n' Cheese (page 247).

**Makes 1 cup
(250 mL)**

Tip

I like to think of the dehydrator as an oven that, instead of cooking food at a high heat, stripping away nutrients, works at a low temperature to slowly concentrate flavors. For example, all the flavors of a roasted pepper can still be achieved in raw food cuisine, but instead of cooking it at 450°F (230°C) for 8 minutes, it can be dehydrated at 105°F (41°C) for 10 hours. It may seem like a long time to wait for your food, but the end result is a healthy body and mind, nourished with the most nutrient-dense food possible.

• **Electric food dehydrator**

1 cup	cherry tomatoes	250 mL
2 tbsp	cold-pressed (extra virgin) olive oil	30 mL
½ tsp	fine sea salt, divided	2 mL
2 tbsp	raw agave nectar	30 mL
2 tsp	apple cider vinegar	10 mL
1 cup	Caramelized Onions (page 292)	250 mL

1. In a bowl, toss tomatoes, olive oil and ¼ tsp (1 mL) salt. Place on a nonstick dehydrator sheet and spread evenly. Dehydrate at 105°F (41°C) for 3 hours, until wilted and soft.

2. Transfer tomato mixture to a bowl and stir in agave nectar, vinegar and remaining salt. Add caramelized onions and stir well. Set aside for 30 to 45 minutes to meld flavors. Serve immediately or cover and refrigerate for up to 3 days.

Variation

The caramelized onions in this recipe can be substituted with ½ cup (125 mL) thinly sliced red onion tossed with 3 tbsp (45 mL) raw agave nectar, 2 tsp (10 mL) apple cider vinegar and a pinch of sea salt. Transfer to a nonstick dehydrator sheet and spread evenly. Dehydrate at 105°F (41°C) for 1 hour or until soft and translucent. Add to softened cherry tomato mixture and stir well.

Pickled Shaved Cucumber

I like to make up a batch of this tangy concoction and keep it in the fridge to nibble on or to use as a condiment on raw sandwiches. It also works as a side dish. Cool and crisp, it pairs well with Asian dishes.

Makes 1 cup (250 mL)

Tip

Cucumbers come in many different varieties. The two most common are field and English cucumbers. You can substitute 2 field cucumbers for the English cucumber called for in this recipe. If you are using an English cucumber, you do not need to remove the seeds before slicing. However, the seeds in a field cucumber are quite large and need to be removed. Before completing Step 1, cut the cucumber in half lengthwise and, using a spoon, scoop out and discard the seeds. Complete the recipe (you will have half-circle slices rather than rounds, which is fine).

- **Mandoline or food processor fitted with the slicing blade**

1	large English cucumber	1
3 tbsp	raw agave nectar	45 mL
2 tbsp	apple cider vinegar	30 mL
1 tbsp	wheat-free tamari	15 mL
2 tsp	black sesame seeds	10 mL
2 tsp	sesame oil (untoasted)	10 mL
1/4 tsp	fine sea salt	1 mL

1. Cut the cucumber in half crosswise. Using a mandoline or a food processor fitted with the slicing blade, cut into slices approximately 1/4 inch (0.5 cm) thick. Transfer to a bowl.

2. In a small bowl, combine agave nectar, vinegar, tamari, sesame seeds, sesame oil and salt. Add to sliced cucumber and toss well. Set aside for 1 hour to soften and meld flavors. Serve immediately or cover and refrigerate for up to 2 days.

Pickled Red Onions

These sweet-and-sour onions are a perfect accompaniment for entrees that need a little zip. They make a great finish for raw sandwiches or burgers. I also like to add them to dishes that use Yellow Coconut Curry Sauce (page 192).

Makes 1 cup (250 mL)

Tip

If you are using a food processor to slice the onions, you will need to halve them lengthwise first so they can fit in the feed tube. Be sure to place them upright in the tube; this will produce half-circles rather than rounds, which is fine.

- Mandoline or food processor fitted with the slicing blade

1	large red onion	1
3 tbsp	raw agave nectar	45 mL
2 tbsp	filtered water	30 mL
1 tbsp	apple cider vinegar	15 mL
¼ tsp	fine sea salt	1 mL

1. Using a mandoline, slice onion into rounds approximately ¼ inch (0.5 cm) thick. Transfer to a bowl and toss with agave nectar, water, vinegar and salt. Cover and set aside for 1 to 2 hours or until soft and translucent. Cover and refrigerate for up to 5 days.

Gremolata

This mixture, Italian in origin, is a flavorful addition to many salads, sauces and dressings. I also enjoy it as a spread on Zucchini Hemp Bread (page 324).

Makes 1 cup (250 mL)

Tip

For this recipe, use flat-leaf parsley, which has more flavor than the curly variety. When parsley needs to be chopped, I usually use curly parsley, as it will oxidize less.

½ cup	chopped parsley leaves (see Tip, left)	125 mL
¼ cup	cold-pressed flax oil	60 mL
3 tbsp	finely grated lemon zest	45 mL
3 tbsp	freshly squeezed lemon juice	45 mL
2	cloves garlic, minced	2
½ tsp	fine sea salt	2 mL

1. In a bowl, combine ingredients. Mix well and set aside for 15 minutes. Serve immediately or refrigerate for up to 5 days.

Variation

For an Asian version of gremolata, substitute ½ cup (125 mL) chopped cilantro for the parsley, ¼ cup (60 mL) sesame oil for the flax oil, 3 tbsp (45 mL) lime juice for the lemon and an equal quantity of lime zest for the lemon zest. Add 1 tbsp (15 mL) raw agave nectar, 2 tsp (10 mL) sesame seeds, 2 tsp (10 mL) wheat-free tamari and 2 tsp (10 mL) chopped gingerroot.

The Main Event

One of the most difficult things when transitioning to a raw food diet is the fear that you will miss many meals you once loved — hot pasta wallowing in tomato sauce, pizza or a great sandwich. Until you've learned how to substitute other, more nutritious dishes for these old favorites, you may find yourself trying to fill this void with less than optimum choices. In this chapter you'll find many main-course recipes to meet that need, from pizza to burgers and burritos — and for those who think they can't live without pasta, there are several recipes, including Pasta Bolognese (page 245).

In a raw food diet, main courses are distinguished by their ingredients. Many traditional main-course dishes include components such as meat and dairy. In the raw food kitchen, ingredients such as nuts, seeds or mushrooms replace meat. They are paired with robust flavors such as wheat-free tamari or nutritional yeast, garlic and other aromatics, herbs and spices, and cold-pressed oils. Substitutes for creamy sauces are easily created from ingredients such as raw cashews and tahini. Successful results depend upon understanding what you are trying to provide in a recipe and creating it with raw, nutrient-dense ingredients.

Many of the dishes in this chapter are particularly satisfying because they create umami. Umami is the fifth flavor, an addition to the traditional four flavors: sweet, sour, salty and bitter. Umami, which means "delicious flavor" in Japanese, describes a kind of savory taste. It is found in foods that contain glutamates, such as some meats, vegetables and cheese. Fortunately, some vegetables — for instance, mushrooms and eggplant — can be flavored to create umami. When you marinate mushrooms in tamari, miso, oil and water, you imbue them with additional flavor and create a particularly pleasing mouth feel. The end result helps you to feel satiated and content.

In raw food cuisine we deliberately use ingredients that help bring umami flavor to foods. These include nutritional yeast, wheat-free tamari and miso. With their encouragement, simple ingredients such as thinly sliced vegetables or seeds are transformed into dishes that are as satisfying as an entire traditional cooked meal.

In raw food cuisine it is important to understand how all the ingredients come together to create something that is greater than the sum of its parts. For example, a simple pâté made from seasoned soaked pumpkin seeds can stand in for traditional refried beans. And when you stuff it into a tortilla made from vegetables and add some guacamole, fresh raw salsa and lettuce, you have a delicious burrito. It is the act of bringing all the ingredients together that creates the unique and satisfying experience of enjoying a well-executed raw food recipe.

Stuffed Portobello Towers

This recipe is a delicious blend of rich, meaty flavors that really complement the chimichurri sauce. I like to serve this with a side of Zucchini Noodles (page 244) tossed in Cashew Alfredo Sauce (page 188). If you're serving more people, double or triple this recipe to suit your needs.

Makes 2 servings

Tips

Be sure to use all the marinade; there needs to be enough so the mushrooms can soften. It is particularly important to wet the gill side well (the dark brown underside of the mushroom). If that side is well soaked, the liquid will spread evenly throughout the mushroom.

If the stacked mushrooms don't fit between the racks of your dehydrator, warm them in a single layer in Step 3, then stack to serve.

While wheat-free tamari is not raw, it is gluten-free. The raw alternative for tamari, nama shoyu, does contain gluten. If you are following a completely raw diet and can tolerate gluten, by all means substitute an equal quantity of nama shoyu.

- **Electric food dehydrator**

½ cup	cold-pressed (extra virgin) olive oil	125 mL
¼ cup	wheat-free tamari (see Tips, left)	60 mL
3 tbsp	chopped fresh thyme leaves	45 mL
1 tbsp	chili powder	15 mL
1 tbsp	finely grated orange zest	15 mL
6	large portobello mushrooms, stems removed	6
1 cup	Pumpkin Seed Chimichurri (page 92), divided	250 mL

1. In a bowl, combine olive oil, tamari, thyme, chili powder and orange zest. Mix well. Brush mixture liberally over mushrooms, making sure all sides of the mushrooms are covered. Place mushrooms on nonstick dehydrator sheets and dehydrate at 105°F (41°C) for 45 to 60 minutes or until soft, basting once or twice with any liquid they expel. Remove from dehydrator.

2. Place 2 of the mushrooms, gill side up, on a work surface. Spread ¼ cup (60 mL) of the chimichurri sauce evenly over each mushroom. Repeat, placing the next 2 mushrooms, gill side up, on top of the first two. Place remaining 2 mushrooms on top, gill side down, and lightly press together.

3. Return stacked mushrooms to dehydrator and dehydrate at 105°F (41°C) for 45 minutes, until firmed up and slightly warm.

Variations

Substitute an equal quantity of Sweet Chili and Pecan Pâté (page 96) or Cashew Spinach Dip (page 83) for the Pumpkin Seed Chimichurri.

Spinach, Mushroom and Red Pepper Quiche

This is a soft and creamy delight. Accompany this tasty quiche with a simple salad and enjoy a wonderful meal. It even makes a delicious breakfast — if you have a busy day ahead and want something substantial, this provides a good amount of protein, which means it will keep you feeling full until lunchtime. Perhaps surprisingly, it is actually time-efficient as a breakfast dish. You can make the crust up to two weeks ahead of time and make the filling the night before and refrigerate it. Simply fill the shell in the morning and set it in the dehydrator to warm while you are showering.

Makes 4 servings

Tip

To soak the cashews for this recipe, place in a bowl and add 6 cups (1.5 L) filtered water. Cover and set aside for 30 minutes. Drain, discarding soaking water. Rinse under cold running water until the water runs clear.

- **Electric food dehydrator**
- **Four 6-inch (15 cm) quiche molds, lined with plastic wrap**

Crust

1 cup	whole raw almonds	250 mL
1/3 cup	ground flax seeds (see Tips, page 213)	75 mL
1/4 cup	(approx.) filtered water	60 mL
3 tbsp	almond butter	45 mL
1 tbsp	chopped fresh thyme leaves	15 mL
1/4 tsp	fine sea salt	1 mL

Filling

3 cups	raw cashews, soaked (see Tip, left)	750 mL
1/4 cup	nutritional yeast (see Tips, page 213)	60 mL
1/4 cup	freshly squeezed lemon juice	60 mL
1 tbsp	fine sea salt	15 mL
3	cloves garlic	3
1 cup	chopped red bell pepper	250 mL
1/2 cup	chopped spinach	125 mL
1/2 cup	Marinated Mushrooms (page 292)	125 mL

1. *Crust:* In a food processor fitted with the metal blade, pulse almonds until flour-like in consistency. Transfer to a bowl. Add flax seeds, water, almond butter, thyme and salt and stir until mixture is the consistency of pastry, adding more water if necessary.

2. Divide mixture into 4 equal parts and press into prepared quiche molds. Dehydrate at 105°F (41°C) for 7 to 8 hours, until firm (you want to be able to peel the crust away from the mold without cracking it). Remove crusts from molds.

Tips

When a recipe calls for flax seeds, you have two options to choose from: golden or brown. They are basically interchangeable except for the effect they have on the color of the product. Golden seeds produce a lighter shade of brown. In this recipe I prefer to use golden flax seeds to keep the color of the crust similar to that of traditional quiche.

Nutritional yeast is used in vegan and raw food diets mainly because it is a source of vitamin B_{12}. It is pasteurized, so technically it does not qualify as a raw food. However, in addition to necessary nutrients, it adds a deep, umami-like flavor to many dishes.

3. Return crusts to dehydrator and dehydrate for 1 to 2 hours at 105°F (41°C) or until completely dry and crisp. Allow to cool and place in an airtight container. Store at room temperature for up to 2 weeks.

4. *Filling:* In a food processor fitted with the metal blade, process nutritional yeast, lemon juice, salt and garlic, until garlic is chopped. Add red pepper and spinach and process until vegetables are puréed. Add soaked cashews and process until puréed, about 2 minutes. Scrape down the sides of the work bowl and process until purée is smooth. Transfer to a bowl and add marinated mushrooms. Stir well.

5. *Assembly:* Divide filling evenly among the crusts. Return to dehydrator and dehydrate at 105°F (41°C) for 30 to 45 minutes, until slightly warmed through.

Sun-Dried Tomato and Basil Tart

This tart is a rich blend of succulent sun-dried tomatoes, aromatic basil and heart-healthy macadamia nuts. Its rich flavor pairs well with a simple salad of fresh romaine lettuce and torn basil leaves tossed in extra virgin olive oil and fresh lemon juice. You can double or triple the recipe to suit your needs.

Makes 2 servings

Tips

To soak the macadamia nuts for this recipe, place them in a bowl with 1 cup (250 mL) water. Cover and set aside for 30 minutes. Drain, discarding soaking water. Rinse under cold running water until the water runs clear.

To soak the sun-dried tomatoes for this recipe, place in a bowl and add 1 cup (250 mL) warm water. Set aside for 30 minutes. Drain, discarding soaking water.

- **Electric food dehydrator**
- **Two 6-inch (15 cm) quiche molds, lined with plastic wrap**

Crust

¾ cup	raw cashews	175 mL
¼ cup	raw pine nuts	60 mL
2 tbsp	ground flax seeds	30 mL
1 tbsp	nutritional yeast (see Tips, page 213)	15 mL
1	clove garlic	1
1 tsp	dried oregano	5 mL
½ tsp	fine sea salt	2 mL
3 tbsp	filtered water	45 mL
1 tbsp	cold-pressed (extra virgin) olive oil	15 mL

Filling

½ cup	raw macadamia nuts, soaked (see Tips, left)	125 mL
¼ cup	dry-packed sun-dried tomatoes, soaked (see Tips, left)	60 mL
2 cups	packed basil leaves	500 mL
¼ cup	chopped tomato	60 mL
2 tbsp	filtered water	30 mL
2 tbsp	freshly squeezed lemon juice	30 mL
2 tbsp	cold-pressed (extra virgin) olive oil	30 mL
1 tbsp	nutritional yeast	15 mL
¼ tsp	fine sea salt	1 mL

1. *Crust:* In a food processor fitted with the metal blade, process cashews, pine nuts, flax seeds, nutritional yeast, garlic, oregano, salt, water and olive oil, until mixture is blended and nuts are broken down but retain some of their texture.

2. Divide mixture into 2 equal portions and, using your fingers, gently press into quiche molds. Dehydrate at 105°F (41°C) for 3 to 4 hours or until firm (you want to be able to peel the crust away from the mold without cracking it). Remove crusts from molds.

Tip

When processing ingredients in a food processor, be aware that they have a tendency to be propelled away from the blade and up the sides of the work bowl. If you see this happening, stop the motor and use a rubber spatula to scrape down the sides of the work bowl.

3. Return crusts to dehydrator and dehydrate for 2 to 3 hours at 105°F (41°C), until completely dry and crisp. Allow to cool and store at room temperature for up to 2 weeks.

4. *Filling:* In a food processor fitted with the metal blade, process soaked macadamia nuts and sun-dried tomatoes, basil, chopped tomato, water, lemon juice, olive oil, nutritional yeast and salt for 2 to 3 minutes or until smooth, stopping the motor and scraping down the sides of the work bowl as necessary.

5. *Assembly:* Divide filling evenly between the crusts. Return to dehydrator and dehydrate at 105°F (41°C) for 1 hour or until warmed through.

Variations

Substitute ¾ cup (175 mL) raw cashews for the macadamia nuts.

Add 1 tsp (5 mL) dried Italian seasoning to the crust in Step 1.

Garlic, Spinach and Mushroom Tarts

These crunchy tarts have a creamy filling with a delectable garlicky flavor. I love this dish because it is satisfying and provides me with some of the traditional flavors of its cooked counterpart. I like to serve it with a simple arugula salad tossed with extra virgin olive oil and lemon juice.

Makes 4 servings

Tips

To soak the cashews for this recipe, place in a bowl and add 2 cups (500 mL) water. Cover and set aside for 30 minutes. Drain, discarding soaking water, and rinse under cold running water until water runs clear.

While wheat-free tamari is not raw, it is gluten-free. The raw alternative for tamari, nama shoyu, does contain gluten. If you are following a completely raw diet and can tolerate gluten, by all means substitute an equal quantity of nama shoyu.

- **Electric food dehydrator**
- **Four 6-inch (15 cm) quiche molds, lined with plastic wrap**

Crust

1 cup	whole raw almonds	250 mL
1/3 cup	ground flax seeds	75 mL
3 tbsp	almond butter	45 mL
1 tbsp	chopped fresh thyme leaves	15 mL
1 tsp	fine sea salt	5 mL
1/4 cup	(approx.) filtered water	60 mL
2 tbsp	cold-pressed (extra virgin) olive oil	30 mL

Filling

1 cup	raw cashews, soaked (see Tips, left)	250 mL
2 cups	Marinated Mushrooms (page 292)	500 mL
2 cups	chopped baby spinach	500 mL
3 tbsp	wheat-free tamari (see Tips, left)	45 mL
3 tbsp	nutritional yeast	45 mL
3	cloves garlic	3
2 tbsp	chopped fresh thyme leaves	30 mL
1 tsp	fine sea salt	5 mL

1. *Crust:* In a food processor fitted with the metal blade, pulse almonds until flour-like in consistency. Transfer to a bowl. Add flax seeds, almond butter, thyme, salt, water and olive oil. Stir until mixture is the consistency of pastry, adding more water if necessary.

2. Divide mixture into 4 equal parts and press into quiche molds. Dehydrate at 105°F (41°C) for 7 to 8 hours, until firm (you want to be able to peel the crust away from the mold without cracking it). Remove crusts from molds.

3. Return crusts to dehydrator and dehydrate for 1 to 2 hours at 105°F (41°C) or until completely dry and crisp. Allow to cool and place in an airtight container. Store at room temperature for up to 2 weeks.

4. *Filling*: In a food processor fitted with the metal blade, process soaked cashews, marinated mushrooms, spinach, tamari, nutritional yeast, garlic, thyme and salt, stopping the motor once or twice and scraping down the sides of the work bowl.

5. *Assembly*: Divide filling evenly among the crusts. Return to dehydrator and dehydrate at 105°F (41°C) for 30 to 45 minutes, until slightly warmed through.

Variations

Substitute the filling with 3 cups (750 mL) Cashew Spinach Dip (page 83) or 3 cups (750 mL) Herbed Mushroom Duxelles (page 102).

Creamy Walnut and Mushroom Stew

> This dish was inspired by traditional beef stroganoff. The wheat-free tamari stands in for veal stock, hearty mushrooms take the place of the beef, and it is finished with dairy-free cashew sour cream instead of the real thing. Serve it over Daikon Radish "Egg Noodles" (page 234) or, for something a little different, pair with Sweet Potato Chips (page 301).

Makes 4 servings

Tips

Substitute up to 2 cups (500 mL) of the button mushrooms with a more exotic type such as chanterelles or king oyster mushrooms.

Add some chopped fresh herbs such as parsley, chives or thyme in Step 2.

I love mushrooms, not only for their meaty texture but also because they provide a savory flavor called umami, which is detected by unique taste receptors on the tongue. Umami is the fifth flavor, in addition to sweet, salty, bitter and sour. It is often found in fermented foods and is particularly abundant in shiitake mushrooms.

- **Electric food dehydrator**

4 cups	quartered trimmed button mushrooms	1 L
1/4 cup	cold-pressed (extra virgin) olive oil	60 mL
1 tbsp	ground cumin	15 mL
1/2 tsp	fine sea salt	2 mL
Pinch	freshly ground black pepper	Pinch
3 tbsp	wheat-free tamari	45 mL
1 cup	Cashew Sour Cream (page 204)	250 mL
1/2 cup	chopped walnut halves	125 mL
3 tbsp	sliced green onions, green part only	45 mL

1. In a bowl, toss together mushrooms, olive oil, cumin, salt, pepper and tamari. Transfer to a nonstick dehydrator sheet and spread evenly. Dehydrate at 105°F (41°C) for 35 to 45 minutes, until mushrooms are soft all the way through and give the appearance of having been lightly sautéed.

2. Transfer to a bowl. Add cashew sour cream, walnuts and green onions. Toss to coat and taste for seasoning, adding more salt if necessary. Serve immediately or transfer to an airtight container and refrigerate for up to 2 days.

Walnut Portobello Burgers

These mushroom burgers are delectable. I like to serve them between two crisp romaine lettuce leaves, garnished with Sun-Dried Tomato Ketchup (page 198), Perfect Guacamole (page 81) and some sliced tomatoes.

Tips

To soak the walnuts and pumpkin seeds for this recipe, place in a bowl and add 2 cups (500 mL) water. Cover and set aside for 1 hour. Drain and rinse.

The outer stalks of celery can be tough and fibrous. For best results, peel the stalk with a vegetable peeler. Save the peel to make soups, sauces or stocks.

When you are dehydrating plant foods with the intention of making them seem like meat, make sure you do not dehydrate too much. The food should be dry on the outside but remain soft in the middle. This will give the mouth feel of meat and help to create a pleasant texture.

• **Electric food dehydrator**

1 cup	walnut pieces, soaked (see Tips, left)	250 mL
¼ cup	raw pumpkin seeds, soaked	60 mL
3 cups	chopped trimmed portobello mushrooms	750 mL
¼ cup	wheat-free tamari	60 mL
3 tbsp	cold-pressed (extra virgin) olive oil	45 mL
1 tsp	fine sea salt	5 mL
½ cup	shredded carrot	125 mL
¼ cup	finely diced celery (see Tips, left)	60 mL
¼ cup	finely diced red onion	60 mL
2 tbsp	chopped fresh thyme leaves	30 mL
¾ cup	ground flax seeds	175 mL

1. In a bowl, combine mushrooms, tamari, olive oil and salt. Mix well and set aside for 30 to 45 minutes, until mushrooms are soft all the way through and look as if they have been lightly sautéed.

2. In a food processor fitted with the metal blade, pulse soaked walnuts and pumpkin seeds until they are the consistency of baby food, stopping the motor and scraping down the sides of the work bowl as necessary.

3. In a separate large bowl, stir carrot, celery and onion. Add mushroom mixture and mix well. Add walnut mixture and mix. Add flax seeds and mix well.

4. Using a ½-cup (125 mL) measure, divide into equal portions and place on nonstick dehydrator sheets at least 2 inches (5 cm) apart. Using the palm of your hand, flatten into patties. Dehydrate at 105°F (41°C) for 3 to 4 hours, until firm enough to handle. Flip and transfer to mesh sheets. Return to dehydrator and dehydrate for another 1 to 2 hours, until they are dry throughout but retain a bit of moisture in the middle.

Variations

Substitute other meaty mushrooms such as creminis or chanterelles for the portobellos. Or try a mixture of mushrooms, for instance, 1 cup (250 mL) each button, shiitake and oyster mushrooms.

Sun-Dried Tomato and Carrot Burgers

These burgers are so rich and meaty they will satisfy any carnivorous cravings. Try spreading Sun-Dried Tomato Ketchup (page 198) on top and serve each burger between two crisp lettuce leaves. Simply delicious!

Makes 10 to 12 burgers

Tips

To soak the sun-dried tomatoes for this recipe, cover with 4 cups (1 L) water. Set aside for 30 minutes. Drain, discarding liquid.

To soak the sunflower seeds for this recipe, cover with 4 cups (1 L) water. Set aside for 30 minutes. Drain, discarding water and any shells or unwanted particles. Rinse under cold running water until the water runs clear.

When processing this mixture, make sure all the ingredients are well incorporated; this will ensure a finished product that truly resembles a traditional hamburger. If the mixture becomes too stiff from the flax seeds, add a little more water until the desired consistency is reached.

When a recipe calls for flax seeds, you have two options to choose from. Golden flax will yield a lighter color, while brown flax seeds will make the final product darker. I like to use brown flax seeds in this recipe to give the burger a darker color, but golden flax seeds will produce an acceptable result.

- **Electric food dehydrator**

2½ cups	dry-packed sun-dried tomatoes, soaked (see Tips, left)	625 mL
2 cups	raw sunflower seeds, soaked (see Tips, left)	500 mL
2 cups	chopped carrots	500 mL
½ cup	chopped red onion	125 mL
2	cloves garlic	2
¼ cup	(approx.) filtered water	60 mL
2 cups	ground flax seeds (see Tips, left)	500 mL

1. In a food processor fitted with the metal blade, process carrots, onion and garlic until smooth and no large pieces of vegetable remain. Transfer to a bowl.

2. Add soaked sun-dried tomatoes, sunflower seeds and water to the food processor and process until smooth, stopping the motor and scraping down the sides of the work bowl as necessary. Add to carrot mixture, along with flax seeds, and mix well.

3. Using a large ice cream scoop, divide mixture into 10 to 12 equal portions and place on nonstick dehydrator sheets at least 2 inches (5 cm) apart. Using the palm of your hand, flatten into patties. Dehydrate at 105°F (41°C) for 5 to 6 hours, until firm enough to handle. Flip and transfer to mesh sheets. Return to dehydrator and dehydrate for 2 to 3 hours or until firm on the outside but still soft in the middle.

Variations

For a spicy Italian sausage flavor, add 2 tbsp (30 mL) whole fennel seeds, 1 tbsp (15 mL) ground cumin and ½ tsp (2 mL) cayenne pepper.

Substitute the sunflower seeds with an equal amount of pumpkin seeds.

Hemp and Sunflower Banquet Burgers

These are my favorite burgers. Their flavor pairs well with many sauces. I enjoy them on Zucchini Hemp Bread (page 324), garnished with crisp lettuce, Sun-Dried Tomato Ketchup (page 198) and Raw Mustard (page 201). For a "bacon cheeseburger," add Cashew Cheddar Cheese (page 105) and Eggplant Bacon (page 41).

Makes 4 burgers

Tips

To soak the sunflower seeds for this recipe, cover with 2 cups (500 mL) water. Set aside for 30 minutes. Drain, discarding water and any shells or unwanted particles. Rinse under cold running water until the water runs clear.

You can purchase flax seeds that are already ground (often described as milled) in vacuum-sealed bags, or you can grind them yourself. Depending upon the quantity you need, grind whole flax seeds in a blender or a spice grinder. Once ground (or after the vacuum-sealed bag has been opened), the beneficial fatty acids begin to dissipate. Store ground flax seeds away from light, in an airtight container in the refrigerator or freezer, for up to 2 months.

Do not over-dehydrate the burgers. Keeping the inside a bit soft gives you the mouth feel of a real burger. To check for doneness, stick a toothpick into the middle of the burger. If it comes out clean, the patty is ready to be removed from the dehydrator.

- **Electric food dehydrator**

1 cup	raw sunflower seeds, soaked (see Tips, left)	250 mL
1 cup	chopped red bell pepper	250 mL
½ cup	chopped celery	125 mL
¼ cup	chopped onion	60 mL
½ cup	filtered water	125 mL
3 tbsp	cold-pressed hemp oil	45 mL
2 tbsp	freshly squeezed lemon juice	30 mL
1 tsp	fine sea salt	5 mL
1 tsp	dried oregano	5 mL
1 tsp	chili powder	5 mL
4	cloves garlic	4
¼ cup	raw shelled hemp seeds	60 mL
½ cup	ground flax seeds (see Tips, left)	125 mL

1. In a food processor fitted with the metal blade, process red pepper, celery, onion, water, hemp oil, lemon juice, salt, oregano, chili powder and garlic, until smooth. Add soaked sunflower seeds and hemp seeds and process until smooth, stopping the motor and scraping down the sides of the work bowl as necessary. Transfer to a bowl.

2. Add flax seeds and mix well. Set aside for 10 minutes so the flax can absorb the liquid and swell.

3. Divide into 4 equal portions and, using your hands, flatten into patties. Place on a nonstick dehydrator sheet at least 2 inches (5 cm) apart. Dehydrate at 105°F (41°C) for 3 to 4 hours or until firm enough to handle. Flip and transfer to mesh sheet. Return to dehydrator and dehydrate for 1 to 2 hours or until firm on the outside but still soft in the middle. Serve immediately with the accompaniments of your choice.

Variation

Replace the hemp seeds with ¼ cup (60 mL) sesame seeds.

Cold Cuts Sandwich

This hearty sandwich is one of the best raw food re-creations ever. The various layers and different textures will make you believe you are eating a traditional sandwich. You can increase the quantity to make as many portions as you like. Serve this with a basic green salad or Simple Marinated Kale Salad (page 142) for a complete meal.

Makes 1 serving

Tip

When making sandwiches, it is always a good idea to spread both sides of the bread with a layer of fat before adding the filling. This will ensure that the bread will not become soggy, because the fat (mayonnaise, in this case) creates a barrier that protects it from moisture in the food.

2 slices	Zucchini Hemp Bread (page 324)	2 slices
¼ cup	Sun-Dried Tomato Hemp Mayonnaise (page 88)	60 mL
¼ cup	thinly sliced romaine lettuce (about 2 leaves)	60 mL
1	small tomato, sliced	1
¼ cup	Eggplant Bacon (page 41)	60 mL
1 slice	Sunflower Date Salisbury Steak (page 253)	1 slice

1. Lay the bread on a flat surface and spread each slice liberally with the mayonnaise. Place lettuce, tomato, Eggplant Bacon and Sunflower Date Salisbury Steak on top of one slice of bread. Top with second slice and cut on the diagonal. Serve immediately.

Sun-Dried Tomato and Zucchini Club Sandwich

This raw sandwich is a standout. It is one of my favorite go-to recipes because it is so easy to make and the flavors combine so well. I love the smoky, salty bacon with the rich avocado. Serve this with simple accompaniments such as Greek Kale Salad (page 143) and Sweet Potato Chips (page 301).

Makes 2 servings

Tip

One of the keys to making this sandwich delicious is to spread enough mayonnaise on the bread. Because the bread is low in fat it needs moisture to create a good mouth feel.

4 slices	Zucchini Hemp Bread (page 324)	4 slices
½ cup	Sun-Dried Tomato Hemp Mayonnaise, divided (page 88)	125 mL
1	large tomato, sliced	1
½ cup	crumbled Eggplant Bacon (page 41), divided	125 mL
½	large avocado, sliced	½
1 tbsp	Lemon Avocado Dressing (page 177), divided	15 mL

1. Spread 2 tbsp (30 mL) mayonnaise on one side of each slice of bread. On one piece, place half of the tomato slices, followed by half the Eggplant Bacon, half the sliced avocado and half of the Lemon Avocado Dressing. Repeat with a second slice.

2. Place remaining bread on top and press down lightly. Slice each sandwich in half diagonally and serve immediately.

Variations

Substitute an equal quantity of Spicy Cashew Mayonnaise (page 87) or Perfect Guacamole (page 81) for the Sun-Dried Tomato Hemp Mayonnaise.

"Barbecue" Pulled Burdock Sandwich

Burdock is a root that can be found in most well-stocked supermarkets as well as natural foods stores. It has a somewhat woody flavor that combines well with barbecue sauce. The end result is a tangy yet slightly sweet filling that can be served on bread, as called for in this recipe, or even between crisp romaine lettuce leaves. I love to slather this sandwich with Caramelized Onions (page 292) and Cashew Sour Cream (page 204). Be sure to start this recipe three days before you want to serve it, because the burdock needs time to pickle.

Makes 4 servings

Tips

Burdock is fibrous in texture. You need to shred or slice it thinly in order to allow the marinade to penetrate.

Burdock will begin to oxidize (turn brown) as soon as it is cut. If you prefer it to remain light colored, prepare your pickling solution before shredding. Transfer the burdock to the liquid immediately after it has been shredded.

You can use a box grater to shred the burdock, but it will be more difficult than using a food processor.

- Box grater or food processor fitted with the shredding blade

1 cup	filtered water	250 mL
¼ cup	apple cider vinegar	60 mL
3 tbsp	raw agave nectar	45 mL
1 tsp	fine sea salt	5 mL
2 cups	shredded peeled burdock root (about 2 medium)	500 mL
1½ cups	Sun-Dried Tomato Barbecue Sauce (page 199)	375 mL
4 slices	Buckwheat Toast (page 36)	4 slices

1. In a deep, non-reactive container, combine water, vinegar, agave nectar and salt. Add shredded burdock and toss well. Cover and set aside for 2 to 3 days, until burdock has become soft enough to chew easily.
2. Transfer to a colander and drain. Rinse well under cold running water and transfer to a bowl.
3. Toss pickled burdock with Sun-Dried Tomato Barbecue Sauce. Place Buckwheat Toast on a serving plate and spoon burdock overtop. Serve immediately as an open-face sandwich.

Variations

Instead of the Buckwheat Toast, substitute an equal quantity of Zucchini Hemp Bread (page 324), or use 8 romaine lettuce leaves to make a sandwich.

If you feel like gilding the lily, top your sandwich with 3 tbsp (45 mL) chopped Caramelized Onions (page 292) and smother it in ¼ cup (60 mL) Cashew Sour Cream (page 204).

Lemon and Cilantro Falafels

This protein-packed treat is much better for you than traditional falafels. The cilantro and lemon provide fabulous flavor. I drizzle these with Lemon Avocado Dressing (page 177) and serve them between two crisp leaves of romaine lettuce.

Makes 10 to 15 falafels

Tips

To soak the chickpeas for this recipe, place in a bowl and add 2 cups (500 mL) water. Cover and set aside for 3 hours. Drain, discarding soaking water. Rinse under cold running water until water runs clear.

You can purchase flax seeds that are already ground (often described as milled) in vacuum-sealed bags, or you can grind them yourself. Depending upon the quantity you need, grind whole flax seeds in a blender or a spice grinder. Once ground (or after the vacuum-sealed bag is opened), the beneficial fatty acids begin to dissipate. Store ground flax seeds in an airtight container in the refrigerator or freezer for up to 2 months.

When a recipe calls for flax seeds, you have two options to choose from: golden or brown. Golden flax seeds will yield a lighter color for the end result, while brown flax seeds will make the final product darker.

- **Electric food dehydrator**

1 cup	chickpeas, soaked (see Tips, left)	250 mL
1 cup	chopped cilantro leaves	250 mL
2 tbsp	finely grated lemon zest	30 mL
¼ cup	freshly squeezed lemon juice	60 mL
¼ cup	cold-pressed flax oil	60 mL
1 tbsp	cumin seeds	15 mL
1 tbsp	ground cumin	15 mL
5	cloves garlic	5
2 tsp	fine sea salt	10 mL
¼ cup	tahini	60 mL
1½ cups	ground flax seeds (see Tips, left)	375 mL
	Filtered water, optional	

1. In a food processor, process cilantro, lemon zest, lemon juice, flax oil, cumin seeds, ground cumin, garlic and salt, until smooth, stopping the motor once and scraping down the sides of the work bowl.
2. Add tahini and soaked chickpeas and process until smooth. If the mixture is too thick, add water 1 tsp (5 mL) at a time until desired consistency is achieved.
3. Transfer to a bowl and stir in flax seeds until well combined. Set aside for 10 to 15 minutes so the flax can absorb the liquid and swell.
4. Using an ice cream scoop or a small ladle, drop 10 to 15 equal portions of the mixture onto nonstick dehydrator sheets at least 2 inches (5 cm) apart. Dehydrate at 105°F (41°C) for 10 to 12 hours or until firm enough to handle. Flip and transfer to mesh sheets. Dehydrate for 2 to 3 hours, until dry on the outside and soft in the middle.

Variations

Substitute an equal quantity of chopped parsley or 2 cups (500 mL) packed fresh basil leaves for the cilantro. If you are using basil, substitute ½ cup (125 mL) chopped tomato for the lemon juice.

Moroccan Chickpea Stew

This slightly sweet and savory dish is perfectly spiced, and I guarantee it will excite your palate. I like to serve this over Cauliflower Rice (page 274). You will need to start this recipe well ahead of time in order to accommodate soaking the chickpeas.

Makes 4 servings

Tips

To soak the chickpeas for this recipe, combine in a bowl with 2 cups (500 mL) water. Cover and set aside in the refrigerator for at least 8 hours or overnight. Drain and rinse well under cold running water.

To soak the sun-dried tomatoes for this recipe, place in a bowl and cover with 1 cup (250 mL) water. Set aside for 30 minutes. Drain, reserving liquid.

If using a spiral vegetable slicer (often called a spiralizer) to make sweet potato strips, fit the machine with the smallest blade. Position the peeled sweet potato according to the manufacturer's instructions and cut into thin strips. If you do not have a spiralizer, use a vegetable peeler, preferably Y-shaped, to make long, thin slices.

If you are using a dehydrator with fixed depth between the racks, divide the mixture between 4 smaller dishes that fit on the racks and use multiple racks, as necessary.

- Spiral vegetable slicer, optional
- Electric food dehydrator

½ cup	dried chickpeas, soaked (see Tips, left)	125 mL
½ cup	dry-packed sun-dried tomatoes, soaked (see Tips, left)	125 mL
3 cups	chopped tomatoes	750 mL
2 tbsp	chopped red onion	30 mL
2	cloves garlic	2
2 tbsp	raw agave nectar	30 mL
1 tbsp	freshly squeezed lemon juice	15 mL
1 tbsp	ground cumin	15 mL
½ tsp	ground cinnamon	2 mL
¼ tsp	ground turmeric	1 mL
Pinch	fine sea salt	Pinch
Pinch	freshly ground black pepper	Pinch
Pinch	cayenne pepper	Pinch
1 cup	sweet potato strips (see Tips, left)	250 mL
1 cup	roughly chopped cilantro leaves	250 mL
½ cup	finely diced carrot	125 mL
½ cup	finely diced red bell pepper	125 mL

1. In a food processor, process chopped tomatoes, onion, garlic, soaked sun-dried tomatoes and ¼ cup (60 mL) of their soaking liquid, until smooth.

2. Add agave nectar, lemon juice, cumin, cinnamon, turmeric, salt, pepper and cayenne and process until incorporated, stopping the machine once to scrape down the sides with a rubber spatula.

3. Transfer to a bowl. Add sweet potato, cilantro, carrot, bell pepper and soaked chickpeas and stir well. Transfer to a shallow casserole-type dish and dehydrate at 105°F (41°C) for 30 minutes, until mixture is warmed through.

Variation

If chickpeas are not available, substitute another legume such as black lentils. Follow the same soaking instructions as for the chickpeas.

Ratatouille

This recipe is a take on a classic French dish with deep tomato and herb flavors that pair perfectly with the peppers, zucchini, eggplant and onion. The dehydrator replaces the oven to deepen the flavor and add texture to the vegetables. I like to serve this over a bowl of Zucchini Noodles (page 244) or Cauliflower Rice (page 274). It also makes a nice side dish with a big bowl of Softened Broccoli (page 140).

Makes 4 servings

Tips

To soak the sun-dried tomatoes for this recipe, combine with 2 cups (500 mL) warm water. Set aside for 30 minutes. Drain, discarding liquid.

If you prefer, combine the ingredients for the marinade in a small bowl before tossing with the vegetables, to ensure even integration.

- **Electric food dehydrator**

½ cup	dry-packed sun-dried tomatoes, soaked (see Tips, left)	125 mL
½ cup	finely diced red bell pepper	125 mL
½ cup	finely diced zucchini	125 mL
¼ cup	finely diced eggplant	60 mL
3 tbsp	finely diced red onion	45 mL
½ cup	cold-pressed (extra virgin) olive oil, divided	125 mL
2 tbsp	dried basil, divided	30 mL
2 tsp	fine sea salt, divided	10 mL
3 cups	chopped tomatoes, divided	750 mL
4	cloves garlic	4
3 tbsp	freshly squeezed lemon juice	45 mL
1 tbsp	dried oregano	15 mL
½ cup	thinly sliced basil leaves	125 mL

1. In a bowl, toss red pepper, zucchini, eggplant, onion, ¼ cup (60 mL) olive oil, 1 tbsp (15 mL) dried basil and 1 tsp (5 mL) salt. Transfer to a nonstick dehydrator sheet and spread evenly. Dehydrate at 105°F (41°C) for 45 minutes to 1 hour, until soft and slightly wilted.

2. In a food processor fitted with the metal blade, process 2½ cups (625 mL) chopped tomatoes, soaked sun-dried tomatoes, garlic, lemon juice, oregano and remaining olive oil, dried basil and salt, until smooth and no large pieces of food remain.

3. Transfer to a bowl and stir in dehydrated vegetables, remaining ½ cup (125 mL) chopped tomatoes and fresh basil. Serve immediately or cover and refrigerate for up to 3 days.

Moussaka

This traditional Greek dish is a classic comfort food. I love how all the ingredients come together. Serve this with a side of Cauliflower Mashed Potatoes (page 273) or a simple salad of fresh romaine lettuce, arugula and baby spinach.

Makes 4 servings

Tips

To soak the cashews for this recipe, place in a bowl and add 4 cups (1 L) water. Cover and set aside for 30 minutes. Drain, discarding soaking water, and rinse under cold running water until the water runs clear.

When arranging the eggplant in the baking dish, it is okay if the slices overlap a bit, but you want most of it to be in a single layer.

If you are using a ring-shaped dehydrator with fixed depth between the racks, you will need to divide the mixture among smaller dishes.

You may want to increase the time a bit if the mixture has been refrigerated.

- **Mandoline**
- **Shallow baking dish**

2 cups	raw cashews, soaked (see Tips, left)	500 mL
1	large Italian eggplant	1
2 tbsp	fine sea salt, divided	30 mL
¼ cup	cold-pressed (extra virgin) olive oil	60 mL
¼ cup	filtered water	60 mL
3 tbsp	wheat-free tamari	45 mL
1 tbsp	chopped thyme leaves	15 mL
1 cup	Tomato Basil Marinara Sauce (page 184)	250 mL
¾ cup	Walnut Mince (page 293)	175 mL
½ cup	filtered water	125 mL
1 tbsp	freshly squeezed lemon juice	15 mL
Pinch	ground nutmeg	Pinch
½ cup	Almond Parmesan Cheese (page 204)	125 mL

1. With a sharp knife, cut off bottom of eggplant to make a flat end. Stand eggplant upright on a cutting board and cut vertically into slices about ½ inch (1 cm) thick, discarding first and last slices. Sprinkle slices on both sides with 1½ tbsp (22 mL) salt. Set aside until water is extracted, removing most of its bitterness, about 1 hour. Rinse under cold running water and pat dry. Transfer to a long, shallow dish.

2. Toss eggplant with olive oil, water, tamari and thyme. Set aside for 1 hour to marinate. Remove from marinade, pat dry and transfer to a baking dish, arranging as much as possible in a single layer (see Tips, left.)

3. In a bowl, combine marinara sauce and walnut mince. Spread evenly over eggplant.

Tip

If you prefer to serve the moussaka warmed, after it has been assembled, place the dish in a dehydrator at 105°F (41°C) for 3 to 4 hours, to warm through and concentrate the flavors.

4. In a food processor fitted with the metal blade, process soaked cashews, water, lemon juice, nutmeg and 1 tsp (5 mL) salt until smooth and creamy, stopping the motor and scraping down the sides of the work bowl as necessary. Spread evenly over moussaka, then spread Almond Parmesan Cheese evenly overtop. Serve immediately or cover and refrigerate. Warm in a dehydrator, if desired (see Tips, page 228), before serving.

Miso Ginger "Stir-Fried" Veggies

> By pulling out some of the moisture, using a dehydrator makes these raw vegetables seem as if they have been quickly stir-fried. The orange juice lends a slightly sweet note to this dish and in combination with the miso creates a wonderful flavor. I like to serve this over Parsnip "Fried Rice" (page 275) with a sprinkling of white sesame seeds.

Makes 4 side or 2 main servings

Tips

Although unpasteurized miso is not 100 percent raw, it is often used in raw food diets because it is fermented, which provides healthy bacteria to aid digestion. Brown rice miso is gluten-free and also contains vitamin B_{12}.

This method gives raw vegetables the texture and mouth feel of those that have been cooked. The lemon juice and salt start to break down the cell walls and the dehydrator completes the softening process.

- **Electric food dehydrator**

Sauce

¼ cup	brown rice miso (see Tips, left)	60 mL
¼ cup	freshly squeezed orange juice	60 mL
3 tbsp	filtered water	45 mL
1 tbsp	freshly squeezed lemon juice	15 mL
2	soft dates, pitted and chopped	2
3 tbsp	chopped gingerroot	45 mL
½ tsp	fine sea salt	2 mL

Veggies

½ cup	thinly sliced red bell pepper	125 mL
¼ cup	thinly sliced carrot	60 mL
¼ cup	thinly sliced celery	60 mL
¼ cup	thinly sliced kale	60 mL
¼ cup	thinly sliced zucchini	60 mL
3 tbsp	cold-pressed hemp oil	45 mL
¼ tsp	freshly squeezed lemon juice	1 mL
¼ tsp	fine sea salt	1 mL

1. *Sauce:* In blender, combine miso, orange juice, water, lemon juice, dates, ginger and salt. Blend at high speed until smooth. Set aside.
2. *Veggies:* In a bowl, combine red pepper, carrot, celery, kale and zucchini. Toss to combine. Add hemp oil, lemon juice and salt and toss well. Transfer to a nonstick dehydrator sheet and spread evenly. Dehydrate at 105°F (41°C) for 15 minutes, until vegetables are slightly wilted. Transfer to a bowl.
3. Add miso mixture to the vegetables and toss to combine. Transfer to a nonstick dehydrator sheet and spread evenly. Return to dehydrator and warm at 105°F (41°C) for 20 minutes. Serve immediately or cover and refrigerate for up to 3 days.

Mixed Vegetable and Shiitake Mushroom "Stir-Fry"

This recipe, with its delicate blend of flavors, is a take on high-fat Chinese takeout. Processed soy sauce is replaced with wheat-free tamari and the dehydrator stands in for a wok. I like to serve this dish over Marinated Kelp Noodles (page 243) sprinkled with hemp seeds and some thinly sliced fresh basil.

Makes 2 servings

Tips

While wheat-free tamari is not raw, it is gluten-free. The raw alternative for tamari, nama shoyu, does contain gluten. If you are following a completely raw diet and can tolerate gluten, by all means substitute an equal quantity of nama shoyu.

When following a completely raw food diet, look for sesame oil that is made from untoasted sesame seeds and is completely unrefined. It will be labeled "cold-pressed."

One of the keys to making this recipe and others successful is to cut all the vegetables to the same size and thickness. This will ensure that they soften at the same rate and are uniformly done.

- Electric food dehydrator

½ cup	thinly sliced shiitake mushrooms	125 mL
¼ cup	thinly sliced kale	60 mL
¼ cup	thinly sliced carrot	60 mL
¼ cup	thinly sliced cauliflower	60 mL
¼ cup	thinly sliced zucchini	60 mL
3 tbsp	wheat-free tamari (see Tips, left)	45 mL
3 tbsp	sesame oil (untoasted) (see Tips, left)	45 mL
2 tbsp	sesame seeds	30 mL
½ tsp	fine sea salt	2 mL

1. In a bowl, toss together mushrooms, kale, carrot, cauliflower, zucchini, tamari, sesame oil, sesame seeds and salt. Place on a nonstick dehydrator sheet and spread evenly. Dehydrate at 105°F (41°C) for 30 to 45 minutes or until slightly wilted. Serve immediately or transfer to an airtight container and refrigerate for up to 4 days.

Variation

Toss the vegetables with your favorite sauce instead of the tamari, sesame oil, sesame seeds and salt. You will need about ½ cup (125 mL) of sauce, such as Spicy Pad Thai Sauce (page 194) or Miso Glaze Sauce (page 196) with 1 tsp (5 mL) freshly grated gingerroot.

Green Coconut Curried Vegetables

> I love the rich, creamy and tangy sauce in this dish. The combination of lime, cilantro and tamari creates a mouth-watering green curry. I like to serve this over Marinated Kelp Noodles (page 243) tossed with hemp seeds and a little fresh basil.

Makes 4 servings

Tips

To soak the cashews for this recipe, place in a bowl and add 1 cup (250 mL) water. Cover and set aside for 30 minutes. Drain, discarding liquid. Rinse under cold running water until the water runs clear.

While wheat-free tamari is not raw, it is gluten-free. The raw alternative for tamari, nama shoyu, does contain gluten. If you are following a completely raw diet and can tolerate gluten, by all means substitute an equal quantity of nama shoyu.

If you have a dehydrator, use it with the vegetables after they have been coated in the sauce (Step 3). Place on a nonstick dehydrator sheet and spread evenly. Dehydrating for 45 to 60 minutes at 105°F (41°C) will slightly warm the vegetables and thicken the sauce a bit.

Vegetables

½ cup	cauliflower florets	125 mL
½ cup	broccoli florets	125 mL
½ cup	thinly sliced carrot	125 mL
½ cup	thinly sliced zucchini	125 mL
½ cup	thinly sliced red bell pepper	125 mL
⅓ cup	cold-pressed flax oil	75 mL
¼ cup	freshly squeezed lemon juice	60 mL
2 tsp	fine sea salt	10 mL

Sauce

½ cup	raw cashews, soaked (see Tips, left)	125 mL
1½ cups	cilantro leaves	375 mL
¾ cup	filtered water	175 mL
¼ cup	coconut butter	60 mL
¼ cup	chopped jalapeño pepper	60 mL
2	cloves garlic	2
3 tbsp	freshly squeezed lime juice	45 mL
2 tbsp	wheat-free tamari (see Tips, left)	30 mL
2 tbsp	chopped gingerroot	30 mL
1 tbsp	raw agave nectar	15 mL
2 tsp	ground cumin	10 mL
1 tsp	ground coriander	5 mL

1. *Vegetables:* In a bowl, toss cauliflower, broccoli, carrot, zucchini, red pepper, flax oil, lemon juice and salt. Set aside for 10 to 15 minutes so the vegetables can soften.

2. *Sauce:* In a food processor fitted with the metal blade, process soaked cashews, cilantro, water, coconut butter, jalapeño, garlic, lime juice, tamari, ginger, agave nectar, cumin and coriander until smooth and creamy.

3. Add sauce to vegetables and toss well. Set aside for 15 minutes to allow vegetables to absorb some of the flavor from the sauce. Serve immediately.

Curried Chickpea Stew

This fragrant stew is a delicate blend of ripe tomatoes, protein-packed chickpeas and spices. I especially enjoy it over a big bowl of Cauliflower Mashed Potatoes (page 273). A sprinkle of chopped fresh cilantro provides a pleasant finish.

Makes 4 to 6 servings

Tips

To soak the chickpeas for this recipe, place in a bowl and add 2 cups (500 mL) water. Cover and set aside for 8 hours, changing the water twice. Drain, discarding liquid.

To soak the sun-dried tomatoes for this recipe, place in a bowl and add 4 cups (1 L) warm water. Set aside for 30 minutes. Drain, discarding liquid.

The outer stalks of celery can be tough and fibrous. For best results, peel the stalk with a vegetable peeler. Save the peel to make soups, sauces or stocks.

If you prefer this dish slightly warm, place it in a shallow baking dish and warm in a dehydrator at 105°F (41°C) for 30 to 45 minutes.

1 cup	chickpeas, soaked (see Tips, left)	250 mL
1 cup	dry-packed sun-dried tomatoes, soaked (see Tips, left)	250 mL
3 cups	chopped tomatoes	750 mL
1/3 cup	coarsely chopped carrot	75 mL
1/3 cup	fresh cilantro leaves	75 mL
1/4 cup	coarsely chopped celery (see Tips, left)	60 mL
3 tbsp	coarsely chopped onion	45 mL
2 tbsp	chopped gingerroot	30 mL
3	cloves garlic	3
1/4 cup	freshly squeezed lemon juice	60 mL
3 tbsp	cold-pressed (extra virgin) olive oil	45 mL
3 tbsp	curry powder	45 mL
2 tbsp	raw agave nectar	30 mL
1 tbsp	ground cumin	15 mL
2 tsp	fine sea salt	10 mL
1 tsp	ground coriander	5 mL
Pinch	cayenne pepper	Pinch

1. In a food processor fitted with the metal blade, process soaked sun-dried tomatoes, chopped tomatoes, carrot, cilantro, celery, onion, ginger, garlic, lemon juice, olive oil, curry powder, agave nectar, cumin, salt, coriander and cayenne until no large pieces of vegetables remain.
2. Transfer to a bowl and add soaked chickpeas. Mix well. Serve immediately or cover and refrigerate for up to 4 days.

Daikon Radish "Egg Noodles"

This recipe is a fresh take on pasta. The daikon has a slightly spicy flavor that pairs well with sauces such as Yellow Coconut Curry Sauce (page 192), Lo Mein "Stir-Fry" Sauce (page 193) or Spicy Pad Thai Sauce (page 194). I love it because it takes virtually no time to prepare and keeps for up to three days.

Yellow Coconut Curry Sauce (page 192), Lo Mein "Stir-Fry" Sauce (page 193) or Spicy Pad Thai Sauce (page 194)

Makes 2 servings

1	medium daikon radish, peeled	1
2 tbsp	cold-pressed (extra virgin) olive oil	30 mL
2 tsp	freshly squeezed lemon juice	10 mL
½ tsp	fine sea salt	2 mL
¼ tsp	ground turmeric	1 mL

Tips

When purchasing extra virgin olive oil, make sure the label says "cold-pressed." Some olive oils are extracted using a centrifuge system, which spins the olives at a very high rate. This heats the olives and the resulting oil, depriving it of its raw status.

To yield the maximum amount of juice from a lemon, make sure it is at room temperature. Rolling the lemon around on the counter while pressing lightly with the palm of your hand also helps by releasing juice from the flesh.

1. Cut the daikon in half lengthwise. Using a vegetable peeler, peel the flat side of one half until you cannot peel any more, transferring the "noodles" to a bowl as completed. Repeat with the remaining half. Save the leftover pieces of daikon to chop up and use in a salad.

2. In a small bowl, mix together olive oil, lemon juice, salt and turmeric. Add to noodles and toss to coat evenly (you want to make sure the turmeric colors all the pieces). Set aside for 1 hour, until noodles are soft and pliable.

Variation

Substitute 1 lb (500 g) parsnips for the daikon. Increase the quantity of olive oil to ¼ cup (60 mL), the lemon juice to 2 tbsp (30 mL) and the salt to 1 tsp (5 mL).

Shaved Asparagus and Squash Fettuccine

This recipe is a simple way to make vegetable pasta using a vegetable peeler and everyday ingredients. The fresh asparagus provides a herbaceous flavor that marries well with the slightly sweet squash. This "pasta" makes a wonderful pairing with sauces such as Cashew Alfredo Sauce (page 188). Sprinkle with hemp seeds to add more nutrients.

Makes 2 servings

Tips

To achieve the best results, use a Y-shaped vegetable peeler. This peeler, which resembles a slingshot, has the blade on top, so it makes jobs such as this more efficient.

Cut the squash into 2 pieces, separating the long, tubular top and the round bottom. Use the top piece to make the pasta. Save the bottom and any leftover pieces for use in sauces or soups.

When using a vegetable peeler to make raw fettuccine, peel repeatedly from the same side to ensure that your strips are uniform in shape and size. Do not rotate the vegetable.

If you prefer, combine the ingredients for the marinade in a small bowl before tossing with the vegetables, to ensure even integration.

6	large stalks asparagus	6
1	piece (6 inches/15 cm) butternut squash, top part only, peeled (see Tips, left)	1
3 tbsp	cold-pressed (extra virgin) olive oil	45 mL
2 tsp	freshly squeezed lemon juice	10 mL
½ tsp	fine sea salt	2 mL

1. Using a vegetable peeler, peel asparagus and squash lengthwise into the longest possible strips, transferring to a bowl as completed. Add olive oil, lemon juice and salt and toss well. Set aside to marinate for 1 hour, until softened. Toss with your favorite sauce and serve immediately or transfer to an airtight container and refrigerate for up to 4 days.

Pesto-Coated Carrot and Parsnip Fettuccine

This dish is a great way to get as many healthy ingredients into your body as possible without having to sacrifice any of the things you love. The softness of the root vegetables makes it reminiscent of traditional al dente pasta.

Makes 2 servings

Tips

Peeling the vegetables lengthwise produces the long, thin strips required for this recipe. For best results use a Y-shaped (slingshot) vegetable peeler. When using a regular peeler, you can glide down the length of the vegetable to make one long, thin strip.

If you prefer, combine the ingredients for the marinade in a small bowl before tossing with the vegetables, to ensure even integration.

3	large carrots, peeled	3
3	large parsnips, peeled	3
1 tbsp	cold-pressed (extra virgin) olive oil	15 mL
¼ cup	freshly squeezed lemon juice, divided	60 mL
1½ tbsp	fine sea salt, divided	22 mL
¾ cup	cold-pressed hemp oil	175 mL
½ cup	raw shelled hemp seeds	125 mL
3	cloves garlic	3
3 cups	chopped fresh cilantro leaves	750 mL

1. Using a vegetable peeler, peel carrots and parsnips into long, thin strips, dropping into a bowl as completed (see Tips, left.) Add olive oil, 1 tsp (5 mL) lemon juice and ¼ tsp (1 mL) salt and toss until vegetables are well coated. Set aside for 10 minutes, until softened.

2. In a food processor fitted with the metal blade, process hemp oil and seeds, garlic and remaining lemon juice and salt, until somewhat smooth but the hemp seeds retain some texture. Add cilantro and process until chopped and blended, stopping the motor once to scrape down the sides of the work bowl. Add pesto to fettuccine, toss well and serve.

Variations

Substitute an equal quantity of parsley leaves for the cilantro.

Toss the fettuccine from Step 1 with another sauce, instead of the pesto. Red Pepper Mole Sauce (page 202), Sweet-and-Sour Thai Almond Butter Sauce (page 191) or Spicy Pad Thai Sauce (page 194) are all good choices.

Red Beet Ravioli

This dish is simple yet elegant, and very versatile. Serve it as a main course accompanied by Simple Marinated Kale Salad (page 142). It also makes a nice side dish, or, for something a little different, make small ravioli for cocktail parties. Whatever your choice, your guests will be impressed. I like to garnish this dish with Sour Cream and Onion Kale Chips (page 298) if I have them on hand. You may also add a sprinkle of thinly sliced fresh basil leaves or chopped fresh chives.

Makes 3 servings

Tips

Slicing the beet thinly and allowing enough time for it to soften in the marinade enables you to form a seal around the cheese so that it resembles traditional ravioli made from pasta.

Mandolines vary dramatically in price. The most functional and cost-efficient version is Japanese-made.

- **Mandoline**

1	large red beet, peeled	1
1 tbsp	cold-pressed (extra virgin) olive oil	15 mL
1 tsp	freshly squeezed lemon juice	5 mL
Pinch	fine sea salt	Pinch
2½ cups	Red Pepper, Dill and Cashew Ricotta (page 103)	625 mL
1 cup	Red Pepper Basil Marinara Sauce (page 184)	250 mL

1. Using a mandoline, slice beet as thinly as possible to create rounds. These will be the ravioli shells, so you'll need at least 60 slices.
2. In a bowl, toss beet slices, olive oil, lemon juice and salt. Set aside to marinate for 10 minutes, until softened.
3. Lay out 30 beet slices on a work surface. Using a tablespoon (15 mL), place one scoop of cashew ricotta on each beet slice. Top with remaining slices.
4. Using your fingers, pick up each ravioli and crimp the edges to form a seal. Arrange finished ravioli neatly on a serving dish and drizzle with Red Pepper Basil Marinara Sauce.

Variations

This recipe can be made substituting parsnip, rutabaga or even squash for the beet. Although each vegetable is a different size, the same technique will work. For larger vegetables such as rutabaga, double the amount of oil, salt and lemon to ensure adequate softening. When using smaller vegetables such as parsnips, be sure to increase the number of slices, as each ravioli will use less filling.

Layered Zucchini Lasagna

Sliced zucchini replaces pasta in this raw version of a traditional Italian recipe. This lasagna has all the traditional flavor components of its cooked counterpart. Although it seems like a lot of work to prepare, the sauces can be made ahead of time and the extra used in other recipes. Serve this as you would a traditional lasagna, with a fork and knife. As you cut through the layers, the sauces will naturally mix together, creating delicious flavor combinations. Increase the quantity to suit your needs.

Makes 1 generous serving

Tips

One key to making this recipe delicious is to slice the zucchini to the correct thickness.

I like to make this recipe ahead of time and let it sit for a few hours. This makes the zucchini noodles softer and allows the flavors to infuse.

- **Mandoline**

1	large zucchini	1
3 tbsp	cold-pressed (extra virgin) olive oil	45 mL
$\frac{1}{2}$ tsp	fine sea salt	2 mL
$\frac{1}{4}$ tsp	freshly ground black pepper	1 mL
$\frac{1}{4}$ cup	Red Pepper, Dill and Cashew Ricotta (page 103)	60 mL
$\frac{1}{4}$ cup	Basil, Spinach and Walnut Pesto (page 186)	60 mL
$\frac{1}{4}$ cup	Tomato Basil Marinara Sauce (page 184)	60 mL
1 tbsp	Almond Parmesan Cheese (page 204)	15 mL

1. Using a mandoline, slice zucchini lengthwise into 9 slices, each approximately $\frac{1}{2}$ inch (1 cm) thick.
2. Transfer to a clean work surface. Drizzle zucchini with olive oil and sprinkle with salt and freshly ground pepper. Set aside for 10 minutes to soften.
3. Lay three strips of zucchini on the bottom of a platter. Spoon 1 heaping tbsp (20 mL) each cashew ricotta, pesto and marinara sauce overtop, dividing evenly in separate areas. Arrange 3 zucchini slices on top, pointing in the opposite direction. Repeat addition of the sauces, spreading them evenly. Arrange remaining zucchini slices overtop, in the original direction, and add remaining sauces, spreading evenly. Garnish with almond Parmesan and serve immediately.

Zucchini Manicotti

These scrumptious zucchini pasta rolls are the perfect way to introduce someone you love to raw food. They take very little time to prepare and are stuffed with a savory cashew cheese that everyone will love.

Makes 2 servings

2	large zucchini	2
2 tsp	cold-pressed (extra virgin) olive oil	10 mL
2 tsp	chopped fresh thyme leaves	10 mL
1/2 tsp	fine sea salt	2 mL
3/4 cup	Red Pepper, Dill and Cashew Ricotta (page 103)	175 mL
1/2 cup	Red Pepper Basil Marinara Sauce (page 184)	125 mL
2 tbsp	Almond Parmesan Cheese (page 204)	30 mL

1. With a sharp knife, cut off one end of each zucchini. Stand zucchini upright and cut vertically into thin slices about 1/4 inch (0.5 cm) thick, discarding the first and last slices (you should have 24 slices). Lay slices on a flat surface, drizzle with olive oil and sprinkle evenly with thyme and salt. Set aside for 15 minutes to soften.

2. Working with 3 zucchini slices at a time, place on a flat work surface. Spread the bottom third of each slice with 2 tsp (10 mL) cashew ricotta. Roll up jelly-roll fashion and place, seam side down, on a serving plate. Repeat until all the slices have been filled. Spread marinara sauce evenly over "manicotti" and garnish each with a small dollop of almond Parmesan. Serve immediately or cover and refrigerate for up to 3 days.

Variation

Many fillings work well with this recipe. After drizzling the zucchini slices with olive oil and sprinkling with thyme and salt, you can fill them with, for instance, Pumpkin Seed "Refried Beans" (page 93) and Perfect Guacamole (page 81) and garnish with Red Pepper Mole Sauce (page 202) for a Mexican twist. Top with a bit of crumbled Eggplant Bacon (page 41) if you have it, or some chopped fresh parsley leaves.

Eggplant Parmesan

This recipe is inspired by a traditional Italian dish of slowly roasted eggplant with rich tomato sauce and Parmesan cheese. I like to serve this with a side of Wilted Spinach Salad (page 140).

Makes 4 servings

Tips

Salting the eggplant removes any bitterness and helps to soften it, a process that is completed with the marinating.

While wheat-free tamari is not raw, it is gluten-free. The raw alternative for tamari, nama shoyu, does contain gluten. If you are following a completely raw diet and can tolerate gluten, by all means substitute an equal quantity of nama shoyu.

1	large Italian eggplant	1
1 tbsp	fine sea salt	15 mL
3 tbsp	cold-pressed (extra virgin) olive oil	45 mL
2 tbsp	wheat-free tamari (see Tips, left)	30 mL
1 tbsp	chopped fresh thyme leaves	15 mL
1 cup	Red Pepper, Dill and Cashew Ricotta (page 103)	250 mL
1 cup	Red Pepper Basil Marinara Sauce (page 184)	250 mL
1/2 cup	Almond Parmesan Cheese (page 204)	125 mL

1. Using a mandoline or a chef's knife, cut the eggplant lengthwise into four slices, each 1 inch (2.5 cm) thick. Sprinkle slices on both sides with salt. Set aside until water is extracted, removing most of its bitterness, about 1 hour. Rinse under cold running water and pat dry. Transfer to a long, shallow dish.

2. In a small bowl, combine olive oil, tamari and thyme. Pour over eggplant, coating all slices evenly. Toss gently to coat and set aside for 10 to 15 minutes, until soft and pliable.

3. Transfer softened eggplant to a flat work surface. Spread each slice with 1/4 cup (60 mL) each cashew ricotta and marinara sauce and 2 tbsp (30 mL) almond Parmesan. Serve immediately or transfer to an airtight container, cover and refrigerate for up to 4 days.

Variation

If you have a dehydrator, use it to finish this dish. It will warm the eggplant through and slightly concentrate the flavors. The sauces will also stick to the eggplant a little better, creating stronger layers of flavor. After completing Step 3, place on a nonstick dehydrator sheet and dehydrate at 105°F (41°C) for 1 to 2 hours, until warmed through.

Stuffed Calzone

These warm and gooey calzone are the perfect meal for anyone transitioning to a healthier diet. They are soft, bread-like and bursting with flavorful tomato and basil, rich cashew cheese and just a hint of oregano. I like to make these for myself for dinner. I serve them with a simple salad of fresh romaine lettuce, tossed with Lemon Avocado Dressing (page 177).

Tips

To soak the buckwheat groats, combine with 2 cups (500 mL) water. Set aside for 30 minutes. Drain, discarding soaking water. Rinse under cold running water until the water runs clear.

To soak the sun-dried tomatoes, add 1 cup (250 mL) warm water. Set aside for 30 minutes. Drain, discarding liquid.

If using a ring-shaped dehydrator, shape the batter into ovals, rather than rounds, to sit on the nonstick sheet. Be sure to keep the ovals 1/2 inch (1 cm) thick.

Vary the fillings to suit your taste. I like to add 1/4 cup (60 mL) Marinated Mushrooms (page 292) and 1/4 cup (60 mL) "Baked" Cheesy Broccoli (page 276) along with the Cashew Ricotta and Marinara Sauce.

- **Electric food dehydrator**

1 cup	buckwheat groats, soaked (see Tips, left)	250 mL
1/4 cup	dry-packed sun-dried tomatoes, soaked (see Tips, left)	60 mL
1/4 cup	chopped carrot	60 mL
1/4 cup	chopped tomato	60 mL
2 tbsp	chopped onion	30 mL
2 tbsp	nutritional yeast	30 mL
4	cloves garlic	4
2 tsp	dried oregano	10 mL
1 tsp	fine sea salt	5 mL
1 cup	ground flax seeds	250 mL
2 cups	Red Pepper, Dill and Cashew Ricotta (page 103)	500 mL
2 cups	Red Pepper Basil Marinara Sauce (page 184)	500 mL

1. In a food processor fitted with the metal blade, process soaked sun-dried tomatoes, carrot, chopped tomato, onion, nutritional yeast, garlic, oregano and salt until well combined. Add soaked buckwheat and process until smooth. Transfer to a bowl. Add flax seeds and mix well. Set aside for 10 minutes so the flax can absorb some of the liquid and swell.

2. Divide batter into 4 equal portions. One at a time, transfer to nonstick dehydrator sheets and, using your hands, shape each into a round approximately 1/2 inch (1 cm) thick and 8 inches (20 cm) in diameter (see Tips, left). Repeat until all the batter has been shaped.

3. Dehydrate at 105°F (41°C) for 5 to 6 hours or until firm enough to handle. Flip and transfer to mesh sheets. Place 1/2 cup (125 mL) cashew ricotta on each round. Spread 1/2 cup (125 mL) marinara sauce over cheese. Fold rounds in half and, using your thumb and forefinger, pinch edges together to seal. Return to dehydrator and dehydrate at 105°F (41°C) for 3 to 4 hours or until warmed through.

Herbed Hemp and Cashew Gnocchi Carbonara

> These tasty little dumplings are easy to make and packed full of flavor. I like to serve them with a rich cream sauce such as Cashew Alfredo Sauce to complement the light texture, but other creamy sauces would be nice too.

Makes 2 servings

Tips

To soak the cashews for this recipe, place them in a bowl with 1 cup (250 mL) water, cover and set aside to soak for 30 minutes. Drain, discarding remaining water, and rinse until water runs clear.

When processing the almonds and unsoaked cashews, do not overprocess. You want the nuts to be broken down and floury but not so processed that they become nut butter.

If you have a high-powered blender, use it to blend the ingredients in Step 1. The gnocchi will be lighter than when made in a food processor.

You can purchase flax seeds that are already ground (often described as milled) in vacuum-sealed bags, or you can grind them yourself. Depending upon the quantity you need, grind whole flax seeds in a blender or a spice grinder. Once ground (or after the vacuum-sealed bag is opened), the beneficial fatty acids begin to dissipate. Store ground flax seeds away from light, in an airtight container in the refrigerator or freezer, for up to 2 months.

- **Electric food dehydrator**

½ cup	raw cashews, soaked (see Tips, left)	125 mL
½ cup	raw shelled hemp seeds	125 mL
½ cup	packed fresh basil leaves	125 mL
¼ cup	filtered water	60 mL
2 tbsp	freshly squeezed lemon juice	30 mL
1 tbsp	chopped fresh thyme leaves	15 mL
2	cloves garlic	2
2 tsp	fine sea salt	10 mL
1 cup	whole raw almonds	250 mL
½ cup	raw cashews	125 mL
¼ cup	ground flax seeds (see Tips, left)	60 mL
½ cup	Cashew Alfredo Sauce (page 188)	125 mL

1. In a food processor, process soaked cashews, hemp seeds, basil, water, lemon juice, thyme, garlic and salt until smooth and creamy. Transfer to a mixing bowl.

2. Rinse out work bowl and blade and dry thoroughly. Reassemble food processor and process almonds and unsoaked cashews until flour-like in consistency.

3. Fold nut flour into hemp mixture and add flax seeds. Mix well. Cover and refrigerate for 2 to 3 hours, until the nut flours and flax seeds have absorbed some of the liquid. The texture should resemble thick bread dough. If it needs to be thicker, process ¼ cup (60 mL) almonds in food processor until flour-like in consistency. Fold into dough 1 tbsp (15 mL) at a time until desired consistency is achieved.

4. Transfer mixture to a clean work surface and, using your hands, shape dough into a log about 16 inches (40 cm) long. Cut into pieces approximately 1 inch (2.5 cm) long. Place on nonstick dehydrator sheets and dehydrate at 105°F (41°C) for 6 to 8 hours or until the surfaces of the gnocchi are no longer wet and they have the texture of cooked traditional pasta. Remove from dehydrator, transfer to a bowl and toss with Alfredo sauce. Serve immediately.

Marinated Kelp Noodles

Kelp noodles are a relatively new product on the market. They are thin, spaghetti-like noodles that are translucent and have a neutral flavor. They are great to use in recipes because they absorb whatever flavors they are matched with. This is a very simple way to prepare them that manipulates the texture to make them soft After marinating, I like to serve them with sauces such as Yellow Coconut Curry Sauce (page 192), Spicy Pad Thai Sauce (page 194) or Sweet-and-Sour Thai Almond Butter Sauce (page 191).

Makes 3 servings

Tips

Although slightly processed, because they are made at temperatures that don't exceed 105°F (41°C), kelp noodles are considered a raw food product. They do not contain any stabilizers, emulsifiers or hidden ingredients.

Kelp noodles have a long shelf life and do not need to be refrigerated until opened. Once opened, transfer to an airtight container and store in the refrigerator for up to one week.

1	bag (16 oz/454 g) kelp noodles	1
3 tbsp	cold-pressed (extra virgin) olive oil	45 mL
2 tsp	freshly squeezed lemon juice	10 mL
¼ tsp	fine sea salt	1 mL

1. Using your hands, separate the noodles until none are stuck together, transferring to a bowl as completed.
2. In a small bowl, whisk olive oil, lemon juice and salt. Add to noodles and toss well. Set aside for at least 30 minutes or overnight, until softened.

Variations

I also like to serve kelp noodles with Brown Rice Miso Broth (page 135), Black Olive Relish (page 205) or Herbed Mushroom Duxelles (page 102). These sauces don't go well with the lemon juice in the marinade, so instead of marinating the noodles, I soak them in warm water for 15 minutes, then rinse under warm running water before tossing with the sauce.

Zucchini Noodles

Zucchini noodles are almost a basic in the raw food kitchen. They have the mouth feel of al dente pasta — even the pickiest eaters won't know they aren't eating cooked pasta if you don't tell them. They are also very easy to prepare and very versatile. My favorite sauces for these are Basil, Spinach and Walnut Pesto (page 186), Tomato Basil Marinara Sauce (page 184), Sweet-and-Sour Thai Almond Butter Sauce (page 191), Spicy Pad Thai Sauce (page 194) and Lo Mein "Stir-Fry" Sauce (page 193).

Makes 4 cups (1 L)

Tips

When securing the zucchini, ensure that it is centered on the blade as much as possible. This will give you the longest possible strands of zucchini pasta, rather than short, broken-up ones.

Although zucchini noodles can be stored for up to 2 days in the refrigerator, for optimum flavor, texture and shape they are best consumed the day they are made.

You will need ½ to ¾ cup (125 to 175 mL) sauce for this quantity of pasta. When you mix zucchini noodles with a sauce that contains sodium (salt), it will draw out the moisture, causing the noodles to quickly become soggy. Once they have been tossed with sauce, it is best to eat them right away.

- **Spiral vegetable slicer, fitted with the smallest blade**

| 4 | large zucchini, ends trimmed | 4 |

1. One at a time, secure zucchini on the spiralizer prongs. Once positioned, rotate the crank while gently pushing the vegetable toward the blade to create long strands of "pasta". Transfer noodles to a bowl as prepared. Use immediately, tossed with your favorite sauce (see Tips, left), or cover with a clean, damp tea towel and refrigerate for up to 2 days.

Variations

Substitute carrots, beets, parsnips or sweet potatoes for the zucchini. You will need 3 cups (750 mL) noodles for a comparable quantity.

I like to spiralize a combination of 1 cup (250 mL) red beet (about 1 medium) and ½ cup (125 mL) sweet potato (about ½ small) and toss with a mixture of ¼ cup (60 mL) Pumpkin Seed "Refried Beans" (page 93) and ¼ cup Cashew Sour Cream (page 204).

For something a little different, try combining zucchini noodles with an equal quantity of Marinated Kelp Noodles (page 243) before tossing with a sauce.

Pasta Bolognese

This dish, which uses zucchini noodles as a base, is full of flavor and texture, yet it is very light. I love serving it with a generous sprinkling of Almond Parmesan Cheese (page 204).

Makes 2 servings

Tips

To cut basil in a chiffonade, pick the leaves off the stems and stack on top of each other in a neat pile. Roll as tightly as possible into a cylinder. Using a chef's knife, slice the rolls 1/4 inch (0.5 cm) thick.

When you mix zucchini noodles with a sauce that contains sodium (salt), it will draw out the moisture, causing the noodles to quickly become soggy. Once they have been tossed with sauce, it is best to eat them right away.

8 cups	Zucchini Noodles (page 244; about 6 large zucchini)	2 L
2 cups	Tomato Basil Marinara Sauce (page 184)	500 mL
1/2 cup	Walnut Mince (page 293)	125 mL
1/4 cup	basil leaves, cut in chiffonade (see Tips, left)	60 mL
1/2 cup	Almond Parmesan Cheese (page 204), optional	125 mL

1. In a bowl, toss together zucchini noodles, marinara sauce, walnut mince and basil, until well coated. Divide into 2 serving bowls and top with almond Parmesan, if using. Serve immediately.

Variation

Substitute an equal quantity of Red Pepper Basil Marinara Sauce (page 184) for the Tomato Basil Marinara Sauce.

Zucchini Pasta Aglio e Olio

This recipe provides a simple way to make a delicious raw pasta dish with high-quality extra virgin olive oil, fresh herbs and garlic, among other ingredients. I like to serve this for dinner with a side of Simple Marinated Kale Salad (page 142) or Wilted Spinach Salad (page 140).

Makes 2 servings

Tip

When you mix zucchini noodles with a sauce that contains sodium (salt), it will draw out the moisture in the zucchini, causing the noodles to become soggy. For that reason, it is best to eat this dish right away.

½ cup	cold-pressed (extra virgin) olive oil	125 mL
¼ cup	cold-pressed hemp or flax oil	60 mL
3 tbsp	freshly squeezed lemon juice	45 mL
5	cloves garlic	5
2 tsp	fine sea salt	10 mL
½ tsp	fennel seeds	2 mL
Pinch	chile flakes	Pinch
2 cups	packed basil leaves	500 mL
1 cup	chopped flat-leaf parsley leaves	250 mL
1 cup	chopped spinach	250 mL
½ cup	chopped cilantro leaves	125 mL
3 tbsp	raw shelled hemp seeds	45 mL
4 cups	Zucchini Noodles (page 244; about 4 large zucchini)	1 L

1. In a food processor fitted with the metal blade, process olive and hemp oils, lemon juice, garlic, salt, fennel seeds and chile flakes until smooth. Add basil, parsley, spinach, cilantro and hemp seeds and process for 2 to 3 minutes, until smooth.
2. Place zucchini noodles in a serving bowl, add sauce and toss well. Serve immediately.

Sweet Potato and Zucchini Mac 'n' Cheese

This recipe is a take on the classic comfort food. The macaroni is replaced by sweet potato and squash, and the creaminess of the sauce comes from cashews. This has a decadent rich and creamy texture that is perfectly balanced by the sweet potato and zucchini. I like to serve it with a simple salad of crisp romaine lettuce tossed with olive oil and lemon juice. For a *pièce de résistance*, top with a generous dollop of Walnut Mince (page 293) and chopped fresh thyme.

Makes 4 servings

Tips

To soak the cashews for this recipe, place in a bowl and cover with 4 cups (1 L) water. Cover and set aside for 30 minutes. Drain, discarding soaking water. Rinse under cold running water until the water runs clear.

A spiral vegetable slicer usually comes with three separate blades: a small one that will make spaghetti-size noodles, a medium-sized one that will make larger noodles, and a blade that will make shreds similar to coleslaw. For this recipe use the medium-sized blade.

If you do not have a spiral vegetable slicer, use a Y-shaped (slingshot) vegetable peeler to cut thin strips off the vegetables.

Turmeric is a great way to produce a bright yellow sauce. A little of this spice goes a long way, so be careful, because it can easily overpower a recipe.

- **Spiral vegetable slicer, fitted with the medium blade**

2 cups	raw cashews, soaked (see Tips, left)	500 mL
2	large zucchini, trimmed	2
1	large sweet potato (or 2 medium)	1
½ cup	nutritional yeast	125 mL
1	clove garlic	1
¾ cup	filtered water	175 mL
2 tbsp	freshly squeezed lemon juice	30 mL
2 tbsp	cold-pressed flax oil	30 mL
2 tsp	brown rice miso	10 mL
1 tsp	ground turmeric (see Tips, left)	5 mL
1 tsp	fine sea salt	5 mL
¼ cup	Almond Parmesan Cheese (page 204)	60 mL

1. Using a spiral vegetable slicer fitted with the medium blade, process zucchini and sweet potato, transferring to a bowl as completed. Set aside.

2. In a food processor fitted with the metal blade, process soaked cashews, nutritional yeast, garlic, water, lemon juice, flax oil, miso, turmeric and salt, until smooth and creamy.

3. Add sauce to zucchini and sweet potato noodles and toss until well combined. Divide into 4 portions and place each in the middle of a plate. Top each with 1 tbsp (15 mL) almond Parmesan. Serve immediately or cover and refrigerate for up to 2 days.

Zucchini Tortillas

These tortillas are thin and delicate, just like crêpes. They are perfect filled with sauces or dips. Some of my favorites include Pumpkin Seed "Refried Beans" (page 93), Sweet Chili and Pecan Pâté (page 96) and Herbed Mushroom and Walnut Pâté (page 100).

Makes 10 to 12 tortillas

Tips

If you have been storing the tortillas in the refrigerator, you may want to warm them in the dehydrator before serving. If they are to be filled, they will need about 60 minutes at 105°F (41°C). If they will not be filled, warm for about 15 minutes at the same temperature.

You can purchase flax seeds that are already ground (often described as milled) in vacuum-sealed bags, or you can grind them yourself. Depending upon the quantity you need, grind whole flax seeds in a blender or a spice grinder. Once ground (or after the vacuum-sealed bag is opened), the beneficial fatty acids begin to dissipate. Store ground flax seeds away from light, in an airtight container in the refrigerator or freezer, for up to 2 months.

When a recipe calls for flax seeds, you have two options to choose from: golden or brown. Golden flax seeds will yield a lighter color for the end result, while brown flax seeds will make the final product darker.

- **Electric food dehydrator**

10 cups	chopped peeled zucchini (about 7 medium)	2.5 L
3 tbsp	cold-pressed (extra virgin) olive oil	45 mL
2 tsp	freshly squeezed lemon juice	10 mL
1 tsp	chili powder	5 mL
1/4 tsp	turmeric	1 mL
Pinch	fine sea salt	Pinch
1/4 cup	ground golden flax seeds (see Tips, left)	60 mL

1. In a blender, combine zucchini, olive oil, lemon juice, chili powder, turmeric and salt. Blend at high speed until smooth. Transfer to a bowl and stir in flax seeds.

2. Using a ladle, measure out 10 to 12 equal portions. Place on nonstick dehydrator sheets at least 2 inches (5 cm) apart and, using the back of the ladle, gently smooth each into a circular shape approximately 1/2 inch (1 cm) thick.

3. Dehydrate at 105°F (41°C) for 4 hours or until firm enough to handle. Flip and transfer to mesh sheets. Return to dehydrator and dehydrate for 30 to 60 minutes, until set all the way through. Serve immediately or allow to cool. Transfer to an airtight container and refrigerate for up to 7 days.

4. To fill, lay a tortilla on a flat surface, place 1/2 cup (125 mL) of the desired filling in the middle and roll up into a cylinder shape. Serve immediately.

Variations

You can vary the seasonings in this recipe to suit the fillings you use. For example, if filling the tortillas with Miso Ginger "Stir-Fried" Veggies (page 230), replace the chili powder and turmeric with 1/2 tsp (2 mL) Chinese five-spice powder and the olive oil with sesame oil. If filling the tortillas with Pumpkin Seed "Refried Beans" (page 93) replace the turmeric with 1/2 tsp (2 mL) ground cumin.

Layered Corn Tostadas

Crispy corn tortillas, layered with guacamole, walnut mince, cashew sour cream, fresh lettuce and ripe tomatoes, make this dish irresistible.

Makes 4 servings

Tips

When spreading out raw bread or cracker dough on a dehydrator sheet, keep a small bowl of room-temperature water off to the side. Use this to wet your hands intermittently to prevent the dough from sticking to your hands.

You can make the shells up to one week ahead of time. After completing Step 2, allow to cool and transfer to an airtight container. Store at room temperature for up to a week.

- **Electric food dehydrator**

2 cups	corn kernels	500 mL
¼ cup	chopped carrot	60 mL
3 tbsp	cold-pressed (extra virgin) olive oil	45 mL
3 tbsp	filtered water	45 mL
1 tbsp	ground cumin	15 mL
2 tsp	fine sea salt, divided	10 mL
Pinch	cayenne pepper	Pinch
½ cup	ground flax seeds	125 mL
1 cup	chopped tomatoes	250 mL
¼ cup	chopped parsley	60 mL
1 tbsp	freshly squeezed lemon juice	15 mL
1 cup	Perfect Guacamole (page 81)	250 mL
1 cup	Walnut Mince (page 293)	250 mL
½ cup	Cashew Sour Cream (page 204)	125 mL
½ cup	thinly sliced lettuce	125 mL
¼ cup	chopped green onion, white and green parts	60 mL

1. In a food processor, process corn, carrot, olive oil, water, cumin, 1 tsp (5 mL) salt and cayenne until smooth, stopping the motor once and scraping down the sides. Transfer to a bowl. Add flax seeds and mix well.

2. Using a ladle, drop 4 equal portions onto a nonstick dehydrator sheet, distributing evenly. Using your hands, spread out until ¾ inch (2 cm) thick. Dehydrate at 105°F (41°C) for 10 to 12 hours, until firm enough to handle. Flip and transfer to mesh sheet. Dehydrate for 3 to 4 hours or until dry and crisp.

3. When you're ready to serve, toss tomatoes with parsley, lemon juice and remaining 1 tsp (5 mL) salt. Set aside.

4. Lay tortillas on a flat surface and spread each with ¼ cup (60 mL) each guacamole and walnut mince and 2 tbsp (30 mL) cashew sour cream. Top with reserved tomato mixture, dividing equally. Scatter lettuce evenly over tomatoes, dividing equally. Sprinkle onion evenly over each, dividing equally. Serve immediately.

Bursting Burritos

The sun-dried tomato and carrot tortillas make this recipe a soft, mouth-watering delight. Moist and delicious, these burritos are bursting with flavor and nutrition. I like to serve them with Avocado and Cucumber Salad (page 155) or Jicama Potato Salad (page 158). Double or triple the recipe to suit your needs.

Makes 4 servings

Tips

To soak the sun-dried tomatoes for this recipe, combine with 4 cups (1 L) warm water. Set aside for 30 minutes. Drain, discarding liquid.

You want the final product to be soft and pliable like a traditional tortilla. Take care not to over-dehydrate.

It's important to spread the mixture to ½ inch (1 cm) thickness, so if you're using a ring-shaped dehydrator, you may need two nonstick sheets, dividing the mixture in half and cutting each portion into two pieces, rather than one large sheet.

- **Electric food dehydrator**

1 cup	dry-packed sun-dried tomatoes, soaked (see Tips, left)	250 mL
2½ cups	chopped carrots	625 mL
¾ cup	parsley leaves	175 mL
2	cloves garlic	2
1 tsp	dried oregano	5 mL
2 tsp	fine sea salt, divided	10 mL
½ cup	(approx.) filtered water	125 mL
¼ cup	freshly squeezed lemon juice, divided	60 mL
2½ cups	ground flax seeds	625 mL
1	small avocado, mashed	1
2 cups	Pumpkin Seed "Refried Beans" (page 93)	500 mL
1 cup	thinly sliced romaine lettuce	250 mL
1 cup	finely diced tomato	250 mL
½ cup	Cashew Sour Cream (page 204)	125 mL

1. In a food processor fitted with the metal blade, process carrots, soaked sun-dried tomatoes, parsley, garlic, oregano, 1 tsp (5 mL) salt, water and 2 tbsp (30 mL) lemon juice, until smooth, stopping the motor once and scraping down the sides of the work bowl.
2. Transfer to a bowl. Add flax seeds and mix until mixture resembles soft bread dough, adding more water if necessary.
3. Transfer to a nonstick dehydrator sheet and, using your hands, spread out until approximately ½ inch (1 cm) thick. Using a knife, cut into 4 equal pieces. Dehydrate at 105°F (41°C) for 5 to 6 hours or until firm enough to handle.

If you have been storing the tortillas in the refrigerator, you may want to warm them in the dehydrator before serving, for about 15 minutes at 105°F (41°C).

4. Flip and transfer to mesh sheet and dehydrate for 2 to 3 hours or until firm and pliable. The tortillas can be made ahead to this point and stored in an airtight container in the refrigerator for up to a week.

5. When you are ready to make the burritos, in a small bowl, mash avocado with remaining 2 tbsp (30 mL) lemon juice and 1 tsp (5 mL) salt.

6. One at a time, lay a tortilla on a flat surface. Spread with one-quarter each of the avocado mixture and "refried beans" and sprinkle with one-quarter of the lettuce and tomato. Repeat until all the tortillas have been filled. Roll into cylinders and garnish each with an equal dollop of cashew sour cream.

Raw Tamales

These delicately sweet and savory little pockets are the perfect addition to any meal. I like to make them ahead of time, refrigerate them and take some with me for a ready-to-eat lunch.

Makes 4 servings

Tips

If you have a dehydrator, toss the corn kernels with 1 tbsp (15 mL) olive oil and spread evenly on a nonstick dehydrator sheet. Dehydrate at 105°F (41°C) for 30 minutes before continuing with the rest of the recipe.

If you have a dehydrator, place finished tamales on a non-stick dehydrator sheet and leave at 105°F (41°F) for 1 hour or until slightly warmed throughout.

Coconut oil is solid at room temperature. It has a melting temperature of 76°F (24°C), so it is easy to liquefy. If you have a dehydrator, place the required amount in a shallow dish and warm at 105°F (41°C) for 15 minutes or until melted. If you do not have a dehydrator, place a shallow glass bowl over a pot of simmering water.

Coconut butter is a blend of coconut oil and coconut meat. You can usually find it in natural foods stores next to the coconut oil. In this recipe, you may substitute an equal quantity of coconut oil, but the dressing will not be as rich and creamy.

2 cups	fresh corn kernels (4 to 5 cobs)	500 mL
¼ cup	melted coconut oil (see Tips, left)	60 mL
2 tbsp	raw shelled hemp seeds, divided	30 mL
1 tbsp	freshly squeezed lemon juice	15 mL
1 tbsp	coconut butter (see Tips, left)	15 mL
1	clove garlic	1
2 tsp	ground cumin	10 mL
½ tsp	chili powder	2 mL
½ tsp	fine sea salt	2 mL
¼ cup	chopped red bell pepper	60 mL
2 tbsp	chopped cilantro leaves	30 mL
¼ cup	Walnut Mince (page 293)	60 mL
4	corn husks, softened in warm water, drained and patted dry	4

1. In a food processor fitted with the metal blade, process corn, coconut oil, 1 tbsp (15 mL) hemp seeds, lemon juice, coconut butter, garlic, cumin, chili powder and salt, until smooth and creamy, stopping the motor and scraping down the sides of the work bowl as necessary.

2. Transfer to a bowl. Add red pepper, cilantro and remaining 1 tbsp (15 mL) hemp seeds and mix well.

3. One at a time, lay the corn husks flat on a work surface. Place 1 tbsp (15 mL) walnut mince on each husk and spread evenly. Spoon one-quarter of the corn filling overtop. Fold over the edges of the husk to form a package. Serve immediately or transfer to an airtight container and refrigerate for up to 3 days. Unwrap tamale before consuming.

Sunflower Date Salisbury Steak

This "meat," made from seeds, is flavorful and dense. It is mildly sweet, thanks to the dates, and the dill, sun-dried tomatoes and tamari make a sumptuous combination. I like to use this as a protein topper for simple salads or in a sandwich between slices of raw bread. Try it with Zucchini Hemp Bread (page 324) spread with Spicy Cashew Mayonnaise (page 87), layered with avocado and tomato slices.

Makes 9 servings

Tips

To soak the sunflower seeds for this recipe, place in a bowl with 4 cups (1 L) water. Cover and set aside for 30 minutes to soak. Drain and discard any remaining water.

To soak the sun-dried tomatoes for this recipe, combine with 1 cup (250 mL) warm water. Set aside for 30 minutes. Drain, discarding liquid.

To soak the dates for this recipe, place them in a bowl with 2 cups (500 mL) warm water. Cover and set aside for 30 minutes. Drain, discarding soaking water.

The key to successfully making this recipe is not to dehydrate it too much. You want the "steak" to be firm on the outside but still soft in the middle.

It's important to spread the mixture to 1-inch (2.5 cm) thickness, if you're using a ring-shaped dehydrator, you may need two nonstick sheets, placing two-thirds on one sheet and one-third on the other. Cut the larger portion into 6 pieces and the smaller portion into 3 pieces.

- **Electric food dehydrator**

2 cups	raw sunflower seeds, soaked (see Tips, left)	500 mL
¼ cup	dry-packed sun-dried tomatoes, soaked (see Tips, left)	60 mL
8	pitted Medjool dates, soaked (see Tips, left)	8
¾ cup	filtered water	175 mL
2 tbsp	cold-pressed (extra virgin) olive oil	30 mL
1 tbsp	wheat-free tamari	15 mL
1 tbsp	nutritional yeast	15 mL
2 tsp	dried dill weed	10 mL
1 cup	ground flax seeds	250 mL

1. In a food processor fitted with the metal blade, process soaked sun-dried tomatoes and dates, water, olive oil, tamari, nutritional yeast and dill until smooth. Add soaked sunflower seeds and process until smooth, stopping the motor once and scraping down the sides of the work bowl. Transfer to a bowl and add flax seeds. Mix well.

2. Transfer to a nonstick dehydrator sheet and, using your hands, spread the dough evenly in a layer approximately 1 inch (2.5 cm) thick (see Tips, left). Using a knife, cut into 9 equal portions. Dehydrate at 105°F (41°C) for 12 to 15 hours, until firm but soft in the middle. Allow to cool, then transfer to an airtight container and refrigerate for up to 7 days.

Variation

If you do not have dates, substitute ¼ cup (60 mL) raw agave nectar in Step 1.

Meatloaf

This scrumptious loaf is full of protein. It is a great recipe for holiday time because the fresh herbs and seasonings seem quite festive. It also makes a great filling for a sandwich. Use crisp romaine leaves as bread and top with fresh tomato slices, Caramelized Onions (page 292) and a dollop of Sun-Dried Tomato Ketchup (page 198).

Makes 6 to 8 servings

Tips

To soak the walnuts for this recipe, place in a bowl and add 2 cups (500 mL) water. Cover and set aside for 30 minutes. Drain, discarding soaking water. Rinse under cold running water until the water runs clear.

To soak the sunflower seeds for this recipe, place in a bowl and add 2 cups (500 mL) water. Cover and set aside for 30 minutes. Drain, discarding water and any shells or unwanted particles. Rinse under cold running water until the water runs clear.

To soak the almonds for this recipe, place in a bowl and add 2 cups (500 mL) water. Cover and set aside for 30 minutes. Drain, discarding soaking water. Rinse under cold running water until the water runs clear.

- **Electric food dehydrator**

1 cup	walnut pieces, soaked (see Tips, left)	250 mL
1 cup	raw sunflower seeds, soaked (see Tips, left)	250 mL
1 cup	whole raw almonds, soaked (see Tips, left)	250 mL
½ cup	chopped carrot	125 mL
¼ cup	filtered water	60 mL
¼ cup	cold-pressed (extra virgin) olive oil	60 mL
6	cloves garlic	6
¼ cup	chopped onion	60 mL
2 tbsp	nutritional yeast	30 mL
2 tsp	fine sea salt	10 mL
1 cup	chopped red bell pepper	250 mL
1 cup	Marinated Mushrooms (page 292)	250 mL
1 cup	ground flax seeds	250 mL
½ cup	chopped celery (see Tips, page 255)	125 mL
½ cup	chopped flat-leaf parsley leaves	125 mL
2 tbsp	chopped fresh rosemary needles	30 mL
1 tbsp	chopped fresh tarragon leaves	15 mL
1 tbsp	chopped fresh thyme leaves	15 mL
2 tsp	ground cumin	10 mL
½ cup	Sun-Dried Tomato Barbecue Sauce (page 199)	125 mL

1. In a food processor fitted with the metal blade, process carrot, water, olive oil, garlic, onion, nutritional yeast and salt, until smooth. Add red pepper and marinated mushrooms and process until smooth. Add soaked walnuts, sunflower seeds and almonds and process until smooth.

Tips

The outer stalks of celery can be tough and fibrous. For best results, peel the stalk with a vegetable peeler. Save the peel to make soups, sauces or stocks.

When you dehydrate recipes that are intended to work as meat substitutes, such as burgers or meatloaf, make sure you do not dehydrate them for too long. They should be dry on the outside but remain soft in the middle. This will give the mouth feel of meat and help to create a pleasing texture.

2. Transfer to a bowl. Add flax seeds, celery, parsley, rosemary, tarragon, thyme and cumin and mix well. Set aside for 10 to 15 minutes so the flax can absorb some of the liquid and swell.

3. Transfer to a nonstick dehydrator sheet and, using your hands, shape into a loaf about 6 inches (15 cm) long and 3 inches (7.5 cm) wide. Dehydrate at 105°F (41°C) for 6 to 8 hours or until firm enough to handle. Flip and transfer to the mesh sheet. Spread Sun-Dried Tomato Barbecue Sauce overtop. Dehydrate for 1 to 2 hours or until firm on the outside and soft in the middle. Serve immediately or transfer to an airtight container and refrigerate for up to 5 days.

Lentil Chili

This take on old-fashioned chili is a scrumptious way to get your fix of that spicy tomato-based stew. The flavors are a perfect balance of tomato, garlic and seasonings. I like to make this on a cold day; it is especially good over Sprouted Quinoa Pilaf (page 269), finished with a large dollop of Cashew Sour Cream (page 204). Just be sure to plan ahead when making it, because soaking the lentils takes 12 hours.

Makes 4 servings

Tips

To soak the lentils for this recipe, place in a bowl with 2 cups (500 mL) water. Cover and set aside for 12 hours, changing the water 3 times. (Alternatively, place in the refrigerator for 18 hours, changing the water once.) Drain, discarding soaking water.

To soak the sun-dried tomatoes for this recipe, combine with 6 cups (1.5 L) warm water in a bowl. Set aside for 30 minutes. Drain, discarding liquid.

½ cup	green lentils, soaked (see Tips, left)	250 mL
1½ cups	dry-packed sun-dried tomatoes, soaked (see Tips, left)	375 mL
4 cups	chopped tomatoes	1 L
3	cloves garlic	3
¼ cup	chili powder	60 mL
2 tbsp	ground cumin	30 mL
2 tbsp	orange juice	30 mL
2 tsp	freshly squeezed lemon juice	10 mL
2 tsp	fine sea salt	10 mL

1. In a food processor fitted with the metal blade, process soaked sun-dried tomatoes, chopped tomatoes, garlic, chili powder, cumin, orange juice, lemon juice and salt, stopping the motor once and scraping down the sides of the work bowl.

2. Transfer to a bowl. Add soaked lentils and mix well. Serve immediately or transfer to an airtight container and refrigerate for up to 4 days.

Ratatouille (page 227) and Cauliflower Rice (page 274)

Pesto-Coated Carrot and Parsnip Fettuccini (page 236)

Zucchini Manicotti (page 239)

Twice "Baked" Stuffed Tomatoes (page 272)

Spicy Orange and Ginger Sesame Watercress (page 278)

Sweet Potato Chips (page 301) and Sour Cream and Onion Kale Chips (page 298)

Buckwheat and Sunflower Seed Pizza Crust (page 326)

Raspberry, Orange and Blueberry Parfait (page 336)

Pecan Pie (page 354)

Cashew Cheesecake (page 360)

Black Lentil Sloppy Joes

This recipe is the perfect potluck dish because it stores well in the refrigerator. Also, the texture and flavor will appeal to people who are new to raw food. I like serving it with a splash of Living Hot Sauce (page 196) and a dollop of Cashew Sour Cream (page 204). You can also serve it over Buckwheat Toast (page 36) or Zucchini Hemp Bread (page 324) with some Cashew Sour Cream.

Makes 4 to 5 servings

Tips

To soak the lentils for this recipe, place in a bowl and add 2 cups (500 mL) water. Cover and set aside for 10 to 12 hours, changing the water every 3 to 4 hours (or place in the refrigerator for 18 hours, changing the water once). Drain and rinse under cold running water until the water runs clear.

To soak the walnuts for this recipe, place in a bowl and add 4 cups (1 L) water. Cover and set aside for 30 minutes. Drain, discarding liquid.

To soak the sun-dried tomatoes for this recipe, combine with 1 cup (250 mL) warm water. Set aside for 30 minutes. Drain, discarding liquid.

Nutritional yeast is used in vegan and raw food diets mainly because it is a source of vitamin B_{12}. It is pasteurized, so technically it does not qualify as a raw food. However, in addition to necessary nutrients, it adds a deep, umami-like flavor to many dishes.

½ cup	black lentils, soaked (see Tips, left)	125 mL
2 cups	walnut pieces, soaked (see Tips, left)	500 mL
¼ cup	dry-packed sun-dried tomatoes, soaked (see Tips, left)	60 mL
1 cup	chopped tomatoes	250 mL
½ cup	chopped red bell pepper	125 mL
¼ cup	chopped green bell pepper	60 mL
3 tbsp	nutritional yeast (see Tips, left)	45 mL
4	cloves garlic	4
2 tbsp	freshly squeezed lemon juice	30 mL
1 tbsp	chopped rosemary needles	15 mL
1 tbsp	ground cumin	15 mL
1 tsp	chili powder	5 mL
1 tsp	fine sea salt	5 mL
Pinch	cayenne pepper	Pinch

1. In a food processor fitted with the metal blade, process soaked sun-dried tomatoes, chopped tomatoes, red and green pepper, nutritional yeast, garlic, lemon juice, rosemary, cumin, chili powder, salt and cayenne until smooth, stopping the motor and scraping down the sides of the work bowl as necessary.

2. Add soaked walnuts and lentils and process until combined and no large pieces remain. Serve immediately or cover and refrigerate for up to 4 days.

Cauliflower Risotto

The cauliflower, cashews and nutritional yeast in this recipe blend together to make a creamy, rich dish that has a slightly cheesy flavor, accented with garlic and herbs. This is one of my favorite comfort foods.

Makes 2 servings

Tips

To soak the cashews for this recipe, place in a bowl and add 2 cups (500 mL) water. Cover and set aside for 30 minutes. Drain, discarding soaking water, and rinse under cold running water until the water runs clear.

To make riced vegetables, chop the ingredients into pieces of similar size. Place in the work bowl of a food processor fitted with the metal blade and pulse until rice-like in consistency. You don't want to overprocess the vegetables, as their cells will begin to break down and they will become soggy.

1 cup	raw cashews, soaked (see Tips, left)	250 mL
3 cups	chopped cauliflower, divided	750 mL
2 tbsp	nutritional yeast	30 mL
1	clove garlic	1
1 tbsp	chopped fresh thyme	15 mL
1 tsp	fine sea salt	5 mL
½ cup	filtered water	125 mL
1 tbsp	freshly squeezed lemon juice	15 mL

1. In a food processor fitted with the metal blade, process soaked cashews, 1 cup (250 mL) cauliflower, nutritional yeast, garlic, thyme, salt, water and lemon juice until smooth and creamy.

2. Transfer to a bowl. Add remaining cauliflower to work bowl and process until broken down into a rice-like consistency. Fold into cashew mixture. Serve immediately or transfer to an airtight container and refrigerate for up to 4 days.

Variation

Use ¾ cup (175 mL) Marinated Mushrooms (page 292) in this recipe, adding ½ cup (125 mL) in Step 1 and folding the remainder in with the cauliflower rice in Step 2.

Braised Cabbage Rolls

These soft, moist cabbage rolls are simple to prepare, and their creamy filling will melt in your mouth. I like to serve these with Arugula and Spinach Salad with Candied Pecans (page 148).

Makes 4 servings

Tips

If your cabbage leaves have a tough spine running through the middle, use a paring knife to remove the more fibrous part.

Substitute collard leaves for the cabbage. Be sure to remove the spine before filling. If using collard leaves for this recipe, you will not need to marinate them ahead of time, so you can omit Step 1.

If you are using a ring-shaped dehydrator, divide the cabbage rolls between two to four smaller dishes that fit on the racks and use multiple racks as necessary.

- **Electric food dehydrator**
- **Shallow baking dish**

3 tbsp	cold-pressed (extra virgin) olive oil	45 mL
3 tbsp	freshly squeezed lemon juice	45 mL
$\frac{1}{2}$ tsp	fine sea salt	2 mL
8	cabbage leaves	8

Filling

1 cup	Cauliflower Mashed Potatoes (page 273)	250 mL
$\frac{1}{4}$ cup	Walnut Mince (page 293)	60 mL
3 cups	Tomato Basil Marinara Sauce (page 184), divided	750 mL

1. In a large bowl, combine olive oil, lemon juice and salt. Add cabbage leaves and toss well. Set aside to marinate for 45 to 60 minutes or until cabbage has softened.

2. *Filling:* In a bowl, combine Cauliflower Mashed Potatoes, Walnut Mince and $\frac{1}{4}$ cup (60 mL) Marinara sauce.

3. One at a time, place softened cabbage leaves on a flat work surface with the natural curve facing up. Spoon about 2 tbsp (30 mL) filling into the middle of each. Wrap leaf around filling, tucking in excess, and roll into a cylinder. Place seam side down in a baking dish. Repeat until all the leaves have been filled.

4. Pour remaining marinara sauce over cabbage rolls. Place in dehydrator and dehydrate at 105°F (41°C) for 3 to 4 hours or until warmed through. Serve immediately.

Jicama Pierogies

These delicious little treats are crisp, refreshing and surprisingly filling. The key to this recipe is to use a mandoline to slice the jicama uniformly.

Tips

The jicama should be sliced into half-moon shapes. The slices need to be thin enough to be pliable. If you cut them too thick, they will break when you attempt to fold them. If the jicama is sliced thinly enough and marinated until soft, the edges should stick together when folded pressed together.

Mandolines come in various sizes and shapes. I recommend purchasing a Japanese-style mandoline because I find them easier to use.

- **Mandoline**

1	large jicama, cut in half	1
3 tbsp	cold-pressed (extra virgin) olive oil	45 mL
2 tsp	freshly squeezed lemon juice	10 mL
1/4 tsp	fine sea salt	1 mL
1 cup	Cauliflower Mashed Potatoes (page 273)	250 mL
1/2 cup	Walnut Mince (page 293)	125 mL
3 tbsp	Cashew Sour Cream (page 204)	45 mL
2 tbsp	chopped green onion, white and green parts	30 mL
1/4 cup	Eggplant Bacon (page 41), chopped	60 mL

1. Using a mandoline (see Tips, left), cut jicama into 12 slices approximately 1/4 inch (0.5 cm) thick. Transfer to a bowl and toss with olive oil, lemon juice and salt. Set aside for 10 to 15 minutes, until softened.

2. Working with one slice at a time, place jicama on a clean work surface. Place 1 heaping tbsp (20 mL) cauliflower mashed potatoes down the middle of each slice and top with 2 tsp (10 mL) walnut mince. Fold one side over the other. Using your forefinger and thumb, press the two sides together to form a seal. Repeat until all slices have been filled.

3. To serve, place 3 pierogies on each plate. Garnish with a dollop of Cashew Sour Cream and sprinkle green onion and Eggplant Bacon overtop.

Variation

Use the sliced marinated jicama with other fillings. You can substitute Pumpkin Seed "Refried Beans" (page 93) for the walnut mince and cauliflower mashed potatoes and roll the sliced jicama into a small, soft taco.

Jerk Veggie Kabobs

The sauce for this recipe was inspired by Caribbean jerk sauce. It's a great way to spice up simple vegetables. This is sure to become a staple in your recipe repertoire.

Makes 4 servings

Tips

If you prefer these skewers to be warm, after the vegetables have been marinated, transfer to a nonstick dehydrator sheet and dehydrate at 105°F (41°C) for 30 to 45 minutes to slightly warm them through and concentrate flavors.

Hemp seeds contain all eight essential amino acids, which makes them a complete protein. One tbsp (15 mL) hemp seeds contains up to 5 grams of complete protein.

- **4 skewers**

Vegetables

½ cup	each broccoli and cauliflower florets	125 mL
½ cup	cubed zucchini (1 inch/2.5 cm)	125 mL
½ cup	diced red bell pepper	125 mL
½ cup	quartered button mushrooms	125 mL
3 tbsp	raw shelled hemp seeds	45 mL
¼ cup	cold-pressed (extra virgin) olive oil	60 mL
2 tbsp	freshly squeezed lemon juice	30 mL
1 tsp	fine sea salt	5 mL

Sauce

¼ cup	cold-pressed flax oil	60 mL
¼ cup	freshly squeezed orange juice	60 mL
3 tbsp	apple cider vinegar	45 mL
3 tbsp	raw agave nectar	45 mL
2 tbsp	freshly squeezed lime juice	30 mL
2 tbsp	wheat-free tamari	30 mL
3 tbsp	chopped green onion	45 mL
3	cloves garlic, minced	3
1 tbsp	chopped fresh thyme leaves	15 mL
1 tsp	ground allspice	5 mL
1 tsp	minced gingerroot	5 mL
½ tsp	each ground nutmeg and cinnamon	2 mL

1. *Vegetables:* In a bowl, toss together broccoli, cauliflower, zucchini, red pepper, mushrooms, hemp seeds, olive oil, lemon juice and salt. Set aside for 10 to 15 minutes.

2. *Sauce:* In a blender, combine flax oil, orange juice, vinegar, agave nectar, lime juice, tamari, green onion, garlic, thyme, allspice, ginger, nutmeg and cinnamon. Blend at high speed until smooth.

3. *Assembly:* Thread 1 broccoli floret on a skewer, followed by 1 piece each of cauliflower, zucchini, pepper and mushroom. Repeat in this order on skewers until all of the vegetables have been used up. Place on a platter.

4. Pour sauce over the vegetables and set aside to marinate for 30 minutes. Serve immediately.

Creamy Spinach and Mushroom Casserole

The creamy spinach and chunky mushrooms in this recipe truly make a delicious combination. When I'm serving this, I like to make it a bit ahead of time and put it in the dehydrator for a few hours to warm slightly. Serve this with Greek Kale Salad (page 143).

Makes 4 servings

Tips

To soak the cashews for this recipe, place in a bowl and add 2 cups (500 mL) water. Cover and set aside for 30 minutes. Drain, discarding soaking water, and rinse under cold running water until the water runs clear.

Nutritional yeast is used in vegan and raw food diets mainly because it is a source of vitamin B_{12}. It is pasteurized, so technically it does not qualify as a raw food. However, in addition to necessary nutrients, it adds a deep, umami-like flavor to many dishes.

- **Shallow casserole dish**

1 cup	raw cashews, soaked (see Tips, left)	250 mL
8 cups	chopped spinach	2 L
1/4 cup	cold-pressed (extra virgin) olive oil, divided	60 mL
1/4 cup	freshly squeezed lemon juice, divided	60 mL
1 tbsp	fine sea salt, divided	15 mL
6	cloves garlic, minced, divided	6
4 cups	sliced white mushrooms	1 L
2 tbsp	wheat-free tamari	30 mL
2 tbsp	chopped green onion, white and green parts	30 mL
2 tbsp	chopped fresh thyme leaves	30 mL
1 tsp	ground cumin	5 mL
1/4 cup	filtered water	60 mL
1/4 cup	nutritional yeast (see Tips, left)	60 mL
1/4 cup	raw shelled hemp seeds	60 mL
1/2 cup	Almond Parmesan Cheese (page 204)	125 mL

1. In a bowl, toss spinach with 2 tbsp (30 mL) olive oil, 2 tbsp (30 mL) lemon juice, 2 tsp (10 mL) salt and 4 cloves minced garlic. Set aside for 30 minutes to soften the spinach.

2. In another bowl, toss mushrooms, remaining 2 tbsp (30 mL) olive oil, tamari, green onion, thyme, cumin and 1/2 tsp (2 mL) salt. Set aside for 30 minutes to soften the mushrooms.

3. In a blender, combine water, nutritional yeast, soaked cashews and remaining garlic, lemon juice and salt. Blend at high speed until smooth and creamy. Add 1 cup (250 mL) of the marinated spinach and blend at high speed until smooth.

4. Spread half of the remaining spinach over the bottom of a baking dish. Cover with half of the marinated mushrooms and half of the cashew sauce from Step 3. Repeat. Spread hemp seeds evenly overtop and finish with a layer of almond Parmesan, spreading evenly. Serve immediately or cover and refrigerate for up to 4 days (see Tip, left).

Variation

Substitute a variety of different mushrooms, such as cremini, shiitake, oyster and chanterelle, for the white mushrooms. If you prefer a chunkier texture, quarter the mushrooms instead of slicing them, in which case increase the quantity to 6 cups (1.5 L).

Macrobiotic Bowl

This recipe is a delicious bowl of healing ingredients. The array of flavors and textures combine very well. I like to have this for dinner along with a glass of Perfect Green Juice (page 18). Double or triple this recipe to suit your needs and be sure to start it well in advance to accommodate soaking the mung beans.

Makes 1 serving

Tips

To soak the mung beans for this recipe, place in a bowl and add 1 cup (250 mL) water. Cover and set aside in the refrigerator for 10 to 12 hours, changing the water once, until beans are softened. Drain, discarding any remaining water.

Arame and wakame are nutritious sea vegetables (seaweed) that need to be soaked before using. To soak the arame and wakame for this recipe, place in a bowl and add 2 cups (500 mL) water. Cover and set aside for 30 minutes. Drain, discarding soaking water. Rinse under cold running water until the water runs clear, to ensure that any sand particles are rinsed away.

If you do not have any seaweed, substitute 1 tbsp (15 mL) each dried kelp and dried dulse.

You may substitute the tabouli in this recipe with an equal quantity of Parsnip "Fried Rice" (page 275).

2 tbsp	mung beans, soaked (see Tips, left)	60 mL
2 tbsp	arame, soaked (see Tips, left)	60 mL
2 tbsp	wakame, soaked	60 mL
1 cup	Cauliflower and Hemp Tabouli (page 280)	250 mL
¼ cup	shredded beet (about ½ small)	60 mL
¼ cup	shredded sweet potato (about ½ small)	60 mL
2 tbsp	Pickled Red Onions (page 208)	30 mL
¼ cup	Spirulina Tahini Ginger Cream (page 180)	60 mL

1. Spread out tabouli on a small platter. Arrange shredded beet and sweet potato, soaked mung beans, arame and wakame and pickled onions overtop. Drizzle with Spirulina Tahini Ginger Cream and serve immediately.

Paella

This Spanish-inspired dish is a luxurious blend of aromatic spices, light vegetable rice and protein. The key to this dish is fragrant saffron.

Makes 2 servings

Tips

In raw food cuisine, vegetables such as cauliflower and parsnips can easily be made into a rice substitute by using the food processor. When making raw "rice" in a food processor, you want to be careful not to overprocess. Always use the Pulse setting, which enables you to control how much the vegetables are broken down. Once the food reaches the point where it resembles rice, stop pulsing. If you continue to process, you will start to break down the cell walls and the texture will become watery.

If you don't have saffron, substitute 1/4 tsp (1 mL) turmeric. It won't give you the flavor, but it will provide color.

1/2 cup	chopped baby spinach	125 mL
1/4 cup	finely diced green bell pepper	60 mL
1/4 cup	finely diced red bell pepper	60 mL
2 tbsp	cold-pressed (extra virgin) olive oil	30 mL
2 tbsp	freshly squeezed lemon juice, divided	30 mL
1/2 tsp	fine sea salt, divided	2 mL
3 tbsp	filtered water	45 mL
2	cloves garlic	2
1 tsp	chopped fresh thyme leaves	5 mL
1/4 tsp	saffron (see Tips, left)	1 mL
2 cups	chopped cauliflower florets	500 mL
1/4 cup	Walnut Mince (page 293)	60 mL
1/4 cup	Sunflower Almond Nuggets (page 316)	60 mL
1/4 cup	chopped flat-leaf parsley leaves	60 mL

1. In a bowl, toss spinach, green and red pepper, olive oil, 1 tbsp (15 mL) lemon juice and 1/4 tsp (1 mL) salt. Set aside for 10 minutes, until ingredients have softened.
2. Meanwhile, in a food processor fitted with the metal blade, process water, remaining lemon juice, garlic, thyme, remaining salt and saffron until garlic has been chopped and liquid has turned yellow.
3. Add cauliflower and pulse until it breaks down to resemble rice.
4. Add cauliflower mixture to spinach mixture and toss to combine. Divide between two bowls. Garnish each equally with Walnut Mince, Sunflower Almond Nuggets and parsley. Serve immediately.

Variation

Substitute 2 cups (500 mL) finely chopped parsnip for the cauliflower. Make sure to chop them finely before adding to the food processor, because parsnip is denser than cauliflower.

No-Crab Cakes

These tasty little cakes are a perfect main-course attraction for any event. The key is to make them wet enough and to use enough flax to hold them together. The taste is reminiscent of real crab cakes and the fresh dill provides a lovely soft herbal undertone. I like to serve these as a main course with sides such as Cauliflower Rice (page 274), or over Sesame, Hemp and Carrot Slaw (page 162). If you have leftovers, use them to garnish a big bowl of Corn and Red Pepper Chowder (page 121).

Makes 4 servings

Tips

When ground flax seeds are combined with liquid, they have a binding property. They can be used to thicken soups, sauces or dips and can hold together raw breads or crackers.

You can purchase flax seeds that are already ground (often described as milled) in vacuum-sealed bags, or you can grind them yourself. Depending upon the quantity you need, grind whole flax seeds in a blender or a spice grinder. Once ground (or after the vacuum-sealed bag is opened), the beneficial fatty acids begin to dissipate. Store ground flax seeds away from light, in an airtight container in the refrigerator or freezer, for up to 2 months.

• **Electric food dehydrator**

1 cup	raw macadamia nuts	250 mL
3	cloves garlic	3
1 cup	chopped zucchini	250 mL
¼ cup	Marinated Mushrooms (page 292)	60 mL
¼ cup	finely diced red bell pepper	60 mL
¼ cup	finely diced celery	60 mL
¼ cup	ground flax seeds	60 mL
¼ cup	chopped fresh dill fronds	60 mL
2 tbsp	nutritional yeast	30 mL
2 tsp	dried dulse flakes	10 mL
½ tsp	chili powder	2 mL
½ tsp	sweet paprika	2 mL
½ tsp	fine sea salt	2 mL
Pinch	cayenne pepper	Pinch
3 tbsp	filtered water	45 mL
2 tbsp	cold-pressed flax oil	30 mL

1. In a food processor fitted with the metal blade, process macadamia nuts and garlic until nuts are broken down. Add zucchini and mushrooms and process until roughly chopped.

2. Transfer to a bowl. Add red pepper, celery, flax seeds, dill, nutritional yeast, dulse, chili powder, paprika, salt, cayenne, water and flax oil and mix well. Set aside for 10 minutes so the flax can absorb some of the liquid and swell.

3. Using a ¼-cup (60 mL) dry measure or ladle, drop equal portions of the mixture onto a nonstick dehydrator sheet at least 2 inches (5 cm) apart and, using your hands, shape into small hockey puck shapes about 2 inches (5 cm) thick. Dehydrate at 105°F (41°C) for 2 to 3 hours or until firm enough to handle. Flip and transfer to the mesh sheet. Dehydrate for 2 to 3 hours or until firm on the outside and soft in the middle. Serve immediately or cover and refrigerate for up to 5 days.

Sides and Small Plates

In raw food cuisine a meal is often a collection of small plates rather than one large main course. This chapter focuses on dishes that work best as smaller portions. Sometimes they work as sides to larger plates such as Bursting Burritos (page 250) or Stuffed Portobello Towers (page 211) in place of a salad. Or they can be combined to create a meal in themselves. For instance, I like to pair Cauliflower Mashed Potatoes (page 273) with Thai Lettuce Wraps (page 290) for a quick meal. There are many different ways to use the recipes in this chapter. By experimenting, you'll find what works best for you.

Sprouted Quinoa Pilaf

Here's a way to enjoy quinoa, a gluten-free seed that is a complete protein, without cooking. This is a simple way to add flavor to sprouted quinoa, which resembles a bowl of rice, with a minimal amount of effort. I love how the parsley, flax oil, hemp seeds and salt combine to create fresh flavors that really stand out. Use this recipe in situations where you would normally use rice. Place in a bowl and top with a serving of Moroccan Chickpea Stew (page 226) or toss with Simple Marinated Kale Salad (page 142). You will need to start well ahead of time in order to sprout the quinoa.

Makes 2 to 3 servings

Tip

To sprout the quinoa for this recipe, place in a bowl and cover with 2 cups (500 mL) water. Cover and set aside for 8 hours, changing the water every 3 hours. Drain and discard any remaining water. Transfer to a colander and rinse under cold running water. Place the colander over a bowl and set aside for 24 hours, rinsing the quinoa every 2 to 3 hours to keep it damp but not moist. Before going to bed, rinse the quinoa and place a damp cloth overtop. In the morning, rinse again. Continue to rinse quinoa every 2 to 3 hours until tails approximately 1/4 inch (0.5 cm) long have sprouted from the seeds. This will take 24 to 30 hours in total. The quinoa is now ready for use in your recipe, or you can cover it and refrigerate for up to 3 days.

1 cup	quinoa, sprouted (see Tip, left)	250 mL
1/2 cup	chopped parsley leaves	125 mL
3 tbsp	cold-pressed flax oil	45 mL
2 tsp	raw shelled hemp seeds	10 mL
1/2 tsp	fine sea salt	2 mL

1. In a bowl, toss sprouted quinoa with parsley, flax oil, hemp seeds and salt until well coated. Serve immediately or cover and refrigerate in an airtight container for up to 3 days.

Variations

I enjoy mixing this pilaf with different sauces. I love it with Olive and Parsley Tapenade (page 91), Basil, Spinach and Walnut Pesto (page 186), Red Pepper Basil Marinara Sauce (page 184) or Lemon Avocado Dressing (page 177).

Portobello Carpaccio

This recipe, a take on traditional beef carpaccio, substitutes thinly sliced portobello mushrooms for the beef. Their meaty texture stands up well to the strong flavorings. I like to serve this on a large, flat plate as an appetizer, followed by Zucchini Noodles (page 244) tossed in Red Pepper Basil Marinara Sauce (page 184).

(page 244) ... (page 184)

Makes 2 servings

Tips

Mushrooms are easier to slice if they are very fresh and cold. Refrigerating them before slicing produces the best results.

This same recipe will work using any mushroom with a large cap, such as shiitakes. You will need approximately 1 lb (500 g) mushrooms. Make sure you add enough dressing to penetrate the mushrooms and soften them.

2	large portobello mushroom caps, chilled (see Tips, left)	2
3 tbsp	cold-pressed (extra virgin) olive oil	45 mL
2 tbsp	wheat-free tamari	30 mL
1 tbsp	chopped fresh thyme leaves	15 mL
2	cloves garlic, minced	2
¼ tsp	fine sea salt	1 mL
2 tbsp	chopped green onion, white and green parts	30 mL
2 tbsp	Cashew Feta Cheese (page 105)	30 mL
2 tsp	Spicy Red Pepper Flax Oil (page 203)	10 mL

1. Place mushroom caps on a cutting board, gill side down, and, using a sharp chef's knife, slice thinly. Transfer to a bowl.

2. In a small bowl, whisk together olive oil, tamari, thyme, garlic and salt, until well incorporated. Add to mushrooms and toss well. Set aside for 45 to 60 minutes or until softened.

3. Arrange sliced mushrooms in a circle on two serving plates, with the slices slightly overlapping. Sprinkle each plate with 1 tbsp (15 mL) green onion and 1 tbsp (15 mL) cashew feta. Drizzle equal portions of red pepper oil around the perimeter of the mushrooms. Serve immediately.

Red Beet Carpaccio with Pumpkin Seed Chimichurri

Thinly sliced beets replace the beef in this recipe. The sauce is South American in origin; it has a herbaceous flavor and is mildly spicy. I like to serve this with Spicy Grapefruit and Chard Salad (page 147) and add a sprinkle of hemp seeds for more protein.

Makes 4 servings

Tips

Wear gloves to keep your hands from being stained by the beet juice.

Make this recipe using golden or rainbow beets instead of red beets.

Substitute 1 large daikon radish, 1 medium turnip or 2 large parsnips for the beets. Just remember to marinate the vegetables for 30 minutes so they soften and become pliable.

- **Mandoline**

2	medium red beets, peeled	2
¼ cup	cold-pressed (extra virgin) olive oil	60 mL
2 tbsp	freshly squeezed lemon juice	30 mL
½ tsp	fine sea salt	2 mL
½ cup	Pumpkin Seed Chimichurri (page 92), divided	125 mL
2 tbsp	Lemon Avocado Dressing (page 177), divided	30 mL

1. Using a mandoline, slice beets approximately ¼ inch (0.5 cm) thick. Transfer to a bowl and toss with olive oil, lemon juice and salt until well coated. Set aside for 30 minutes, until beets begin to emit juice and soften.

2. Arrange sliced beets in a circle on four serving plates, with the slices slightly overlapping. Spread chimichurri over beets and drizzle Lemon Avocado Dressing overtop.

Twice "Baked" Stuffed Tomatoes

This recipe is a twist on a classic French dish. Soft, delicious tomatoes are filled with a rich and delectable cashew cheese, and the accompanying dill, garlic and lemon juice make a great flavor combination. I like to serve this with Eggplant Parmesan (page 240) or Sprouted Quinoa Croquettes (page 285).

(page 240) or Sprouted Quinoa Croquettes (page 285).

Makes 4 side servings

Tips

To make this recipe you will need a dehydrator with adjustable racks that can be spaced apart to allow the tomatoes to stand upright.

The trick with the almonds is to process them enough that no large pieces remain, but not to overprocess until they begin to clump and stick together.

Almonds are very nutritious. They include phytochemicals, protein, fiber and healthy fats, as well as vitamin E, magnesium, phosphorus, potassium, manganese and a small amount of B vitamins.

- Electric food dehydrator (see Tips, left)

4	large tomatoes	4
2 tbsp	cold-pressed (extra virgin) olive oil	30 mL
Pinch	fine sea salt	Pinch
Pinch	freshly ground black pepper	Pinch
1 cup	Red Pepper, Dill and Cashew Ricotta (page 103)	250 mL
¼ cup	whole raw almonds	60 mL

1. Cut a piece from the stem end of each tomato and scoop out the seeds and pulp, hollowing out the inside. Discard tops, seeds and pulp.

2. Brush tomatoes inside and out with olive oil and sprinkle with salt and freshly ground pepper. Place on a nonstick dehydrator sheet, distributing evenly. Dehydrate at 105°F (41°C) for 10 to 12 hours or until softened all the way through. Remove from dehydrator and set aside to cool.

3. Using a large spoon, stuff tomatoes with cashew ricotta in equal amounts.

4. In a food processor fitted with the metal blade, pulse almonds until they become flour-like in consistency (see Tips, left). Sprinkle tomatoes evenly with almond flour and return to dehydrator. Dehydrate at 105°F (41°C) for 1 to 2 hours or until slightly warm throughout.

Cauliflower Mashed Potatoes

This delicious side is very creamy and pairs well with virtually any dish. It makes a great substitute for mashed potatoes. I especially enjoy it as an accompaniment to Sunflower Date Salisbury Steak (page 253).

Makes 4 servings

Tips

Nutritional yeast is used in vegan and raw foods diets mainly because it is a source of vitamin B_{12}. It is pasteurized, so technically it does not qualify as a raw food. However, in addition to necessary nutrients, it adds a deep, umami-like flavor to many dishes.

Although it is not necessary to refrigerate nutritional yeast, make sure to store it in an airtight container away from light. This will extend its shelf life, help to retain its B vitamins and keep the flavor more potent.

The smaller you cut the cauliflower, the easier it will be for the food processor to purée the mix into a smooth, homogenized mixture.

Although this dish will keep in the refrigerator, it is best eaten immediately after preparation.

¼ cup	nutritional yeast (see Tips, left)	60 mL
2 tbsp	filtered water	30 mL
1	clove garlic	1
1 tsp	freshly squeezed lemon juice	5 mL
¼ tsp	fine sea salt	1 mL
2 tbsp	cold-pressed flax oil	30 mL
3 cups	chopped cauliflower florets	750 mL
¼ cup	chopped parsley leaves	60 mL

1. In a food processor fitted with the metal blade, process nutritional yeast, water, garlic, lemon juice and salt until smooth and no pieces of garlic remain. Add cauliflower and process until smooth and creamy. Transfer to a bowl and stir in parsley. Serve immediately or cover and refrigerate for up to 2 days (see Tips, left).

Variations

For a heartier version of this dish, along with the cauliflower add ½ cup (125 mL) cashews, soaked in 1 cup (250 mL) water for 30 minutes, then drained and rinsed.

Add any dried spice or fresh herb to suit your taste.

For a curry cauliflower mash, add 1 tbsp (15 mL) curry powder, ¼ tsp (1 mL) turmeric and 1 tsp (5 mL) ground cumin.

Cauliflower Rice

This recipe is a light and fluffy alternative to starches such as potatoes and rice. I like to serve it alongside Bursting Burritos (page 250) or Mixed Vegetable and Shiitake Mushroom "Stir-Fry" (page 231.)

Tip

When pulsing the cauliflower, be sure not to overprocess. Otherwise the cell walls of the cauliflower will break down and the "rice" will become soggy.

4 cups	chopped cauliflower florets	1 L
¼ cup	chopped parsley leaves	60 mL
2 tbsp	freshly squeezed lemon juice	30 mL
1 tsp	fine sea salt	5 mL

1. In a food processor fitted with the metal blade, pulse cauliflower until it breaks down to a rice-like consistency, 10 to 15 times (see Tip, left).
2. Transfer to a bowl. Add parsley, lemon juice and salt and stir well. Serve immediately or place in an airtight container and refrigerate for up to 4 days.

Variations

Use this as a basic recipe that you can build upon to create different flavor profiles. For a curry-style rice, along with the parsley add 1 tbsp (15 mL) curry powder, 1 tbsp (15 mL) chopped gingerroot, ½ tsp (2 mL) ground cumin and ¼ tsp (1 mL) ground turmeric.

For Italian-style rice, add ¼ cup (60 mL) thinly sliced fresh basil leaves, 1 tbsp (15 mL) dried oregano and ½ tsp (2 mL) whole fennel seeds along with the parsley.

Parsnip "Fried Rice"

This Asian-inspired dish is very reminiscent of traditional fried white rice. The slightly salty flavor provided by the tamari helps to carry the flavors of the green onion and sesame oil. I like to pair this with many vegetable dishes, including Mixed Vegetable and Shiitake Mushroom "Stir-Fry" (page 231), Collard Wrap Spring Rolls (page 291) and Sunflower Maki Rolls (page 288).

Makes 4 servings

Tips

Be sure to chop the parsnip to the right consistency. If overprocessed, the water it contains will bleed and the mixture will become mushy. Use the Pulse function to process a little at a time. This will take no longer than one minute.

Be sure to use white sesame seeds in this recipe.

When following a strictly raw diet, use unrefined sesame oil made from seeds that haven't been toasted. Look for it in the condiments and dressings section of well-stocked supermarkets or natural foods stores.

1 tbsp	freshly squeezed lemon juice	15 mL
1 tbsp	chopped gingerroot	15 mL
2	cloves garlic	2
1 tsp	wheat-free tamari	5 mL
½ tsp	fine sea salt	2 mL
2 cups	chopped parsnip	500 mL
3 tbsp	finely sliced green onion, white and green parts	45 mL
2 tsp	sesame seeds	10 mL
2 tsp	sesame oil (untoasted)	10 mL

1. In a food processor fitted with the metal blade, process lemon juice, ginger, garlic, tamari and salt until no large pieces of ginger or garlic remain.
2. Add parsnip and pulse until it becomes rice-like in consistency. Transfer to a bowl and stir in green onion, sesame seeds and sesame oil until well incorporated. Serve immediately or cover and refrigerate for up to 4 days.

Variations

Substitute an equal quantity of chopped cauliflower florets for the parsnip. Again, make sure not to overprocess the cauliflower.

For a take on sushi rice, stir in 3 tbsp (45 mL) agave nectar and 2 tbsp (30 mL) rice wine vinegar along with the green onion.

"Baked" Cheesy Broccoli

This recipe reminds me of dishes I enjoyed as a child, made from canned Cheddar cheese soup and freeze-dried broccoli. This version is healthier, and it tastes better.

Makes 4 servings

Tips

If you are using broccoli florets in a recipe, don't discard the stems — they are very flavorful and contain a lot of nutrition. Peel the stem to expose the tender core and slice thinly. Toss ½ cup (125 mL) thinly sliced broccoli stems with 1 tbsp (15 mL) extra virgin olive oil, 2 tsp (10 mL) lemon juice and ½ tsp (2 mL) sea salt. Set aside to marinate for 15 minutes until softened.

If you are using a ring-shaped dehydrator, divide the mixture among four smaller dishes that fit on the racks and use multiple racks, as necessary.

Broccoli belongs to a group of vegetables called crucifers that also includes arugula, cauliflower, radishes and Brussels sprouts. Crucifers contain cancer-fighting phytochemicals. These cancer fighters are very susceptible to high temperatures and are water-soluble, which means their nutritional benefit is maximized when they are eaten raw.

- Electric food dehydrator
- Shallow baking dish

3 cups	coarsely chopped broccoli florets	750 mL
3 tbsp	cold-pressed flax oil	45 mL
2 tbsp	raw shelled hemp seeds	30 mL
2 tsp	freshly squeezed lemon juice	10 mL
½ tsp	fine sea salt	2 mL
2 cups	Cashew Cheddar Cheese (page 105)	500 mL
1 cup	chopped red bell pepper	250 mL
½ cup	Almond Parmesan Cheese (page 204)	125 mL

1. In a bowl, toss together broccoli, flax oil, hemp seeds, lemon juice and salt. Set aside to marinate for 10 to 15 minutes, until broccoli has softened and taken on a lightly steamed appearance.
2. In a food processor fitted with the metal blade, process cashew Cheddar and red pepper until smooth. Add to marinated broccoli and mix well.
3. Transfer to a baking dish (see Tips, left). Sprinkle almond Parmesan evenly overtop and dehydrate at 105°F (41°C) for 30 to 45 minutes or until warmed through. Serve immediately or cover and refrigerate for up to 2 days.

Variations

Substitute other green vegetables such as kale for the broccoli. I use 4 cups (1 L) chopped trimmed kale.

Substitute 2 tbsp (30 mL) sesame seeds for the hemp seeds.

Creamed Greens with Pumpkin Seeds and Lemon

This rich, creamy blend of Swiss chard, spinach, lemon and tahini is a delectable alternative to dairy-based creamed greens. I like to eat this on its own as a midday snack or as a side with dishes such as Red Beet Ravioli (page 237) or Eggplant Parmesan (page 240). It is also delicious tossed with Zucchini Noodles (page 244).

Makes 2 servings

Tips

Before slicing the chard, remove the long stem that runs up through the leaf almost to the top of the plant. Use only the leafy green parts.

You can make this recipe without a dehydrator. Complete Step 1, then cover spinach and set aside at room temperature for 1 hour or until soft. However, be aware that the dehydrator creates the mouth feel of a sautéed food, which marinating can't duplicate.

- Electric food dehydrator, optional (see Tips, left)

2 cups	Swiss chard, trimmed and cut into 1-inch (2.5 cm) slices	500 mL
1 cup	baby spinach	250 mL
3	cloves garlic, divided, minced	3
3 tbsp	cold-pressed (extra virgin) olive oil	45 mL
1/4 cup	freshly squeezed lemon juice, divided	60 mL
1 tsp	fine sea salt, divided	5 mL
1/2 cup	filtered water	125 mL
1/4 cup	tahini	60 mL
2 tbsp	cold-pressed hemp oil	30 mL
1/4 cup	raw pumpkin seeds	60 mL

1. In a bowl, toss chard, spinach, 2 cloves minced garlic, olive oil, 2 tbsp (30 mL) lemon juice and 1/2 tsp (2 mL) salt.
2. Transfer to a nonstick dehydrator sheet, spreading evenly. Dehydrate at 105°F (41°C) for 30 to 45 minutes or until soft and slightly wilted.
3. In a blender, combine water, tahini, remaining garlic and lemon juice and salt, and hemp oil. Blend at high speed until emulsified.
4. Pour tahini sauce over wilted greens. Add pumpkin seeds and toss well. Serve immediately.

Spicy Orange, Ginger and Sesame Watercress

This is a light side dish that is packed full of flavor and nutrition. Watercress is an underused product that has a very positive nutritional profile. I love how the flavors of the sweet orange, spicy cayenne and slightly bitter sesame seeds play on each other. I like to serve this as a side with Sweet Potato and Zucchini Mac 'n' Cheese (page 247), Daikon Radish "Egg Noodles" (page 234) or Layered Zucchini Lasagna (page 238).

Makes 2 servings

Tips

If you do not have a dehydrator, complete Step 1, tossing the mixture in a long, flat dish rather than a bowl. Set aside to marinate for 1½ hours, stirring the mixture 5 or 6 times.

A dehydrator is a great tool for softening leafy greens. Allow enough time for the greens to soften, but not so much that they become crispy. For the best results, make sure the greens are cut to the same size.

The easiest and best method for zesting citrus fruit is to use a sharp-toothed grater such as those made by Microplane. You can also use the small shredding holes on a box grater, in which case, be careful not to shred too deeply and remove the bitter white pith.

- Electric food dehydrator, optional (see Tips, left)

4 cups	lightly chopped watercress, leaves and tender stems	1 L
3 tbsp	cold-pressed (extra virgin) olive oil	45 mL
2 tbsp	minced gingerroot	30 mL
1 tbsp	finely grated orange zest	15 mL
¼ cup	chopped orange segments (see Tips, page 67)	60 mL
3 tbsp	freshly squeezed orange juice	45 mL
2 tbsp	freshly squeezed lemon juice	30 mL
2 tbsp	sesame seeds	30 mL
1 tsp	fine sea salt	5 mL
½ tsp	cayenne pepper	2 mL

1. In a bowl, toss watercress with olive oil, ginger, orange zest, chopped orange, orange juice, lemon juice, sesame seeds, salt and cayenne, until well coated.
2. Transfer to a nonstick dehydrator sheet and spread evenly. Dehydrate at 105°F (41°C) for 45 minutes or until slightly wilted. Serve immediately or cover and refrigerate for up to 2 days.

Variation

Substitute an equal quantity of black kale for the watercress. Make sure to chop it finely to ensure that the marinade penetrates. Kale is a little more fibrous than watercress, so it must be marinated for a longer time, about 2 hours.

Jicama Fries

This recipe is a delectable and much healthier replacement for French fries. It makes a great snack as well as a side. My favorite accompaniment is Sun-Dried Tomato Ketchup (page 198). I also like to scatter these fries with some chopped green onion.

Makes 4 servings

Tips

Jicama tastes like a blend of apple, potato and celery. It is mildly sweet and has a high water content.

To trim the jicama, use a chef's knife to remove a small slice from all four sides to square it off before peeling.

If, like me, you prefer fatter fries, after cutting the jicama into slices, cut it into strips that are approximately 1 inch (2.5 cm) wide.

- **Mandoline**

1	large jicama, peeled and trimmed (see Tips, left)	1
3 tbsp	cold-pressed (extra virgin) olive oil	45 mL
1 tbsp	freshly squeezed lemon juice	15 mL
1 tsp	fine sea salt	5 mL

1. Using a mandoline, cut jicama into $1/2$-inch (1 cm) slices. Stack pieces and cut into long strips approximately $1/2$ inch (1 cm) wide. The pieces should resemble French fries.
2. In a bowl, toss jicama slices, olive oil, lemon juice and salt. Set aside to marinate for 20 to 30 minutes or until slightly soft. Serve immediately or transfer to an airtight container and refrigerate for up to 2 days.

Variation

Most mandolines come with a selection of blades. If you have one that will make shoestring potatoes, use it to make shoestring jicama fries. After marinating the "fries," toss them with black sesame seeds to add color and a bit of calcium to your diet.

Cauliflower and Hemp Tabouli

This dish is wonderfully light and flavorful, bursting with the fresh flavors of parsley, lemon and sweet pepper. I like to serve it as a topping on a simple salad of crisp romaine lettuce tossed with a little extra virgin olive oil and fresh lemon juice, or even on a more complex salad such as Greek Kale Salad (page 143). It also makes a great accompaniment for Lemon and Cilantro Falafels (page 225).

Makes 4 servings

Tip

Hemp seeds are considered a complete protein, meaning they contain all eight essential amino acids. One tablespoon (15 mL) of raw shelled hemp seeds provides up to 5 grams of protein and contains appreciable amounts of vitamins B_1 (thiamine) and B_6 (pyridoxine), folate, phosphorus, magnesium, zinc and manganese. Two tablespoons (30 mL) of hemp seeds essentially meets your daily requirement for omega-3 fatty acids.

3 cups	chopped cauliflower florets	750 mL
1 cup	chopped flat-leaf parsley leaves	250 mL
1/4 cup	finely diced red bell pepper	60 mL
1/4 cup	raw shelled hemp seeds	60 mL
3 tbsp	cold-pressed hemp oil	45 mL
2 tbsp	freshly squeezed lemon juice	30 mL
1 tsp	apple cider vinegar	5 mL
1/2 tsp	fine sea salt	2 mL

1. In a food processor fitted with the metal blade, pulse cauliflower until it breaks down to the consistency of rice. It is important not to overprocess, or the cauliflower will become soft and mushy. Transfer to a bowl.
2. Add parsley, red pepper, hemp seeds, hemp oil, lemon juice, vinegar and salt and mix well. Serve immediately or cover and refrigerate for up to 2 days.

Variation

If you prefer a slightly spicier result, along with the salt add 1 tsp (5 mL) curry powder, 1/2 tsp (2 mL) ground cumin, 1/4 tsp (1 mL) ground coriander and a pinch each of cayenne and turmeric.

Avocado Tartare

A chunky avocado treat that bursts with flavor and nutrition, this dish is easy to prepare and even easier to devour. I like to serve it with Eggplant Parmesan (page 240), Stuffed Portobello Towers (page 211), or Pasta Bolognese (page 245). The richness of the avocado also makes this a perfect appetizer, served in smaller portions, for any dinner party.

Makes 2 servings

Tips

Don't crush all the avocado in Step 1. You want to keep some of its texture to provide contrast when biting into the fresh vegetables.

I like to add 1 tsp (5 mL) sweet smoked paprika along with the dressing, to add a hint of smoky flavor.

1 cup	cubed avocado (about 1 medium)	250 mL
¼ cup	finely diced red bell pepper	60 mL
¼ cup	finely diced tomato	60 mL
¼ cup	thinly sliced romaine lettuce	60 mL
3 tbsp	Marinated Mushrooms (page 282)	45 mL
2 tbsp	raw shelled hemp seeds	30 mL
1 tbsp	sesame seeds	15 mL
¼ tsp	fine sea salt	1 mL
¼ cup	Red Pepper Basil Marinara Sauce (page 184)	60 mL
2 tbsp	Lemon Avocado Dressing (page 177)	30 mL

1. In a bowl, toss together avocado, red pepper, tomato, lettuce, marinated mushrooms, hemp seeds, sesame seeds and salt. Using a rubber spatula, lightly crush some of the avocado.
2. Add marinara sauce and Lemon Avocado Dressing and fold gently to combine.

Jalapeño Poppers

Stuffed jalapeño peppers are a popular dish. The problem is, traditional versions are stuffed with cheese, coated in bread crumbs and deep-fried. This healthier raw version couldn't be easier to make, and they are even more delicious. I like to serve these as a side dish with Bursting Burritos (page 250) or Zucchini Tortillas (page 248), or on their own as a small plate with a side of Red Pepper Mole Sauce (page 202).

Makes 4 poppers

Tips

This method for softening peppers can be used with any variety of pepper, sweet or spicy. The key is to coat the peppers with a bit of oil before they go in the dehydrator. This ensures that the heat will penetrate the flesh of the pepper and help to soften it.

Studies have found that capsaicin, the heat source in chile peppers, possesses anti-inflammatory properties, which may benefit health conditions with low-grade inflammation, such as heart disease, arthritis and diabetes. Capsaicin has also been shown to improve digestive health and reduce the tendency for blood cells to clump (platelet aggregation), which helps to improve circulation and may reduce the risk for stroke.

- **Electric food dehydrator**

4	jalapeño peppers	4
2 tbsp	cold-pressed (extra virgin) olive oil	30 mL
½ tsp	fine sea salt, divided	2 mL
½ cup	Red Pepper, Dill and Cashew Ricotta (page 103)	125 mL
½ cup	raw whole almonds	125 mL
1 tbsp	nutritional yeast	15 mL

1. Using a paring knife, make a small incision down one side of each pepper. Use your fingers to gently open it without tearing. Scoop out seeds and discard. Repeat with remaining peppers. Place in a bowl and toss with olive oil and a pinch of salt. Transfer to a nonstick dehydrator sheet, spacing evenly, and dehydrate at 105°F (41°C) for 3 to 4 hours or until soft.

2. Remove from dehydrator and gently fill each pepper with 2 tbsp (30 mL) cashew ricotta (try to stuff in as much cheese as you can).

3. In a food processor fitted with the metal blade, process almonds, nutritional yeast and remaining salt until almonds become flour-like in consistency (you want them to be broken down but not processed to the point that they become almond butter). Spread evenly over a large plate.

4. One at a time, gently roll each jalapeño in the almond flour mixture until thoroughly coated. Return to nonstick sheet and dehydrate at 105°F (41°C) for 2 to 3 hours or until warmed through and peppers are a bit more shriveled. Serve immediately.

Variations

Fill the peppers with another dense stuffing such as Sweet Chili and Pecan Pâté (page 96), Cashew Spinach Dip (page 83) or Basil, Spinach and Walnut Pesto (page 186). I also like to use Cashew Cheddar Cheese (page 105) and serve a small bowl of Red Pepper Mole Sauce (page 202) alongside for dipping. Be creative and develop your own filling for the peppers.

Stuffed Bell Peppers

These soft peppers are an easy side dish to prepare. I like to serve them alongside Cauliflower Rice (page 274) drizzled with Red Pepper Mole Sauce (page 202).

Tips

This recipe will also work with green, yellow or orange bell peppers, although I prefer the taste of the red ones.

If you have a dehydrator with racks that are not moveable and therefore won't accomodate whole peppers, cut the peppers in half lengthwise, remove stems, cores and seeds, then toss with olive oil and salt. Place cut side up on a nonstick dehydrator sheet and proceed with dehydrating as directed. Mound about ¼ cup (60 mL) filling in each half in Step 2.

When purchasing extra virgin olive oil, make sure the label says "cold-pressed." Some olive oils are extracted using a centrifuge system, which spins the olives at a very high rate. This heats the olives and the resulting oil, depriving it of its raw status.

- **Electric food dehydrator**

4	medium red bell peppers	4
2 tbsp	cold-pressed (extra virgin) olive oil	30 mL
¼ tsp	fine sea salt	1 mL
1 cup	Walnut Mince (page 293)	250 mL
½ cup	Tomato Basil Marinara Sauce (page 184)	125 mL
½ cup	Cashew Alfredo Sauce (page 188)	125 mL

1. In a bowl, toss peppers, olive oil and salt. Place on a nonstick dehydrator sheet, spacing evenly. Dehydrate at 105°F (41°C) for 8 to 10 hours or until softened.
2. Remove peppers from dehydrator and, using a sharp knife, slice a piece off the top of each. Scoop out seeds and discard. In a bowl, combine walnut mince and marinara and Alfredo sauces. Mix well. Stuff each pepper with ½ cup (125 mL) filling.
3. Return peppers to the dehydrator and dehydrate at 105°F (41°C) for 30 to 45 minutes or until slightly warmed through.

Variations

Stuff the peppers with different fillings. Substitute an equal quantity of Parsnip "Fried Rice" (page 275) for the walnut mince or Mixed Vegetable and Shiitake Mushroom "Stir-Fry" (page 231) and Miso Glaze Sauce (page 196) for the marinara and Alfredo Sauces.

Chickpea and Zucchini Fritters

These slightly crunchy fritters are delicious and packed with protein. They can be made ahead of time and stored in an airtight container for up to a week.

Makes 10 to 15 fritters

Tips

To soak the chickpeas for this recipe, place in a bowl and add 2 cups (500 mL) water. Cover and set aside for 2 hours. Drain, discarding liquid. Rinse under cold running water until the water runs clear.

Instead of the chickpeas, substitute 1 cup (250 mL) sunflower seeds soaked in 2 cups (500 mL) water for 30 minutes, drained and rinsed.

To shred the zucchini for this recipe, use the large holes of a box grater or the shredding blade of your food processor.

- **Electric food dehydrator**

½ cup	dried chickpeas, soaked (see Tips, left)	125 mL
½ cup	chopped zucchini	125 mL
2 tbsp	cold-pressed (extra virgin) olive oil	30 mL
2 tbsp	freshly squeezed lemon juice	30 mL
2 tsp	ground cumin	10 mL
1 tsp	fine sea salt	5 mL
¼ tsp	ground turmeric	1 mL
1 cup	shredded zucchini (about 1 small; see Tips, left)	250 mL
1 cup	ground flax seeds	250 mL
2 tbsp	sesame seeds	30 mL

1. In a food processor fitted with the metal blade, process chopped zucchini, olive oil, lemon juice, cumin, salt and turmeric, until smooth. Add soaked chickpeas and pulse for 30 to 45 seconds, until slightly broken down and chunky (do not overprocess).

2. Transfer to a bowl. Add shredded zucchini and flax and sesame seeds and mix well. Set aside for 10 to 15 minutes so the flax can absorb the liquid and swell.

3. Using a small ice cream scoop or ladle, drop 10 to 15 equal portions of the batter onto a nonstick dehydrator sheet, distributing evenly. Dehydrate for 10 to 12 hours at 105°F (41°C) or until firm enough to handle. Flip fritters onto a mesh sheet and dehydrate for 3 to 4 hours or until dry and firm on the outside and soft in the middle. Serve immediately or transfer to an airtight container and refrigerate for up to 5 days.

Sprouted Quinoa Croquettes

These delicious little cakes are a take on the French classic, potato croquettes. I love to serve them with small dollop of Sun-Dried Tomato Hemp Mayonnaise (page 88) on top. They are also good with Creamed Greens with Pumpkin Seeds and Lemon (page 277) and Pesto-Coated Carrot and Parsnip Fettuccine (page 236).

Makes 8 servings

Tips

To sprout the quinoa for this recipe, place in a bowl and cover with 2 cups (500 mL) water. Cover and set aside for 8 hours, changing the water every 3 hours. Drain and discard any remaining water. Transfer to a colander and rinse under cold running water. Place the colander over a bowl and set aside for 24 hours, rinsing the quinoa every 2 to 3 hours to keep it damp but not moist. Before going to bed, rinse the quinoa and place a damp cloth overtop. In the morning, rinse again. Continue to rinse quinoa every 2 to 3 hours until tails approximately ¼ inch (0.5 cm) long have sprouted from the seeds. This will take 24 to 30 hours in total. The quinoa is now ready for use in your recipe, or you can cover it and refrigerate for up to 3 days.

If you have a dehydrator, use it to add a little texture and to warm the croquettes. Drop the batter onto a nonstick dehydrator sheet and dehydrate at 105°F (41°C) for 1 to 2 hours, until slightly warm. Serve immediately or transfer to an airtight container and refrigerate for up to 3 days.

1 cup	quinoa, sprouted (see Tips, left)	250 mL
¼ cup	Sun-Dried Tomato Hemp Mayonnaise (page 88)	60 mL
3 tbsp	ground flax seeds	45 mL
2 tbsp	chopped fresh dill fronds	30 mL
¼ cup	finely diced red bell pepper	60 mL
¼ cup	chopped parsley leaves	60 mL
½ tsp	fine sea salt	2 mL

1. In a bowl, combine sprouted quinoa, mayonnaise and flax seeds until well combined. Set aside for 10 minutes so the flax can absorb some of the liquid and swell.
2. Add dill, red pepper, parsley and salt and mix well.
3. Using a ¼-cup (60 mL) dry measure, drop 8 equal portions of the mixture onto a serving plate (see Tips, left). Using your hands, shape into small rounds resembling hockey pucks. Serve immediately or cover and refrigerate for up to 3 days.

Variations

Substitute an equal quantity of Hemp Avocado Mayonnaise (page 89) or Spicy Cashew Mayonnaise (page 87) for the Sun-Dried Tomato Hemp Mayonnaise.

Spicy Kimchi

This fermented Korean side dish lends a spicy crunch to any meal. The healthy bacteria created in this process make it great for the digestion.

Makes 6 to 8 servings

Tips

Look for Korean chili powder in well-stocked Asian markets. If you can't find it, substitute 2 tsp (10 mL) paprika and 1 tsp (5 mL) dried chile flakes.

You want to make sure that you don't have large chunks of salt remaining after rinsing. Gently grinding the salt in a mortar or with a rolling pin on a cutting board, will achieve this result.

- **Sealable glass container, approximately 16 cups (4 L)**

8 cups	packed chopped napa cabbage (2-inch/2.5 cm squares)	2 L
1 cup	coarse sea salt, gently ground (see Tips, left)	250 mL
¼ cup	chopped green onions, white and green parts	60 mL
3 tbsp	Korean chili powder (see Tips, left)	45 mL
2 tbsp	wheat-free tamari	30 mL
2 tbsp	raw agave nectar	30 mL
2 tsp	chopped gingerroot	10 mL
2	cloves garlic, minced	2

1. In a bowl, combine cabbage and salt and toss until well combined. Cover and set aside at room temperature for 2 to 4 hours, until wilted. Transfer to a colander and rinse well under cold running water. Drain well and use your hands to squeeze out any excess liquid.

2. Transfer to a clean bowl and add green onions, chili powder, tamari, agave nectar, ginger and garlic. Toss until well combined.

3. Transfer to a sealable glass container and pack down tightly, using your hands or a wooden spoon to press out as much air as possible. Place plastic wrap directly on the surface of the kimchi to prevent contact with air and seal the lid tightly. Store in a cool, dry place for 4 to 5 days or until the mixture begins to take on a slightly sour taste. Transfer to the refrigerator and store for up to a month.

Miso "Baked" Eggplant

This recipe is a take on a classic Japanese dish that usually involves fish. It is tangy, sweet and rich. I like to serve this with Mixed Vegetable and Shiitake Mushroom "Stir-Fry" (page 231) and Parsnip "Fried Rice" (page 275).

Makes 4 servings

Tips

Eggplant comes in many different varieties, shapes and sizes. My favorite is Japanese eggplant, which is far less bitter than the Italian variety. If you are using Japanese eggplant in this recipe, you will need 2 medium-size eggplants to replace the one called for. Because it is less bitter, you can skip the salting step.

When following a completely raw food diet, look for sesame oil that is made from untoasted seeds and is completely unrefined. It will be labeled "cold-pressed."

- **Electric food dehydrator**

1	large Italian eggplant (see Tips, left)	1
1 tsp	fine sea salt	5 mL
2 tbsp	cold-pressed (extra virgin) olive oil	30 mL
¼ cup	brown rice miso	60 mL
¼ cup	filtered water	60 mL
2 tbsp	raw agave nectar	30 mL
2 tbsp	sesame oil (untoasted)	30 mL
1 tsp	apple cider vinegar	5 mL

1. Slice eggplant crosswise into 2-inch (5 cm) rounds. Using a paring knife, gently score each side in a crisscross pattern, taking care not to cut through. Sprinkle both sides of the slices with salt and set aside in a colander for 1 hour.

2. Gently squeeze eggplant to remove excess water and rinse under running water. Pat dry and brush both sides with olive oil. Place on mesh dehydrator sheets, distributing evenly. Dehydrate at 105°F (41°C) for 1 to 2 hours or until slightly softened.

3. In a blender, combine miso, water, agave nectar, sesame oil and vinegar. Blend at high speed until smooth.

4. Remove eggplant from dehydrator. Brush both sides with miso mixture (about 1 tbsp/15 mL per side). Return to dehydrator and dehydrate for 5 to 6 hours, until eggplant is soft and slightly wilted. Serve immediately.

Sunflower Maki Rolls

One of the keys to successfully switching to a raw food diet is to replace dishes you once ate with those that are similar. This vegan version of sushi is very satisfying.

Makes 4 servings

Tips

If you don't have a sushi mat, use a sheet of waxed paper. However, be aware that your maki rolls will not be as tight as when made using a mat. It takes some time to get used to working with a sushi mat, but once you do, it is very simple.

Dipping Sauce: In a small bowl, combine ¼ cup (60 mL) each wheat-free tamari and raw agave nectar, and 2 tsp (10 mL) freshly squeezed lemon juice. Mix well.

- Sushi mat, optional (see Tips, left)

2	sheets nori	2
1 cup	Parsnip "Fried Rice" (page 275)	250 mL
½ cup	avocado slices (about 1 small)	125 mL
½ cup	thinly sliced red bell pepper	125 mL
¼ cup	thinly sliced carrot	60 mL
¼ cup	thinly sliced cucumber	60 mL
	Dipping Sauce (see Tips, left)	

1. Place sushi mat on a flat surface with bamboo strips running crosswise. Place nori on mat, shiny side down. Spread Parsnip "Fried Rice" over nori, pressing it out until it is about ¼ inch (0.5 cm) thick and leaving a 1½-inch (3.5 cm) border along the edge farthest away from you. Place avocado slices on top in a crosswise line about 1 inch (2.5 cm) from the nearest edge. Lay rows of red pepper, carrot and cucumber slices crosswise at the upper edge of the avocado row.

2. Place your thumb under the bottom of the sushi mat and your index finger on top. Using your remaining fingers to hold the filling in place, gently roll the nori with the mat, tucking in the edge as you roll to make a cylinder shape. Continue to roll the sushi, taking care to tuck nori as you roll but not the mat itself. Using both hands, grab the mat and roll a few times to tighten. Repeat a few times to make the roll as tight as possible.

3. Once you have rolled all the way to the top, wet your finger with a little water and lightly moisten the top free edge of the nori. Make one final roll to seal the top. Remove the mat and cut the roll crosswise into 6 equal slices. Serve immediately with Dipping Sauce.

Variation

Substitute an equal quantity of Sweet Chili and Pecan Pâté (page 96) for the Parsnip "Fried Rice". Omit the avocado and red pepper and substitute ¼ cup (60 mL) shredded carrot and 2 tbsp (30 mL) thinly sliced cucumber.

Nori Hand Rolls

These hand rolls are an easy and delicious way to consume protein along with nutrient-dense seaweed. I like the mild ginger flavor paired with the lemon juice and dill. Serve these with something rich, such as Marinated Kelp Noodles (page 243) tossed with Sweet-and-Sour Thai Almond Butter Sauce (page 191).

Makes 4 rolls

Tips

To soak the sunflower seeds for this recipe, place in a bowl and add ½ cup (125 mL) water. Cover and set aside for 30 minutes. Drain, discarding soaking water and any shells or unwanted particles. Rinse under cold running water until the water runs clear.

Be sure to use high-quality nori that is labeled "raw." Purchase your nori from a reputable source such as your favorite raw food retailer, health food store or well-stocked grocery store.

Tahini, or sesame seed paste/butter, has a wonderful creamy texture and provides calcium, phosphorus, vitamin E and mono- and polyunsaturated fats.

¼ cup	raw sunflower seeds, soaked (see Tips, left)	60 mL
2 tbsp	filtered water	30 mL
1 tbsp	freshly squeezed lemon juice	15 mL
1 tsp	chopped gingerroot	5 mL
¼ tsp	dried dill weed	1 mL
¼ tsp	fine sea salt	1 mL
2 tbsp	tahini	30 mL
2	nori sheets, cut in half	2

1. In a food processor fitted with the metal blade, process soaked sunflower seeds, water, lemon juice, ginger, dill and salt until smooth. Add tahini and process until creamy.
2. Place nori, shiny side down, in your left hand, long edge facing you. Arrange filling on a diagonal on the left side of the nori. Fold bottom left corner of nori over the filling and roll into a cone shape. Enjoy immediately.

Variation

Nori hand rolls are an easy way to combine a favorite dip or pâté and nutrient-dense nori. Before rolling, top the filling with ¼ cup (60 mL) each thinly sliced red pepper and cucumber and a few avocado slices.

Thai Lettuce Wraps

This is a deliciously crunchy side dish or small plate that is also sweet and spicy — the perfect solution for Thai food cravings. I like to serve these with Parsnip "Fried Rice" (page 275) and Miso "Baked" Eggplant (page 287).

Makes 8 wraps

Tip

Hemp seeds are considered a complete protein, meaning they contain all eight essential amino acids. One tablespoon (15 mL) of raw shelled hemp seeds provides up to 5 grams of protein and contains appreciable amounts of vitamins B_1 (thiamine) and B_6 (pyridoxine), folate, phosphorus, magnesium, zinc and manganese. Two tablespoons (30 mL) of hemp seeds essentially meets your daily requirement for omega-3 fatty acids.

2 cups	thinly sliced romaine lettuce	500 mL
½ cup	Marinated Kelp Noodles (page 243)	125 mL
¼ cup	Sweet-and-Sour Thai Almond Butter Sauce (page 191)	60 mL
¼ cup	thinly sliced red bell pepper	60 mL
¼ cup	chopped cilantro leaves	60 mL
¼ cup	finely diced tomato	60 mL
2 tbsp	finely diced red onion	30 mL
2 tbsp	raw shelled hemp seeds	30 mL
1 tbsp	cold-pressed hemp oil	15 mL
2 tsp	freshly squeezed lemon juice	10 mL
4	collard or Swiss chard leaves	4

1. In a bowl, toss together kelp noodles, almond butter sauce, red pepper, cilantro, tomato, onion, hemp seeds, hemp oil and lemon juice until well combined.
2. Place collard leaves on a flat surface. Using a paring knife, remove the long vein from the center of each leaf so it is pliable. Continue cutting to the end so that each leaf produces 2 pieces.
3. Divide filling into 8 equal portions. Place one portion on uncut end of leaf and roll up until you reach the middle of the leaf. Fold in the sides and continue rolling into a tight cylindrical package. Repeat until all the leaves have been filled. Serve immediately or cover and refrigerate for up to 2 days.

Variation

If you are feeling ambitious, add ½ cup (125 mL) Simple Marinated Kale Salad (page 142) to the filling.

Collard Wrap Spring Rolls

These tasty little treats are easy to make. They are perfect for taking with you in an airtight container to work or to eat on the go.

Makes 8 rolls

Tip

In many recipes that call for olive oil, it can be substituted with another high-quality oil such as flax, hemp or pumpkin seed oil. The only factor to consider — so long as you are using good-quality cold-pressed oils — is the flavor profile you are trying to achieve.

¼ cup	shredded carrot	60 mL
¼ cup	shredded beet	60 mL
¼ cup	thinly sliced red bell pepper	60 mL
¼ cup	thinly sliced mango	60 mL
1 tbsp	cold-pressed (extra virgin) olive oil	15 mL
1 tsp	freshly squeezed lemon juice	5 mL
¼ tsp	fine sea salt	1 mL
4	large collard or Swiss chard leaves	4
¼ cup	Sweet-and-Sour Thai Almond Butter Sauce (page 191)	60 mL

1. In a bowl, toss together carrot, beet, red pepper and mango. Add olive oil, lemon juice and salt and toss well. Set aside to marinate for 10 minutes.

2. Place collard leaves on a flat surface. Using a paring knife, remove the long vein from the center of each leaf so it is pliable. Continue cutting to the end so that each leaf produces 2 pieces.

3. Add almond butter sauce to the carrot mixture and toss well.

4. Divide filling into 8 equal portions. Place one portion on uncut end of leaf and roll up until you reach the middle of the leaf. Fold in the sides and continue rolling into a tight cylindrical package. Repeat until all the leaves have been filled. Serve immediately or cover and refrigerate for up to 2 days.

Variations

For the olive oil, substitute an equal quantity of another high-quality oil such as flax, hemp or pumpkin seed oil.

Use different combinations of vegetables in this recipe, such as shredded parsnip or thinly sliced celery. The mango adds sweetness and a touch of acid, but an equal quantity of pineapple or thinly sliced papaya would make a good substitute.

I also like to add ¼ cup (60 mL) chopped cilantro and 3 tbsp (45 mL) chopped almonds or cashews to the filling for additional protein.

Caramelized Onions

This recipe is very versatile. It is used in many other recipes in this book, such as Walnut Portobello Burgers (page 219) and Sun-Dried Tomato and Carrot Burgers (page 220).

Makes 3 cups (750 mL)

Tips

Be sure to use a mandoline or the slicing blade of a food processor to slice your onions. They should be no thicker than 1/4 inch (0.5 cm).

I prefer to use red onions because they are slightly sweeter and do not have quite as strong a flavor as white or yellow onions.

• **Mandoline or food processor (see Tips, left)**

1/4 cup	filtered water	60 mL
2 tbsp	wheat-free tamari	30 mL
1 tbsp	cold-pressed (extra virgin) olive oil	15 mL
1 cup	chopped pitted dates	250 mL
4	large red onions, thinly sliced (see Tips, left)	4

1. In a blender, combine water, tamari, olive oil and dates. Blend at high speed until smooth.
2. In a bowl, toss sliced onions with date purée until well coated. Transfer to nonstick dehydrator sheets and spread evenly. Dehydrate at 105°F (41°C) for 2 to 3 hours, until onions are slightly dehydrated and begin to look cooked. Serve immediately or transfer to an airtight container and refrigerate for up to 7 days.

Marinated Mushrooms

This recipe helps to create mouth-watering, meaty mushrooms that you will not believe aren't cooked. They are used in many recipes in this book.

Makes 3 servings

Tips

If you do not have a dehydrator, complete Step 1. Cover and set aside for 1 1/2 hours, until softened.

Use any variety of mushroom. If using a denser mushroom such as portobello, add twice as much olive oil and tamari to ensure softening. Whatever kind of mushrooms you are using, ensure they are liberally covered by the marinade.

• **Electric food dehydrator (see Tips, left)**

2 cups	quartered button mushrooms	500 mL
3 tbsp	cold-pressed (extra virgin) olive oil	45 mL
2 tbsp	wheat-free tamari	30 mL
1/2 tsp	fine sea salt	2 mL

1. In a bowl, toss together mushrooms, olive oil, tamari and salt.
2. Transfer to a nonstick dehydrator sheet and spread evenly. Dehydrate at 105°F (41°C) for 30 to 45 minutes or until soft and mushrooms begin to look as if they have been sautéed.

Walnut Mince

This recipe is rich and savory and makes a great substitute for traditional ground meat. The crumbled walnuts really stand out: not only do they add great flavor, their texture is superb. I like to add a dollop as a finish to salads such as Wilted Spinach Salad (page 140). It turns even the simplest dish into a substantial main course and also works as a stuffing for collard green roll-ups or in more complex dishes such as Moussaka (page 228). This recipe can be doubled or tripled to make larger quantities.

Makes 4 servings

Tip

Walnuts provide alpha-linolenic acid (ALA), the omega-3 fat that is the essential fatty acid — without it, we could not survive. It is called "essential" because our bodies are unable to make it and must obtain it from food. Other good sources of ALA include flax and chia seeds. Research has demonstrated ALA's ability to reduce chronic inflammation and other risk factors for diabetes, heart disease and stroke. It is estimated that North Americans get an average of about 1.5 grams ALA per day. Some experts recommend an intake of 2.3 to 3 grams per day. Reaching this goal is easy if you include ALA-rich foods as part of your daily diet.

2 cups	walnut pieces	500 mL
1 tbsp	ground cumin	15 mL
1 tsp	chili powder	5 mL
1/4 tsp	fine sea salt	1 mL
1 tsp	wheat-free tamari	5 mL
2 tbsp	cold pressed (extra virgin) olive oil	30 mL

1. In a food processor fitted with the metal blade, process walnuts, cumin, chili powder and salt for 2 minutes or until walnuts become crumbly and begin to resemble ground meat.

2. Add tamari and pulse 2 to 3 times to combine. With the motor running, drizzle olive oil through the feed tube, processing until well combined. Transfer to an airtight container. Serve immediately or refrigerate for up to 5 days.

Samosas

These traditional Indian snacks are perfect for cocktail parties or as a side dish.

Makes 8 samosas

Tips

To soak the cashews for this recipe, place in a bowl and add ½ cup (125 mL) water. Cover and set aside for 30 minutes. Drain, discarding soaking water, and rinse under cold running water until the water runs clear.

If you are serving these as an appetizer, accompany them with Yellow Coconut Curry Sauce (page 192) for dipping.

- Electric food dehydrator

Wrappers

10 cups	chopped peeled zucchini	2.5 L
3 tbsp	cold-pressed (extra virgin) olive oil	45 mL
2 tsp	freshly squeezed lemon juice	10 mL
1 tsp	curry powder	5 mL
¼ tsp	turmeric	1 mL
Pinch	fine sea salt	Pinch
¼ cup	ground flax seeds	60 mL

Filling

¼ cup	raw cashews, soaked (see Tips, left)	60 mL
1 cup	chopped cauliflower florets	250 mL
¼ cup	chopped tomato	60 mL
2	cloves garlic	2
2 tbsp	filtered water	30 mL
2 tbsp	freshly squeezed lemon juice	30 mL
1 tsp	ground cumin	5 mL
1 tsp	caraway seeds	5 mL
1 tsp	fine sea salt	5 mL

1. *Wrappers:* In a food processor fitted with the metal blade, process zucchini, olive oil, lemon juice, curry powder, turmeric and salt until smooth. Transfer to a bowl. Add flax seeds and mix well.

2. Transfer mixture to a nonstick dehydrator sheet and, using your hands, spread evenly in a thin layer approximately ½ inch (1 cm) thick. Using a small knife, cut into 8 rectangles. Dehydrate at 105°F (41°C) for 5 to 6 hours or until firm. Remove from dehydrator and set aside or transfer to an airtight container and refrigerate for up to 7 days.

3. *Filling:* In a food processor, process soaked cashews, cauliflower, tomato, garlic, water, lemon juice, cumin, caraway seeds and salt until smooth and creamy.

4. *Assembly:* Place one wrapper on a flat surface, long side facing you. Spread ¼ cup (60 mL) filling on left side of wrapper. Fold bottom left corner of wrapper over filling, then continue rolling to make a cone. Brush edges with water to seal. Repeat with remaining ingredients.

Snacks and Breads

Snacking is inevitable. Between major meals our blood sugar levels drop, and it is important to eat throughout the day to maintain them within the appropriate range. So long as you don't overdo it, the only problem with snacking is making sure that the treats you enjoy between meals are as healthy as your meals themselves. While potato chips might be tasty, they do nothing for your waistline and do not provide your body with any real nutrition. Quite the contrary, in fact, since they are usually loaded with refined salt and unhealthy fats.

Snacking on a raw food diet can be as simple as munching on an apple or as complex as making Pizza Bites (page 313), which, while not difficult to assemble, need dehydrating time. But because the prepared foods in a raw food diet have usually been dehydrated, they can be kept for longer periods of time and are easy to transport. One secret to eating healthy snacks is to make sure you always have some that you can carry with you. This reduces the likelihood that you will succumb to eating junk food when temptation strikes.

Although a dehydrator is not commonly found in homes, I recommend purchasing this appliance. Among its other benefits, it is very useful for creating raw snacks that can be made ahead, stored for a relatively long time and easily transported. A dehydrator comes in handy for making things such as kale chips, raw crackers, seasoned nuts and raw breads, all of which can be enjoyed on the go.

Although many of these snack recipes need to be prepared well in advance, often they can be cooked overnight and once they are finished, you can enjoy them for days at a time.

Cauliflower Popcorn

Make this and I guarantee you will never again want the movie-theatre version, loaded with refined salt and saturated fat. It is so delicious you will savor every bite. Double or triple the recipe to suit your needs.

Makes 2 cups (500 mL)

Tip

Use a paring knife to cut the florets into 1-inch (2.5 cm) pieces. This may seem large, but they will shrink drastically in the dehydrator. Make sure all the pieces are uniformly sized so they dehydrate in the same amount of time.

- **Electric food dehydrator**

3 cups	bite-sized cauliflower florets (see Tip, left)	750 mL
½ cup	nutritional yeast	125 mL
¼ cup	cold-pressed (extra virgin) olive oil	60 mL
½ tsp	fine sea salt	2 mL

1. In a bowl, toss cauliflower, nutritional yeast, olive oil and salt.
2. Spread evenly on nonstick dehydrator sheets in a single layer and dehydrate at 105°F (41°C) for 4 to 5 hours, until the cauliflower shrinks to the size of traditional popcorn. Serve immediately.

Variations

Add 1 tbsp (15 mL) curry powder along with the salt for delicious Indian-themed popcorn.

For a bit of texture, add 3 tbsp (45 mL) Almond Parmesan Cheese (page 204) along with the seasonings. Increase the dehydrating time by 30 minutes.

Sour Apple Chips

These easy-to-make snacks are a great addition to any packed lunch. I like to nibble on them when I am relaxing.

Makes 2 cups (500 mL)

Tip

Use a mandoline to cut the apple into thin, uniform slices approximately ¼ inch (0.5 cm) thick.

- **Mandoline**
- **Electric food dehydrator**

2 cups	thinly sliced green apple (about 1 large; see Tip, left)	500 mL
¼ cup	freshly squeezed lemon juice	60 mL
2 tbsp	raw agave nectar	30 mL

1. In a bowl, toss together apple, lemon juice and agave nectar until well coated. Spread out on nonstick dehydrator sheets in a single layer and dehydrate at 105°F (41°C) for 8 to 10 hours or until dry and crisp. Serve immediately or allow to cool, transfer to an airtight container and store at room temperature for up to 7 days.

Sour Cream and Onion Kale Chips

These crunchy snacks are a perfect excuse to sit on the couch on Sunday afternoon and indulge without feeling guilty. They are great on their own, but if you feel like gilding the lily, dip them in Pumpkin Seed "Refried Beans" (page 93) or Cashew Spinach Dip (page 83).

Makes 4 portions (4 cups/1 L)

Tips

To soak the cashews for this recipe, place in a bowl and cover with 3 cups (750 mL) water. Cover and set aside for 30 minutes. Drain, discarding soaking water, and rinse under cold running water until the water runs clear.

You don't need to break the dehydrated kale into chips. The pieces will break naturally after being dehydrated.

- **Electric food dehydrator**
- **Mandoline**

1½ cups	raw cashews, soaked (see Tips, left)	375 mL
1	bunch green kale (see Tips, page 299)	1
1	small red onion	1
½ cup	filtered water	125 mL
¼ cup	freshly squeezed lemon juice	60 mL
1½ tbsp	apple cider vinegar	22 mL
¼ tsp	fine sea salt	1 mL

1. Starting at the bottom of each stem, strip away the frilly green leaves of the kale and, if necessary, tear into small pieces (about 2 inches/5 cm). Discard stems and transfer leaves to a bowl. Set aside.
2. Using a mandoline, slice onion very thinly. Break up the rounds with your fingers and add to kale.
3. In a blender, combine soaked cashews, water, lemon juice, vinegar and salt. Blend at high speed until smooth and creamy. Add to kale mixture and toss until thoroughly combined.
4. Spread out on nonstick dehydrator sheets in a single layer and dehydrate at 105°F (41°C) for 10 to 12 hours or until crispy. Serve immediately or allow to cool, transfer to an airtight container and store for up to 7 days.

Variation

Add ¼ cup (60 mL) raw shelled hemp seeds to the kale and onion mixture in Step 2. This will add up to 20 grams of complete protein to the recipe.

Creamy Ranch Kale Chips

These tangy, crispy chips are the perfect healthy snack. I enjoy them with a glass of Perfect Green Juice (page 18) or a green smoothie such as The Gardener (page 59). The greens in the drinks and the flavors of the fresh herbs in the chips complement each other very well.

**Makes 6 to
8 portions
(8 cups/2 L)**

Tips

To soak the cashews for this recipe, place in a bowl and add 4 cups (1 L) water. Cover and set aside for 30 minutes. Drain, discarding soaking water, and rinse under cold running water until the water runs clear.

When making any type of kale chip, it is best to use green kale, also known as curly kale. This variety is easier to tear into bite-sized pieces and is less likely to crumble after dehydrating.

When tearing kale to make chips, be aware that the strips should be two to three times larger than the size you want the finished product to be. They will break apart naturally after being dehydrated.

Substitute 1 tsp (5 mL) dried dill weed for the fresh dill.

- **Electric food dehydrator**

2 cups	raw cashews, soaked (see Tips, left)	500 mL
2	bunches green kale	2
1½ cups	filtered water	375 mL
½ cup	chopped green onions, green part only	125 mL
½ cup	chopped fresh dill fronds	125 mL
3	cloves garlic	3
1 tbsp	apple cider vinegar	15 mL
2 tsp	freshly squeezed lemon juice	10 mL
2 tsp	fine sea salt	10 mL

1. Starting at the bottom of each stem, strip away the frilly green leaves of the kale and, if necessary, tear into small pieces (about 2 inches/5 cm). Discard stems and transfer leaves to a bowl. Set aside.

2. In a blender, combine soaked cashews, water, green onions, dill, garlic, vinegar, lemon juice and salt. Blend at high speed until smooth and creamy. Add to kale and toss well.

3. Spread out on nonstick dehydrator sheets in a single layer and dehydrate at 105°F (41°C) for 10 to 12 hours or until dry and crisp. Serve immediately or allow to cool, transfer to an airtight container and store for up to 7 days.

Variations

To make a simple dip for the chips, soak 2 cups (500 mL) cashews in 4 cups (1 L) water for 30 minutes. Drain, rinse and add 1½ cups (375 mL) filtered water. Blend at high speed until smooth and creamy.

Try adding different seasonings to the cashew mixture to create different flavors. I enjoy 1 tsp (5 mL) ground cumin, ½ tsp (2 mL) smoked paprika and ¼ tsp (1 mL) cayenne pepper for a spicy cream. A good curried version is 1 tbsp (15 mL) curry powder, ½ tsp (2 mL) ground cumin, ½ tsp (2 mL) chili powder and ¼ tsp (1 mL) ground turmeric.

Apple, Ginger and Sesame Kale Chips

I like to make a batch of these tasty treats and keep them in an airtight container for when I get the munchies. I love their sweet and tangy flavor, and the sesame seeds add a nice crunch.

Makes 4 cups (1 L)

Tips

To soak the sesame seeds for this recipe, place in a bowl with 1 cup (250 mL) water. Cover and set aside for 30 minutes. Drain, discarding liquid, and rinse under cold running water.

Once cut, apples will start to oxidize (turn brown). To prevent this from happening, place them in acidulated water: 1 cup (250 mL) water with 2 tbsp (30 mL) lemon juice added.

- **Electric food dehydrator**

½ cup	sesame seeds, soaked, divided (see Tips, left)	125 mL
1	bunch green kale (see Tips, page 299)	1
1 cup	apple juice	250 mL
3 tbsp	cold-pressed flax oil	45 mL
2 tbsp	chopped gingerroot	30 mL
¼ tsp	fine sea salt	1 mL
½ cup	shredded apple	125 mL

1. Starting at the bottom of each stem, strip away the frilly green leaves of the kale and, if necessary, tear into small pieces (about 2 inches/5 cm). Discard stems and transfer leaves to a bowl. Set aside.

2. In a blender, combine apple juice, ⅓ cup (75 mL) soaked sesame seeds, flax oil, ginger and salt. Blend at high speed until smooth and creamy.

3. Add sesame seed mixture, apple and remaining soaked sesame seeds to kale and toss well.

4. Spread out on nonstick dehydrator sheets in a single layer and dehydrate at 105°F (41°C) for 10 to 12 hours or until dry and crisp. Serve immediately or allow to cool, transfer to an airtight container and store at room temperature for up to 7 days.

Sweet Potato Chips

These sweet potato chips are so crisp and thin you won't believe they aren't fried. I like to serve them with Pumpkin Seed "Refried Beans" (page 93), Cashew Spinach Dip (page 83), Sweet Chili and Pecan Pâté (page 96) or Perfect Guacamole (page 81).

Makes about 80 chips

Tips

The trick to making these chips is to slice the sweet potatoes as thinly as possible.

Mandolines come in various sizes and shapes. I recommend purchasing a Japanese-style mandoline because I find them easier to use.

- **Electric food dehydrator**
- **Mandoline**

2	medium sweet potatoes	2
3 tbsp	cold-pressed (extra virgin) olive oil	45 mL
½ tsp	fine sea salt	2 mL

1. Using a mandoline, slice sweet potatoes lengthwise into thin slices approximately ¼ inch (0.5 cm) thick. Transfer to a bowl and toss with olive oil and salt.
2. Spread slices out in a single layer on nonstick dehydrator sheets. Dehydrate at 105°F (41°C) for 10 to 12 hours or until crisp and dry. Serve immediately or allow to cool, then store in an airtight container at room temperature for up to 7 days.

Chili Cumin Almonds

These crunchy snacks are perfect to have with you at all times. I love how easy they are to prepare and how long they keep once finished.

Makes 2 cups (500 mL)

Tip

To soak the almonds for this recipe, place in a bowl and add 4 cups (1 L) water. Cover and set aside for 30 minutes. Drain, discarding soaking water. Rinse under cold running water until the water runs clear.

- **Electric food dehydrator**

2 cups	whole raw almonds, soaked (see Tip, left)	500 mL
3 tbsp	wheat-free tamari	45 mL
2 tbsp	raw agave nectar	30 mL
1 tbsp	ground cumin	15 mL
2 tsp	chili powder	10 mL
Pinch	fine sea salt	Pinch

1. In a bowl, toss together soaked almonds, tamari, agave nectar, cumin, chili powder and salt.
2. Spread evenly on nonstick dehydrator sheets and dehydrate at 105°F (41°C) for 5 to 6 hours or until dry. Allow to cool, transfer to an airtight container and store at room temperature for up to 2 weeks.

Spicy Curried Cashews

These cashews are perfect to have on hand. If you're experiencing a midday slump, they provide a quick hit of protein and healthy fats.

Makes 2 cups (500 mL)

Tips

To soak the cashews for this recipe, place in a bowl and cover with 4 cups (1 L) water. Cover and set aside for 1 hour. Drain, discarding soaking water, and rinse under cold running water until the water runs clear.

Always allow any food that is warm to cool off before placing it in a container with a lid. Otherwise, the heat in the food creates steam, making it soft and soggy instead of crunchy.

- **Electric food dehydrator**

2 cups	raw cashews, soaked (see Tips, left)	500 mL
¼ cup	cold-pressed (extra virgin) olive oil	60 mL
2 tsp	curry powder	10 mL
1 tsp	ground cumin	5 mL
½ tsp	fine sea salt	2 mL
¼ tsp	turmeric	1 mL
Pinch	cayenne pepper	Pinch
Dash	freshly squeezed lemon juice	Dash

1. In a bowl, combine soaked cashews, olive oil, curry powder, cumin, salt, turmeric, cayenne and lemon juice. Toss until well combined.
2. Transfer to nonstick dehydrator sheets and spread evenly. Dehydrate at 105°F (41°C) for 10 to 12 hours or until dry and crispy. Allow to cool, transfer to an airtight container and store at room temperature for up to 2 weeks.

Variation

To make Greek-seasoned cashews, substitute 1 tbsp (15 mL) dried oregano, 1 tsp (5 mL) lemon zest and 1 tsp (5 mL) freshly squeezed lemon juice for the curry powder, cumin, turmeric and cayenne.

Avocado Fries

These "fries" are soft on the inside and lightly crunchy on the outside. I love the way the spices and the ground flax seeds combine to make a perfectly seasoned and textured breading. These pair well with Sun-Dried Tomato Ketchup (page 198).

(page 198)

Makes 4 servings

Tip

To ripen avocados, place them in a brown paper bag with a tomato or an apple. If your avocado is ripe and won't be consumed within a day or two, place it in the coolest part of the refrigerator to lengthen its life by up to a week. Once you take an avocado out of the fridge, do not put it back in, or it will turn black.

• **Electric food dehydrator**

1 cup	ground flax seeds	250 mL
2 tbsp	chili powder	30 mL
1 tsp	ground cumin	5 mL
½ tsp	fine sea salt	2 mL
Pinch	cayenne pepper	Pinch
2	large avocados (or 3 medium)	2

1. In a large bowl, toss together flax seeds, chili powder, cumin, salt and cayenne.
2. Cut the avocados in half lengthwise and remove the pit. Scoop out the flesh in one piece and cut each half lengthwise into 4 equal slices. (If you're using medium-sized avocados, cut each half into 3 slices.) Add to flaxseed mixture and, using a rubber spatula, toss gently until avocado is well coated.
3. Arrange avocado slices evenly in a single layer on nonstick dehydrator sheets and dehydrate at 105°F (41°C) for 7 to 8 hours, until the exterior is slightly crunchy. Serve immediately.

Crispy Kale Spears

This recipe takes five minutes to prepare and can stay fresh in an airtight container for up to a week. Its simplicity is beautiful. Use these spears to garnish dishes that use Zucchini Noodles (page 244), or as dippers.

Makes 10 to 12 spears

Tip

Kale comes in various forms: green (curly) kale, red kale and black kale. Black kale is also called dinosaur kale or lacinato kale. Black kale is particularly nutritious, but it also has the toughest texture and is the most costly.

- **Electric food dehydrator**

1	bunch black kale, separated into leaves	1
¼ cup	cold-pressed (extra virgin) olive oil	60 mL
1 tsp	fine sea salt	5 mL
Pinch	freshly ground black pepper	Pinch

1. In a bowl, toss together kale leaves, olive oil, salt and pepper.
2. Spread kale evenly in a single layer on nonstick dehydrator sheets and dehydrate at 105°F (41°C) for 10 to 12 hours or until crispy. Allow to cool completely and transfer to an airtight container. Store at room temperature for up to 2 weeks.

Sweet Potato Hickory Sticks

These little treats take just five minutes to prepare. They are crispy and satisfying — try not to eat the whole batch!

Makes 4 cups (1 L)

Tips

For curry sweet potato hickory sticks, substitute 1 tsp (5 mL) curry powder, ½ tsp (2 mL) ground coriander and ¼ tsp (1 mL) turmeric for the cumin, chili powder and paprika.

When shredding, aim for the longest pieces possible.

- **Electric food dehydrator**
- **Box grater**

2	large sweet potatoes, peeled and quartered	2
¼ cup	cold-pressed (extra virgin) olive oil	60 mL
½ tsp	fine sea salt	2 mL
1 tsp	ground cumin	5 mL
½ tsp	chili powder	2 mL
½ tsp	smoked sweet paprika	2 mL
Dash	wheat-free tamari	Dash

1. Using the large holes of a box grater, shred sweet potatoes lengthwise. Transfer to a bowl.
2. Add olive oil and salt and toss well. Spread evenly in a single layer on nonstick dehydrator sheets. Dehydrate at 105°F (41°C) for 7 to 8 hours or until dry and crispy.
3. Transfer to a bowl. Add cumin, chili powder, paprika and tamari and toss to coat evenly.

Red Pepper Jerky

These mouth-watering strips are perfect for packing in your lunch for an additional hit of protein and vitamin C. They also make a great topping for simple salads.

Makes 2 portions

Tips

To soak the cashews for this recipe, place in a bowl and add ½ cup (125 mL) water. Cover and set aside for 30 minutes. Drain, discarding soaking water. Rinse under cold running water until the water runs clear.

You may need to dehydrate the peppers for longer than the suggested time, as the amount of moisture they contain will play a role in the final texture. You want the end result to look wilted and slightly roasted. You may need to increase the dehydrating time by as much as 2 hours to achieve this result.

- Electric food dehydrator

3 tbsp	raw cashews, soaked (see Tips, left)	45 mL
2 tbsp	wheat-free tamari	30 mL
1 tbsp	filtered water	15 mL
1 tbsp	lime juice	15 mL
¼ tsp	ground cumin	1 mL
¼ tsp	ground cinnamon	1 mL
Pinch	cayenne pepper	Pinch
Pinch	ground nutmeg	Pinch
1	red bell pepper, seeded and thickly sliced	1
1 tbsp	raw shelled hemp seeds	15 mL

1. In a blender, combine soaked cashews, tamari, water, lime juice, cumin, cinnamon, cayenne and nutmeg. Blend at high speed until smooth and creamy.
2. Transfer to a bowl. Add red pepper strips and hemp seeds and toss well.
3. Place strips on nonstick dehydrator sheets in a single layer, distributing evenly, and dehydrate at 105°F (41°C) for about 7 hours (see Tips, left) or until strips are slightly wilted and appear to be lightly cooked. Allow to cool, transfer to an airtight container and refrigerate for up to 7 days.

Variation

Substitute a fruit such as mango, papaya or pineapple for the red pepper. Peel the fruit and cut into strips approximately ½ inch (1 cm) thick.

Cheesy Nori Snacks

These nori bites are deliciously cheesy and rich. I like to serve them on a platter alongside crispy Corn and Carrot Nachos (page 325) with some Perfect Guacamole (page 81). They are ideal for making in large batches ahead of time because they will keep for up to two weeks.

Makes 18 bars

Tip

Nori sheets come in both raw and cooked versions. Make sure you purchase raw nori, which is a bit more pricey and slightly more difficult to find.

- **Electric food dehydrator**

¾ cup	Cashew Cheddar Cheese (page 105)	175 mL
3	raw nori sheets	3

1. Lay the nori sheets flat on a clean work surface. Place ¼ cup (60 mL) of the cheese on each sheet and, using an offset spatula, spread evenly in a layer about ⅛ inch (3 mm) thick. Cut each sheet in half crosswise, then into 3 equal pieces lengthwise, to make 6 equal bars.
2. Arrange evenly on nonstick dehydrator sheets and dehydrate at 105°F (41°C) for 10 to 12 hours or until dry. Allow to cool and transfer to an airtight container. Store, refrigerated, for up to 2 weeks.

Variation

Substitute an equal quantity of Lemon-Ginger-Dill Sunflower Seed Pâté (page 97) for the cashew Cheddar.

Ants on a Log

This snack, although super easy and quite quick to make, is a wonderful way to add protein and heart-healthy fats to your diet. It will keep you feeling full for hours.

Makes 2 portions

Tip

Replace the almond butter with any other nut or seed butter, such as pumpkin, sunflower, cashew or hazelnut.

½ cup	almond butter	125 mL
3 tbsp	melted coconut oil (see Tips, page 334)	45 mL
1 tsp	ground cinnamon	5 mL
4 to 6	stalks celery (see Tips, page 255)	4 to 6
¼ cup	raisins	60 mL

1. In a bowl, combine almond butter, coconut oil and cinnamon. Stir well. Refrigerate for 30 minutes, until slightly firm.
2. Spread celery sticks evenly with almond butter mixture, dividing equally. Arrange raisins in a neat row on top. Serve immediately.

Saucy Lettuce Sandwiches

Wrapping a nutritious filling in lettuce is one of the easiest ways to create an enjoyable snack. I like to prepare the ingredients (but not the avocado, which will oxidize on contact with air) ahead of time and assemble the sandwiches as needed.

Tips

Try using various kinds of lettuce, such as romaine, red leaf or iceberg, to hold sandwiches or snacks together.

For additional flavor, sprinkle with chopped cilantro. If you like heat, add a little chopped jalapeño chile pepper.

½ cup	Sweet-and-Sour Thai Almond Butter Sauce (page 191)	125 mL
8	large romaine lettuce leaves	8
1 cup	sliced avocado (about 1 medium)	250 mL
½ cup	Walnut Mince (page 293)	125 mL
	Cashew Sour Cream (page 204), optional	

1. Spread 2 tbsp (30 mL) of the almond butter sauce on each of 4 lettuce leaves. Top each with one-quarter of the avocado and 2 tbsp (30 mL) walnut mince. Add a dollop of cashew sour cream, if using, and top with remaining lettuce leaves. Serve immediately.

Pad Thai Lettuce Wraps

I love the spicy, tangy flavor, the soft texture of the Boston lettuce, the crisp red pepper and the slightly nutty hemp seeds in these little bites. It's a great combination — I'm sure this is a recipe you will return to time and again.

Tips

Use leafy lettuce (red or green) or romaine in place of the Boston lettuce.

Using lettuce leaves in place of wraps such as pita breads is an easy way to cut gluten from your diet.

4	Boston lettuce leaves (see Tips, left)	4
½ cup	Walnut Mince (page 293)	125 mL
¼ cup	Spicy Pad Thai Sauce (page 194)	60 mL
¼ cup	raw shelled hemp seeds	60 mL
¼ cup	thinly sliced red bell pepper	60 mL
2 tsp	chopped green onion, white and green parts	10 mL

1. Working with one leaf at a time, spread 2 tbsp (30 mL) walnut mince along the wide end of a leaf, leaving a border 1½ inches (4 cm) wide at the top and sides. Top with 1 tbsp (15 mL) pad thai sauce, 1 tbsp (15 mL) hemp seeds, 1 tbsp (15 mL) red pepper and ½ tsp (2 mL) green onion, distributing evenly. Roll up leaf until you reach the middle. Fold in the sides and continue rolling into a tight cylindrical package. Repeat until all the leaves have been filled. Serve immediately.

Ginger Sesame Snaps

These crispy treats are similar in texture to peanut brittle. Don't spread the mixture too thickly on the dehydrator sheet. Otherwise, the snaps won't have a beautiful crunch. If necessary, use a second sheet.

Makes about 32 pieces

Tips

To soak the sesame seeds for this recipe, place in a bowl and add 4 cups (1 L) water. Cover and set aside for 30 minutes. Drain, discarding water.

If you do not have nonstick sheets for your dehydrator, use unbleached parchment paper as a substitute.

- **Electric food dehydrator**

2 cups	raw sesame seeds, soaked (see Tips, left)	500 mL
¾ cup	filtered water	175 mL
½ cup	raw agave nectar	125 mL
½ cup	chopped gingerroot	125 mL
1 tsp	freshly squeezed lemon juice	5 mL
Pinch	fine sea salt	Pinch
2 cups	raw sesame seeds	500 mL

1. In a food processor fitted with the metal blade, process soaked sesame seeds, water, agave nectar, ginger, lemon juice and salt until a thick paste forms. Transfer to a bowl and set aside.

2. Add the unsoaked sesame seeds and mix well. With slightly wet hands, spread mixture out on a nonstick dehydrator sheet in a single layer about ½ inch (1 cm) thick, using a second sheet if necessary. Dehydrate at 105°F (41°C) for 9 to 10 hours, until firm enough to handle. Flip in one piece and transfer to mesh sheet. Dehydrate for 3 to 4 hours or until crispy. Using your hands, break the crisp into pieces about the size of traditional ginger snaps. Serve immediately or transfer to an airtight container and store for up to 7 days.

Variations

For a multicolored version of this snack, substitute 1 cup (250 mL) black sesame seeds for an equal quantity of the unsoaked white sesame seeds.

To give this snack a holiday feel, add 1 tbsp (15 mL) beet juice and ¼ cup (60 mL) finely chopped parsley, in Step 1 along with the soaked sesame seeds.

Buckwheat Pretzels

These crunchy treats are perfectly seasoned and crunchy on the outside with a soft, dough-like consistency in the middle. I like them because they don't contain gluten or yeast but still have the flavor of traditional ballpark pretzels.

Makes 8 pretzels

Tips

To soak the buckwheat for this recipe, combine with 6 cups (1.5 L) water. Cover and set aside for 2 hours, changing the water every 30 minutes. Drain, discarding soaking water. Rinse under cold running water until the water runs clear.

When soaking buckwheat, it is important to change the water every 30 minutes to ensure that it does not begin to ferment. Because buckwheat is extremely high in protein, it is very easy for it to become sour and grow bacteria. Always use cool water to soak, and if any bubbles start to form, immediately change the water.

- **Electric food dehydrator**

3 cups	buckwheat groats, soaked	750 mL
3 tbsp	cold-pressed (extra virgin) olive oil	45 mL
2 tbsp	filtered water (approx.)	30 mL
1 tsp	fine sea salt	5 mL
1/2 cup	ground flax seeds	125 mL
2 tbsp	chopped fresh thyme leaves	30 mL

1. In a food processor fitted with the metal blade, process soaked buckwheat, olive oil, water and salt until smooth, scraping down the sides of the work bowl as necessary. Gradually add more water, 1 tbsp (15 mL) at a time if mixture is too stiff to process.

2. Transfer to bowl and add flax seeds and thyme. Mix well.

3. Divide dough into 8 equal portions. Roll each into a 12-inch (30 cm) log. Bring the ends up to start to form a circle, then cross them over each other and press on the bottom of the circle to make a traditional pretzel shape. Place on nonstick dehydrator sheets at least 2 inches (5 cm) apart. Dehydrate at 105°F (41°C) for 7 to 9 hours, until firm enough to handle.

4. Flip and transfer to the mesh sheet and dehydrate for 3 to 4 hours or until pretzels are hard on the outside and slightly soft in the middle. Serve immediately or allow the pretzels to cool and transfer to an airtight container. Store, refrigerated, for up to 5 days.

Variation

For an Indian-spiced buckwheat pretzel, add 1 tbsp (15 mL) curry powder, 1 tsp (5 mL) ground cumin and 1/4 tsp (1 mL) turmeric powder in Step 1.

Chocolate Date Protein Bars

These dense treats are perfect for midday hunger and take very little time to prepare. Try making a double batch and freezing some of the mixture for future use.

Makes 8 to 10 bars

Tips

To soak the dates for this recipe, place them in a bowl and cover with 4 cups (1 L) water. Cover and set aside to soak for 30 minutes. Drain, discarding any remaining water.

Dates provide iron, fiber and potassium and they are also a good source of antioxidants. Although dates are a healthy whole food, they are high in sugar. When you find yourself craving refined sugar, reach for one or two dates and you will find the craving goes away.

If caffeine is a concern, substitute raw carob powder in place of the cacao.

- Baking sheet

2 cups	pitted dates, soaked (see Tips, left)	500 mL
¼ cup	freshly squeezed orange juice	60 mL
¼ cup	raw agave nectar	60 mL
½ cup	raw cacao powder	125 mL
1 cup	raw shelled hemp seeds	250 mL

1. In a food processor fitted with the metal blade, process soaked dates, orange juice, agave nectar and cacao powder until smooth, stopping the motor once and scraping down the sides of the work bowl. Add hemp seeds and pulse several times until well integrated.

2. Transfer onto baking sheet and, using your hands, press out until approximately 8 inches (20 cm) square and 1 inch (2.5 cm) thick. Refrigerate for 1 hour to firm up. Remove and cut into bars. Transfer to an airtight container and store, refrigerated, for up to 7 days.

Energizing Trail Mix

This mix is very simple to prepare and can be made days in advance for a quick snack on the run.

Makes 4 to 6 servings

Tip

To soak the almonds, walnuts and sunflower and pumpkin seeds for this recipe, place in a bowl and cover with 5 cups (1.25 L) water. Cover and set aside for 30 minutes. Drain, discarding soaking water and any bits of shells. Rinse under cold running water until the water runs clear.

• **Electric food dehydrator**

1 cup	whole raw almonds, soaked (see Tip , left)	250 mL
½ cup	walnuts, soaked	125 mL
½ cup	raw pumpkin seeds, soaked	125 mL
½ cup	raw sunflower seeds, soaked	125 mL
¼ cup	dried shredded coconut	60 mL
¼ cup	cold-pressed hemp oil	60 mL
2 tbsp	goji berries	30 mL
1 tsp	ground cumin	5 mL
1 tsp	fine sea salt	5 mL
½ tsp	chili powder	2 mL
¼ tsp	smoked sweet paprika	1 mL

1. In a bowl, toss together soaked almonds, walnuts and pumpkin and sunflower seeds, coconut, hemp oil, goji berries, cumin, salt, chili powder and paprika.
2. Transfer to a nonstick dehydrator sheet and spread evenly. Dehydrate at 105°F (41°C) for 7 to 8 hours or until dry and crisp. Allow to cool, transfer to an airtight container and store at room temperature for up to 7 days.

Variation

This recipe is great because you can add many things to the mix. I like to include ¼ cup (60 mL) raw shelled hemp seeds and 2 tbsp (30 mL) chia seeds for additional protein and omega fatty acids.

Thai-Style Nuts 'n' Bolts

This protein-dense snack is great to keep in the cupboard to satisfy any late-night cravings. The sweet, spicy and slightly salty flavors really enhance the nuts and seeds. In addition to being a delicious snack, this is excellent as a garnish sprinkled over dishes made with Marinated Kelp Noodles (page 243) or Sweet-and-Sour Thai Almond Butter Sauce (page 191).

Makes 2 cups (500 mL)

Tips

To soak the almonds, cashews, buckwheat and sesame seeds for this recipe, combine in a bowl and add 2½ cups (625 mL) water. Cover and set aside for 30 minutes. Drain, discarding soaking water, and rinse under cold running water until the water runs clear.

After dehydrating you will have a large tray full of well-seasoned nuts, seeds and buckwheat groats — the perfect bar mix snack.

- **Electric food dehydrator**

½ cup	whole raw almonds, soaked (see Tips, left)	125 mL
½ cup	raw cashews, soaked	125 mL
¼ cup	buckwheat groats, soaked	60 mL
2 tbsp	sesame seeds, soaked	30 mL
¼ cup	almond butter	60 mL
3 tbsp	lime juice	45 mL
2 tbsp	filtered water	30 mL
2 tbsp	raw agave nectar	30 mL
1 tbsp	wheat-free tamari	15 mL
1 tbsp	chopped gingerroot	15 mL
¼ tsp	fine sea salt	1 mL
Pinch	cayenne pepper	Pinch
2 tbsp	raw shelled hemp seeds	30 mL
2 tsp	ground cumin	10 mL
½ tsp	chili powder	2 mL

1. In a blender, combine almond butter, lime juice, water, agave nectar, tamari, ginger, salt and cayenne. Blend at high speed until smooth.

2. In a bowl, combine soaked almonds, cashews, buckwheat and sesame seeds. Add almond butter mixture, hemp seeds, cumin and chili powder and toss to coat evenly.

3. Transfer to a nonstick dehydrator sheet and, using your hands, spread evenly. Dehydrate at 105°F (41°C) for 6 to 8 hours or until dry and crispy. Allow to cool and transfer to an airtight container. Store at room temperature for up to 7 days.

Variation

Substitute ⅓ cup (75 mL) Sweet-and-Sour Thai Almond Butter Sauce (page 191) for the ingredients in Step 1. Begin with Step 2.

Pizza Bites

These tasty little snacks are the perfect solution for mid-afternoon hunger pangs, and they also do double duty as simple hors d'oeuvres for a cocktail party. Serve them as is or spread with Red Pepper, Dill and Cashew Ricotta (page 103) and Red Pepper Basil Marinara Sauce (page 184). They are also good topped with fresh tomato slices, a bit of kale and a dollop of Almond Parmesan Cheese (page 204).

Makes 16 bites

Tips

To soak the whole flax seeds for this recipe, place in a bowl and cover with 1 cup (250 mL) water. Set aside for 30 minutes. Drain, discarding any remaining soaking water. Rinse under cold running water until the water runs clear.

To soak the sun-dried tomatoes for this recipe, combine with 1 cup (250 mL) warm water. Set aside for 30 minutes. Drain, discarding liquid.

When a recipe calls for flax seeds, you have two options to choose from: golden or brown. Golden flax seeds will yield a lighter color in the end result of the recipe while brown flax seeds will make the final product darker. I prefer to use golden flax seeds in this recipe because they produce a crust that is lighter in color.

If you are using a ring-shaped dehydrator, divide the mixture in half before spreading on the sheet. Spread each half into a 4-inch (10 cm) square about 1/2 inch (1 cm) thick and cut each one into 8 squares.

- **Electric food dehydrator**

1/2 cup	whole flax seeds, soaked (see Tips, left)	125 mL
1/4 cup	dry-packed sun-dried tomatoes, soaked (see Tips, left)	60 mL
1/4 cup	chopped tomato	60 mL
3	cloves garlic	3
3 tbsp	cold-pressed (extra virgin) olive oil	45 mL
1 tsp	freshly squeezed lemon juice	5 mL
1/2 tsp	dried oregano	2 mL
1/2 tsp	dried basil	2 mL
1/4 cup	ground flax seeds	60 mL

1. In a food processor fitted with the metal blade, process soaked sun-dried tomatoes, chopped tomato, garlic, olive oil, lemon juice, oregano and basil until smooth.
2. Transfer to a bowl. Add ground flax seeds and soaked whole flax seeds and mix well.
3. Spread mixture out on a nonstick dehydrator sheet in a single layer approximately 8 inches (20 cm) square and 1/2 inch (1 cm) thick (see Tips, left). Using a knife, cut into 16 equal squares. Dehydrate at 105°F (41°C) for 5 to 6 hours or until firm enough to handle. Flip and transfer to mesh sheet and dehydrate for 7 to 8 hours or until dry and crisp. Serve immediately or allow to cool and transfer to an airtight container. Store, refrigerated, for up to 7 days.

Sunflower Seed Croutons

These crunchy little bites are great with crispy romaine lettuce, Creamy Sunflower Seed Dressing (page 178), a little chopped Eggplant Bacon (page 41) and some Almond Parmesan Cheese (page 204). You can also use them to add protein and crunch to your favorite meal; I enjoy them scattered over dishes made with Zucchini Noodles (page 204). They also make a perfect addition to a green salad.

Makes 15 to 20 croutons

Tips

To soak the sunflower seeds for this recipe, place in a bowl and add 2 cups (500 mL) water. Cover and set aside for 30 minutes. Drain, discarding water and any shells or unwanted particles.

You can purchase flax seeds that are already ground (often described as milled) in vacuum-sealed bags or you can grind them yourself. Depending upon the quantity you need, grind whole flax seeds in a blender or a spice grinder. Once ground (or after the vacuum-sealed bag is opened), the beneficial fatty acids begin to dissipate. Store ground flax seeds away from light, in an airtight container in the refrigerator or freezer, for up to 2 months.

- **Electric food dehydrator**

1 cup	raw sunflower seeds, soaked (see Tips, left)	250 mL
1/4 cup	cold-pressed (extra virgin) olive oil	60 mL
2 tbsp	freshly squeezed lemon juice	30 mL
3	cloves garlic	3
2 tsp	caraway seeds	10 mL
1 tsp	dried oregano	5 mL
1 tsp	fine sea salt	5 mL
1/4 cup	ground flax seeds	60 mL

1. In a food processor fitted with the metal blade, process soaked sunflower seeds, olive oil, lemon juice, garlic, caraway seeds, oregano and salt until smooth, stopping the motor once and scraping down the sides of the work bowl.

2. Transfer to a bowl. Add ground flax seeds and stir well. Set aside for 10 minutes so the flax can absorb some of the liquid and swell.

3. Using a small ice cream scoop or ladle, scoop out 15 to 20 equal portions of batter and arrange evenly on a nonstick dehydrator sheet. Dehydrate at 105°F (41°C) for 10 to 12 hours or until dry through the middle. Transfer to an airtight container and store at room temperature for up to 2 weeks.

Variations

Substitute 1 cup (250 mL) pumpkin seeds, soaked and drained, for the sunflower seeds.

I like to try various seasonings in this recipe. Substitute 2 tsp (10 mL) ground cumin and 1 tsp (5 mL) curry powder or chili powder for the caraway and oregano.

Butternut Squash Garlic Bites

You'll be surprised by how much these little bites taste like traditional garlic bread. I enjoy them as a midday pick-me-up with a Beta-Carotene Burst (page 68).

Makes 15 to 20 bites

Tips

Working with peeled butternut squash can cause your hands to become dry. To prevent this, wear gloves.

When shaping raw bread dough on a dehydrator sheet, have a small bowl containing room-temperature water handy. Use this to wet your hands intermittently to prevent the dough from sticking.

- **Electric food dehydrator**

¼ cup	cold-pressed (extra virgin) olive oil	60 mL
3 tbsp	filtered water	45 mL
6 to 8	cloves garlic	6 to 8
2 tsp	fine sea salt	10 mL
1 tsp	dried oregano	5 mL
4 cups	finely diced peeled butternut squash	1 L
¾ cup	ground flax seeds	175 mL

1. In a food processor fitted with the metal blade, process olive oil, water, garlic, salt and oregano until no large pieces of garlic remain. Add squash and process until it has been broken down to the consistency of soft dough, stopping the motor and scraping down the sides of the work bowl as necessary.
2. Transfer to a deep bowl. Add flax seeds and mix well.
3. Divide the dough in half and divide each half into 10 equal pieces. Place on nonstick dehydrator sheets, distributing evenly. Using your hands, flatten each until approximately ½ inch (1 cm) thick. Dehydrate at 105°F (41°C) for 12 to 15 hours or until dry and crisp. Serve immediately or allow to cool and transfer to an airtight container. Store, refrigerated, for up to 5 days.

Variations

Substitute an equal quantity of diced sweet potato for the squash.

Substitute the oregano with 1 tsp (5 mL) ground cinnamon and a pinch each of ground nutmeg and cloves.

Substitute the garlic with 3 tbsp (45 mL) raw agave nectar and the olive oil with an equal quantity of liquid coconut oil (see Tips, page 334).

Sunflower Almond Nuggets

Enjoy these little morsels as the protein component of a main course as well as a snack. They are perfect with Sun-Dried Tomato Ketchup (page 198).

Makes about 25 pieces

Tips

To soak the almonds for this recipe, place them in a bowl and add 2 cups (500 mL) water. Cover and set aside for 45 minutes. Drain, discarding remaining water. Rinse under cold running water until the water runs clear.

To soak the sunflower seeds for this recipe place in a bowl and add 2 cups (500 mL) water. Cover and set aside for 30 minutes. Drain, discarding water and any shells or unwanted particles. Rinse under cold running water until the water runs clear.

To soak the sun-dried tomatoes for this recipe, combine with 2 cups (500 mL) warm water. Set aside for 30 minutes. Drain, discarding liquid.

When you dehydrate foods that are intended to work as meat substitutes such as burgers or meatloaf, make sure you do not dehydrate them for too long. They should be firm on the outside but soft in the middle. This will give the mouth feel of meat and help to create a pleasing texture.

- **Electric food dehydrator**

1 cup	whole raw almonds, soaked (see Tips, left)	250 mL
1 cup	raw sunflower seeds, soaked	250 mL
½ cup	dry-packed sun-dried tomatoes, soaked (see Tips, left)	125 mL
1 cup	whole raw almonds	250 mL
¼ cup	chopped onion	60 mL
¼ cup	nutritional yeast	60 mL
1 tbsp	brown rice miso	15 mL
4	cloves garlic	4
½ cup	filtered water	125 mL
3 tbsp	cold-pressed flax oil	45 mL
½ cup	sesame seeds	125 mL

1. In a food processor fitted with the metal blade, process unsoaked almonds until they become flour-like in consistency. Transfer to a bowl and set aside.
2. Add onion, nutritional yeast, miso, garlic, water and flax oil to food processor work bowl and process until smooth. Add soaked almonds, sunflower seeds and sun-dried tomatoes and process until smooth, stopping the motor once and scraping down the sides of the work bowl.
3. Transfer to a bowl. Add reserved almond flour and sesame seeds and mix well. Set aside for 10 to 15 minutes, until the almond flour absorbs some of the liquid.
4. Using an ice cream scoop or small ladle, drop about 25 equal portions of dough onto nonstick dehydrator sheets, distributing evenly. Dehydrate at 105°F (41°C) for 8 to 10 hours or until firm (see Tips, left). Serve immediately or store in an airtight container for up to 7 days.

Variations

Substitute soaked walnuts for the almonds.

For a Southwest flavor profile, add ¼ cup (60 mL) chopped cilantro, 1 tbsp (15 mL) ground cumin and 2 tsp (10 mL) chili powder along with the other ingredients in Step 2.

Cinnamon Buckwheaty Squares

These crispy little treats are perfect when you are craving a little protein or something that seems slightly sinful. I love the way the flavors of the sweet agave nectar, rich dates and aromatic cinnamon combine. They remind me of the holiday season.

Makes 25 to 30 squares

Tips

To soak the buckwheat for this recipe, combine with 4 cups (1 L) water. Set aside for 2 hours, changing the water every 30 minutes. Drain, discarding soaking water. Rinse under cold running water until the water runs clear.

To soak the dates for this recipe, place them in a bowl with 2 cups (500 mL) warm water, cover and set aside to soak for 30 minutes. Drain, discarding any remaining water.

It's important to spread the mixture to 2-inch (5 cm) thickness, so if you're using a ring-shaped dehydrator, you may need two nonstick sheets, dividing the mixture in half and spreading into two smaller rather than one large square.

• **Electric food dehydrator**

2 cups	buckwheat groats, soaked (see Tips, left), divided	500 mL
½ cup	chopped pitted Medjool dates, soaked (see Tips, left)	125 mL
½ cup	raw agave nectar	125 mL
¼ cup	filtered water	60 mL
1 cup	ground flax seeds	250 mL
2 tbsp	ground cinnamon	30 mL
1 tsp	fine sea salt	5 mL

1. In a food processor fitted with the metal blade, process 3 cups (750 mL) soaked buckwheat, soaked dates, agave nectar and water until smooth, stopping the motor once and scraping down the sides of the work bowl.

2. Transfer to a bowl. Add remaining 1 cup (250 mL) soaked buckwheat, flax seeds, cinnamon and salt and mix well. Set aside for 10 minutes so the flax can absorb some of the liquid and swell.

3. Transfer mixture onto a nonstick dehydrator sheet and, using your hands, spread evenly in a square approximately 2 inches (5 cm) thick (see Tips, left). Using a knife, cut into approximately 1-inch (2.5 cm) squares. Dehydrate at 105°F (41°C) for 10 to 12 hours or until firm enough to handle.

4. Flip and transfer to mesh sheet. Dehydrate for 4 to 5 hours, until dry and crispy. Serve immediately or allow to cool, then transfer to an airtight container and store at room temperature for up to 7 days.

Variation

To keep these squares slightly soft in the center, remove them from the dehydrator after completing Step 3. Allow to cool and transfer to an airtight container. Store, refrigerated, for up to 7 days.

Apple Chia Crackers

These crispy and sweet little crackers are great with dips such as Sweet-and-Sour Thai Almond Butter Sauce (page 191), Sweet Chili and Pecan Pâté (page 196) or Cashew Sour Cream (page 204). They make a great snack on the go. You can prepare a large batch ahead of time and keep them in an airtight container for up to two weeks.

Makes approximately 30 crackers

Tips

To soak the chia seeds for this recipe, cover with 1 cup (250 mL) water. Stir to moisten evenly. Cover and set aside to soak for 30 minutes.

Two tablespoons (30 mL) of chia seeds provides about 7 grams of alpha-linolenic acid (ALA), the omega-3 fat that is the essential fatty acid; without it, we could not survive. It is called "essential" because our bodies are unable to make it and must obtain it from food. Good sources of ALA include flax and chia seeds, walnuts and walnut oil. Research has demonstrated ALA's ability to reduce chronic inflammation and other risk factors for diabetes, heart disease and stroke. It is estimated that North Americans get an average of about 1.5 grams ALA per day. Some experts recommend an intake of 2.3 to 3 grams per day.

Chia seeds will double in size when they are soaked, so that ½ cup (125 mL) will turn into 1 cup (250 mL) after they have been in the water for 30 minutes or more.

- **Electric food dehydrator**

½ cup	chia seeds, soaked (see Tips, left)	125 mL
1 cup	chopped apple	250 mL
¼ cup	apple juice	60 mL
¼ cup	chopped parsley leaves	60 mL
3 tbsp	cold-pressed (extra virgin) olive oil	45 mL
½ tsp	fine sea salt	2 mL

1. In a food processor fitted with the metal blade, process apple, apple juice, parsley, olive oil and salt until smooth.

2. Transfer to a bowl. Add soaked chia seeds and stir well. Set aside for 5 to 10 minutes to allow chia seeds to absorb the liquid and swell.

3. Using your hands, spread mixture out on a nonstick dehydrator sheet until it is approximately ¼ inch (0.5 cm) thick. Dehydrate at 105°F (41°C) for 8 to 10 hours or until firm enough to handle. Flip and transfer to mesh sheet. Dehydrate for 5 to 6 hours or until dry and crisp. Allow to cool, break into about 30 pieces and transfer to an airtight container. Store at room temperature for up to 2 weeks.

French Onion Flax Crackers

These crackers are crisp and light. They pair well with Herbed Mushroom and Walnut Pâté (page 100) or Herbed Mushroom Duxelles (page 102).

Makes 10 crackers

Tips

To soak the whole flax seeds for this recipe, place in a bowl and add 2 cups (500 mL) water. Cover and set aside for 30 minutes. Drain, discarding soaking water. Rinse under cold running water until the water runs clear.

When spreading out raw bread or cracker dough on a dehydrator sheet, keep a small bowl of room-temperature water off to one side. Use this to wet your hands intermittently to prevent the dough from sticking to them.

- **Electric food dehydrator**

1 cup	whole flax seeds, soaked (see Tips, left)	250 mL
2 cups	filtered water	500 mL
¼ cup	wheat-free tamari	60 mL
3 tbsp	raw agave nectar	45 mL
2 tsp	apple cider vinegar	10 mL
½ cup	shredded red onion (about ½ medium)	125 mL
2 tbsp	chopped fresh thyme leaves	30 mL
5	cloves garlic	5
2 cups	ground golden flax seeds	500 mL
2 tsp	fine sea salt	10 mL

1. In a food processor fitted with the metal blade, process water, tamari, agave nectar, vinegar, onion, thyme and garlic for 1 minute or until garlic has been chopped fine.
2. Transfer to a bowl. Add ground flax seeds, salt and soaked whole flax seeds. Mix well. Set aside for 20 minutes so the flax can absorb some of the liquid and swell.
3. Transfer mixture to a nonstick dehydrator sheet and, using the palm of your hand, spread evenly in a layer approximately ½ inch (1 cm) thick. Use a small knife to cut the dough into 10 equal slices. Dehydrate at 105°F (41°C) for 8 to 10 hours or until firm enough to handle. Flip onto mesh sheet and dehydrate for 2 to 3 hours or until crisp and dry. Allow to cool and transfer to an airtight container. Store at room temperature for up to 7 days.

Buckwheat, Sunflower and Almond Breadsticks

> These crunchy snacks are perfect to use with dips such as Pumpkin Seed "Refried Beans" (page 93), Cashew Sour Cream (page 204), or Perfect Guacamole (page 81).

Makes 48 breadsticks

Tips

To soak the almonds for this recipe, place in a bowl and add 4 cups (1 L) water. Cover and set aside for 1 hour. Drain, discarding water, and rinse under cold running water until the water runs clear.

To soak the buckwheat for this recipe, combine with 8 cups (2 L) water. Set aside for 30 minutes. Drain, discarding soaking water. Rinse under cold running water until the water runs clear.

To soak the sunflower seeds for this recipe, place in a bowl and add 3 cups (750 mL) water. Cover and set aside for 30 minutes. Drain, discarding water and any shells or unwanted particles. Rinse under cold running water until the water runs clear.

To soak the sesame seeds for this recipe, place in a bowl and add 4 cups (1 L) water. Cover and set aside for 30 minutes. Drain, discarding water.

To soak the whole flax seeds for this recipe, place in a bowl and add 4 cups (1 L) water. Cover and set aside for 30 minutes. Drain, discarding any remaining water.

- **Electric food dehydrator**

2 cups	whole raw almonds, soaked (see Tips, left)	500 mL
4 cups	buckwheat groats, soaked (see Tips, left)	1 L
2½ cups	raw sesame seeds, soaked (see Tips, left)	625 mL
1½ cups	sunflower seeds, soaked (see Tips, left)	375 mL
1 cup	whole flax seeds, soaked (see Tips, left)	250 mL
3 cups	chopped red bell peppers	750 mL
1 cup	nutritional yeast (see Tips, page 273)	250 mL
¼ cup	freshly squeezed lemon juice	60 mL
7	cloves garlic	7
1 tbsp	each fine sea salt and dried oregano	15 mL
Pinch	cayenne pepper	Pinch
1 cup	ground golden flax seeds	250 mL

1. In a food processor fitted with the metal blade, process red peppers, nutritional yeast, lemon juice, garlic, salt, oregano and cayenne until smooth, stopping the motor once and scraping down the sides of the work bowl.
2. Add soaked almonds and buckwheat and process until smooth, scraping down the sides as necessary.
3. Transfer to a bowl. Add soaked sesame, sunflower and flax seeds, plus the ground flax seeds, and mix well.
4. Divide batter into three equal portions Shape each into a 8-inch square about 1-inch (2.5 cm) thick. Place squares at least 2 inches (5 cm) apart on nonstick dehydrator sheets. Cut each square into 16 thin sticks.
5. Dehydrate at 105°F (41°C) for 10 to 12 hours or until firm enough to handle. Separate into individual sticks and transfer to mesh sheets. Dehydrate for 6 to 8 hours or until completely dry and crispy. Allow to cool and transfer to an airtight container. Store at room temperature for up to 7 days.

Herbed Pumpkin Seed Flatbread

This flatbread is a delicious alternative to store-bought breads. I like to dip it into Perfect Guacamole (page 81) or Pumpkin Seed "Refried Beans" (page 93). It makes a great accompaniment to raw soups such as Red Pepper and Tomato Bisque (page 113).

Makes 15 to 20 slices

Tips

To soak the pumpkin seeds for this recipe, place them in a bowl and cover with 6 cups (1.5 L) water. Cover and set aside for 30 minutes. Drain, discarding liquid.

To soak the sun-dried tomatoes for this recipe, combine with 1 cup (250 mL) warm water. Set aside for 30 minutes. Drain, discarding liquid.

After refrigeration, place the bread in the dehydrator at 105°F (41°C) for 30 minutes to 1 hour to crisp it up.

• **Electric food dehydrator**

3 cups	raw pumpkin seeds, soaked (see Tips, left), divided	750 mL
¼ cup	dry-packed sun-dried tomatoes, soaked (see Tips, left)	60 mL
½ cup	chopped tomato	125 mL
½ cup	chopped parsley leaves	125 mL
5	cloves garlic	5
1 tbsp	dried basil	15 mL
1 tsp	fine sea salt	5 mL
½ cup	filtered water	125 mL
¼ cup	cold-pressed (extra virgin) olive oil	60 mL
2 tbsp	freshly squeezed lemon juice	30 mL
2 cups	ground brown flax seeds	500 mL

1. In a food processor fitted with the metal blade, process soaked sun-dried tomatoes, chopped tomato, parsley, garlic, basil, salt, water, olive oil and lemon juice until no large pieces remain. Add 2 cups (500 mL) soaked pumpkin seeds and process until smooth.

2. Transfer to a bowl. Add remaining soaked pumpkin seeds and ground flax seeds and mix well. Set aside for 10 minutes so the flax can absorb liquid and swell.

3. Transfer to a nonstick dehydrator sheet and spread evenly in a layer approximately ¾ inch (2 cm) thick. Use a small knife to cut the dough into 16 equal slices and dehydrate at 105°F (41°C) for 10 to 12 hours or until firm. Flip the bread onto the mesh sheet and dehydrate for an additional 3 to 4 hours or until dry on the outside but slightly soft in the center. Allow to cool and transfer to an airtight container. Store in the refrigerator for up to 7 days.

Variation

Soak 1 cup (250 mL) almonds and 2 cups (500 mL) sunflower seeds for 30 minutes. Process the almonds and 1 cup (250 mL) of the sunflower seeds in Step 1. Add the remaining sunflower seeds in Step 2.

Carrot Zucchini Loaf

Once you make this savory bread I'm sure it will become a favorite snack. I enjoy it on its own or spread with Raw Chickpea Hummus (page 94) and topped with avocado slices.

(page 94)

Makes 10 to 15 servings

Tips

To soak the buckwheat for this recipe, combine with 2 cups (500 mL) water. Set aside for 1 hour, changing the water once. Drain, discarding soaking water. Rinse under cold running water until the water runs clear.

When soaking buckwheat, it is important to change the water frequently to ensure that it does not begin to ferment. Because buckwheat is extremely high in protein, it is very easy for it to become sour and grow bacteria. Always use cool water to soak, and if any bubbles start to form, immediately change the water.

When spreading out raw bread or cracker dough on a dehydrator sheet, keep a small bowl of room-temperature water off to one side. Use this to wet your hands intermittently to prevent the dough from sticking to them.

• **Electric food dehydrator**

1 cup	buckwheat groats, soaked (see Tips, left)	250 mL
¼ cup	cold-pressed (extra virgin) olive oil	60 mL
3 tbsp	freshly squeezed lemon juice	45 mL
3 tbsp	chopped fresh thyme leaves	45 mL
2	cloves garlic	2
2 tsp	fine sea salt	10 mL
1 cup	chopped carrot	250 mL
1 cup	shredded zucchini (about ½ large)	250 mL
1 cup	ground flax seeds	250 mL

1. In a food processor fitted with the metal blade, process olive oil, lemon juice, thyme, garlic and salt for 1 minute. Add soaked buckwheat and process until smooth, stopping the motor and scraping down the sides of the work bowl as necessary. Add carrot and process until smooth.

2. Transfer to a bowl. Add shredded zucchini and ground flax seeds and mix well. Using your hands, shape mixture into a loaf approximately 3 inches (7.5 cm) wide and 6 inches (15 cm) long. Place on a nonstick dehydrator sheet and dehydrate at 105°F (41°C) for 6 to 7 hours or until firm enough to handle.

3. Flip onto the mesh sheet and dehydrate for 2 to 3 hours or until desired consistency has been reached. You want the outside of the loaf to be firm and somewhat crisp and the inside to be soft but not gummy. Allow to cool and transfer to an airtight container. Store in the refrigerator for up to 7 days.

Banana Raisin Bread

This banana bread is light, fluffy and sweet. I like to eat it warm, right out of the dehydrator, with a big spoonful of almond butter and a glass of cold Almond Milk (page 45).

Makes 12 slices

Tips

You want the bread in this recipe to be firm but still soft in the middle. When the bread is close to be being ready, check once every hour or so for the desired texture.

When dehydrating raw breads, you have different options in terms of texture. For crispier, firmer bread, dehydrate until all of the moisture has been removed. This will make storing the bread easy, as it cannot spoil without moisture present. For softer, chewier bread, dehydrate for less time to retain more moisture in the middle. Make sure to store breads that contain moisture in the refrigerator, as bacteria can grow even with only filtered water present.

● **Electric food dehydrator**

8 cups	chopped banana	2 L
¼ cup	raw agave nectar	60 mL
2 tbsp	cinnamon	30 mL
1 tsp	fine sea salt	5 mL
4 cups	ground brown flax seeds	1 L
1 cup	raisins	250 mL

1. In a food processor fitted with the metal blade, process banana, agave nectar, cinnamon and salt until smooth and creamy.
2. Transfer to a bowl. Add ground flax seeds and raisins and stir well. Set aside for 10 minutes so the flax can absorb the liquid and swell.
3. Transfer to a nonstick dehydrator sheet and, using your hands, spread evenly in a layer approximately 2 inches (5 cm) thick. Dehydrate at 105°F (41°C) for 10 to 12 hours or until firm enough to flip.
4. Flip onto a cutting board and cut the bread into 12 equal portions. Transfer to a mesh sheet, distributing evenly, and continue to dehydrate for 3 to 4 hours or until the outside of the bread is firm and the middle is soft but not gummy in consistency. Allow to cool and transfer to an airtight container. Store, refrigerated, for up to 7 days.

Variation

For a holiday bread, add ¼ cup (60 mL) dried cranberries, 2 tbsp (30 mL) chopped gingerroot, ½ tsp (2 mL) ground allspice and a pinch of freshly grated nutmeg. Process with the banana.

Zucchini Hemp Bread

This recipe is perfect if you are craving a slice of bread. It is also very versatile; I enjoy it with crisp romaine lettuce, Sun-Dried Tomato Hemp Mayonnaise (page 88) and some slices of avocado.

Sun-Dried Tomato Hemp Mayonnaise (page 88)

Makes about 12 pieces

Tips

To soak the sun-dried tomatoes for this recipe, combine with 6 cups (1.5 L) water. Set aside for 30 minutes. Drain, discarding liquid.

If you have a high-powered blender, use it to make this batter.

To shred vegetables, use the shredding blade attachment of a food processor. If you are shredding a large quantity, this will save you time and effort.

It's important to spread the mixture to a ¾-inch (2 cm) thickness. Depending on your dehydrator, you may need two or more nonstick sheets for this recipe.

- **Electric food dehydrator**

2 cups	dry-packed sun-dried tomatoes, soaked (see Tips, left)	500 mL
5 cups	chopped zucchini (about 4 medium)	1.25 L
½ cup	filtered water	125 mL
½ cup	cold-pressed hemp oil	125 mL
1 tbsp	fine sea salt	15 mL
4 cups	ground brown flax seeds	1 L
3 cups	shredded zucchini (about 3 large)	750 mL
2 cups	raw shelled hemp seeds	500 mL

1. In a food processor fitted with the metal blade, process chopped zucchini, water, hemp oil, salt and soaked sun-dried tomatoes until smooth. Transfer to a large bowl.

2. Add ground flax seeds, shredded zucchini and hemp seeds and mix well.

3. Transfer to nonstick dehydrator sheets, dividing as necessary (see Tips, left) and using your hands spread evenly in a layer approximately ¾ inch (2 cm) thick. Cut into squares (you should have about 12).

4. Dehydrate at 105°F (41°C) for 5 to 6 hours, until firm enough to handle. Flip and transfer to a mesh sheet (do not separate squares). Return to dehydrator and dehydrate for 2 to 3 hours, until soft like traditional bread (you do not want it to become hard, but on the other hand, it should not be soggy in the middle). Serve warm or allow to cool. Transfer to an airtight container and refrigerate for up to 5 days.

Corn and Carrot Nachos

These crispy chips are a perfect stand-in for your favorite junk food. You will never feel guilty again after making this recipe. I like to crush these into salads to create a little crunch or serve them as a side with Perfect Guacamole (page 81) and some Cashew Sour Cream (page 204).

Makes 20 to 30 chips

Tips

To remove the kernels from a cob of corn, place the cob upright on the counter. Using a chef's knife, run the blade along the kernels, being careful not to cut too far into the cob, as this will remove the fibrous part of the corn.

Always use freshly picked corn if possible. As corn sits, the sugar converts to starch and creates a less pleasant flavor.

If you want to make a larger batch of these nachos, simply double or triple the recipe and lay the mixture out on several dehydrator sheets.

- **Electric food dehydrator**

4 cups	fresh corn kernels (see Tips, left)	1 L
½ cup	chopped carrot	125 mL
2 tbsp	cold-pressed (extra virgin) olive oil	30 mL
2 tsp	chili powder	10 mL
1 tsp	ground cumin	5 mL
Pinch	cayenne pepper	Pinch
1¼ cups	ground flax seeds	300 mL
¼ cup	sesame seeds	60 mL
2 tsp	fine sea salt	10 mL

1. In a food processor fitted with the metal blade, process corn, carrot, olive oil, chili powder, cumin and cayenne until smooth, stopping the motor once and scraping down the sides of the work bowl. Transfer to a bowl.
2. Add flax and sesame seeds and salt and mix well. Set aside for 10 to 15 minutes, until the flax absorbs some of the liquid and swells.
3. Transfer mixture onto a nonstick dehydrator sheet and, using your hands, spread the dough evenly in a thin layer approximately ¼ inch (0.5 cm) thick. Dehydrate at 105°F (41°C) for 12 to 15 hours or until firm enough to handle. Flip and transfer to mesh sheet. Dehydrate for 5 to 6 hours or until dry and crispy.
4. Remove from the mesh sheet and allow to dry completely. Break into bite-sized pieces. Transfer to an airtight container and store at room temperature for up to 7 days.

Buckwheat and Sunflower Seed Pizza Crust

When I make this recipe, I usually prepare four small crusts and store them in the refrigerator. When I feel a craving for a pizza, I take one out and add my favorite toppings (see Variations, page 327). Let your imagination run wild and see what flavor combinations you can come up with to make the perfect raw pizza.

Makes 1 large pizza

(approximately 16 inches/40 cm) or 4 mini pizzas (4 inches/10 cm)

Tips

To soak the buckwheat for this recipe, place in a bowl and add 4 cups (1 L) water. Set aside for 30 minutes. Drain, discarding soaking water. Rinse under cold running water until the water runs clear.

To soak the sunflower seeds for this recipe, combine with 2 cups (500 mL) water. Cover and set aside for 30 minutes. Drain, discarding water and any shells or unwanted particles. Rinse under cold running water until the water runs clear.

When a recipe calls for flax seeds, you have two options to choose from: golden or brown. Golden flax seeds will yield a lighter color in the end result, while brown flax seeds will make the final product darker.

• **Electric food dehydrator**

2 cups	buckwheat groats, soaked (see Tips, left)	500 mL
¾ cup	raw sunflower seeds, soaked (see Tips, left)	175 mL
¾ cup	chopped carrot	175 mL
½ cup	chopped red bell pepper	125 mL
¼ cup	cold-pressed (extra virgin) olive oil	60 mL
2	cloves garlic	2
1 tsp	dried oregano	5 mL
½ tsp	fine sea salt	2 mL
½ cup	filtered water	125 mL
1 cup	ground flax seeds (see Tips, left)	250 mL

1. In a food processor fitted with the meal blade, process carrot, red pepper, olive oil, garlic, oregano and salt until smooth, stopping the motor and scraping down the sides of the work bowl as necessary.

2. Add soaked buckwheat and sunflower seeds and water and process until smooth, stopping the motor and scraping down the sides of the work bowl as necessary.

3. Transfer to a bowl and stir in ground flax seeds. Set aside for 10 minutes so the flax can absorb some of the moisture and swell.

4. Transfer to a nonstick dehydrator sheet and, using your hands, work into a circular shape about ½ inch (1 cm) thick. (If making mini pizzas, divide the dough into four equal portions before flattening, see Tips, page 327.) Dehydrate at 105°F (41°C) for 5 to 6 hours or until firm enough to handle.

5. Flip and transfer to mesh sheet. Dehydrate at 105°F (41°C) for 2 to 3 hours or until dry on the outside and soft in the middle. The finished product should be similar to a traditional pizza crust. Allow to cool and transfer to an airtight container. Store in the refrigerator for up to 7 days.

Tips

The trick to making this pizza crust perfect is to dehydrate it for the right amount of time. It is a great gluten-free substitute for any cooked version of pizza. Just dehydrate it first and then use it as you would any other crust.

When spreading out raw bread or cracker dough on a dehydrator sheet, keep a small bowl of room-temperature water off to one side. Use this to wet your hands intermittently to prevent the dough from sticking to them.

If you have a ring-shaped dehydrator, make the mini pizza version and use 2 nonstick sheets, if necessary.

Variations

Replace the sunflower seeds with pumpkin seeds and follow the same soaking instructions.

Base: Spread with $\frac{1}{4}$ cup (60 mL) Red Pepper and Dill Cashew Ricotta (page 103), Pumpkin Seed "Refried Beans" (page 93), Pumpkin Seed Chimichurri (page 92), Macadamia Mozzarella (page 106), Cashew Spinach Dip (page 83), Raw Chickpea Hummus (page 94) or Sweet Chili and Pecan Pâté (page 96).

Toppings: Top base with a sauce such as Red Pepper Basil Marinara Sauce (page 184), Tomato Basil Marinara Sauce (page 184), Red Pepper Mole Sauce (page 202), Cashew Sour Cream (page 204), Cashew Alfredo Sauce (page 188), Herbed Pumpkin Seed and Hemp Oil Pesto (page 187) or Basil and Spinach Cream Sauce (page 186).

Final Finish: You can also vary the flavor profile by adding something unusual, such as Spicy Pad Thai Sauce (page 194) paired with Macadamia Mozzarella (page 106). Finish the pizza with 2 to 3 tbsp (30 to 45 mL) Almond Parmesan Cheese (page 204), Simple Marinated Kale Salad (page 142), Wilted Spinach Salad (page 140), Softened Broccoli (page 140), Sun-Dried Tomato, Red Onion and Parsley Slaw (page 163) or crumbled Chili Cumin Almonds (page 301).

Add $\frac{1}{2}$ cup (125 mL) torn basil leaves and $\frac{1}{4}$ cup (60 mL) raw shelled hemp seeds immediately before consuming for an additional boost of complete protein.

Soft-Shell Tortillas

These soft corn tortillas are easy to prepare and can be stuffed with many different fillings. A delicious combination is Walnut Mince (page 293), Perfect Guacamole (page 81), Pumpkin Seed "Refried Beans" (page 93) and Cashew Sour Cream (page 204). They can also replace the bread in sandwiches. Try using Lemon-Ginger-Dill Sunflower Seed Pâté (page 97) or Sweet Chili and Pecan Pâté (page 96) as a sandwich spread.

Makes 4 tortillas

Tip

When spreading out raw bread or cracker dough on a dehydrator sheet, keep a small bowl of room-temperature water off to one side. Use this to wet your hands intermittently to prevent the dough from sticking to them.

2 cups	fresh corn kernels	500 mL
1/4 cup	chopped carrot	60 mL
3 tbsp	cold-pressed (extra virgin) olive oil	45 mL
3 tbsp	filtered water	45 mL
1 tbsp	ground cumin	15 mL
1 tsp	fine sea salt	5 mL
Pinch	cayenne pepper	Pinch
1/2 cup	ground flax seeds	125 mL

1. In a food processor fitted with the metal blade, process corn, carrot, olive oil, water, cumin, salt and cayenne until smooth, stopping the motor once and scraping down the sides of the work bowl.
2. Transfer to a bowl. Add ground flax seeds and mix well.
3. Using an ice cream scoop or a small ladle, drop 4 equal portions of dough onto a nonstick dehydrator sheet, distributing evenly and leaving plenty of space between them. Using your hands, pat down until they are 1/2 inch (1 cm) thick.
4. Dehydrate at 105°F (41°C) for 5 to 6 hours or until firm enough to handle. Flip and transfer to mesh sheet. Dehydrate for an hour or so, until tortillas are firm but still pliable enough to use as wraps. Use immediately or transfer to an airtight container and store, refrigerated, for up to 7 days.

Desserts

When we hear the word "dessert," we usually think of rich, sweet treats such as whipped cream, ice cream, chocolate and cake. For most people, dessert is a special-occasion indulgence, and there are good reasons for this. Most conventional desserts contain an abundance of refined sugar and flour, not to mention hidden ingredients such as emulsifiers and preservatives, which should be avoided. They are simply not good for you.

On a raw food diet, you can enjoy dessert knowing that you are consuming healthful ingredients. Instead of sugar, raw food desserts are sweetened with dates or raw agave nectar, a sap that is extracted at low temperatures from the piña, or center, of the agave plant, which is native to Mexico. Instead of high-fat dairy, a creamy texture is achieved by using ingredients such as nuts, nut butters and coconut products. Soaked seeds such as flax seeds or even finely ground almonds are used as binders, taking the place of refined flour and eggs.

Some raw foods, such as cacao powder, coconut and hemp seeds, are delicious by any standard, as well as containing ingredients such as phytonutrients that help to keep us healthy. Raw food desserts can be just as rich and sinfully delicious as their traditional counterparts. Because all the ingredients are fresh and unrefined, their luscious flavors shine through. Next time you are having friends over, serve them Cashew Cheesecake (page 360), Lemon Avocado Mousse (page 363), Apple Crumble (page 333) or any other raw dessert that catches your eye. I know you will have a hit on your hands and that even the most skeptical guest will be asking for more.

Macerated Berries

Here's a simple and easy technique for softening berries. This dessert is quick to make and can be prepared ahead of time and refrigerated until you're ready to eat.

Makes 2 servings

Tip

Substitute any soft berry for those called for in this recipe, so long as the total amount adds up to 1½ cups (375 mL). You can add finely grated lemon zest as well.

1 cup	sliced hulled strawberries (about ½ pint)	250 mL
¼ cup	blueberries	60 mL
¼ cup	blackberries	60 mL
3 tbsp	raw agave nectar	45 mL
2 tbsp	freshly squeezed lemon juice	30 mL
Dash	raw vanilla extract (see page 336)	Dash

1. In a bowl, toss strawberries, blueberries, blackberries, agave nectar, lemon juice and vanilla. Set aside for 30 to 45 minutes or until berries are soft and liquid is seeping out of the fruit. Serve immediately or cover and refrigerate for up to 3 days.

Poached Pears

I love the way the agave nectar and beet juice in this recipe combine to provide such an intriguing background flavor to the pears. The orange zest and cinnamon add pleasant zing and the beet juice gives the dish a beautiful pink hue. Double or triple the quantities to suit your needs.

Makes 2 servings

Tips

For a slightly less sweet result with a background flavor of cloves and allspice, substitute 2 cups (500 mL) freshly squeezed orange juice, 1 cup (250 mL) water, 1 cup (250 mL) beet juice, 1 tsp (5 mL) ground allspice and a pinch of ground cloves for the poaching liquid ingredients called for.

If you are using a ring-shaped dehydrator, divide the mixture between two smaller dishes that will fit on the racks.

- **Electric food dehydrator**
- **Baking dish**

3 cups	filtered water	750 mL
½ cup	beet juice	125 mL
¼ cup	raw agave nectar	60 mL
1 tbsp	finely grated orange zest	15 mL
1 tsp	ground cinnamon	5 mL
2	pears, peeled, halved and cored	2

1. In a bowl, whisk together water, beet juice, agave nectar, orange zest and cinnamon.
2. Place pears in baking dish, cut side down, and add poaching liquid. Pears should be submerged in the liquid; if not, add water to cover. Dehydrate at 105°F (41°C) for 12 to 15 hours or until soft. Serve immediately or allow to cool. Cover and refrigerate for up to 3 days.

Chocolate-Dipped Strawberries

These tantalizing treats are perfect for special occasions or when you are craving something sweet and fruity.

Makes 15 to 20 strawberries

Tip

When dipping strawberries in chocolate sauce, make sure not to submerge the entire berry. Dip it about halfway in and then move it from side to side. This will keep your fingers from getting dirty and the strawberry will look neat and clean.

- Baking sheet

½ cup	melted coconut oil (see Tips, page 334)	125 mL
½ cup	filtered water	125 mL
⅓ cup	raw cacao powder	75 mL
¼ cup	raw agave nectar	60 mL
15 to 20	strawberries	15 to 20

1. In a blender, combine coconut oil, water, cacao powder and agave nectar. Bend at high speed until smooth.
2. Transfer to a bowl. One at a time, grab the strawberries by their green stems and dip them in the chocolate sauce. Place on a baking sheet as completed. Once all the strawberries have been dipped, refrigerate for 20 to 30 minutes or until the chocolate has firmed up. Serve immediately or transfer to an airtight container and refrigerate for up to 2 days.

"Baked" Stuffed Apples

I like to serve these warm out of the dehydrator with a big bowl of Cashew Ice Cream (page 362). Double or triple the quantity to suit your needs.

Makes 2 servings

Tips

To make this recipe, you will need a dehydrator with adjustable racks that will allow the apples to stand upright.

You can make these ahead of time. After dehydrating, allow to cool, then transfer to an airtight container and refrigerate for up to 2 days. To reheat, dehydrate at 105°F (41°C) for 2 hours or until slightly warmed.

- Electric food dehydrator (see Tips, left)

2	firm apples (such as Red Delicious)	2
½ cup	Date Paste (page 80)	125 mL
2 tsp	ground cinnamon	10 mL

1. Remove cores from apples, leaving bottoms intact. In a small bowl, combine cinnamon and date paste.
2. Fill each apple with ¼ cup (60 mL) date paste. Place on a nonstick dehydrator sheet and dehydrate at 105°F (41°C) for 6 to 8 hours or until soft throughout. Serve immediately (see Tips, left).

Apple Crumble

This dessert is one of my all-time favorites. The soft apples tossed with sweet dates, walnuts and cinnamon make a perfect combination. In my opinion there is no better flavor pairing than apples and cinnamon.

Makes 6 servings

Tips

Once the apples are sliced they will turn brown fairly quickly. Make sure to toss them with the other ingredients within a few minutes. Failing that, toss them in 2 tsp (10 mL) freshly squeezed lemon juice.

Walnuts and cold-pressed walnut oil are a good source of alpha-linolenic acid (ALA), an omega-3 fat that is the essential fatty acid; without it, we could not survive. It is called "essential" because our bodies are unable to make it and must obtain it from food. Research has demonstrated ALA's ability to reduce chronic inflammation and other risk factors for diabetes, heart disease and stroke. North Americans get an average of about 1.5 grams of ALA per day. Some experts recommend an intake of 2.3 to 3 grams per day. Reaching this goal is easy if you include ALA-rich foods as part of your daily diet.

- 9-inch (2.5 L) square baking dish

Filling

6 cups	sliced apples	1.5 L
1 cup	Date Paste (page 80)	250 mL
1 tbsp	ground cinnamon	15 mL
2 tsp	melted coconut oil	10 mL

Crust

2 cups	walnut halves or pieces	500 mL
4	pitted dates, chopped	4
2 tsp	ground cinnamon	10 mL
Pinch	fine sea salt	Pinch

1. *Filling:* In a bowl, toss apples, date paste, cinnamon and coconut oil until well coated. Transfer to a baking dish.
2. *Crust:* In a food processor fitted with the metal blade, pulse walnuts, dates, cinnamon and salt, until mixture is blended but some visible pieces of walnuts remain.
3. *Assembly:* Using a spatula, spread crust evenly over filling. Refrigerate for 45 minutes to firm up. Serve immediately or cover and refrigerate for up to 3 days.

Variation

Add 1 tsp (5 mL) finely grated orange zest to the filling. Substitute ½ cup (125 mL) of the date paste with ¼ cup (60 mL) raisins, soaked in 1 cup (250 mL) water for 30 minutes and drained.

Peach and Blueberry Cobbler

This is a perfect dessert when peaches and blueberries are in season. I love its summery taste. The light touch of melted coconut oil provides a delicate creaminess that pairs well with the crunch from the walnuts.

Makes 4 servings

Tips

To slice peaches, run a paring knife around the middle of the peach through to the stone. Twist and divide into two halves, using your hands. Slice the half without the stone into the desired pieces. For the half with the stone, use your knife to loosen and remove it before slicing.

Coconut oil is solid at room temperature. It has a melting temperature of 76°F (24°C), so it is easy to liquefy. To melt it, place near a source of heat. If you have a dehydrator, you can place the required amount of coconut oil in a shallow bowl and warm at 100°F (38°C) for 5 to 6 minutes, until melted. If you do not have a dehydrator, place a shallow glass bowl over a pot of simmering water.

- Four ³⁄₄-cup (175 mL) ramekins or custard cups

Filling

2 cups	blueberries, divided	500 mL
2 cups	sliced peaches, divided	500 mL
3 tbsp	raw agave nectar	45 mL
1 tbsp	melted coconut oil (see Tips, left)	15 mL
1 tsp	ground cinnamon	5 mL
Pinch	fine sea salt	Pinch

Crust

2 cups	walnut halves or pieces	500 mL
2 tsp	ground flax seeds	10 mL
4	pitted Medjool dates, chopped	4
2 tbsp	melted coconut oil	30 mL
1 tsp	ground cinnamon	5 mL
Pinch	fine sea salt	Pinch

1. *Filling:* In a food processor fitted with the metal blade, process 1 cup (250 mL) blueberries, 1 cup (250 mL) peaches, agave nectar, coconut oil, cinnamon and salt, until smooth.
2. Transfer to a bowl and stir in remaining blueberries and peaches. Cover and refrigerate for 30 minutes.
3. *Crust:* In a food processor fitted with the metal blade, process walnuts, flax seeds and dates until mixture is crumbly and sticking together. Add coconut oil, cinnamon and salt and process until well incorporated.
4. *Assembly:* Divide filling equally among ramekins. Top each with one-quarter of the crust mixture and press lightly. Serve immediately or cover and refrigerate for up to 3 days.

Variation

Place filled baking dishes on a nonstick dehydrator sheet and dehydrate at 105°F (41°C) for 30 minutes, until slightly warm. Serve topped with a dollop of Cashew Ice Cream (page 362).

Raspberry Parfait

You'll want to make this divine dessert time and time again. I love using freshly picked raspberries when they are at their peak of flavor. Double or triple the recipe to suit your needs.

Tips

To soak the dates for this recipe, place in a bowl and add 2 cups (500 mL) warm water. Cover and set aside to soak for 30 minutes. Drain, discarding remaining water.

Hemp seeds are considered a complete protein, meaning they contain all eight essential amino acids. One tablespoon (15 mL) of raw shelled hemp seeds provides up to 5 grams of protein and appreciable amounts of vitamins B_1 (thiamine) and B_6 (pyridoxine), folate, phosphorus, magnesium, zinc and manganese. Two tablespoons (30 mL) of hemp seeds essentially meets your daily requirement for omega-3 fatty acids.

- **2 parfait glasses**

$\frac{1}{2}$ cup	pitted dates, soaked (see Tips, left)	125 mL
2 cups	raspberries, divided	500 mL
1 tbsp	raw agave nectar	15 mL
2 tsp	freshly squeezed lemon juice	10 mL
$\frac{1}{2}$ cup	Cashew Whipped Cream (page 367)	125 mL
3 tbsp	raw shelled hemp seeds, divided	45 mL
$\frac{1}{4}$ cup	Caramel Sauce (page 369)	60 mL

1. In a blender, combine soaked dates, $1\frac{1}{2}$ cups (375 mL) raspberries, agave nectar and lemon juice. Blend at high speed until smooth.
2. Place a layer of whole raspberries in each of the parfait glasses. Add a layer of raspberry purée and a layer of cashew whipped cream. Sprinkle with hemp seeds and drizzle with caramel sauce. Repeat 3 or 4 times until all the ingredients are used up. Serve immediately or cover and refrigerate for up to 2 days.

Variations

Substitute an equal quantity of sliced hulled strawberries for the raspberries.

Instead of puréeing the berries with the dates, you can marinate the raspberries in 2 tsp (10 mL) lemon juice, 1 tbsp (15 mL) agave nectar and a dash of vanilla extract.

Substitute $\frac{3}{4}$ cup (175 mL) Date Paste (page 80) for the soaked dates. Sprinkle with ground cinnamon just before serving.

Raspberry, Orange and Blueberry Parfait

> This parfait is a mixture of ripe fresh berries and the perfect amount of juicy orange. The combination is mouthwatering, especially when finished with sinful caramel sauce. Double or triple the quantity to suit your needs.

Makes 2 servings

Tips

To soak the cashews for this recipe, place in a bowl and add 1 cup (250 mL) water. Cover and set aside for 30 minutes. Drain, discarding soaking water. Rinse under running water until the water runs clear.

If you have a high-powered blender, use it to make the raspberry purée. It will be smoother and creamier than when made in a regular blender.

When following a strictly raw food diet, make sure to purchase vanilla extract that has been processed using a cold extraction method. Many commercial vanillas are processed using high heat, rendering them a non-raw food product. Some vanilla beans are put into an oven after being harvested, so if you're using whole beans, make sure to look for those that have been sun-dried and are labeled "raw." If you prefer, substitute ¼ tsp (1 mL) vanilla seeds for the extract in this recipe.

- **2 parfait glasses**

½ cup	raw cashews, soaked (see Tips, left)	125 mL
1 cup	raspberries	250 mL
½ cup	raw agave nectar, divided	125 mL
3 tbsp	filtered water	45 mL
1 cup	blueberries	250 mL
2 tsp	freshly squeezed lemon juice	10 mL
1 tsp	raw vanilla extract (see Tips, left)	5 mL
¼ cup	sliced orange	60 mL
1 tsp	ground cinnamon	5 mL
1 tbsp	raw shelled hemp seeds	15 mL
1 tbsp	Caramel Sauce (page 369)	15 mL

1. In a blender, combine soaked cashews, raspberries, 2 tbsp (30 mL) agave nectar and water. Blend at high speed until smooth. Set aside.
2. In a bowl, toss the blueberries, lemon juice, vanilla and 3 tbsp (45 mL) agave nectar. Using a fork, lightly crush the blueberries, releasing some of their juice. Set aside.
3. In a bowl, toss orange, cinnamon and 3 tbsp (45 mL) agave nectar. Set aside.
4. To serve, place a layer of raspberry purée in each of the parfait glasses. Add a layer of blueberries and then one of orange. Repeat 3 or 4 times. Finish with a sprinkling of hemp seeds and a drizzle of caramel sauce, dividing equally. Serve immediately.

Pear Crisp

This versatile crisp is a great replacement for pastry in many recipes and takes only minutes to prepare. It can be used as a base for toppings or you can use it in layers, with fillings in between. I like serving it with Macerated Berries (page 331) topped with Citrus Cream (page 366). Chocolate Fondue (page 368), Mango and Ginger Cashew Mousse (page 364), Cinnamon Almond Cream (page 366) and Cashew Ice Cream (page 362) also work well.

Makes 4 servings

Tips

When a recipe calls for flax seeds, you have two options to choose from: golden or brown. Golden flax seeds will yield a lighter color in the end result, while brown flax seeds will make the final product darker. I like to use golden flax seeds in this recipe because I prefer a lighter result, but brown is fine too.

Items that are meant to be crispy will often be a bit soft when first removed from the dehydrator but will crisp up as they cool. Make sure to store dehydrated foods in an airtight container, away from moisture or humidity, to retain texture and freshness.

- **Electric food dehydrator**

2 cups	chopped peeled pears	500 mL
¼ cup	filtered water	60 mL
¼ cup	raw agave nectar	60 mL
Pinch	fine sea salt	Pinch
¾ cup	ground flax seeds (see Tips, left)	175 mL

1. In a blender, combine pears, water, agave nectar and salt. Blend at high speed until smooth.
2. Transfer to a bowl and stir in flax seeds. Set aside for 10 minutes so the flax can absorb the moisture and swell.
3. Using your hands, spread out the mixture on a nonstick dehydrator sheet in a single layer approximately ½ inch (1 cm) thick. Dehydrate at 105°F (41°C) for approximately 10 to 12 hours or until firm enough to handle. Flip and transfer to a mesh sheet and dehydrate for 2 to 3 hours or until crispy. Break into 4 equal pieces. Allow to cool and transfer to an airtight container. Store at room temperature for up to 7 days.

Variation

Add 1 tbsp (15 mL) chopped gingerroot and 1 tsp (5 mL) ground cinnamon before processing.

Pecan Banana Cinnamon Cookies

These cookies are soft and delicious, even better than those you buy from a bakery — and they are so much better for you. They are delicious either soft or crunchy.

Makes about 2 dozen cookies

Tips

To soak the pecans for this recipe, place in a bowl and add 4 cups (1 L) water. Cover and set aside to soak for 30 minutes. Drain, discarding remaining water.

When following a strictly raw food diet, make sure to purchase vanilla extract that has been processed using a cold extraction method. Many commercial vanillas are processed using high heat, rendering them a non-raw food product. Some vanilla beans are put into an oven after being harvested, so if you're using whole beans, make sure to look for those that have been sun-dried and are labeled "raw."

- **Electric food dehydrator**

2 cups	pecans, soaked (see Tips, left)	500 mL
1/4 cup	chopped banana (about 1/2 small)	60 mL
1/4 cup	raw agave nectar	60 mL
2 tsp	ground cinnamon	10 mL
1 tsp	raw vanilla extract or 1/4 tsp (1 mL) vanilla seeds	5 mL

1. In a food processor fitted with the metal blade, process banana, agave nectar, cinnamon and vanilla until smooth. Add soaked pecans and process until no large pieces remain.

2. Using a tablespoon (15 mL), drop dough onto a nonstick dehydrator sheet and flatten lightly to 1 inch (2.5 cm) in diameter. Dehydrate at 105°F (41°C) for 4 to 5 hours, until firm enough to handle. Flip and transfer to mesh sheets. Dehydrate for 2 to 3 hours for a soft cookie or 5 to 6 hours for a crisp cookie. Allow to cool and transfer to an airtight container. Store soft cookies in the refrigerator for 4 to 5 days. Store crisp cookies at room temperature for up to a week.

Variations

Add 2 tbsp (30 mL) chopped gingerroot to the dough along with the banana to give the cookie a nice kick of spice.

After the cookies are laid out on the dehydrator sheet, make a small indentation in the middle of each with your index finger. Dehydrate as directed and allow to cool. Fill cooled cookies with Caramel Sauce (page 369).

Banana Cinnamon Goji Berry Cookies

These tasty little cookies are perfect as a snack. They also make a full-blown dessert course at dinner when topped with Macerated Berries (page 331) and a dollop of Cashew Whipped Cream (page 367).

Makes 12 to 15 cookies

Tips

Coconut oil is solid at room temperature. It has a melting temperature of 76°F (24°C), so it is easy to liquefy. To melt it, place near a source of heat. If you have a dehydrator, you can place the required amount of coconut oil in a shallow bowl at 100°F (38°C) for 5 to 6 minutes, until melted. If you do not have a dehydrator, place a shallow glass bowl over a pot of simmering water.

To ripen bananas, place them in a paper bag with an uncut apple and fold over the end of the bag to seal it. The apple will emit ethylene gas, which helps to speed ripening. Place the bag in a warm, dry area to finish ripening.

Goji berries are native to China and Tibet. They provide vitamin C and are thought to be high in antioxidants.

1 cup	raw cashews	250 mL
¼ cup	whole raw almonds	60 mL
1 tbsp	ground cinnamon	15 mL
½ cup	goji berries	125 mL
½ cup	chopped banana	125 mL
½ cup	melted coconut oil (see Tips, left)	125 mL
¼ cup	raw agave nectar	60 mL

1. In a food processor fitted with the metal blade, process cashews, almonds and cinnamon until crumbly but not smooth. Add goji berries and process until broken into pieces about the same size as the nuts. Add banana, coconut oil and agave nectar and pulse just until the mixture comes together.

2. Transfer to a bowl and, using a tablespoon (15 mL), drop 12 to 15 portions of dough onto a baking sheet lined with parchment. Refrigerate for 1 to 2 hours or until set. These are best served immediately, but they can be refrigerated for up to 2 days.

Gingerbread Cookies

Perfectly spiced cookies with the snap and home-style taste of those your grandmother made. I like to serve these with a tall glass of Almond Milk (page 45).

(page 45)

Makes 12 to 15 cookies

Tips

To soak the dates for this recipe, place them in a bowl and add 3 cups (750 mL) warm water. Cover and set aside to soak for 30 minutes. Drain, discarding remaining water.

When purchasing agave nectar, be sure to look for products labeled "raw." Most of the agave nectar on the market has been heated to a high temperature and does not qualify as raw food. If you have concerns, ask your purveyor.

• **Electric food dehydrator**

1 cup	chopped pitted dates, soaked (see Tips, left)	250 mL
2 cups	whole raw almonds	500 mL
¼ cup	freshly squeezed orange juice	60 mL
3 tbsp	raw agave nectar (see Tips, left)	45 mL
3 tbsp	chopped gingerroot	45 mL
½ tsp	ground allspice	2 mL
Pinch	ground cloves	Pinch
Pinch	fine sea salt	Pinch

1. In a food processor fitted with the metal blade, process almonds until they become flour-like in consistency. (You don't want any large pieces but you do not want them to move toward becoming almond butter.)

2. Add soaked dates, orange juice, agave nectar, ginger, allspice, cloves and salt and process until well incorporated.

3. Using a tablespoon (15 mL), drop 12 to 15 equal portions of dough onto a nonstick dehydrator sheet, at least 2 inches (5 cm) apart. Flatten lightly. Dehydrate at 105°F (41°C) for 8 to 10 hours or until firm enough to handle. Flip and transfer to mesh sheet. Dehydrate for 3 to 4 hours or until crispy. Serve warm or allow the cookies to cool and transfer to an airtight container. Store at room temperature for up to a week.

Variation

If you prefer a softer cookie, dehydrate on the first side for 6 to 7 hours and on the second side for 2 to 3 hours or until the desired consistency has been reached. Allow the cookies to cool and transfer to an airtight container. Store, refrigerated, for up to 5 days.

Almond Biscuits

These biscuits are soft on the inside and crisp on the outside. They are delicious served with Green Tea Metabolizer (page 72). They hold up well and can be kept in an airtight container for up to two weeks.

(page 72)

Makes about 30 biscuits

Tips

To soak the almonds for this recipe, place in a bowl and add 4 cups (1 L) water. Cover and set aside to soak for 45 minutes. Drain, discarding remaining liquid. Rinse under running water until water runs clear.

When it is humid or exceptionally hot outside, dehydrated foods can pick up moisture easily. You can store them in an airtight container at room temperature, but check periodically to see if the food has picked up any moisture. If so, refrigerate. If you want a crispy texture, dehydrate again until desired texture is achieved.

• **Electric food dehydrator**

2 cups	whole raw almonds, soaked (see Tips, left)	500 mL
5 tbsp	filtered water	75 mL
$\frac{1}{4}$ cup	raw agave nectar	60 mL
3 tbsp	freshly squeezed lemon juice	45 mL
1 tsp	raw vanilla extract	5 mL
Pinch	sea salt	Pinch

1. In a food processor fitted with the metal blade, process water, agave nectar, lemon juice and vanilla until incorporated. Add soaked almonds and salt and process until incorporated.

2. Using a tablespoon (15 mL), drop dough onto a nonstick dehydrator sheet at least 2 inches (5 cm) apart. Using your hand, flatten to about $\frac{1}{4}$ inch (0.5 cm) thickness.

3. Dehydrate at 105°F (41°C) for 6 to 7 hours, until firm enough to handle. Flip and transfer to the mesh sheet. Dehydrate for 3 to 4 hours, until crispy. Serve warm or allow the cookies to cool and transfer to an airtight container. Store at room temperature for up to 2 weeks.

Almond Quinoa Raisin Cookies

These crunchy treats are particularly delicious just out of the dehydrator and still warm. I enjoy them as a light snack or even for dessert, paired with a big bowl of Cashew Ice Cream (page 362) drizzled with Caramel Sauce (page 369).

Makes 12 to 15 cookies

Tips

To soak the quinoa for this recipe, place in a bowl and add 2 cups (500 mL) water. Cover and set aside for 3 hours. Drain, discarding remaining liquid. Rinse under running water until the water runs clear.

Quinoa is one of the best sources of complete protein, as it contains all the essential amino acids. It is also easily digestible. Soaked quinoa is a great topper for salads — an easy way to boost your protein intake.

- **Electric food dehydrator**

½ cup	quinoa, soaked (see Tips, left)	125 mL
1½ cups	whole raw almonds	375 mL
½ cup	raw agave nectar	125 mL
½ cup	chopped banana	125 mL
¼ cup	filtered water	60 mL
¼ cup	raisins	60 mL
2 tsp	ground cinnamon	10 mL

1. In a food processor fitted with the metal blade, process almonds until they are broken down but not flour-like in consistency. With the motor running, drizzle agave nectar through the feed tube, processing until the almonds start to stick together.

2. Add soaked quinoa, banana, water, raisins and cinnamon and process until combined, about 30 to 45 seconds.

3. Using an ice cream scoop or small ladle, drop 12 to 15 equal portions of dough onto a nonstick dehydrator sheet, at least 2 inches (5 cm) apart. Using your hand, flatten slightly. Dehydrate at 105°F (41°C) for 5 to 6 hours or until firm enough to handle (the cookies will be dry on the outside but soft in the middle). Serve warm or allow to cool, then transfer to an airtight container. Store, refrigerated, for up to a week.

Variations

Replace the agave nectar in this recipe with ¾ cup (175 mL) Date Paste (page 80).

Substitute an equal quantity of dried cranberries or finely diced dried apricots or prunes for the raisins. If using dried apricots, stir them in after completing Step 2 rather than processing them in the food processor.

Lemon Raspberry Thumbprint Cookies

> These are easy to prepare. I enjoy them topped with Cashew Whipped Cream (page 367) alongside a nice glass of Spicy Cinnamon Lemonade (page 63).

Makes 12 to 15 cookies

Tips

To soak the almonds for this recipe, place in a bowl and add 4 cups (1 L) water. Cover and set aside for 1 hour. Drain, discarding soaking water, and rinse under cold running water until the water runs clear.

To soak the dates for this recipe, place them in a bowl and cover with 2 cups (500 mL) warm water. Cover and set aside to soak for 30 minutes. Drain, discarding any remaining water.

Use golden flax seeds, if possible, to produce a lighter cookie.

- Electric food dehydrator

Cookies

2 cups	whole raw almonds, soaked (see Tips, left)	500 mL
3 tbsp	finely grated lemon zest	45 mL
¼ cup	freshly squeezed lemon juice	60 mL
½ cup	raw agave nectar	125 mL
¼ cup	ground flax seeds	60 mL
Pinch	sea salt	Pinch

Raspberry Sauce

½ cup	chopped pitted dates, soaked (see Tips, left)	125 mL
1 cup	raspberries	250 mL
3 tbsp	raw agave nectar	45 mL
1 tbsp	freshly squeezed lemon juice	15 mL

1. *Cookies:* In a food processor, process soaked almonds, lemon zest and juice, agave nectar, flax seeds and salt until smooth, stopping the motor and scraping down the sides of the work bowl as necessary.

2. Using a small ice cream scoop or ladle, drop 12 to 15 equal portions of dough onto a nonstick dehydrator sheet, at least 2 inches (5 cm) apart. Using your hand, flatten them slightly. Using your thumb, make a small indentation in the center of each cookie. Dehydrate for 8 to 10 hours at 105°F (41°C) or until firm on the outside and soft in the middle.

3. *Raspberry Sauce:* In a blender, combine soaked dates, raspberries, agave nectar and lemon juice. Blend at high speed until smooth.

4. *Assembly:* Remove cookies from the dehydrator. Spoon about 1 tbsp (15 mL) raspberry sauce into the middle of each cookie. Serve immediately. If you prefer to serve the cookies later, do not fill them. Allow to cool, then transfer to an airtight container and refrigerate for up to 7 days. When you are ready to serve, return to the dehydrator for 30 to 45 minutes at 105°F (41°C). Fill and serve immediately.

Chocolate Banana Walnut Cookies

These cookies are decadent. I love how the rich chocolate flavor, which comes from using raw cacao, combines with the slightly bitter walnuts and sweet banana. They're a great midday pick-me-up served with a tall glass of Almond Milk (page 45).

Makes 12 to 15 cookies

Tips

Be sure to use ripe bananas. They will provide all the sweetness you need.

After processing the walnuts, it is okay if some small pieces of nut remain.

The agave nectar in this recipe is optional because bananas are naturally sweet. Add it if you have a sweet tooth.

Use unsweetened medium shredded unsulfured coconut. Not only is this type of coconut nutritionally beneficial, the medium shred size will help the cookies hold together during the drying process.

• **Electric food dehydrator**

2 cups	walnuts, halves or pieces	500 mL
4 cups	chopped ripe bananas (see Tips, left)	1 L
½ cup	raw cacao powder	125 mL
¼ cup	raw agave nectar, optional (see Tips, left)	60 mL
¼ cup	dried shredded coconut (see Tips, left)	60 mL
¼ cup	raw pumpkin seeds	60 mL
¼ cup	raw sunflower seeds	60 mL

1. In a food processor fitted with the metal blade, process walnuts until they are flour-like in consistency. (You don't want any large pieces but you do not want them to move toward becoming walnut butter.) Transfer to a bowl.

2. Add bananas, cacao powder and agave nectar, if using, to food processor and process until smooth and creamy. Add to walnuts along with coconut and pumpkin and sunflower seeds. Mix well.

3. Using a small ice cream scoop or ladle, drop 12 to 15 equal portions of dough onto a nonstick dehydrator sheet, about 2 inches (5 cm) apart. Using your hand, flatten to ½ inch (1 cm) thick. Dehydrate at 105°F (41°C) for 8 to 10 hours or until firm enough to handle.

4. Flip and transfer to the mesh sheet. Dehydrate for 2 to 3 hours or until dry on the outside and soft in the middle. Serve warm or allow the cookies to cool and transfer to an airtight container. Store, refrigerated, for up to 3 days.

Variation

Substitute 2 cups (500 mL) whole raw almonds for the walnuts.

Blueberry Banana Cookies

These mouth-watering little cookies are packed full of nutrition and flavor. You will find yourself making them over and over again. I enjoy them both for dessert and as a snack on the go. The addition of zucchini helps to provide a dense texture, which gives the cookies a nice mouth feel.

Makes 12 to 15 cookies

Tip

When making raw cookies, before dehydrating make sure the dough feels thick enough to hold together. You can use many kinds of puréed fruit, or even vegetables, as a base, but the puréed ingredients need to be bound together with something. I like using almond flour, but virtually any ground nut or seed will work as a binder. If the batter is still too thin after adding your binder, try adding whole ingredients such as raisins or goji berries to absorb some of the liquid and give the cookie body.

- **Electric food dehydrator**

1 cup	blueberries, divided	250 mL
1/3 cup	raw agave nectar	75 mL
1/2 cup	chopped banana	125 mL
1/2 cup	chopped peeled zucchini	125 mL
1/4 cup	coconut butter (see Tips, page 365)	60 mL
1/2 tsp	ground cinnamon	2 mL
1 cup	whole raw almonds	250 mL
1/2 cup	ground flax seeds	125 mL
Pinch	fine sea salt	Pinch

1. In a food processor fitted with the metal blade, process 2/3 cup (150 mL) blueberries, agave nectar, banana, zucchini, coconut butter and cinnamon until smooth, stopping the motor and scraping down the sides of the work bowl as necessary. Transfer to a bowl and set aside.

2. Rinse out work bowl and blade and dry thoroughly. Reassemble food processor. Add almonds and process until finely ground. Add ground flax seeds and pulse just until combined. Add to puréed blueberry mixture and stir in remaining whole blueberries. Mix well, until mixture has a dough-like consistency.

3. Using a small ice cream scoop or ladle, drop 12 to 15 equal portions of dough onto a nonstick dehydrator sheet, about 2 inches (5 cm) apart. Using your hand, flatten to approximately 1/2 inch (1 cm) thick. Dehydrate at 105°F (41°C) for 8 to 10 hours or until firm enough to handle. Flip and transfer to the mesh sheet. Dehydrate for 2 to 3 hours or until the cookies are soft in the middle and slightly crunchy on the outside. Serve immediately or allow to cool and transfer to an airtight container. Store, refrigerated, for up to 5 days.

Variation

To make these into chocolate chip cookies, add 1/2 cup (125 mL) raw cacao powder in Step 1 and stir in 1/4 cup (60 mL) raw cacao nibs in place of the blueberries.

Lemon Almond Biscotti

These divinely crisp little treats have the same texture and taste as traditional biscotti made with white flour and refined sugar. The dough takes no more than 10 minutes to prepare. I like to dip these in a bowl of Chocolate Fondue (page 368), along with some fresh strawberries.

Makes 16 biscotti

Tips

To soak the almonds for this recipe, place in a bowl and add 6 cups (1.5 L) water. Cover and set aside for 1 hour. Drain, discard soaking water and rinse under cold running water until the water runs clear.

If you prefer, substitute ¾ tsp (3 mL) vanilla seeds for the vanilla extract in this recipe.

After storage, place the biscotti in the dehydrator at 105°F (41°C) for 30 minutes to 1 hour , to crisp it up.

Almonds are very nutritious. They contain phytochemicals, protein, fiber and healthy fats, as well as vitamin E, magnesium, phosphorus, potassium, manganese and a small amount of B vitamins.

- **Electric food dehydrator**

3 cups	whole raw almonds, soaked (see Tips, left)	750 mL
3 tbsp	finely grated lemon zest	45 mL
¼ cup	freshly squeezed lemon juice	60 mL
½ cup	filtered water	125 mL
¼ cup	raw agave nectar	60 mL
1 cup	ground flax seeds	250 mL
1 tbsp	raw vanilla extract (see Tips, left)	15 mL
½ tsp	fine sea salt	2 mL

1. In a food processor fitted with the metal blade, process soaked almonds, lemon zest and juice, water and agave nectar until smooth, about 2 to 3 minutes, stopping the motor and scraping down the sides of the work bowl as necessary. Add flax seeds, vanilla and salt and process until smooth.

2. Divide the dough into quarters. Working with one quarter at a time, transfer to nonstick dehydrator sheets and shape each into a rectangle approximately 5 inches (12.5 cm) long, 3 inches (7.5 cm) wide and 1 inch (2.5 cm) thick, placing at least 2 inches (5 cm) apart. Cut each lengthwise into 4 slices. Dehydrate at 105°F (41°C) for 9 to 12 hours or until firm enough to handle.

3. Separate into individual biscotti and place cut-side down on mesh sheets. Dehydrate for 4 to 5 hours or until crispy. Serve immediately or allow to cool and transfer to an airtight container. Store for up to 14 days.

Variation

If you have made Almond Milk (page 45) you can use the leftover pulp in this recipe. Spread out on a nonstick dehydrator sheet and dehydrate at 105°F (41°C) until crisp, about 6 hours. Use 2 cups (500 mL) dehydrated pulp and ¼ cup (60 mL) melted coconut oil in place of the whole almonds in this recipe.

Strawberry Sesame Banana Chews

These chewy treats are quite heavenly. They are simple to prepare and can be enhanced by dipping in Cashew Whipped Cream (page 367). I also enjoy them accompanied by a Cake Batter Smoothie (page 53).

Makes 16 to 20 cookies

Tip

Dehydrated foods will pick up moisture from the air unless they are stored in an airtight container away from sunlight. If the food was crispy when removed from the dehydrator but has become soft again, simply return it to the dehydrator until crisp.

- **Electric food dehydrator**

3 cups	chopped bananas	750 mL
2 cups	chopped hulled strawberries	500 mL
3 tbsp	raw agave nectar	45 mL
2 tbsp	sesame seeds	30 mL

1. In a food processor fitted with the metal blade, process bananas, strawberries and agave nectar until smooth (no visible pieces of fruit should remain). Transfer to a bowl and stir in sesame seeds.

2. Transfer mixture to a nonstick dehydrator sheet and, using your hands, spread evenly in a thin layer approximately 1/2 inch (1 cm) thick. Using a small knife, score into 16 to 20 equal portions. Dehydrate at 105°F (41°C) for 8 to 10 hours or until firm enough to handle. Serve immediately or allow to cool and transfer to an airtight container. Store, refrigerated, for up to 5 days.

Variation

Substitute 2 cups (500 mL) blueberries, 1 tsp (5 mL) ground cinnamon and a dash of vanilla extract for the strawberries.

Coconut Macaroons

These flavorful chews take very little time to create. I love the combination of coconut and vanilla. The healthy fats in the tahini help to hold these tasty little treats together. I enjoy them after dinner.

Makes 10 to 12 macaroons

Tips

Use unsweetened medium shredded unsulfured coconut. Not only is this type of coconut nutritionally beneficial, the medium shred size will help the macaroons hold together during the drying process.

Using your hands to mix the batter helps to ensure that you don't end up with chunks of tahini. Your fingers are more efficient than a spoon. When mixing, make sure the coconut is completely covered in tahini and agave nectar so that it can stick together. If the mixture is not holding together, you may need to add a bit more tahini.

For convenience I've called for vanilla extract, but in my opinion, the best-tasting and healthiest form of vanilla is the seeds that come directly from the pod. They are easy to use: split the pod lengthwise down the middle with a paring knife and, using the back of the knife, scrape the seeds away from you in one clean motion. If you prefer, substitute ½ tsp (2 mL) vanilla seeds for the extract.

- Baking sheet lined with parchment

1 cup	dried shredded coconut (see Tips, left)	250 mL
½ cup	tahini	125 mL
¼ cup	raw agave nectar	60 mL
2 tsp	raw vanilla extract (see Tips, left)	10 mL

1. In a bowl, combine coconut, tahini, agave nectar and vanilla. Using your hands, work together until well incorporated.
2. Using a small ice cream scoop or ladle, scoop out 10 to 12 equal portions of batter and drop onto prepared baking sheet. Refrigerate for 1 hour or until firm. Serve immediately or transfer to an airtight container and store, refrigerated, for up to 7 days.

Variations

For chocolate macaroons, add ¼ cup (60 mL) raw cacao powder in Step 1.

This recipe can be used as a carrier for many healthy ingredients. Add 3 tbsp (45 mL) raw shelled hemp seeds, 2 tbsp (30 mL) chopped almonds or 2 tbsp (30 mL) chopped walnuts.

For holiday macaroons, add 2 tsp (10 mL) finely grated orange zest, 1 tsp (5 mL) ground cinnamon and a pinch each of ground allspice, nutmeg and cloves.

Chocolate Walnut Brownies

These rich and decadent brownies are easy to make and even easier to eat. I like to make a large batch and keep them in the fridge for snacking. They are great with fresh strawberries drizzled with Chocolate Fondue (page 368). Double or triple the recipe to suit your needs.

Makes 6 brownies

Tips

Be sure not to overprocess the walnuts in the food processor, because the fats will begin to break down and you will be left with a product that resembles walnut butter.

Be sure to use high-quality raw cacao powder to achieve a rich chocolate flavor.

Vary the amount of agave nectar to suit your sweet tooth. If you are not fond of sweets, use ¼ cup (60 mL). Add 1 tbsp (15 mL) agave at a time until it is sweet enough for you.

Walnuts provide omega-3 fats, which are essential for overall health and well-being. They help to reduce inflammation and other risk factors for diabetes, heart disease and stroke. Include foods rich in omega-3 fats, such as walnuts, chia and flax, in your diet every day.

- **Small baking dish**

2 cups	walnuts	500 mL
½ cup	raw cacao powder	125 mL
¼ to ½ cup	raw agave nectar (see Tips, left)	60 to 125 mL

1. In a food processor fitted with the metal blade, process walnuts until broken down but not smooth. (Do not process into a paste; you want to retain texture and body.)
2. Add cacao powder and pulse to combine. With the motor running, drizzle agave nectar slowly through the feed tube until the walnuts become sticky and start to clump together (see Tips, left).
3. Transfer to baking dish and spread evenly. Refrigerate for 1 hour until set. Cut into brownies. Serve immediately or refrigerate for up to 1 week.

Variations

Substitute the walnuts with 1½ cups (375 mL) cashews or 1 cup (250 mL) each almonds and walnuts.

I sometimes add 2 tbsp (30 mL) finely grated orange zest along with the cacao powder to make chocolate orange brownies.

Raspberry Chocolate Hemp Squares

This recipe is a perfect finger food for parties or potlucks. I love the high protein content of these squares and, from time to time, enjoy one after working out. For a special treat, top with fresh raspberries and drizzle with Caramel Sauce (page 369). These are great with a tall glass of Almond Milk (page 45).

Makes 16 squares

Tips

To soak the hemp seeds for this recipe, place in a bowl and cover with 2 cups (500 mL) water. Cover and set aside for 30 minutes. Drain, discarding remaining liquid.

Coconut oil is solid at room temperature. It has a melting temperature of 76°F (24°C), so it is easy to liquefy. If you have a dehydrator, place the required amount in a shallow dish and warm at 100°F (38°C) for 15 minutes or until melted. If you do not have a dehydrator, place a shallow glass bowl over a pot of simmering water.

Hemp seeds are considered a complete protein, meaning they contain all eight essential amino acids. One tablespoon (15 mL) of raw shelled hemp seeds provides up to 5 grams of protein and contains appreciable amounts of vitamins B_1 (thiamine) and B_6 (pyridoxine), folate, phosphorus, magnesium, zinc and manganese. Two tablespoons (30 mL) of hemp seeds essentially meets your daily requirement for omega-3 fatty acids.

- 8-inch (20 cm) square baking dish

1½ cups	raw shelled hemp seeds, soaked (see Tips, left)	375 mL
2 cups	raspberries	500 mL
½ cup	raw cacao powder	125 mL
⅓ cup	raw agave nectar	75 mL
¼ cup	filtered water	60 mL
¼ cup	melted coconut oil (see Tips, left)	60 mL

1. In a blender, combine soaked hemp seeds, raspberries, cacao powder and agave nectar. Blend at high speed until smooth. You will need to stop the blender once and scrape down the sides with a rubber spatula.
2. Add water and coconut oil and blend until smooth.
3. Transfer to baking dish and refrigerate for 3 to 4 hours or until firm enough to cut. Cut into 16 squares and refrigerate until ready to use, for up to 5 days.

Variations

Substitute the raspberries with 1 cup (250 mL) sliced hulled strawberries and add an additional ¼ cup (60 mL) agave nectar.

You can double this recipe and use it as the filling for a cake. Make a crust by processing 2 cups (500 mL) walnuts, ½ cup (125 mL) pitted dates and 2 tbsp (30 mL) agave nectar in a food processor until mixture sticks together. Press into the bottom of an 8-inch (20 cm) springform pan. Add filling and refrigerate until firm enough to slice. Serve with Blueberry Ginger Coulis (page 371).

Chocolate Coffee Cake

This delectable dessert is sure to be a crowd-pleaser, and not only for coffee drinkers. It is velvety smooth, with a delicious chocolate coffee flavor. I like to make this dessert for large dinner parties. Try drizzling the cake with a little Caramel Sauce (page 369) just before serving.

Makes 16 servings

Tips

To soak the cashews for this recipe, place in a bowl and cover with 8 cups (2 L) water. Cover and set aside for 30 minutes. Drain, discarding soaking water, and rinse under cold running water until the water runs clear.

To give this dessert as much flavor as possible, use high-quality organic raw coffee extract. It will have been extracted using a cold-press method. Some extracts are processed using heat, so be sure to read the label or follow up with the supplier.

To check whether a raw dessert is frozen in the middle, insert a toothpick or other tester into the center. If it comes out clean, then the dessert is firm enough to be removed from the freezer.

When purchasing agave nectar, be sure to look for products labeled "raw." Most of the agave nectar on the market has been heated to a high temperature and does not qualify as raw food. If you have concerns, ask your purveyor.

- 10-inch (25 cm) springform pan

Filling

4 cups	raw cashews, soaked (see Tips, left)	1 L
1 cup	melted coconut oil (see Tips, page 350)	250 mL
1 cup	raw agave nectar	250 mL
¾ cup	filtered water	175 mL
½ cup	raw cacao powder	125 mL
1 tbsp	raw coffee extract (see Tips, left)	15 mL
2 tsp	raw vanilla extract or 1 tsp (5 mL) vanilla seeds	10 mL

Crust

1 cup	whole raw almonds	250 mL
1 cup	walnuts, halves or pieces	250 mL
¼ cup	raw agave nectar	60 mL
3 tbsp	raw cacao powder	45 mL
Pinch	fine sea salt	Pinch

1. *Filling:* In a food processor fitted with the metal blade, process soaked cashews, coconut oil, agave nectar, water, cacao powder, coffee extract and vanilla until smooth and creamy, stopping the motor and scraping down the sides of the work bowl as necessary. Set aside.

2. *Crust:* In a clean, dry food processor fitted with the metal blade, process almonds and walnuts until crumbly. (You want the nuts to be broken down into small pieces but not overprocessed, or they will start to become nut butter.) Add agave nectar, cacao powder and salt and process until well combined.

3. Transfer to springform pan and press till firm (you may use the flat bottom of a glass or mug for this).

4. *Assembly:* Transfer filling to pan and distribute evenly over crust. Freeze for at least 4 hours or until firm all the way through.

5. When you're ready to serve, allow cake to sit at room temperature for 30 to 45 minutes or until soft enough to slice. Refrigerate leftovers for up to 5 days.

Chocolate Avocado Torte

This recipe has the feel of a classic smooth chocolate torte, but the addition of chili powder, cinnamon and avocado makes it unique. I like to serve this after a light meal such as a salad or Zucchini Noodles (page 244) tossed in Red Pepper Basil Marinara Sauce (page 184). Because it has a high fat content I find that it complements a lighter meal well.

Makes 16 servings

Tips

To remove the pit from an avocado, use a paring knife to remove the nib at the top. Insert the blade of the knife where the nib was and turn the avocado from top to bottom to split it in half lengthwise. Twist the two halves apart. Stick the knife into the pit and with one motion turn it 90 degrees, pulling out the pit as you twist the knife.

Coconut oil is solid at room temperature. It has a melting temperature of 76°F (24°C), so it is easy to liquefy. If you have a dehydrator, place the required amount in a shallow dish and warm at 100°F (38°C) for 15 minutes or until melted. If you do not have a dehydrator, place a shallow glass bowl over a pot of simmering water.

- 9-inch (15 cm) springform pan

Crust

1 cup	raw sunflower seeds	250 mL
½ cup	dried shredded coconut	125 mL)
5	pitted soft dates	5
Pinch	fine sea salt	Pinch

Filling

6 cups	chopped avocados (about 6 medium)	1.5 L
1 cup	raw cacao powder	250 mL
¾ cup	raw agave nectar	175 mL
½ cup	melted coconut oil (see Tips, left)	125 mL
½ tsp	chili powder	2 mL
¼ tsp	ground cinnamon	1 mL
⅛ tsp	cayenne pepper	0.5 mL
Pinch	fine sea salt	Pinch

1. *Crust:* In a food processor fitted with the metal blade, process sunflower seeds, coconut, dates and salt until a smooth paste is formed. Press into springform pan and set aside.

2. *Filling:* In a food processor fitted with the metal blade, process avocado, cacao powder, agave nectar, coconut oil, chili powder, cinnamon, cayenne and salt until smooth, stopping the motor once and scraping down the sides of the work bowl.

3. Spread filling evenly over crust and refrigerate for 2 to 3 hours or until set. To remove from the springform pan, gently open the hinges and place the torte, still on the pan bottom, on a flat surface. Using either a large chef's knife or a cake server, gently remove the bottom of the pan from the crust. Cut into desired number of slices. Transfer leftovers to an airtight container and store, refrigerated, for up to 5 days.

Pumpkin Pie

Serve this dessert for Thanksgiving dinner and you will never regret leaving the baked version behind. I also like to serve this during the holidays, topped with a large dollop of Cashew Whipped Cream (page 367) and drizzled with Caramel Sauce (page 369).

Makes 8 servings

Tips

To soak the dates for this recipe, add 2 cups (500 mL) water, cover and set aside for 20 minutes. Drain, discarding any remaining water.

When buying pumpkin to make pumpkin pie, look for a pie pumpkin (also known as sugar pumpkin). These are sweeter and much smaller (about 6 inches/90 cm in diameter) than Halloween pumpkins.

You need a high-powered blender for this recipe. Otherwise the pumpkin will not be smooth enough.

If pumpkin is not available, substitute an equal amount of shredded sweet potato.

Substitute walnuts for the pecans in the crust.

- **High-powered blender**
- **9-inch (23 cm) springform pan**

Filling

1 cup	pitted dates, soaked (see Tips, left)	250 mL
4 cups	shredded pumpkin (about 1 small)	1 L
¼ cup	Almond Milk (page 45)	60 mL
½ cup	melted coconut oil (see Tips, page 352)	125 mL
2 tbsp	chopped gingerroot	30 mL
1 tsp	freshly grated nutmeg	5 mL
Pinch	ground cloves	Pinch
1 tsp	raw vanilla extract or ¼ tsp (1 mL) vanilla seeds	5 mL

Crust

2 cups	pecans	500 mL
½ cup	soft pitted dates	125 mL
½ tsp	fine sea salt	2 mL

1. *Filling:* In a high-powered blender (see Tips, left), combine pumpkin and almond milk. Blend at high speed until smooth.
2. Add soaked dates, coconut oil, ginger, nutmeg, cloves and vanilla and blend at high speed until incorporated.
3. *Crust:* In a food processor fitted with the metal blade, process pecans, dates and salt until crumbly. Press mixture into pan.
4. *Assembly:* Pour filling over crust and refrigerate for 2 hours or until set. Remove from refrigerator 10 minutes before serving to allow flavors to bloom. Serve immediately. Store leftovers in an airtight container for up to 3 days.

Pecan Pie

This heavenly dessert is definitely decadent — creamy, luscious and smooth. This is a great recipe to make for people who are new to raw food, because it is so rich and delicious it's sure to make a convert of even the most skeptical guest.

Makes 16 servings

Tips

To soak the pecans for this recipe, place them in a bowl and cover with 8 cups (2 L) water. Cover and set aside to soak for 30 minutes. Drain, discarding remaining water.

Coconut oil is solid at room temperature. It has a melting temperature of 76°F (24°C), so it is easy to liquefy. If you have a dehydrator, place the required amount in a shallow dish and warm at 100°F (38°C) for 15 minutes or until melted. If you do not have a dehydrator, place a shallow glass bowl over a pot of simmering water.

- 10-inch (25 cm) springform pan

Filling

4 cups	pecans, soaked (see Tips, left)	1 L
1 cup	filtered water	250 mL
1 cup	raw agave nectar	250 mL
1 cup	melted coconut oil (see Tips, left)	250 mL
2 tbsp	ground cinnamon	30 mL
2 tsp	raw vanilla extract	10 mL

Crust

2 cups	whole raw almonds	500 mL
6	chopped pitted soft dates	6
2 tbsp	raw agave nectar	30 mL
Pinch	sea salt	Pinch

1. *Filling:* In a blender, combine soaked pecans, water and agave nectar. Blend at high speed until smooth. Add coconut oil, cinnamon and vanilla and blend until smooth and creamy.

2. *Crust:* In a food processor fitted with the metal blade, pulse almonds until crumbly. Add dates, agave nectar and salt and pulse until combined, with no large pieces of almonds or dates remaining. Press into bottom of springform pan and set aside.

3. *Assembly:* Pour filling over crust and freeze for 5 to 6 hours or until firm. About half an hour before you are ready to serve, remove from the freezer (pie needs to be soft enough to slice). Serve immediately. Transfer leftovers to an airtight container and refrigerate for up to 5 days.

Variations

Pecan Almond Custard: Omit the crust, pour the filling into dessert-size ramekins and freeze.

Add a layer of date frosting. Soak 1 cup (250 mL) pitted dates in 2 cups (500 mL) water for 30 minutes, then drain. Blend with ¼ cup (60 mL) water, ¼ cup (60 mL) raw agave nectar, 2 tsp (10 mL) ground cinnamon and a pinch of sea salt, until smooth. Spread over defrosted cake. Refrigerate for 1 to 2 hours to firm up the frosting.

Caramelized Peach Tart

I like to make this dessert when peaches are in season My favorite garnish is a large dollop of Cashew Whipped Cream (page 367) and some fresh raspberries or blueberries.

Makes 2 servings

Tips

Once they are assembled, I like to warm these tarts slightly before serving by placing in the dehydrator at 105°F (41°C) for 20 to 30 minutes.

If you prefer, instead of using the Cinnamon Almond Cream, substitute the following: 1 cup (250 mL) sliced peaches; ½ cup (125 mL) cashews soaked in 1 cup (250 mL) water for 30 minutes, then drained and rinsed; ¼ cup (60 mL) raw agave nectar; 1 tsp (5 mL) ground cinnamon; and a dash of water, all combined in a blender until smooth.

- Two 6-inch (15 cm) quiche molds, lined with plastic wrap
- Electric food dehydrator

Crust

1 cup	walnuts, halves or pieces	250 mL
¼ cup	chopped pitted soft dates	60 mL
2 tbsp	raw agave nectar	30 mL
Pinch	sea salt	Pinch

Filling

2 cups	sliced peaches (about 6)	500 mL
3 tbsp	raw agave nectar	45 mL
2 tsp	freshly squeezed lemon juice	10 mL
1 tsp	ground cinnamon	5 mL
½ cup	Cinnamon Almond Cream (page 366)	125 mL
¼ cup	Caramel Sauce (page 369)	60 mL

1. *Crust:* In a food processor fitted with the metal blade, pulse walnuts and dates until they are broken down and stick together. Add agave nectar and salt and pulse until combined.
2. Divide crust equally between quiche molds. Using the palm of your hand, firmly press the crust into the mold. Refrigerate for 1 hour.
3. *Filling:* In a bowl, toss peaches, agave nectar, lemon juice and cinnamon. Transfer to a nonstick dehydrator sheet and dehydrate at 105°F (41°C) for 2 to 3 hours or until peaches are softened and some of the juices begin to run out. Remove from dehydrator and set aside to cool.
4. *Assembly:* Remove crusts from molds. Working with one crust at a time, spoon ¼ cup (60 mL) Cinnamon Almond Cream onto the base. Top with half of the dehydrated peaches and finish with 2 tbsp (30 mL) caramel sauce. Repeat with the second tart. Serve immediately.

Pear and Apple Tartlets

Although this dessert takes a bit of time to prepare, it is well worth the extra effort. The combination of soft pear and crisp apple offers great contrasting flavor and texture. I like to serve this in the fall, when locally grown apples and pears are at their peak. I often bring this to family gatherings in place of traditional apple pie.

Makes 4 servings

Tips

When grinding the almonds into flour, be sure not to overprocess them. Otherwise, they will begin to become almond butter.

Once cut, apples and pears will start to oxidize (turn brown). To prevent this from happening, toss with a touch of lemon juice as soon as they are cut.

I like using Red Delicious apples in any recipe where the flesh of an apple needs to be softened. This apple stands up to heat and won't become mushy.

There are many different types of dates but, by far, Medjool dates are the easiest to work with. Because they are particularly soft, they are easier to blend and purée.

- **Four 4-inch (10 cm) quiche molds, lined with plastic wrap**
- **Electric food dehydrator**

Crust

2 cups	whole raw almonds	500 mL
½ cup	Date Paste (page 80)	125 mL
¼ cup	ground flax seeds	60 mL
¼ cup	filtered water	60 mL
2 tsp	finely grated lemon zest	10 mL
2 tbsp	freshly squeezed lemon juice	30 mL
2 tbsp	raw agave nectar	30 mL
Pinch	fine sea salt	Pinch

Filling

2 cups	sliced pears, divided	500 mL
1 cup	sliced apple	250 mL
3 tbsp	raw agave nectar, divided	45 mL
2 tbsp	freshly squeezed lemon juice, divided	30 mL
Pinch	fine sea salt	Pinch
3 tbsp	filtered water	45 mL
2 tbsp	chia seeds	30 mL

1. *Crust:* In a food processor fitted with the metal blade, process almonds until they become flour-like in consistency (see Tips, left).

2. Transfer to a bowl and add date paste, flax seeds, water, lemon zest, lemon juice, agave nectar and salt. Mix well, until dough-like in consistency. Set aside for 10 minutes so the flax can absorb some of the liquid and swell.

3. Divide dough into 4 equal portions and press into prepared quiche molds. Place on mesh sheet and dehydrate at 105°F (41°C) for 5 to 6 hours or until firm. Remove crusts from molds. The crusts can be made ahead and refrigerated in an airtight container for up to 5 days.

4. *Filling*: In a bowl, toss 1 cup (250 mL) sliced pears and the apple with 2 tbsp (30 mL) agave nectar, 2 tsp (10 mL) lemon juice and salt. Transfer fruit to nonstick dehydrator sheet and dehydrate at 105°F (41°C) for 1 to 2 hours or until slightly softened. Remove from dehydrator. Transfer to a bowl and set aside to cool.

5. In a food processor fitted with the metal blade, process remaining pears, agave nectar and lemon juice, water and chia seeds until smoothly blended. Add to softened fruit and toss well.

6. *Assembly*: Divide filling equally among the crusts. Serve immediately.

Salted Chocolate Hemp Truffles

These scrumptious little bites make a perfect afternoon snack. Packed full of protein and healthy antioxidants, they are a true chocolate lover's delight.

Makes 12 to 15 truffles

Tips

Salt and chocolate are a perfect pairing. Salt enhances the nuances of cacao, helping to bring out its natural flavor.

Cacao powder is powdered raw chocolate. Is it similar to cocoa powder but tastes even better, with a deeper, richer flavor. Cacao powder is available in well-stocked supermarkets, natural foods stores and online. If you are transitioning to a raw foods diet and can't find it, substitute an equal quantity of good-quality cocoa powder.

1 cup	raw pecans	250 mL
¼ cup	raw cacao powder (see Tips, left)	60 mL
¼ cup	raw agave nectar	60 mL
3	pitted Medjool dates, chopped	3
1 tsp	fine sea salt	5 mL
¼ cup	Coconut Chocolate Mousse (page 364)	60 mL
¼ cup	raw shelled hemp seeds	60 mL

1. In a food processor fitted with the metal blade, process pecans, cacao powder, agave nectar, dates and salt until well combined, with no large pieces of pecan remaining. Transfer to a bowl. Stir in Coconut Chocolate Mousse.

2. Using a melon baller, scoop up 12 to 15 equal portions of the mixture. Roll each between your hands to make a small ball. Spread hemp seeds on a piece of parchment and roll balls in them, coating evenly. Refrigerate for 30 minutes, until set. Serve immediately or refrigerate for up to 5 days.

Variations

Substitute an equal quantity of walnuts or almonds for the pecans. If using almonds, add 2 more pitted Medjool dates and an additional dash of agave nectar.

For a holiday version of this recipe, add 2 tsp (10 mL) finely grated orange zest and a pinch each of ground cloves and allspice.

Brazil Nut Mango Cheesecake Pops

These tasty little treats are a perfect way to get healthy fats into your kids' diets. They will never know they are free of refined sugars or dairy.

Makes 15 to 20 pops

Tips

To soak the Brazil nuts for this recipe, place in a bowl with 2 cups (500 mL) water. Cover and set aside for 1 hour. Drain and rinse under cold running water until water runs clear.

To soak the cashews for this recipe, place in a bowl and cover with ½ cup (125 mL) water. Cover and set aside for 30 minutes. Drain, discarding soaking water, and rinse under cold running water until the water runs clear.

You can double this recipe and have extra on hand in your freezer for a hot summer day.

- Ice cube or Popsicle tray
- Toothpicks or Popsicle sticks

½ cup	Brazil nuts, soaked (see Tips, left)	125 mL
¼ cup	raw cashews, soaked (see Tips, left)	60 mL
½ cup	chopped mango	125 mL
⅓ cup	raw agave nectar	75 mL
⅓ cup	melted coconut oil (see Tips, page 361)	75 mL
¼ cup	filtered water	60 mL
1 tbsp	freshly squeezed lemon juice	15 mL

1. In a blender, combine soaked Brazil nuts and cashews, mango, agave nectar, coconut oil, water and lemon juice. Blend at high speed until smooth.
2. Transfer to ice cube tray and place a toothpick or Popsicle stick in each cube. Freeze for at least 3 hours or until firm enough to remove from tray. Serve immediately or keep frozen until ready to use.

Variations

Substitute an equal quantity of chopped hulled strawberries or blueberries for the mango.

If you do not have Brazil nuts, increase the amount of cashews to 1 cup (250 mL) and the coconut oil to ½ cup (125 mL).

Spirulina Cashew Cheesecake Squares

These delicious dessert bites contain spirulina, a blue-green alga that is reputed to have many health benefits (see Tips, below). They are sinfully sweet — a perfect balance of vanilla, rich cashews and sweet agave nectar. You can double or triple this recipe to suit your needs.

Makes 16 squares

Tips

To soak the cashews for this recipe, place in a bowl and add 2 cups (500 mL) water. Cover and set aside for 30 minutes. Drain, discarding soaking water, and rinse under cold running water until the water runs clear.

If you prefer, substitute 1 tsp (5 mL) vanilla seeds for the extract.

Some vanilla beans are put into an oven after being harvested, so if you're using vanilla seeds, make sure to look for vanilla beans that have been sun-dried and are labeled "raw."

Spirulina is a blue-green alga that has many healthful properties. It has trace amounts of vitamins and minerals and is a source of phytonutrients with antioxidant properties; it is also thought to be extremely detoxifying. Spirulina can be found in the supplements section of your health food store. You may also find it in the natural foods section of a well-stocked grocery store.

- **8-inch square (2 L) baking dish**

1 cup	raw cashews, soaked (see Tips, left)	250 mL
1/3 cup	raw agave nectar	75 mL
1/3 cup	melted coconut oil (see Tips, page 361)	75 mL
1/4 cup	filtered water	60 mL
1 tbsp	freshly squeezed lemon juice	15 mL
2 tsp	raw vanilla extract (see Tips, left)	10 mL
1/2 tsp	spirulina powder	2 mL

1. In a food processor fitted with the metal blade, process soaked cashews, agave nectar, coconut oil, water, lemon juice, vanilla and spirulina until smooth and creamy.
2. Transfer to baking dish and freeze for at least 4 hours or until firm. When you're ready to serve, remove from the freezer and allow to sit at room temperature for 30 minutes to thaw slightly. Cut into squares. Serve immediately or refrigerate for up to 5 days.

Variation

Strawberry Cinnamon Cheesecake Squares: Substitute 1/4 cup (60 mL) chopped strawberries and 2 tsp (10 mL) ground cinnamon for the spirulina.

Cashew Cheesecake

This rich cake is particularly delicious served with fresh berries and a sprinkle of cinnamon. I like to save this for special occasions. You will need a high-powered blender to achieve the smoothest consistency possible.

Makes 16 servings

Tips

To soak the cashews for this recipe, cover with 8 cups (2 L) water. Set aside for 1 hour. Drain, discarding soaking water, and rinse under cold running water until the water runs clear.

To check if the cake is frozen all the way through, insert a tester such as a wooden skewer or toothpick. If it comes out clean, then the cake is ready to be thawed.

For decades, coconut products (coconut oil, milk and flesh) have been painted with the anti–saturated fat brush, based on the assumption that saturated fat increases the risk for cardiovascular disease. However, recent studies have found otherwise, so long as the coconut products are unprocessed. In fact, an impressive benefit of coconut products is their ability to boost HDL ("good cholesterol"), which helps to reduce the risk for cardiovascular disease. Coconut is high in a type of saturated fat called medium-chain triglycerides (MCTs), which are unique in the sense that they are burned for energy and are less likely to be stored as body fat.

- **High-powered blender**
- **9-inch (23 cm) springform pan**

Filling

4 cups	raw cashews, soaked (see Tips, left)	1 L
1 cup	filtered water	250 mL
1 cup	raw agave nectar	250 mL
1 cup	melted coconut oil (see Tips, page 361)	250 mL
1 tbsp	raw vanilla extract	15 mL
2 tsp	freshly squeezed lemon juice	10 mL

Crust

2 cups	whole raw pecans	500 mL
¼ cup	chopped pitted soft dates	60 mL
½ tsp	fine sea salt	2 mL

1. *Filling:* In a high-powered blender, combine soaked cashews, water, agave nectar, coconut oil, vanilla and lemon juice. Blend at high speed until smooth and creamy. Set aside.

2. *Crust:* In a food processor, pulse pecans, dates and salt until smooth (no large pieces should remain). Press into bottom of pan, ensuring that there are no gaps.

3. *Assembly:* Pour filling over crust and freeze for at least 2 hours or until firm in the center. This dessert can be made ahead and kept in the freezer for up to 1 month.

4. When you are ready to serve, remove from freezer and set aside to thaw for 15 to 20 minutes. Remove pan sides and slice. Serve immediately or cover and refrigerate for up to 1 week.

Variation

Blueberry Cheesecake: Before processing filling in Step 1, set aside 1 cup (250 mL) of the soaked cashews and ¼ cup (60 mL) of the agave nectar. Add to blender along with ½ cup (125 mL) blueberries. Blend until smooth. Cover and refrigerate. When cake is frozen, spread mixture evenly over the top. Freeze for 3 hours, until top is frozen. Proceed to Step 4.

Almond Cacao Bars

These bars are a nutrition-packed treat, perfect to make ahead and freeze. They will keep you feeling nourished while you're on the go. They are rich, soft and melt-in-the-mouth good.

Makes 18 bars

Tips

Allow the almond butter to come to room temperature before stirring in the other ingredients, so that everything is able to come together and incorporate properly.

The best place to purchase almond butter is bulk food stores, as it can be quite pricey when purchased in small quantities. When purchasing nut butters, make sure they are raw and organic. Find a favorite brand or source and stick with it.

Coconut oil is solid at room temperature. It has a melting temperature of 76°F (24°C), so it is easy to liquefy. If you have a dehydrator, place the required amount in a shallow dish and warm at 100°F (38°C) for 15 minutes or until melted. If you do not have a dehydrator, place a shallow glass bowl over a pot of simmering water.

- 8-inch (20 cm) square glass baking dish

2 cups	almond butter (see Tips, left)	500 mL
¾ cup	raw agave nectar	175 mL
½ cup	melted coconut oil (see Tips, left)	125 mL
¼ cup	raw cacao powder	60 mL

1. In a bowl, combine almond butter, agave nectar, coconut oil and cacao powder. Mix well.
2. Transfer to a baking dish and freeze for at least 2 hours or until firm in the center, or for up to 2 weeks.
3. When you are ready to serve, remove from freezer and set aside at room temperature for 20 to 30 minutes to thaw slightly. Cut into 18 bars (3 rows of 6). Serve immediately or cover and refrigerate for up to a week.

Variation

If you prefer denser bars, blend the agave nectar with ¼ cup (60 mL) coconut butter before adding to the remaining ingredients in Step 1. Coconut butter has a higher fat content than almond butter, which makes the dessert richer and denser.

Chocolate Mint Bites

These tasty little bites are perfect for making in large batches and keeping in the freezer as a snack.

Tip

Most flavoring extracts are not raw. Check the labels or contact purveyors (see Buying Raw Ingredients, page 373) if you have concerns. However, in raw food cuisine most organic extracts are acceptable, even those that have been distilled with steam.

- **Small (approx. 2-inch/10 cm) nonstick molds**

1 cup	melted coconut oil (see Tips, page 361)	250 mL
½ cup	raw cacao powder	125 mL
¼ cup	raw agave nectar	60 mL
1 tsp	raw mint extract (see Tip, left)	5 mL

1. In a food processor fitted with the metal blade, process coconut oil, cacao powder, agave nectar and mint extract until smooth. Pour into molds and freeze for 1 to 2 hours or until firm. Remove from freezer and allow to sit at room temperature for 15 minutes or until soft enough to remove from molds. Serve immediately or transfer to an airtight container and store, refrigerated, for up to 7 days or freeze for up to 2 weeks.

Cashew Ice Cream

This is a simple way to make raw ice cream, which is very delicious — as creamy and rich as its dairy counterpart. I love the strong vanilla flavor with the luscious cashews. I like to serve this on its own with Chocolate Fondue (page 368). It also makes a great finish for many desserts from this book. If you are lucky enough to own a high-powered blender, use it to make this recipe. It will produce the creamiest ice cream.

Makes 4 cups (1 L)

Tips

To soak the cashews for this recipe, cover with 2 cups (500 mL) water. Set aside for 30 minutes. Drain, discarding soaking water, and rinse under cold running water until the water runs clear.

Substitute 2 tsp (10 mL) vanilla seeds for the extract.

- **Ice-cream maker**

1 cup	raw cashews, soaked (see Tips, left)	250 mL
¾ cup	melted coconut oil (see Tips, page 361)	175 mL
½ cup	raw agave nectar	125 mL
¼ cup	Cashew Milk (page 46)	60 mL
1 tsp	raw vanilla extract	5 mL
1 tsp	freshly squeezed lemon juice	5 mL

1. In a blender, combine ingredients. Blend at high speed until smooth and creamy.
2. Transfer to ice-cream maker and freeze according to manufacturer's instructions. Transfer to an airtight container and store in the freezer for up to 2 weeks.

Mango and Pineapple Gelato

I love this light and fruity take on the traditional Italian favorite. I like to serve this with Pear Crisp (page 337) and Pecan Pie (page 354), among other desserts.

Makes 3 cups (750 mL)

Tip

To soak the cashews for this recipe, place in a bowl and add ½ cup (125 mL) water. Cover and set aside for 30 minutes. Drain, discarding soaking water, and rinse under cold running water until the water runs clear.

- **Ice-cream maker**

¼ cup	raw cashews, soaked (see Tip, left)	60 mL
1 cup	Almond Milk (page 45)	250 mL
1 cup	chopped mango (about 1 medium)	250 mL
½ cup	chopped pineapple (about ¼ medium)	125 mL
½ cup	raw agave nectar	125 mL
¼ cup	melted coconut oil (see Tips, page 361)	60 mL
¼ cup	coconut butter (see Tips, page 370)	60 mL
2 tbsp	freshly squeezed lemon juice	30 mL

1. In a blender, combine almond milk, mango, pineapple and agave nectar. Blend at high speed until smooth. Add soaked cashews, coconut oil, coconut butter and lemon juice. Blend at high speed until smooth and creamy.
2. Transfer to ice-cream maker and freeze according to manufacturer's instructions. Transfer to an airtight container and store in the freezer for up to 2 weeks.

Lemon Avocado Mousse

This dessert has a creamy, smooth pudding-like consistency that melts in the mouth.

Makes 4 servings

Tip

To use the flesh of a lemon, place on a cutting board and cut slices from the top and bottom to create flat surfaces. Using a sharp knife in a downward motion, remove the skin and the pith. Shave off any remaining bits of pith, then cut between the membranes to produce wedges of pure citrus flesh.

2 cups	chopped avocado	500 mL
½ cup	freshly squeezed lemon juice	125 mL
¼ cup	lemon segments (see Tip, left)	60 mL
¾ cup	raw agave nectar	175 mL

1. In a food processor fitted with the metal blade, process avocado, lemon juice and lemon segments until smooth, stopping the motor and scraping down the sides of the work bowl as necessary. With the motor running, drizzle agave nectar through the feed tube, combining well. Serve immediately or transfer to an airtight container and refrigerate for up to 3 days.

Coconut Chocolate Mousse

This is a velvety blend of creamy coconut, cashews and rich raw cacao. It is also decadently chocolaty. I like to serve this over a bowl of fresh strawberries.

Makes 4 servings

Tip

To soak the cashews for this recipe, place in a bowl and add ½ cup (125 mL) water. Cover and set aside for 30 minutes. Drain, discarding soaking water, and rinse under cold running water until the water runs clear.

¼ cup	raw cashews, soaked (see Tip, left)	60 mL
1 cup	melted coconut oil (see Tip, page 365)	250 mL
½ cup	coconut butter (see Tips, page 370)	125 mL
½ cup	raw cacao powder	125 mL
½ cup	raw agave nectar	125 mL
½ cup	filtered water	125 mL

1. In a food processor fitted with the metal blade, process coconut oil and coconut butter until smooth. Add cacao powder, agave nectar, water and soaked cashews and process until smooth and creamy, stopping the motor once and scraping down the sides of the work bowl. Serve immediately or transfer the mixture to an airtight container and refrigerate for up to 7 days.

Mango and Ginger Cashew Mousse

This light and creamy mousse pairs particularly well with tropical fruits. I like to serve this with Pear Crisp (page 337). True confession: I sometimes find myself eating it right out of the bowl, with just a spoon and a smile.

Makes 2 cups (500 mL)

Tip

To soak the cashews for this recipe, place in a bowl and add 2 cups (500 mL) water. Cover and set aside for 30 minutes. Drain, discarding soaking water, and rinse under cold running water until the water runs clear.

1 cup	raw cashews, soaked (see Tip, left)	250 mL
1 cup	chopped mango	250 mL
¼ cup	filtered water	60 mL
3 tbsp	raw agave nectar	45 mL
2 tbsp	chopped gingerroot	30 mL
2 tsp	freshly squeezed lemon juice	10 mL

1. In a blender, combine soaked cashews, mango, water, agave nectar, ginger and lemon juice. Blend at high speed until smooth and creamy.

Variation

For a slightly tarter version of this mousse, substitute ½ cup (125 mL) chopped pineapple and ¼ cup (60 mL) chopped peeled apple for the mango.

Avocado Lemon Curd

This slightly sweet yet pleasantly tangy dessert melts in your mouth.

Makes 4 servings

Tip

Coconut butter is a blend of coconut oil and coconut meat that is high in healthy fats and adds creaminess to smoothies and sauces. It is available in the nut butter section of natural foods stores or well-stocked supermarkets. Don't confuse it with coconut oil, because they are different.

- **Four ½-cup (125 mL) ramekins**

2 tsp	finely grated lemon zest	10 mL
⅓ cup	freshly squeezed lemon juice	75 mL
⅓ cup	raw agave nectar	75 mL
¼ cup	chopped avocado	60 mL
¼ cup	coconut butter (see Tip, left)	60 mL
¼ cup	melted coconut oil (see Tips, page 361)	60 mL
2 tbsp	almond butter	30 mL
2 tbsp	cashew butter	30 mL

1. In a blender, combine lemon zest and juice, agave nectar, avocado and coconut butter. Blend until smooth and creamy. Add coconut oil, almond butter and cashew butter and blend until smooth.
2. Transfer to ramekins and refrigerate for at least 2 hours or up to 3 days. When you're ready to serve, remove from molds and serve.

Fig-Blueberry Macadamia Cream

This enticing cream is a perfect finish for fresh peach slices. I love to spoon it over a bowl of fresh berries and garnish it with hemp seeds for a dinner-party dessert.

Makes 2 cups (500 mL)

Tips

To soak the macadamia nuts, cover with 2 cups (500 mL) water. Set aside for 30 minutes. Drain and rinse under running water until the water runs clear.

To soak the figs, cover with 1 cup (250 mL) warm water. Set aside to soak for 30 minutes. Drain, discarding remaining water.

½ cup	macadamia nuts, soaked (see Tips, left)	125 mL
¼ cup	dried figs, soaked (see Tips, left)	60 mL
1 cup	blueberries	250 mL
¼ cup	filtered water	60 mL
¼ cup	raw agave nectar	60 mL
1 tbsp	cold-pressed flax oil	15 mL

1. In a food processer fitted with the metal blade, process soaked macadamia nuts and figs, blueberries, water, agave nectar and flax oil until smooth and creamy. Transfer to an airtight container and store, refrigerated, for up to 5 days.

Cinnamon Almond Cream

This can be used very simply, as a finish for a dish of fresh fruit. It also makes a great filling for sandwich cookies.

Makes 1½ cups (375 mL)

Tip

To soak the almonds, add 3 cups (750 mL) water. Cover and refrigerate for 10 to 12 hours or until the skins can easily be peeled away. Drain and rinse.

- High-powered blender

1 cup	whole raw almonds, soaked and peeled (see Tip, left)	250 mL
⅓ cup	raw agave nectar	75 mL
¼ cup	filtered water	60 mL
1 tbsp	ground cinnamon	15 mL
¼ tsp	freshly squeezed lemon juice	1 mL

1. In a high-powered blender, place soaked almonds, agave nectar, water, cinnamon and lemon juice. Blend at high speed until smooth and creamy.

Citrus Cream

This delectable cream pairs well with many recipes in this book. It can be frozen for use later.

Makes 4 cups (1 L)

Tip

To soak the cashews for this recipe, cover with 2 cups (500 mL) water. Set aside for 30 minutes. Drain, discarding soaking water, and rinse under cold running water until the water runs clear.

1 cup	raw cashews, soaked (see Tips, left)	250 mL
1 tbsp	finely grated orange zest	15 mL
½ cup	chopped orange segments (see Tips, page 67)	125 mL
¼ cup	filtered water	60 mL
¼ cup	raw agave nectar	60 mL
1 tbsp	finely grated lemon zest	15 mL
3 tbsp	chopped lemon segments	45 mL
1 tbsp	finely grated grapefruit zest	15 mL
3 tbsp	chopped grapefruit segments	45 mL
1 tsp	ground cinnamon, optional	5 mL

1. In a blender, combine all ingredients. Blend at high speed until smooth and creamy. Serve immediately or transfer to an airtight container and store, refrigerated, for up to 5 days.

Variation

For a slightly less acidic sauce, substitute ¼ cup (60 mL) chopped lime segments and 1 tsp (5 mL) finely grated lime zest for the lemon and zest.

Cashew Whipped Cream

This cream is light and fluffy and tastes just as delicious as the dairy version. It is a perfect finish for Macerated Berries (page 331), among other desserts.

Makes 3½ cups (875 mL)

Tips

To soak the cashews for this recipe, place in a bowl and add 4 cups (1 L) water. Cover and set aside for 30 minutes. Drain, discarding soaking water, and rinse under cold running water until the water runs clear.

If you have a high-powered blender, use it to make this cream. It will be smoother and creamier than when made in a regular blender.

2 cups	raw cashews, soaked (see Tips, left)	500 mL
1 cup	filtered water	250 mL
½ cup	raw agave nectar	125 mL
1 tsp	raw vanilla extract (see Tips, page 338)	5 mL
¼ tsp	freshly squeezed lemon juice	1 mL

1. In a blender (see Tips, left), combine soaked cashews, water, agave nectar, vanilla and lemon juice. Blend at high speed until smooth and creamy. Transfer to a bowl, cover and refrigerate for up to 5 days.

Variations

Vanilla Pine Nut Whipped Cream: Substitute 2 cups (500 mL) pine nuts for the cashews.

Brazil Nut Whipped Cream: Substitute 2 cups (500 mL) Brazil nuts for the cashews.

Almond Whipped Cream: Substitute 2 cups (500 mL) almonds for the cashews. Follow the soaking instructions in the Tips on page 341. If you prefer, substitute raw almond extract for the vanilla.

Coconut Whipped Cream

This light yet decadent topping makes a great substitute for whipped cream.

Makes 1 cup (250 mL)

Tip

To soak the cashews for this recipe, combine in a bowl with ½ cup (125 mL) water. Cover and set aside for 30 minutes. Drain, discarding soaking water. Rinse under cold running water until the water runs clear.

¼ cup	raw cashews, soaked (see Tip, left)	60 mL
½ cup	young Thai coconut meat	125 mL
3 tbsp	raw agave nectar	45 mL
1 tbsp	filtered water	15 mL
½ tsp	freshly squeezed lemon juice	2 mL
1 tsp	raw vanilla extract or ¼ tsp (1 mL) vanilla seeds	5 mL

1. In a food processor fitted with the metal blade, process soaked cashews, coconut, agave nectar, water, lemon juice and vanilla until smooth. Transfer to a bowl and serve immediately or cover and refrigerate for up to 3 days.

Chocolate Fondue

This makes a thick, rich and decadent chocolate sauce.

Makes 2 cups (500 mL)

Tip

This is delicious over Macerated Berries (page 331) or as a dip with fresh apples and bananas.

¾ cup	raw agave nectar	175 mL
¾ cup	raw cacao powder	175 mL
½ cup	melted coconut oil	125 mL
¼ to ½ cup	filtered water	60 to 125 mL

1. In a blender, combine agave nectar, cacao powder, coconut oil and ¼ cup (60 mL) water. Blend at high speed until smooth. If sauce seems too thick, add 1 tbsp (15 mL) water at a time until the sauce thins out to the consistency of a traditional fondue or thick chocolate sauce.

Strawberry Chocolate Fondue

Use this thick and delicious fondue as a dipping sauce for fresh strawberries. You can also freeze it and enjoy it as a frozen chocolate treat. I like to serve it slightly warm over Macerated Berries (page 331), finished with a sprinkling of hemp seeds.

Makes 1½ cups (375 mL)

Tips

Coconut oil is solid at room temperature. It has a melting temperature of 76°F (24°C), so it is easy to liquefy. If you have a dehydrator, place the required amount in a shallow dish and warm at 100°F (38°C) for 15 minutes or until melted. If you do not have a dehydrator, place a shallow glass bowl over a pot of simmering water.

To serve this fondue slightly warm, place it in a bowl and dehydrate at 105°F (41°C) for 15 minutes.

1 cup	chopped banana	250 mL
¾ cup	melted coconut oil (see Tips, left)	175 mL
½ cup	raw cacao powder	125 mL
½ cup	chopped hulled strawberries	125 mL
¼ cup	raw agave nectar	60 mL

1. In a blender, combine banana, coconut oil, cacao powder, strawberries and agave nectar. Blend at high speed until smooth and creamy. Serve immediately.

Variation

Substitute the strawberries with 1 cup (250 mL) blueberries and 2 tbsp (30 mL) freshly squeezed orange juice.

Chocolate Sauce

This rich syrup is delicious served on Almond Biscuits (page 341). It is very versatile and makes a perfect accompaniment to many desserts.

Makes 1 cup (250 mL)

Tips

If you prefer a richer, thicker sauce, add up to 2 tbsp (30 mL) melted coconut oil.

If the sauce becomes too thick after sitting, place it over a small pot of simmering water and stir gently just until melted.

½ cup	raw cacao powder (see Tips, page 357)	125 mL
¼ cup	melted coconut oil (see Tips, page 368)	60 mL
½ cup	raw agave nectar	125 mL
2 tbsp	filtered water	30 mL

1. In a bowl, combine cacao powder, coconut oil, raw agave nectar and water. Whisk until smooth. Use immediately or cover and refrigerate for up to 7 days.

Variation

If you are avoiding caffeine, replace the raw cacao with an equal amount of carob powder.

Caramel Sauce

This thick and delicious sauce can replace any traditional version made from refined sugar and dairy. I love it as a dip for apple slices. It is perfect paired with, among other dishes, Pecan Pie (page 354) and "Baked" Stuffed Apples (page 332).

Makes 2 cups (500 mL)

Tip

To soak the dates for this recipe, place them in a bowl with 2 cups (500 mL) warm water, cover and set aside to soak for 30 minutes. Drain, discarding any remaining water.

½ cup	pitted dates, soaked (see Tip, left)	125 mL
1½ cups	raw agave nectar	375 mL
1 tbsp	ground cinnamon	15 mL
Pinch	fine sea salt	Pinch

1. In a blender, combine soaked dates, agave nectar, cinnamon and salt. Blend at high speed until smooth. Transfer to an airtight container and store, refrigerated, for up to 7 days.

Variation

If you prefer a sauce that isn't quite as sweet as this version, blend 1 cup (250 mL) soaked dates, ½ cup (125 mL) raw agave nectar, 2 tsp (10 mL) ground cinnamon and a pinch of salt.

Coconut Butter Vanilla Icing

Here's a rich and creamy vanilla frosting that is actually good for you. I love to make a large batch and keep it in the fridge for when I am craving something sweet. It makes a perfect frosting for Chocolate Walnut Brownies (page 349). I also like to spread it on a sliced banana and enjoy it just like that.

Makes 2 cups (500 mL)

1½ cups	coconut butter (see Tips, left)	375 mL
½ cup	raw agave nectar	125 mL
2 tsp	vanilla seeds (about 1 whole pod) or 2 tsp (10 mL) raw vanilla extract	10 mL
¼ cup	(approx.) filtered water, optional	60 mL

Tips

Coconut butter is a blend of coconut oil and coconut meat. You can usually find it in natural foods stores next to the coconut oil.

Some coconut oils are softer than others, so it is often necessary to add liquid to adjust the consistency of recipes containing coconut oil or coconut butter.

Some vanilla beans are put into an oven after being harvested, so if you're using whole beans, make sure to look for those that have been sun-dried and are labeled "raw."

1. In blender, combine coconut butter, agave nectar and vanilla seeds. Blend at high speed until smooth and creamy. If necessary, add water 1 tbsp (15 mL) at a time, pulsing after each addition, until desired consistency has been achieved.

Variation

Chocolate Coconut Butter Frosting: Add ½ cup (125 mL) raw cacao powder and an additional 3 tbsp (45 mL) raw agave nectar.

Peach Mango Ginger Coulis

This sauce is a perfect blend of sweet, ripe peaches, savory ginger and flavorful sesame seeds. I like using it a garnish for Fruit Gazpacho (page 110) or generously drizzled over a bowl of fresh peaches and blueberries.

Makes ¾ cup (175 mL)

Tips

Peaches generally ripen quickly, so if they are not ripe when you purchase them, do not forget about them. They will go from rock-hard to perfectly ripe in 2 to 3 days.

To remove the skin from gingerroot with the least amount of waste, use the edge of a teaspoon. Use a brushing motion to scrape the skin off to reveal the yellow root.

½ cup	chopped peach	125 mL
¼ cup	chopped mango (about ¼ medium)	60 mL
2 tbsp	filtered water	30 mL
1 tbsp	chopped gingerroot	15 mL
1 tbsp	raw agave nectar	15 mL
2 tsp	sesame seeds	10 mL

1. In a food processor fitted with the metal blade, process peach, mango, water, ginger, agave nectar and sesame seeds until smooth. Transfer to a bowl and serve immediately or cover and refrigerate for up to 3 days.

Variation

Peach Mango Hemp Cream: Substitute ¼ cup (60 mL) raw shelled hemp seeds, soaked in ½ cup (125 mL) water for 10 minutes and drained, for the ginger and sesame seeds.

Blueberry Ginger Coulis

This tasty sauce makes a perfect finish for many desserts. I love it with Peach and Blueberry Cobbler (page 334) and Raspberry Parfait (page 335), among others.

Makes 2 cups (500 mL)

Tip

"Coulis" is a French term for a purée, usually of fruit or vegetables, that is used as a sauce. It can be sweet or savory.

1½ cups	blueberries	375 mL
¼ cup	raw agave nectar	60 mL
2 tbsp	chopped gingerroot	30 mL
1 tsp	freshly squeezed lemon juice	5 mL

1. In a blender, combine blueberries, agave nectar, ginger and lemon juice. Blend at high speed until smooth. Serve immediately or cover and refrigerate for up to 3 days.

Variation

Use ½ cup (125 mL) orange flesh blended with 1 cup (250 mL) blueberries, 2 tbsp (30 mL) raw agave nectar and 2 tsp (10 mL) orange zest.

Strawberry Date Sauce

This sauce is absolutely delicious on Cashew Ice Cream (page 362). It is also wonderful as a sauce on many breakfast dishes such as Blueberry Scones (page 32).

Makes 2 cups (500 mL)

Tip

Substitute raspberries, blueberries or blackberries for the strawberries. Or create a bumbleberry sauce by using a mixture of whatever berries you have on hand, such as blackberries, blueberries, strawberries and raspberries.

2 cups	hulled strawberries (about 1 pint)	500 mL
½ cup	chopped pitted soft dates (about 5 large)	125 mL
⅓ cup	raw agave nectar	75 mL
Pinch	fine sea salt	Pinch

1. In a food processor fitted with the metal blade, process strawberries, dates, agave nectar and salt until smooth. Serve immediately or cover and refrigerate for up to 1 week.

Variation

Substitute 2 tbsp (30 mL) freshly squeezed orange juice for the agave nectar.

Orange-Melon-Cranberry Sauce

This tart and sweet sauce is a take on the traditional version. Using fresh oranges sweetens the sauce and mitigates the bite of the cranberries. I like to toss this sauce with chopped fresh fruit or use as a complement to many desserts, such as Cashew Cheesecake (page 360).

Makes 2 cups (500 mL)

Tip

If fresh cranberries are not available, substitute ½ cup (125 mL) dried cranberries, soaked in ½ cup (125 mL) additional orange juice for 30 minutes. When purchasing dried fruits, look for those that are free of added sugars or preservatives and are organic.

¾ cup	fresh cranberries (see Tip, left)	175 mL
½ cup	freshly squeezed orange juice	125 mL
½ cup	chopped cantaloupe	125 mL
¼ cup	chopped orange segments (see Tips, page 153)	60 mL
3 tbsp	raw agave nectar	45 mL

1. In a blender, combine cranberries, orange juice, cantaloupe, chopped orange and raw agave nectar. Blend at high speed until smooth. Transfer to a bowl and serve immediately or cover and refrigerate for up to 5 days.

Buying Raw Ingredients

Because it is often difficult to recognize food products that qualify as raw, to help you through the transitioning process I have noted a few brands that pass muster. With the passage of time, others will no doubt appear in the marketplace. As you become more comfortable with purchasing raw food products, you will be able to identify them yourself. If you have trouble locating some of the products, I have also included the names of several websites where you can order online. As people become more aware of raw foods, I'm confident more and more of these products will become stock items at grocery stores.

Raw cacao powder: Raw cacao can be found in natural foods stores and some well-stocked supermarkets. Brands to look for include Navitas Naturals, Mum's Original and Organic Traditions.

Nut and seed butters: Most well-stocked grocery stores carry raw nut and/or seed butters. You will certainly be able to find them in natural foods stores. Check the label before purchasing to make sure that they are labeled "raw." Brands to look for include Artisana and Nuts to You nut butters.

Raw agave nectar: Agave nectar can be found on the shelves of most well-stocked supermarkets and in all natural foods stores. When purchasing agave nectar, make sure the label identifies it as raw and/or that it has been processed at acceptable temperatures. Brands to look for include Wholesome Sweeteners, Madhava Natural Sweeteners (raw grade) and Xagave.

Vanilla beans: You can find raw vanilla beans in most natural foods stores or at online specialty suppliers. Some well-stocked grocery stores also carry raw vanilla beans. You do not want vanilla beans that have been processed using heat or roasted. Brands to look for include Nielsen-Massey, Lochhead, Arizona Vanilla Company and Vanillabazaar.

Vanilla extract: You can find raw vanilla extract in most natural foods stores or at online specialty suppliers. Some well-stocked grocery stores will also carry the product. Brands to look for include Nielsen-Massey, Lochhead, Arizona Vanilla Company and Vanillabazaar.

Protein powder: Raw protein powders can be found in natural foods stores and some well-stocked supermarkets. When purchasing protein powders, look for ones that have been sprouted and/or are labeled "raw." Some of my favorite brands include Manitoba Harvest, Sunwarrior, Garden of Life, Forever Healthy, Navitas Naturals and Ruth's Hemp Foods.

Wheat-free tamari: Wheat-free tamari can be found in natural foods stores and well-stocked supermarkets. Although not a raw product, wheat-free tamari is gluten-free. My favorite brands include San-J, Amano and Eden Foods.

Nutritional yeast: Nutritional yeast flakes can be found in well-stocked supermarkets and natural foods stores. Although not a raw product, nutritional yeast is fortified with vitamin B_{12}. When purchasing nutritional yeast, make sure it has been fortified. My favorite brands include Red Star, KAL and Lynside.

Brown rice miso: Brown rice miso is made from whole fermented brown rice grains. Although not a raw food, it is commonly used in raw cuisine because it is gluten-free, mineral-rich and great for the digestion. You can find brown rice miso at well-stocked supermarkets and natural foods stores. Brands to look for include Eden Foods, Tradition and South River.

Sea vegetables: Sea vegetables (seaweed) can be found in most well-stocked supermarkets and natural foods stores. Some are roasted before being packaged, so make sure to check the label to see if this is the case. Generally they will not be labeled "raw." Consequently it is best to become familiar with brands that are raw, which include Eden Foods and Maine Coast Sea Vegetables.

Online Sources for Certified Raw Food Products

The following are leading websites for raw food products. I have included their geographic location to assist you when ordering.

- Blue Mountain Organics (Floyd, Virginia)
  http://www.bluemountainorganics.com/

- Raw Utopia (Denver, Colorado)
  http://shop.rawutopia.com/

- Sunfood (San Diego, California)
  http://www.sunfood.com

- Real Raw Food (Vancouver, British Columbia)
  http://www.realrawfood.com/

- Upaya Naturals (Toronto, Ontario)
  www.upayanaturals.com

- The Fresh Network (Norwich, United Kingdom)
  http://www.fresh-network.com/

- Raw Pleasure (Queensland, Australia)
  http://raw-pleasure.com.au/

- Raw Power Australia (Queensland, Australia)
  http://www.rawpower.com.au/

Library and Archives Canada Cataloguing in Publication

McNish, Douglas
    Eat raw, eat well : 400 raw, vegan & gluten-free recipes / Douglas McNish.

Includes index.
ISBN 978-0-7788-0295-2

1. Raw foods. 2. Raw food diet. 3. Vegan cooking. 4. Gluten-free diet—Recipes. 5. Cookbooks—I. Title.

TX837.M29 2012   641.5'636   C2011-907497-4

Index